M000275211

Godwired

Godwired offers an engaging exploration of religious practice in the digital age. It considers how virtual experiences, like stories, games and rituals, are forms of world-building or "cosmos construction" that serve as a means of making sense of our own world. Such creative and interactive activity is, arguably, patently religious.

This book examines:

- the nature of sacred space in virtual contexts
- technology as a vehicle for sacred texts
- who we are when we go online
- how religious ritual works in virtual spaces
- whether it is possible to gather for worship in online space.

Rachel Wagner suggests that whilst our engagement with virtual reality can be viewed as a form of religious activity, today's virtual religion marks a radical departure from traditional religious practice – it is ephemeral, transient, rapid, disposable, hyper-individualized, hybrid, and in an ongoing state of flux.

Rachel Wagner is an associate professor of religion and culture at Ithaca College, USA.

Media, Religion and Culture
Edited by Stewart M. Hoover, Jolyon Mitchell and David Morgan

Media, Religion and Culture is an exciting series which analyzes the role of media in the history of contemporary practice of religious belief. Books in this series explore the importance of a variety of media in religious practice and highlight the significance of the culture, social and religious setting of such media.

Religion in the Media Age
Stewart M. Hoover

The Lure of Images
A history of religion and visual media in America
David Morgan

Brands of Faith
Marketing religion in a commercial age
Mara Einstein

When Religion Meets New Media
Heidi Campbell

Godwired

Religion, Ritual and Virtual Reality

Rachel Wagner

Routledge
Taylor & Francis Group

LONDON AND NEW YORK

First published 2012
by Routledge
2 Park Square, Milton Park, Abingdon, Oxon OX14 4RN

Simultaneously published in the USA and Canada
by Routledge
711 Third Avenue, New York, NY 10017

Routledge is an imprint of the Taylor & Francis Group, an informa business

© 2012 Rachel Wagner

The right of Rachel Wagner to be identified as author of this work has been asserted by her in accordance with sections 77 and 78 of the Copyright, Designs and Patents Act 1988.

All rights reserved. No part of this book may be reprinted or reproduced or utilised in any form or by any electronic, mechanical, or other means, now known or hereafter invented, including photocopying and recording, or in any information storage or retrieval system, without permission in writing from the publishers.

Trademark notice: Product or corporate names may be trademarks or registered trademarks, and are used only for identification and explanation without intent to infringe.

British Library Cataloguing in Publication Data
A catalogue record for this book is available from the British Library

Library of Congress Cataloging in Publication Data
Wagner, Rachel.
Godwired : religion, ritual, and virtual reality / Rachel Wagner.
p. cm. - - (Media, religion, and culture series)
Includes bibliographical references (p.) and index.
1. Virtual reality- -Religious aspects. I. Title.
BL65.V57W34 2011
204.0285'68- -dc23
2011025265

ISBN: 978-0-415-78144-2 (hbk)
ISBN: 978-0-415-78145-9 (pbk)
ISBN: 978-0-203-14807-5 (ebk)

Typeset in Sabon
by Taylor & Francis Books

Printed and bound in Great Britain by MPG Printgroup

Contents

Acknowledgements   vi

1   Walkthrough   1

2   The stories we play: interactivity and religious narrative   16

3   The games we pray: what is this ritual–game–story thing?   54

4   The Other right here: in search of the virtual sacred   78

5   Me, myself and iPod: hybrid, wired and plural selves   99

6   God-mobs: virtually religious community   126

7   What you play is what you do? Procedural evil and video game violence   162

8   Xbox apocalypse: video games, interactivity and revelatory literature   187

9   Making belief: transmedia and the hunger for the real   205

10   Expansion pack   235

Notes   243
Bibliography   245
Index   262

Acknowledgements

The study of religion and media is just beginning to include elements of video game analysis. As with any new field of inquiry, the best insights are the result of conversations and collaborations with kindred spirits.

I have received much appreciated support from my series editors Stewart Hoover, David Morgan, and Jolyon Mitchell. I also deeply appreciate collaborative conversations with fellow scholars John Lyden, Greg Grieve, Chip Callahan, Jim Thrall, Gary Laderman, Amanullah DeSondy, Eric Michael Mazur, Craig Detweiler, Dan Clanton, Angela Zito, Dan Boscaljon, Jeffrey Mahan, J. Sage Elwell, S. Brent Plate, Mara Einstein, and a host of others.

I received needed and welcome support for research through grants and release time provided by Ithaca College; through conversation and research support fromthe CrossCurrents Foundation in cooperation with Union Theological Seminary; and through fellowship support for early project development from the Wabash Center for Teaching and Learning in Theology and Religion, funded by the Lilly Endowment.

Much affection and appreciation also goes out to the Ithaca College students who, over the past three years, participated in the seminar classes and independent studies that nurtured and developed the ideas in this book: Scott Berg, John Borchert, Grant Carnes, Marissa DeMello, Stephen Gleason, Jonathan Hirschberg, Benjamin Miller, Mallory Moser, Allison Musante, Amanda Pelliciari, Christa Petruzzi, Joni Sweet, Robert Walsh, Becky Zaremba, Mark Glaser, Chris Hendrickson, Liz Kranz, Ashley May, Peter Motzenbecker, Harry Muniz, Angelo Peters, Nikki Quarrier, Greg Rappaport, Tim Schmitz, Robert Woods, Matt Broadhead, Shayn Campbell, Miles Chickering, Devin Dawson, Rob Engelsman, Jessie Mitchell, Mary O'Connell, Michael Radzwilla, Margaret Riley, Cody Ripa, Rachel Rothenberg, Xandra Seidner, Dylan Lowry, and Tyler DeHaven. Charlotte Roberts graciously read the final manuscript for grammatical errors. Brilliant thinkers, every one.

I also thank my son Isaac, who has watched me move from struggling student and single mother to tenured professor, and along the way grew up to be a very talented and generous young man. I owe final thanks to my partner, John, who has listened to me wax enthusiastically and often about the ideas in this book, and who came into my life at just the right time.

Chapter I

Walkthrough

Avid players of video games will recognize the title here, which refers to a user-created set of instructions for making it through a video game. A walkthrough tells you where you can go, what it's possible to do in a game, what the goals are, and how to survive. It also often tells you a few cheatcodes, or points you to the best parts of the game's optional experiences. This introduction is, then, a sort of walkthrough, showing you how and why this book is worth your time as an introduction to the complex relationship between religion and virtual reality. Why should we care about this relationship, you ask?

In 2007, the Anglican Church threatened to sue Sony over a video game that depicted a violent shoot-out staged in a digital replica of Manchester Cathedral, claiming that the game enacted a form of "virtual desecration." In 2009 in India, a group of clerics ruled that it would be a sin for Muslims to take a cell phone into the bathroom if it rang near the toilet with Quranic chanting. Also in 2009, a New York Church "tweeted" the Passion play, complete with "tweets" from Mary, the disciples and Jesus, who "tweeted" his last words from the cross. Increasingly around the world, Hindus conduct puja online using digital images of the gods; Muslims and others can conduct a virtual hajj in the online world of *Second Life*; and the Dalai Lama has approved the spinning of virtual prayer wheels on a computer's hard drive. Lubavitcher Rabbi Yosef Y. Kazen recently claimed that a *minyan* (required quorum of Jews for a prayer service) cannot be accomplished online because real physical bodies are required, but at the same time, there are synagogues functioning in *Second Life* populated by virtual worshippers who clearly feel otherwise. As I demonstrate in *Godwired*, rapid and incredible changes are taking place in religious practice today due to interfacing with virtual reality, and these experiences are raising profound questions about the nature of sacred space, about technology as a vehicle for sacred texts, about who we are when we go online, about how religious ritual works, and about whether or not it is possible to gather for worship in online space.

Godwired addresses this rich relationship between religion and "virtual reality" (which I define as any form of digital technology that involves user engagement with software via a screen interface). I argue throughout the book that our cultural fascination with virtual reality reflects a deeper and more basically human fascination with world-building, or what we might also call cosmos construction: that is, the imagining of a world in which we are in control, in which things make sense, in which what we do has profound meaning, and in which we can enact our ideal selves: activities that have long been viewed as forms of the religious imagination. A consideration of how such scripted, ordered spaces work in a world that many increasingly view as chaotic is a conversation worth having, as it may illuminate for us what some of the attraction is. As I argue in the following chapters, this fascination has some religious roots to it.

As Egenfeldt-Nielsen, Smith and Tosca (2008) put it, games create ordered spaces too, and I suggest this is part of what identifies them as being at least in some respects "religious." To play a game means "setting oneself apart from the outside world, and surrendering to a system that has no effect on anything which lies beyond the circle" (24). Both religion and virtual reality can be said to be deeply concerned with some sense of the "other." That is, both are concerned with a mode of being that lies beyond our ordinary day-to-day experience. This mode or realm of being is typified by imagination of the ideal, that hope for a mode of existence enables us to bypass normal physical limitations, and that presents itself, at least in some respects, as eternal. Are both forms of engagement with the other equally valuable? That remains to be seen, but I raise a number of questions about this proposition throughout the book.

More than half a century ago, Johan Huizinga noted the deep kinship between ritual and play – and thus implicitly also between religion and games – when he noted that "the indissoluble connection between sacred earnest and 'make-believe' or 'fun,' [is] best understood in the concept of play itself" (1955, 24). The ritual act, he says, "has all the formal and essential characteristics of play ... in so far as it transports the participants to another world" (18). This means, says Huizinga, that "archaic ritual is thus sacred play, indispensable for the well-being of the community, fecund of cosmic insight and social development but always play in the sense Plato gave to it – an action accomplishing itself outside and above the necessities and seriousness of everyday life" (25). Ritual and play, then, both set apart a time and space in which special happenings occur, shaped by rules and in some ways different from our daily life, somehow nurturing in their predictability and in their "otherworldliness."

When we play a game, we enter into what Bernard Suits has called the "lusory attitude" or "the state of mind whereby game players consciously take on the challenges and obstacles of a game in order to experience the play of the game itself" through "accepting the artificial authority of the magic circle, submitting behavior to the constraints of rules in order to experience the free movement of play." In other words, "playing a game means submitting to the authority of the magic circle, which includes the cultural conventions expressed through implicit rules" (1990, 574). If such games are appealing because they provide us with intentional challenges and predictable rules, then one could see an intriguing parallel between the "lusory attitutude" and the "faith attitude." Both assume a purpose to challenges, a discoverable set of rules, and both involve the voluntary submission to these mindsets.

Play is like ritual in that it is "not 'ordinary' or 'real' life." Instead, play is "a stepping out of 'real' life into a temporary sphere of activity with a disposition all of its own" (Huizinga 1955, 8). Play, like ritual, is a form of order-making. Play "creates order, is order. Into an imperfect world and into the confusion of life it brings a temporary, a limited perfection" (10). Through the institution of rules and the engagement with an idealized, structured mode of being, play, like ritual, offers us a temporary escape from the disorder in our daily lives. Indeed, the rules themselves seem to offer a degree of this comfort: we know what we are supposed to do, and for the duration of play time, these simple rules adhere. Ritual, too, offers us an ordered mode of escape. Huizinga describes the world-making potential of sacred rituals:

> The sacred performance is more than an actualization in appearance only, a sham reality; it is also more than a symbolical actualization – it is a mystical one. In it, something invisible and inactual takes beautiful, actual, holy form. The participants in the rite are convinced that the action actualizes and effects a definite beatification, brings about an order of things higher than that in which they customarily live.
>
> (1955, 14)

The sacred space is "a temporarily real world of its own" and "continues to shed its radiance on the ordinary world outside" even after the ritual of its creation and performance has ended (1955, 14). For Huizinga, rituals and play both evoke in us, and are reflections of, our desire for purpose and meaning, instantiated through engagement in temporary "worlds" that make sense, and that allow us an escape from the daily grind. In ritual and in play, we invest ourselves in rules that work, in systems that make sense, and in places that are set apart from the things we cannot control. The best kinds of play and ritual offer us an ongoing sense of belonging when they end, spilling their sense of order over into our regular lives, and giving us the strength to deal with adversity. Is it any surprise, then, that we are so drawn both to programmed virtual spaces and to ritual ones?

We can see similar concerns expressed by video game theorists, who argue that games are not just discrete experiences with no effect whatsoever on daily life. Games can and do affect us when we put down the joysticks and turn off our screens. Salen and Zimmerman argue that

> [T]he wider our cultural frame grows in defining games as culture, the more their artificiality begins to unravel. As culture, games are open systems. They are not isolated from their environment, but are intrinsically part of

it, participating in the ebb and flow of ideas and values that make up a larger cultural setting ... the magic circle is not an impermeable curtain but is instead a border that can be crossed. Cultural elements from outside the circle enter in and have an impact on the game; simultaneously, cultural meanings ripple outward from the game to interact with numerous cultural contexts.

(2004, 572)

If games are viewed as open systems, then for some games, we find that "the boundary is so completely erased that it is difficult to distinguish the space of play from ordinary life." In such games, there is a "heightened overlap between the artificial space of the game and the physical spaces and lifestyles of their players. They blur the distinction between players and non-players. ... [and] raise fundamental questions about the artificiality of games and their relationship to real life" (572). It's easy to see that their argument has a lot in common with Huizinga's argument, even if they never mention ritual at all. The "magic circle" of a game is crossed anytime that game has meaning for our daily lives. And that activity, the order-making property, is a key feature of rituals as well. Religion and virtual reality, it seems, may offer some of the same benefits and by implication, some of the same risks as well.

In the following chapters, I examine a series of carefully chosen themes relating to the study of religion and virtual reality to argue that the relationship between religion and virtual reality is more than a casual affiliation. My interest here includes the appearance of explicitly religious themes and images within virtual reality, but also includes the ways that virtual spaces can work *like* religion. As I argue throughout the book, the kinds of fascination we have with *virtual* places and modes of being look an awful lot like a fascination with *religious* places and modes of being. Both religion and virtual reality can be viewed as manifestations of the desire for transcendence, the wish for some mode of imagination or being that lies just beyond the reach of our ordinary lives. Both raise profound questions about what it means to be human, to be embodied, and to be more than *just* in bodies. Both invite scripted engagement with stories and experiences, drawing on vast wells of myth and ritual. Both encourage self-reflection on who we are, and on what we could be. Maybe Ken Hillis is right that our fascination with virtual reality reveals "an individual and a collective need to confer meaning on an otherwise disenchanted world" (2009, 19). Of course, religion used to meet this need for much of the world's population. With the decline and the transformation of institutionalized religion in many parts of the world, perhaps virtual reality is stepping in to fill the gap.

An interesting example of the similar modes of encounter practiced by those engaged with virtual reality and with religion is evident in one Christian's advice for adopting technological metaphors for living the Christian life. Drawing on the metaphor of "augmented reality" (the ability to overlay digital information onto images viewed through a mobile phone's camera), Tony Whittaker suggests that "we already have augmented reality as Jesus-followers." Before people become Christians, he argues, they can't see the "deeper meaning or true value" in the things around them, but once they become Christians, they are "able to overlay [their] perception of everything with a new layer," what for him is the Christian "layer." He advises evangelists to tell potential converts that there is "an 'augmented reality' overlay that they can apply to the world and themselves" (2010b). In other words, let Christianity be the "screen" through which you view reality; let Jesus be your operating system. This example is remarkable not for its use of contemporary metaphors, which is a staple tool of many evangelists. Rather, the compelling issue here is the author's easy assumption that engagement with virtual reality is similar to engagement with religion as an enchanted mode of being. Throughout *Godwired*, I raise numerous examples of Christians drawing on what they see to be poignant parallels between similar modes of engagement with an "other" realm.

An easy place to see the intersection between religion and virtual reality is in video games, which can be understood as one of the most poignant "ritual" components of the virtual world. As I argue throughout the book, ritual and video games are both scripted ways of interacting with virtual (or sacred) space. Because rituals and games are both contested terms that exhibit immense diversity of practice, all comparative observations must be generalizations. But even the most obvious comparisons reveal that both video games and ritual may be doing some similar things for the people who use them, performing what David Chidester calls "religious work" even if they aren't explicitly or traditionally "religious" (2005, 18).[1]

First of all, both rituals and video games are often concerned with *storytelling*, an issue addressed in Chapter 2 most directly, but which colors my analysis of many different modes of virtual encounter. Scholars have long noticed the close relationship between myth and ritual in religious contexts, as when sacred stories are recited in a ritual context, or when rituals are themselves dramatic re-enactments of these stories. Similarly, video games are often infused with a complex mythology that is revealed and enacted via the player's performance of the game. Some games even have associated novels, websites, comic books, films, and other media to enhance the experience of the story offered in the game. However, most players would be less than satisfied with mere walkthroughs or descriptions of a game's mythology. They want to perform the story, and in so doing, in some ways to live it.

Rituals and games are also both deeply *interactive*. Despite the contested nature of the concept of interactivity, few would deny that both games and rituals draw people in and create a feedback loop of experience. Rituals are often driven by liturgy, or scripts, describing how the ritual is meant to unfold. Similarly, many video games are also scripted via the computer programming and story-writing behind the scenes. Both, however, require human interaction and performance for the "script" to become something more than just the potential for experience. And both, one could argue, shape the performer through his or her movement *through* the scripted experience. Thus both video games and rituals are "emergent" in the sense that meaning arises largely via play/ performance, and depends upon the inputted actions of the player–performer. Due to the similarly scripted qualities of rituals as kinds of "programmed" experiences, it should come as no surprise that religious rituals increasingly find new homes online and in mobile devices, a phenomenon that both challenges and in some cases enriches religious experience in surprising ways. I address this phenomenon in some depth in Chapter 3, although the translation of rituals into virtual contexts is an issue also pertinent to the concept of religious community (Chapter 6) and the analysis of virtual violence (Chapter 7).

The idea of *performance* is an important one for game players and ritual theorists, and is of course deeply tied in with storytelling and interactivity. As ritual theorist Roy Rappaport notes, "performance as well as formality is necessary for ritual" (1996, 428). That is, *doing* as well as scripting is required. This performance is often thought of as shaping our larger view of how to be in the world. In other words, rituals are often viewed as telling us something about how the world works, by helping us learn foundational stories that offer some meaning for how we are to live, or by reaffirming some sense of cosmic structure and order. The "arena" of gameplay, however, by contrast is often seen by players as having little to no meaningful effect on life beyond the game, apart from perhaps some sense of cathartic purging of intense emotions or an appreciation for camaraderie achieved in multiple-player games. The issues raised by the conflict of "play" with the "seriousness" assumed to be associated with ritual, color many facets of the intersection of religion and virtual reality, and are considered especially in my treatment of the "ritual–game–story thing" (Chapter 3) and the development of transmedia as a performance of belief (Chapter 9). For many users of virtual reality today, whether we read a specific experience as a game or as something else (like ritual) "depends on the player's attitude towards the activity" (Egenfeldt-Nielson *et al.* 2008, 35). Can intention alone, though, determine the effect that a given experience has upon us?

Both rituals and games are defined by *rules*, or structures that regulate and limit performance, shaping the player–performer's experience. Rules, in this sense, are the structure-providing mechanisms that shape experience. Both games and rituals set limits on what we can do and what we cannot, and thereby give shape and structure to an emerging experience. When we enter a virtual space, we can be assured that there are rules to be followed, whether they are loosely or rigidly defined. There are, for example, only a certain number of paths we can follow in a video game. There are also only certain modes of building things in online worlds like *Second Life*. There are, typically, defined quests in adventure games, and even if we are allowed to design our avatars to look however we please in a particular virtual context, there are always some rules to be discerned, since things cannot become virtual without a programmer defining the bounds of our experiences in some form. Even our online engagement with social media is scripted. In short, anything that we encounter behind a digital screen has been, in some way, scripted, limited, programmed, coded.

Both rituals and games draw on previous stereotypes or genre specifications, creating expectations and familiarity in performer–players, who know what to do in new manifestations of the game or ritual since they have seen this kind of thing before. Rules tell us what is possible and what is not possible to do. If there is anything to the claim that both rituals and video games can shape our view of the world, then looking at what the rules are in any ritual or gaming experience could tell us something about what we are meant to derive from the experience. This, in turn, should enable us to be critically aware participants in *any* rule-based environment. In a way, then, we could argue that religion itself can work as a sort of game, shaped by an agreed-upon set of rules, defining how we should act, what's possible, and what the goals are. Of course, not all forms of religious experience are "played" in such limited ways, but noticing the ones that are invites more comparisons between religious rituals and games.

Although it may seem to some that "religion" is on the decline, human beings are notoriously creative, imaginative creatures and will find ways to craft meaningful experiences whether or not we feel comfortable labeling them as explicitly "religious." Our engagement with virtual reality clearly reveals our desire for "religious" things and provides us with secular forms of ritual that offer us meaning, imaginative engagement, enchantment, desire and temporary escape from our ordinary routines. Games may even offer us kinds of proxy religions, giving us a temporary sense of structure and order in an increasingly chaotic world. The virtual "worlds" we enter into offer us a means of escape, a mode of imagining, and a never-depleted well of possibility for imagining ourselves all-powerful, infinite, beautiful, desired, even worshipped.

Of course, engagement with virtual reality can range well beyond video game play to include a host of online rituals, experiences, and forms of communal bonding that also do religious work. Indeed, the visual and literary arts have always been more than mere images that passively flit before our eyes. Literature and painting have the ability to draw us into other worlds, to engage us in thinking of the "what if," imagining ourselves other than we are, and the world other than it is. Books too are portals into other spaces, other modes of being. The ancient Jewish apocalypticists recognized this when they recorded their elaborate otherworldly journeys to the heavens in written texts, intended to be read by the initiated and protected, in some cases after utilizing mystical passwords. Painters recognized art's ability to create new worlds when they created vast frescoes drawing us into the spiritual spaces they imagined, some of which, like Michelangelo's paintings in the Sistine Chapel, for example, present the world of the Bible to us as a visual space to be explored. Even our prehistoric ancestors seem to have been fascinated with the idea of entry into other realms via visual imagination; cave paintings from 15,000 years ago suggest that the best place to encounter the spirit world was in a place that was different from ordinary life: in this case, the recesses of a physical structure that itself resembles a portal (Coppens 2003).

Contemporary theorists of religion and culture have spent the past several decades analyzing the means by which we replicate our urge toward other spaces in contemporary popular culture. John Lyden's groundbreaking *Film as Religion* (2003) was the first to pull all of these threads together into one coherent argument for film as a contemporary form of religion and ritual. Others, including Jolyon Mitchell, Conrad Ostwalt, Adele Reinhartz, Michael Bird, Joel Martin, Paul Schrader, Robert Johnston, Clive Marsh and John May, have added substantial insight to these claims. Brent Plate's *Religion and Film: Cinema as the Re-creation of the World* tackles this issue directly, arguing persuasively for the ability of both religion and film to envision a "re-created world." For Plate, film and religion are both mediators of reality. He is especially interested in "the connection of the world 'out there' [in real life], and the re-created world onscreen and at the altar, and how these worlds have a mutual impact on one another" (2008, 3). The academic study of video games and virtual reality is even newer than the academic study of film, with full-length academic studies of video games appearing only in the past decade and most related courses on college campuses appearing only in the past few years. Accordingly, the study of the intersection of religion and video games is just beginning now.

But who should define the new field of study of virtual reality? In what kinds of departments and programs should its academic study be housed? As Jesper Juul explains, "it is only around the turn of the millennium that video game studies began to come together as a field with its own conferences, journals, and organizations." What has resulted is a "jumble of disagreements" and a "gold rush and a race toward the being the first to point out special aspects of games, to format the field, to define words, and to point to similarities and dissimilarities between games and other cultural forms" (Juul 2005, 11). Scholars from a host of disciplines are engaging in the study of virtual reality, with some of the most notable including anthropology (Celia Pearce's *Communities of Play*, 2009); sociology (i.e. Howard Rheingold's *Smart Mobs* and Henry Jenkins' *Convergence Culture*, 2006); psychology (Sherry Turkle's *Life on the Screen*, 1997); and theater (Richard Schechner's *Performance Studies: An Introduction*, 2002, on performance theory and virtuality).

The best work is interdisciplinary, drawing from the new academic work in video game studies, and drawing on the expertise of actual game designers and theorists. This interdisciplinarity, however, seems to be yielding a new discipline – one drawing on the wisdom of pre-existing modes of inquiry but focusing on virtual reality and gaming as emergent phenomena worthy of academic specialization and uniquely designed modes of study. Important recent books that are defining the field of video game studies and virtual reality theory as independent fields of study in their own right include books like

Noah Wardrip-Fruin and Pat Harrigan's (eds) *First Person: New Media as Story, Performance and Game* (2004), Simon Egenfeldt-Nielsen *et al.*'s *Understanding Video Games* (2008), Heidi Campbell's *When Religion Meets New Media* (2010), Katie Salen and Eric Zimmerman's *Rules of Play* (2004) and Noah Wardrip-Fruin and Nick Montfort's (eds) *The New Media Reader* (2003). Jane McGonigal's *Reality Is Broken* (2011), Celia Pearce's *Communities of Play* (2009) and Sherry Turkle's *Alone Together* (2011) represent degrees of optimism and concern over what our love affair with the virtual might mean for human relationships and for society at large.

Godwired integrates these theoretical discussions with issues pertinent to contemporary religious studies, not with the hope of claiming the field for itself but rather in the spirit of interdisciplinary inquiry, arguing implicitly that the best scholarship is a conversation not a claim to territory. The shared concerns of those in a variety of other fields all looking at virtual reality and the traditional modes of inquiry in religious studies reveal that religion *ought* to be one of the voices considering these new phenomena: theories about violence, about identity, about ritual performance, and about storytelling all have a powerful place in existing studies of religious experience, and are key modes of inquiry in the study of video games by theorists in other fields as well. Once illuminated, the deep similarities in form and function between many virtual reality experiences and religious practices today are compelling, marking our seemingly secular culture as more "religious" than we might first realize.

Even as *Godwired* pushes the study of virtual reality into new realms, it also draws upon the strong scholarship of a few pioneering thinkers in recent decades. Only a few scholars were at work directly on the question of religion and virtual reality before 2002. Because technology changes so rapidly, research is quickly dated in these first-wave books by analysis of old technologies such as chat-based religious experiences, text-based games, or use of websites as organizational hubs for existing religious groups. Nonetheless, the conceptual frameworks and paradigms created by these authors are still shaping analysis today. Some of the most important books from this time period include: Brenda Brasher's *Give Me That Online Religion* (2001), Tom Beaudoin's *Virtual Faith* (2000), Jennifer Cobb's *Cybergrace: The Search for God in the Digital World* (1998), Margaret Wertheim's *The Pearly Gates of Cyberspace* (1999), Jeffrey Zaleski's *The Soul of Cyberspace: How New Technology Is Changing Our Lives* (1997), David Noble's *The Religion of Technology* (1999) and Quentin J. Schultze's *Habits of the High-Tech Heart: Living Virtuously in the Information Age* (2002). In addition to other important areas of inquiry, these works consider the nature of online worship, the thorny issue of depiction of sacred space in virtual contexts, and the moral implications of virtual actions. These are all issues that remain pertinent, and that I address in various ways in the following chapters.

The books that come closest to the aims of this book all have been published in the past six years, and deal with theoretical issues of religion practiced online, but often come at the topic from fields outside religious study, or they focus primarily on case studies. These works are indispensable in making sense of the phenomenon of religion understood through a virtual context. My own book takes their insights, weaving them into a larger discussion about key issues occupying those interested in religion and virtual reality broadly conceived. The most important of these foundational works are Heidi Campbell's *Exploring Religious Community Online: We Are One in the Network* (2005), Lorne L. Dawson and Douglas E. Cowan's (eds) *Religion Online: Finding Faith on the Internet* (2004b), Morton Højsgaard and Margit Warburg's (eds) *Religion and Cyberspace* (2005), Ken Hillis's *Online a Lot of the Time* (2009) and most recently, Craig Detweiler's (ed.) *Halos and Avatars* (2010).

The chapters here are thematically organized, each one focusing on an issue commonly addressed by scholars in a variety of overlapping disciplines all interested in the phenomenon of virtual reality. *Godwired* illuminates what these common themes are and brings these disparate conversations together. Even in such seemingly different fields, the most basic considerations reveal a shared interest in thinking about structure, storytelling, and an urge toward other realms and transcendent modes of being. In terms of the human quest for meaning, virtual reality is as potent a site for this endeavor as any existing religious institution.

Chapter 2. This chapter focuses on the issue of storytelling as a religious phenomenon and addresses the transformation of storytelling from a linear or cinematic form to an interactive form in virtual reality, including the translation of sacred texts into SMS (short message service, texting language) and the development of video games that enact stories from the Bible. Looking at a spectrum of different types of interactivity in storytelling, I move from the least interactive new religious stories to the most interactive: from hypertext (and its similarity to rituals like the stations of the cross) to cyberdrama (interactive storytelling with predetermined plot options) to video games (experiential stories with possible trajectories) to online worlds (environments in which our own stories take place). I also look at the notion of "play" as a means of thinking about hermeneutical inquiry, cinematic production (especially of religious stories), and biblical interpretation. I argue that both stories and games involve forms of rich interactivity that draw reader–players in and invite investment and immersion in experiences that can be deemed religious through their form and their function.

Chapter 3. In this chapter, I build upon the work on storytelling in Chapter 2 to argue that it is impossible to understand new virtual religious experiences without looking at rituals, stories and games as hybrid entities. What I call the "ritual–game–story thing" is a complex blend of different types of interactivity, a kind of demarcation of sacred space and time that has been going on throughout human history, but which is also at the heart of popular culture today. Video games are enactments of Huizinga's "magic circle" of play, but they also exhibit obvious characteristics of story through the implementation of a procedural dramatic arc and experiential catharsis. Furthermore, video games act like ritual when they evoke a liminal space and invite participatory identification by viewer–players with the unfolding narrative experience. The shared features and functions of rituals, games and stories reveal that these are in fact not separate types of experiences but rather overlapping forms of human meaning-making, differentiated primarily by the intentions of the player–performer.

Chapter 4. The distinction between virtual "sacred" space and "brick-and-mortar" sacred space raises some compelling questions about what makes a space "sacred" in the first place. Using Mircea Eliade's (1961) perhaps too easy distinction between "sacred" and "profane," I explore how these concepts are increasingly complicated by today's virtual environments. What makes a space sacred? Can a virtual space (such as an online church or temple) be "sacred," and if so, under what circumstances? For some online religious folk, the construction of sacred space itself can be viewed as an act of transforming the "chaos" of cyberspace into the "cosmos" of religious order. For others, the online world can be nothing more or less than a place for play, rendering any sacred space constructed there merely a prop on the digital playground and inviting intentional and unintentional sacrilege. It turns out that in consideration of virtual sacred space, as with so many of the topics that arise in thinking about the virtual, what makes something "sacred" is more a matter of intention and perspective than anything else.

Chapter 5. In this chapter, I look at online experiences with religious significance that involve forms of hybrid identity, and often multiple identities, for the user–participant. For game designer Richard Bartle, player involvement ranges from seeing the avatar online as an utterly separate object on-screen, to viewing it as a sort of puppet as a "conduit" into the online world, to seeing the avatar as a "character" that represents some facet of the player's own personality, to viewing it as a persona identical to oneself in some meaningful way. Accordingly, as I explore specific examples of hybrid and multiple identity online, I address issues such as Victor Turner's (1969) exploration of the role of masks in tribal ritual and the hybrid identities they introduce. It turns out that the issue of identity is a deeply rich one for making sense of religious experience in virtual contexts, since it represents the entry point for our "selves" into new online experiences and contexts, and because our online identities are typically plural, fluid, and perpetually in process.

Chapter 6. This chapter integrates discussions about online communities from a variety of perspectives, including (among others) game developers, computer studies theorists, anthropologists and religious studies experts. Online communities tend to be informal, transient, and governed by temporary rules. Drawing in particular on the Durkheimian sense of the "sacred" as based on community identity, the chapter explores the problems of how one defines a community (religious or not) in virtual space and how religious communities make use of virtual space today: as a site for information-sharing, as a medium for religious rituals, and as a sacred space in and of itself. The discussion about religion and its moral rules inevitably intersects with those about game communities, as both types of discussion involve some similar structural components in the "rules" they invoke, the roles player–performers adopt, and the improvisational character of interactions alongside the rigidity of agreed-upon limitations of gameplay. This chapter explores the implications of community formation online, looking at community-based virtual phenomena, such as religious dating sites, wikis, discussion boards, blogs and religious communities in *Second Life* and *World of Warcraft*. Victor Turner's notion of *communitas* is also helpful in making sense of the function of video games and online worlds as liminal spaces in which taboo behavior can be enacted, where ordinary hierarchical structures of given communities are disrupted, and where temporary experimentation in identity can occur. However, disputes abound in regard to the ability of virtual spaces to provide the kind of communal space that Durkheim and Turner envisioned, recalling issues raised in previous chapters about embodiment, presence, sacred space and agency.

Chapter 7. This chapter explores video games, virtual worlds, and other violent virtual experiences as mimetic enactments of symbolic sacrifice. Numerous video games and online immersive experiences have made use of violence as a device to propel the storyline forward, and can accordingly be viewed as instantiations of mimetic violence as a ritual salve for societal angst and violent impulses. In this chapter, I focus on some particularly controversial examples of virtual violence, each of which has explicit religious themes: the online *KumaWar* series of virtual "re-enactments" of the war in Iraq, the controversial *Left Behind: Eternal Forces* PC video game, and the staging of a violent battle in a virtual rendering of Manchester Cathedral in Sony's Playstation 3 game *Resistance: Fall of Man*. I also apply a Girardian reading to less explicitly religious examples of virtual violence, notably the controversial game *Super Columbine Massacre RPG!* and to a number of 9/11-based online games like *New York Defender* and *9/11 Survivor*, comparing the use of memory of victims as a defense for a game's violence with similar debates about the mimetic violence of the crucifixion. I argue that an examination of such virtually violent experiences reveals the importance of player intent and the role of reflexivity in meaning-making in video games, and I suggest that if Girard is right about religion and violence, then video games may be providing some of the same religious functions that violent religious ritual has historically provided.

Chapter 8. This chapter builds upon Chapter 7's discussion about violence, but tackles the specific issue of genre, arguing that violent video games (typically first-person shooters) can be aptly viewed as an experiential form of the genre of apocalypse as defined by the Society of Biblical Literature "Apocalypse Group" in 1979 (see Collins 1979). Such video games, like apocalypses, can be viewed as revelatory literature disclosing an otherworldly realm, evoking visionary hope of eschatological salvation in both a temporal and a spatial sense, often including vivid descriptions of the destruction of "evil" forces by

the forces of "good." However, unlike traditional Jewish and Christian apocalypses, video games are inherently interactive and thus require the agency of
the player to enact the violence of the end times. Video games, especially first-
person shooters, place the player directly in a "messianic" role, urging players
to see themselves as the primary agent of destruction of "evil" in a replayable
imagined battle against one's enemies. Furthermore, today's violent video games
allow players to imagine their enemies in endlessly variable, programmable ways.
Through an analysis of select examples of popular video games in comparison
with traditional apocalypses, I argue that video games are the most poignant site
for contemporary renegotiation of the genre of apocalypse, and I offer
some insights on what this might mean for our contemporary understanding
of "evil."

Chapter 9. In this chapter, I bring together the threads of the individual
chapters by looking at the most prominent theme that recurs in my examination
of religion and virtual reality: the phenomenon of world-building (as a religious
activity). In particular, I look at the emerging concept of transmedia storytelling as a kind of world-building, arguing that religion and transmedia have a
lot in common as types of streaming storytelling based upon a common story
hub. Drawing on the insights of emerging transmedia theorists, I propose that
transmedia, even in its secular forms, functions like religion in its ability to
engender hunger in consumers, a sort of existential desire for inhabitation of
another world and a fascination with rule-based environments outside of our
daily lives. Drawing on popular examples of transmedia like the *Harry Potter*
and *Avatar* franchises, I consider how the performance of belief via new media
storytelling compares to traditional notions of faith. Whereas traditional religion
is characterized by the fixedness of ritual and texts, by recognizable modes of
performance, and by predictable methods of engagement and interpretation,
today's new transmediated experiences are indeed sometimes rule-based, but they
are also often commodified, temporary distractions characterized by fluidity,
plasticity and multiple modes of performance.

Chapter 10. Every good online game offers "expansion packs," new material
devoted to enhancing the play experience and offering new quests. This chapter
is an "expansion pack" for the book, and pulls together threads from throughout
to see where all of this talk leaves us, to suggest new directions for research and
analysis, and to invite further academic play with the resonances suggested here.
There is much more to be done; our fascination with the coded, the screened, the
mediated, and the scripted is here to stay, and if it is shaping us in deep ways,
we ought to at least notice that it's happening and think about what it means.

Godwired asks why we are so drawn to such programmed environments, to
virtual places in which we know there is some order, where we hope for connection, where we enter into a mode of being that both is and isn't the same as
our ordinary lives. In our messy, postmodern world values are often seen as up
for grabs; institutionalized religion is largely in decline; and people increasingly
craft their own moral codes from scratch. So might our fascination with virtual

experiences reveal, at least in some respects, a desire for greater order and structure? Is there some kind of existential comfort in the assumption of a programmer, and for fixed trajectories of experiences that mimic the notion of predestination? Do we long for experiences, however temporary, in which we know exactly who the bad guys are, in which we know there is some order to be discerned, in which we can assume the well-ordered hand of a programmer at work, guiding the unfolding of our quest and directing us about what we should do? If this notion is combined with the increasing modes of immersion apparent in new technological developments, then an argument for a hunger for the real, the ordered, is even stronger.

So might it be fair to suggest that our fascination with virtual reality is a signal of our disillusionment with the postmodern, the fragmented, the uncertain? And thus, might we see our investment in virtual spaces as a reflection of what in other contexts we might easily consider the "religious" impulse? If viewed this way, then our desire for the virtual can in fact be viewed at least in part also as a hunger for the real – for a sense of meaning, order and definition in our own real lives. If religion is about finding meaning, order and a sense of predictability – if it is about imagining the way the world might be – if it is about stories that animate our lives, rituals that shape our consciousness, and modes of interacting that define who we are, then it seems to me that virtual engagement is doing some of the very same things. Our desire for greater and greater immersion, coupled with the structure and order that come with that very immersion, may signal a hunger for the real that suggests a religious function for some of our most popular pastimes.

Douglas Rushkoff astutely observes that the screens we use to engage with virtual reality "are the windows through which we are experiencing, organizing, and interpreting the world in which we live." For Rushkoff, when we engage with virtual reality "we are doing more than extending human agency through a new linguistic or communications system. We are replicating the very function of cognition with external, extra-human mechanisms." We can and should look at how these programs work, and how they shape us when we use them. Furthermore, if we think about the digital things we make as kinds of human expression, then "recognizing how the programs we do use really work is revolutionary in itself" because "once people come to see the way their technologies are programmed, they start to recognize the programs at play everywhere else – from the economy and education to politics and government" (Rushkoff 2010). Religion is just one mode of human expression, but it too is a mode of encounter, a set of processes or programs that shape us and that we also program for ourselves.

In an interview with an Amish man about religiously motivated restriction of technology (including the internet), Howard Rheingold was advised: "It's not just how we use the technology that concerns us. We're also concerned about what kind of people we become when we use it" (2002, 185). *Godwired* is an invitation to think precisely about these questions: How do we use technology, especially in terms of its virtual experiences, and how might thinking about the relationship between religion and virtual reality enhance our ability to make reasoned, thoughtful and healthy decisions about what it means to live a good life in a digital age? How is humanity being shaped and changed by the questions raised through our engagement with virtual environments? In what ways are these experiences akin to those traditionally labeled as "religious," and what can we learn by drawing such comparisons? This is the experience you are invited to enter into with *Godwired*. Your password is curiosity. Your username is human being. Now you can log in.

Chapter 2

The stories we play

Interactivity and religious narrative

We might be tempted to think that "playing" stories is something new, but interactivity has long played a pervasive role in religious storytelling. Every religious tradition has stories of its founders, its practitioners or its legendary figures, and many of these stories have "interactive" forms, what we might call the "stories we play." The Exodus is remembered in Jewish tradition in the *seder* meal with symbolic associations for the food that is eaten alongside a retelling of the story. The Quran (and the stories in it) is recited in full by Muslims during the month of Ramadan. Christians regularly retell the story of Jesus, through a re-enactment of the Nativity story or in the dozens of Hollywood films that focus on his life and death. Buddhists remember stories about Gautama Siddhartha: the four noble truths are taught within the context of the story of his enlightenment. Hindus have a rich panoply of narratives about the gods and goddesses who once walked the earth, with associated television shows ritually enjoyed by viewers and local re-enactments of their stories as well. Even Taoists tell the story of Lao Tzu's leaving behind of all he had known to go into the wild and experience nature directly and see this as a model for the good life. There is a long-standing and deep connection between stories and interactivity in religious life.

Today, interactivity with sacred texts is taking on new hues, as we are given the immediate and easy power to treat sacred texts as streaming bits of information rather than as physical objects endowed with singular meaning. The fluidity of digital texts creates a cascade of possible uses, interpretations, and alterations that frustrate the assumption that the text can be used as a sort of singular portal into divine will. The exploration of wired textuality invites us to consider texts *as* texts, and thus also as material objects transformed into information streams, with profound impacts for how they are used and treated. In the transformation of material books into downloadable information streams, we are witnessing also the transformation of sacred texts from a fixed series of words on a page – God's will typeset and printed – into fluid, shapable and playable streams. The first section of this chapter is devoted to an examination of the implications of these changes.

But it is not enough to just consider the problem of fluid textuality and sacred writ; the transformation of sacred texts into new formats also profoundly affects the stories *within* those texts. In the second section of this chapter, I look at how our fascination with fluidity results in a transformation from stories as fixed texts to stories as fictional worlds, pools of possibility that invite transformation in the form of games, personal retellings, and other forms of "play." Indeed, the emerging recognition of kinship between games and stories gestures toward a fundamental shared enterprise of these media as different modes of world-building – an activity that has traditionally been ascribed to God. Today, we are all creators. And as might be expected, the degree of interactivity in religious storytelling and story-hearing varies tremendously in different virtual contexts.

As we look at sacred stories in their contexts as video games, instant messages, web pages, or blends of cut and pasting in email tags, we might ask with Foucault, "What is a work? What is this curious unity which we designate as a work? Of what elements is it composed?" The impossibility of answering this question leads Foucault to conclude that "the word *work* and the unity that it designates are probably as problematic as the status of the author's individuality" (1998, 207–8). Nowhere are these remarks as true as they are in today's virtual contexts, where stories are frequently composed by multiple individuals, designed by a team of game designers, cribbed and copied from other media objects, and enacted through the emergent storytelling of the player. They might even have a second life as parts of mash-ups, mods, user-created sequels, or other blended digital creations. If these stories happen to be religious ones, the evocative nature of interactive storytelling invites a host of intriguing questions about the relationship between play and sacred writ.

Sacred texting: when religious writ gets wired

David Morgan defines textuality as "practices of reading, writing, and performing texts that are grounded in print. A text is something written, published, stored, read silently or aloud, purchased and shared, traded, displayed. [A text] is cited, edited, rewritten, compared with other texts, and taught" (2005, 89).[1] Today, we would need to also include as forms of textuality the host of new wired modes of interaction that people use as they engage with sacred writ. Simply transferring written text into virtual forms brings with it some surprising consequences. Religious texts can now be searched, hyper-linked, downloaded, spliced, copied, truncated, e-mailed, text-messaged, recited with video accompaniment, chanted on iPod, and piped from mobile devices into earplugs. They can be streamed, tweeted, mashed-up and modded. Religious texts are available in as many digital forms as there are devices to access them. Hopeful worshippers are constructing their own transformations of existing texts in the form of digitized prayers, video accompaniment to existing religious texts, and the recording and sharing of recitation of prayers and liturgy. Now believers must ask some awkward questions like: once a sacred text is digitized, can the new "sacred" file be "profaned," by placement next to less holy texts?

secular

Others wonder, now that any text can be copied in seconds, what was the original text to begin with?

For believers, especially in revealed traditions, the text is often assumed to be a perfect copy of a heavenly Original. Believers typically assume the integrity of their sacred text in its "Original" form because the text is seen as a window or heirophany tapping into the divine realm. For example, many Jews believe God's hand shaped the writing of the Bible. Many Christians believe the same about their own received version of the text and about the words of Jesus they find in the New Testament. Muslims believe the Quran was delivered without error to Muhammad. For such believers, the sacred text may originally have been a streaming revelation from God downloaded into human form – but this happened *one* time and it was received, recorded, and fixed. Morgan explains that textuality assumes authorship, producing the "constellation" of reader, text, referent and writer. When we're looking at a sacred text, this "constellation" implies that God is the author of the Original Text, that God gave the Text to us as passive if devoted readers, receptacles of the divine words therein (2005, 89).

One of the primary means of disruption of sacred texts is in the receptacle itself. The written book that we can hold, caress, care for, and lift up is no longer fixed. It has become a stream of information – a copiable file based at its root on simple binary code. "Sacred" files can now be streamed into digital devices that are used for a host of savory and unsavory activities. Furthermore, if we wish we can simply delete them to make room for other preferred files! Such fluidity creates confounding theological problems for how we understand the sacred and the profane, how we relate to the potentially "corrupting" influences of other nearby digital files.

For the Buddhists who follow the teachings of Thich Nhât Hanh, the problem is not the availability of religious texts online, but rather the spiritual temptations that new media pose in their ability to distract monks from meditation and study. This concern has prompted the Plum Village community in France to adopt a revision to monastic rules that had remained unchanged since the time of the first followers of the Buddha. In the "*Revised Pratimoksha*," monks are instructed that any monk who "keeps a television, video player, karaoke player, electronic games' machine, and any other kind of equipment used for showing worldly films, listen[s] to worldly music, and play[s] electronic games" is subject to a statement of "Release and Expression of Regret." Similarly, a monk who "goes on to the Internet alone without another monk next to him as a protection against getting lost in toxic websites" has committed an "Expression of Regret" offense (Nhât Hanh 2004, 60).

Some religious officials are less worried about the corrupting influence of new media at large than they are about unsavory mixing of sacred digitized files with more plebeian or even offensive digital files. For example, how should a Muslim treat an iPod once he or she has downloaded the entire Quran onto it? Is there a difference between downloading the Quran onto an iPod intended solely for worship purposes and downloading into on an iPod intended also to store a host of other (perhaps less pious) media? What about the physical nature of video iPods as devices that must be held and viewed? One new Muslim asked recently on the turntoislam.com discussion board if he could use an iPod as a hand-held prompt while he learned to recite the prayers. In response, one poster quotes the twentieth-century Saudi Arabian Muslim scholar Sheikh Muhammad b. Sâlih al-'Uthaymîn in his own argument against the use of a text to guide one in prayer, since such a practice distracts from the bodily movements required in Muslim prayer ("Tahajud") (TurnToIslam n.d.). The poster likens this fatwa's proscriptions to the use of iPods and advises the new Muslim not to use one during prayer.

There is also the issue of the virtual relay of religiously significant messages and the implications this may have for God's ability to "hear" prayer wherever it is uttered, as well as the concern that digital technology might somehow dilute the sacredness of a religious message. Is something important lost in the 2005 translation of the entire Bible into SMS, when the first passage in Genesis becomes: "In da Bginnin God cre8d da heavens & da earth?" And what are we to make of the "Text Mary" service, embraced in 2005 in the Philippines, which allows worshippers to send text prayers via cell phones to then be included in the Catholic Mass ("Text Mary")? Should Muslims consider a divorce legitimate if the husband, who is required to tell his wife three times that he wishes to divorce her before it is final, simply texts her or emails her instead of telling her personally, a problem that Malaysian Muslims have recently been addressing (Kent 2003)? In Malaysia, the practice was banned, but in Saudi Arabia, a Jeddah-based Shariah court approved its practice in 2009 (Arab News 2009).

Michelle Boorstein of the *Washington Post* points out that these questions can get thornier still, when she asks: "Is it rude to watch your phone in church – if that's where you've downloaded your Bible? Can text-message blessings be spiritually enriching? Is there a sense of religious community on a cellular phone?" (2006). As Tony Dokoupil of *Newsweek* asks: "[S]hould Jesus and Madonna (the singing one) go on the same iPod?" Dokoupil wryly observes that "downloading the Word through the same fiber-optic cables as the latest Korn album sounds like a bad idea, given that Roman Catholics dispose of holy water through special pipes to keep it from touching sewage" (2007). The implicit question here is about the boundaries of sacred literature in a digitized world. Should digitized sacred texts be viewed as confined to the digital file alone, or if, once a sacred text has been downloaded onto a digital device, should the entire hardware device then be considered the "vessel" for the sacred text, and treated accordingly? In other words, if you download a religious text as a file onto your iPod, is it the *file alone* that is sacred, the iPod *itself*, or something else entirely, and if so, *what*?

For some religious people, concerns about digital technology even spill over into the *potential* polluting uses to which that technology *could* be put, whether it actively is now or not. Concerned about the mere *ability* of cell phones to be used for impure activities, some Jewish cell phone users have requested so-called "kosher" phones, an issue explored in some depth recently by Heidi Campbell (2010, 162–78). The idea is to offer conservative Jews a phone that is free of "corrupting influences" of the sort that are already avoided by ultra-orthodox Jews through a ban on television and some radio (MacKinnon 2005). Reuters reported in February 2008 that Bezeq Israel Telecom had launched a new "kosher" landline phone service, which will block calls to porn and other "improper" destinations for these conservative groups (Reuters 2008). The same sentiment troubled religious courts in the United Kingdom, where judges heard a case about whether or not church steeples can host mobile phone masts, since the masts *might* be used to relay porn (Petre 2007). Ultimately the practice was approved, with the recognition that software-based protections are typically in place to prevent unseemly consumption (Malkin 2007). For Campbell, the best means of understanding religious use of new technology is to look at the complex social formations that inform initial use and then shape its continuing place in religious community. Thus, for Jews interested in the kosher phone, the symbolism of technology is as important as the technology itself: "The potential invasion of forbidden content which might cause community members to sin was seen as a threat that could not be ignored" (2010, 165). The phone itself (and the information that might flow through it) became a focus for religiously informed renegotiation, and the *kosher* phone became a recommended solution for maintaining the idea of purity and impurity, while still participating in contemporary technological society. A key issue, it seems, is authority.

Authority

When religious texts become information, new issues of authority also arise, concerning the ability of these texts to be used by more people in more new ways. As Bill Seaman remarks, "the volume of virtual space is quantitatively different from that of the bound volume" and has, in effect, "become unhinged" from its materiality (2004, 228). Digital texts are streaming texts; they are simulacra that can be multiplied endlessly and thus become nearly impossible for religious authorities to control. As fluid as any digital text, they become astonishingly easy to copy and manipulate, creating new challenges for those who may wish to control their distribution or interpretation.

Some religious groups see the transference of sacred texts into digital forms as a positive means of preserving texts that otherwise might be lost or forgotten. The Asian Classics Input Project (ACIP) is the result of tens of thousands of hours put in by Tibetan monks and others supportive of their cause, all transcribing woodblock and other handwritten texts into digital formats. The *User Manual* on the ACIP website (ACIP n.d.) explains that the mission of the group is finding, organizing, "digitally preserving and disseminating rapidly disappearing Tibetan and Sanskrit manuscripts that hold the philosophical, cultural, and religious heritage of endangered cultures dating back more than 2000 years," and to "make these books and ideas accessible to the world at large." Now, the website offers thousands of texts, some removed from Chinese-controlled Tibet and available for the first time through ACIP. In their digitized form, then, the texts have a sort of durability and accessibility that they do not have in their original physical form. They also serve as a sort of digital defense against the loss of Tibetan culture, since once texts have become digitally copied and distributed, it is almost impossible to eradicate them.

Other religious authorities register increasing concern about easy digital access to controlled religious texts by those who previously would not have the ability or perhaps even the desire to access them. For example, the ease with which a Muslim can now read and search online databases of the *Hadith* (sayings and deeds of Muhammad) has made some Muslim scholars nervous. The University of Southern California (USC) offers a searchable online Hadith collection, in English (USC n.d.), which is prefaced by a "warning" issued "especially for Muslims." The warning explains that the early scholars of Hadith were experts in the "critical science of collecting and evaluating aha-deeth" and that students were required first to learn from the scholars how to utilize the Hadith correctly. Today, "there is a real danger that Muslims will fall under the impression that owning a book or having a database is equivalent to being a scholar of *ahadeeth*. This is a great fallacy." The archivists of the USC online database explain that it is "merely a tool, and not a substitute for learning, much less scholarship in Islam." Particularly problematic are wide-stream availability and ease of manipulability. Not only can any internet users get hold of almost any sacred text they wish, but they can access numerous commentaries and interact with them through cut-and-paste, through searches, through the easy movement of portions of them, and through the delivery of texts to others as a form of communication and religious devotion. In so doing, a user "takes a fluid role in the construction of meaning through different levels and qualities of interaction" (Utterback 2004, 231). Put another way, they use the texts in unintended, sometimes theologically dangerous ways.

Despite warnings by some religious scholars, new technology is changing the ways that Muslims and others access and assimilate religious rulings. In addition to using searchable digitized sources, Muslims today turn to imams online, call imams live on television shows, and even access imams via cell phones to receive new *fatwas* (religious rulings). The recent proliferation of people claiming to have credentials to issue fatwas has created confusion and frustration among some Muslims. Who should decide, if anyone, what authoritative texts should be accessible, and to whom – when anyone with an internet hook-up and a laptop can find whatever he or she desires at the click of a mouse? As argued by Dale Eickelman, Jon Anderson and the other contributors to *New Media in the Muslim World* (Eickelman and Anderson 2003), new media access to traditional Muslim authoritative resources is forcefully challenging the most conservative modes of Islamic authority, allowing those who previously had no voice to decide for themselves what to believe and why to believe it, whether those in traditional positions of authority like it or not.

One recent ruling by a group of Muslim jurists in India forbids the use of recitation of the Quran as a ringtone for one's cell phone. Why? There are two reasons: First, if one's phone rings, one will certainly answer it – and in so doing, cut off the recitation of the Quranic verse midstream, a sign of profound disrespect to God. Second, and perhaps even more importantly, one's cellphone might ring in the bathroom – thus allowing God's holy word to be recited in the most profane of places, a despicable act, and one that would never be committed by a human – but apparently can, and occasionally is, committed by a cell phone! Thus, responsibility must be shifted back to the *owner* of the cell phone, who is required to turn it off before entering the bathroom – or better yet, not to even download the recitation of the Quran for use as a ringtone in the first place (Daily Times 2009).

For Christians, the problem of increasing accessibility of religious texts is just as intense, but takes a different form: anxiety over easy public access to texts that were rejected in the formation of the New Testament, but which offer compelling and problematic portraits of Jesus and the early Christian community. The *Nag Hammadi Library*, the collection of ancient Gnostic manuscripts discovered in Egypt in 1945, was first published in an English translation by James Robinson in 1977, with a paperback version appearing in 1981. Public awareness about the Nag Hammadi materials grew consistently in the following two decades, but exploded in 2003 with the publication of Dan Brown's *The Da Vinci* Code, which exhibits Brown's muddled but provocative interpretation of elements from the Gnostic worldview. Today, fans of *The Da Vinci Code* don't need to buy their own copy of James Robinson's translation of the Gnostic manuscripts, but can simply read the Gnostic texts for themselves online at the *Gnosis Archive*. Or, if they are interested in other early contenders for New Testament inclusion such as the Gospel of Peter, they can scan through the *Early Christian Writings* online database, where well over a hundred New Testament-era texts appear, many of which were hotly contested in their time period and most of which did not make it into the New Testament.

The sticky problem for Christians, then, is also authority. With individual access to a host of early Christian texts, and spurred to question the New Testament's authority by Brown's reassessment of early Christian history, what should people believe? Today's Christians must decide for *themselves* which texts "should" have been included in the New Testament and why, and they must do so with limited information about the history and context in which these texts were composed. The implications of such explorations are obvious: given the competing accounts available both in the New Testament and in other ancient Christian texts, how do Christians know what Jesus *really* said and did? Although many Christians obviously struggled with such questions a long time before the internet, today the stakes are higher and more people are exposed to the possibilities. The very format of hyperlinked and digitally archived searchable religious texts presents a given book of the Bible in its digital form as simply one of many files to be perused, considered, copied-and-pasted, and integrated into the reader's ever-changing interpretive worldview. The Bible itself has become fluid, its fixed covers dissolving into a host of linked sites that describe competing biblical histories, alternate non-canonical gospels, and previously unavailable literature from the first few centuries of the Common Era.

The virtual as medium

Some groups seem to have recognized the dangers of textual manipulation today, and thus argue for digital communications as mere tools for communication. In 2002, Pope John Paul II announced at the World Communications Day that: "While the Internet can never replace that profound experience of God which only the living, liturgical and sacramental life of the Church can offer, it can certainly provide a unique supplement and support in both preparing for the encounter with Christ in community, and sustaining the new believer in the journey of faith which then begins" (cited in Charny 2004). For John Paul, digital communications are to be used as supports, not substitutes, for formal religious life.

Maybe the problem is media competition. After all, popes are sort of like spiritual screens, delivering to us God's wishes for us from a remote location. Grimes, in discussing the relationship between ritual and media, remarks that the two ideas are closely connected, prompting us to ask "in what respect [media] is ritual" (2006, 10). Although not all ritual is religious, the relationship between religious ritual and media is particularly evident in the view that human beings can serve as hierophanies, that is, as mediators between the heavenly realm and the human realm. In this respect, then, Catholics are apt to see the pope as the most important medium, as the window or "device" streaming God's wishes to us. The internet could be seen as a potential upstart, mediating from the "other" realm into our daily lives and disrupting traditional channels of authority.

In his statement on World Communications day in 2010, Pope Benedict declared that:

> The increased availability of the new technologies demands greater responsibility on the part of those called to proclaim the Word, but it also requires them to become more focused, efficient and compelling in their efforts. Priests stand at the threshold of a new era: as new technologies create deeper forms of relationship across greater distances, they are called to respond pastorally by putting the media ever more effectively at the service of the Word.
>
> (2010a)

Echoing John Paul's earlier remarks, Benedict argues that the internet should be viewed as a *supplement* but not a *source* for religious life. As Benedict argues, priests should "be present in the world of digital communications as faithful witnesses to the Gospel, exercising their proper role as leaders of communities which increasingly express themselves with the different 'voices' provided by the digital marketplace." Priests, he proposes, "are thus challenged to proclaim the Gospel by employing the latest generation of audiovisual resources (images, videos, animated features, blogs, websites) which, alongside traditional means, can open up broad new vistas for dialogue, evangelization and catechesis." Technology is to be used simply as an effective vehicle for transmission of the gospel, not a replacement for it.

Pope John Paul II was the first pope to use SMS (short message service, i.e. "texting") technology to send out a "daily papal message" to believers (Charny 2004). Pope John Paul also oversaw the creation in 1995 of the Vatican's online website, complete with searchable encyclicals, and in 1999 he named the sixth-century scholar St Isidore as the patron saint of computers and the internet. After succeeding John Paul II, Pope Benedict XVI arranged for SMS messages to be sent to the cell phones of youth attending World Youth Day, a practice that has now become standard and is an apt model for how Catholic leadership views the benefits of virtual reality. Pope Benedict text-messaged a reminder about evangelism to all subscribers to the SMS service: "The Holy Spirit gave the Apostles and gives u the power boldly 2 proclaim that Christ is risen! – BXVI" (Wooden 2008). Such messages are *one-way*, sent from above and received below. Such a view of technology echoes the church's traditional view about the pope as mediator, transmitter of God's wishes, in similar one-way delivery. Technology can also be used, with the proper leadership, to wall off elements of the world that threaten religious belief. Bishop Anthony Fisher recently announced the development of a social networking site for Catholic youth called Xt3.com, which Fisher describes as similar to *Facebook*. The Vatican's spokesperson on these new developments, Cardinal Pell, has a page on Xt3.com, and invites Catholics to "come online and become one of my friends." But despite the new technology of connection, friendship here retains all of the Church's pre-existing authoritative structures.

World Youth Day for 2008 included a new feature: a "digital prayer wall" to which participants could text-message prayer requests from their cell phones. One important element was the public display of the prayers onto a large digital screen. Such a move might seem a democratic mode of encounter, flattening Catholic religious hierarchy. It seems Protestant, even, in its apparent bypassing of the church's rite of confession. However, the *framing* of the activity within the World Youth Day experience emphasizes the prayer wall as merely a means of aggregating messages to God without disrupting the belief that God is in heaven, degrading sacred texts, or disturbing the church's authority. In other words, prayer became a sacred spectacle housed within the larger Church-sanctioned ritual event.

More problematic for church hierarchy are the numerous prayer walls available on websites and in mobile device apps (applications), since these prayer walls invite user participation without any sanction or even participation from religious hierarchy. For example, consider the non-denominational Christian answer to *YouTube* called *GodTube*. *GodTube* used to include a digital prayer wall, available online at any time. The wall has now migrated to crosswalk.com, where a forum hosts it; an affiliated *Twitter* feed operates under the username "theprayerwall." The use of digital prayer walls like this one that exist *only* in virtual spaces raises the puzzling questions of who these prayers are *really* addressed to, and why posters felt the need to publicly display them. A quick read of the posted prayers on *GodTube* in 2009 revealed that some prayers are invitations to other readers to pray "with" the poster, and others are addressed directly to God, as if God must "read" the prayer wall to learn the poster's desires. Does this mean that God must "enter" into virtual reality to read these prayers? If not, then why post them there at all, instead of directly praying quietly to God?

Prayer apps available for the iPhone raise similar questions. For example, an app called simply "Prayer Wall" is designed to "unite Christians around the world in prayer for each other" as Christians identify particular prayers and promise, via a message, to pray for the selected person. A new feature identifies those posters who have not yet been chosen: "The yellow star is a visual cue that the individual is still waiting for someone to accept this Prayer." Such a feature implies that the real point of the app is not prayer to God, but rather the satisfaction that comes through socializing prayer and the sense of "acceptance" that can be achieved digitally through another person's selection of your prayer.

Other apps are more theologically challenging, such as the app entitled "Pray," which simply offers users a blank space in which to type a prayer. At the bottom of the screen is a button labeled "Send Prayer." Hitting this button results in a message (similar to one received when sending a text message) that "Your Prayer has been Sent." The prayer doesn't go to a public prayer wall, nor is it received by other users at all (unless the creators have set up a hidden system to collect prayers). Rather, the point of this prayer app is the sheer performance of sending a "message" to God. In this case, the "space" of virtual reality is identified with the "space" of heaven, and God is implicitly presented as a media user too, receiving messages in a digital prayer box.

The app "Box for Prayer" is similar in its representation of messages as presumably being sent to God via digital delivery; however, "Box for Prayer" offers a response. Users type a message into a message box, hit "send," and receive back an inspiring message that appears to have been composed by the designers, since none of them is biblical. After entering several generic prayers, I received the messages: "May the Lord smile upon you" and "The Lord listens to all of his children." A third time I got the advice: "Let go and Let God." Certainly, none of these messages presume to speak as God, but they do depend upon the assumption that the prayer, once "sent," will be delivered to God via the iPhone delivery system. Such programming suggests that increasingly we *do* view digital space as identified in some ways with sacred heavenly space, and we see messages sent via virtual reality as having the ability to be delivered to God via that space. In fact, such prayers may arguably have *more* potency, having been sent through the most reliable message-delivery system available for most people today.

Digital prayer delivery services resemble in some ways the Jewish Wailing Wall's email prayer service. However, for those who email prayers to the Wailing Wall, there is a tangible material object involved: the Wall itself. Worshippers email a prayer to Jerusalem, where it is printed out by a courier and physically inserted into the wall on their behalf. If they still wish to pray "at" the wall via their computers, 24-hour webcams record what is happening there (Spiegel Online 2006). Worshippers can even use their iPhones to send messages directly to Jerusalem to be put in the wall. This digital practice begs the question of what it means to actually go to the wall yourself. Is God "closer" if you visit the physical wall than if you simply view a digital image of it? And if you aren't actually engaging in the ritual yourself, can the same intent be realized by sending a virtual message to a virtual wall?

To make things even more complicated, a replica of the Wailing Wall has been constructed in *Second Life*. The creator of the virtual Wailing Wall, who adopts the user name "Xanadu," explains that the digital wall "is a peaceful spot to sit and grieve, pray, meditate or comfort a friend. The wall accepts self-created notecards that are immediately deleted. The idea is to allow The Wailing Wall to bear away your burden" (Xanadu 2008). Given the fact that both the *physical* wall in Jerusalem and the *virtual* wall in *Second Life* each seem to function as a sort of "go-between" for the worshipper wanting to communicate with God, it makes you wonder which version is more "real," and what is "spiritual" or "virtual" about prayer, or about the Wall as sacred space.

The transmission of religious texts in virtual space can clearly result in new forms of interactivity, such that religious stories may be remade, retold, and altered in ways that affect the characters, plots, events, and thus also their religious significance and theological import. It would be comforting if the questions posed here had obvious answers. But today it seems we are shaped precisely by the uncertainties. We have already seen how sacred texts are subject to increasing fluidity by a movement into virtual space. Now we will look at how the stories within these texts are also transformed in new virtual contexts.

Stories and interactivity

What happens to the shape, style and authority of biblical stories when they are transformed into video games? Why are some religious stories more suited for film than for interactive games? How do different degrees of reader control over a story's outcome affect its ability to work theologically? Religious stories can undergo radical changes simply by their placement in a new interactive medium. Suddenly characters that were passive become agents that we can control. Outcomes that we have taken for granted in sacred history, as recorded in received scriptural stories, are called into question as we are invited to enact alternate outcomes. Agency that has been attributed to God can now be transferred to the human being responsible in the new context for the story's unfolding. Indeed, in some cases, the linear trajectory of received stories is abandoned altogether as they become mere environments in which players can enact fantasies.

Stories today are increasingly shaped by player choices. The rapid individualization of experience that we expect – as players of video games, as intentional surfers of the internet, as consumers with a seemingly infinite selection of media items – is also shaping our use of sacred stories, which are less often viewed as fixed evidence of a heavenly determined story and more often as grist in the imaginative mill of gameplay. Hermeneutics becomes malleable, and we are less "readers" than "users" of the system of the Bible, an imaginative worldview that we integrate as one of many cultural resources helpful in the shaping of our personal values. As a means of examining the implications of interactive storytelling in twenty-first-century wired society, I integrate components of media theory into the study of religious texts to look at five different ways of thinking about stories: (1) stories as games; (2) stories as fate; (3) stories as potential narratives; (4) stories as catharsis; and (5) stories as interactive systems. All of these ways of thinking about stories have distinctive implications in virtual contexts.

Stories as games

So what is a story, anyway? This seemingly simple question has resulted in a messy stew of arguments, comparisons, new definitions, and theoretical disputes in recent decades. As Jesper Juul has remarked, "one of the most contested terrains in the study of games is that of games and narrative" which "can only be characterized as a tangled mess of intersecting positions, counterpositions, retractions, qualifications, sidesteps, and reframings" (2006, 33). Salen and Zimmerman agree, referring to the "turf wars" about games and narrative that are "surprisingly contentious" (2004, 379). Zimmerman remarks that "there are as many approaches to the question of 'games and stories' as there are designers, artists, technologists, and academics asking the questions" (155).[2] It seems that there is no easy answer to the problem.

Some scholars are loathe to consider games as stories. They seem to believe that something important is lost if we emphasize narrative over interactivity. Instead, they privilege what Markku Eskelinen calls "an ergodic dominant" (2004, 37). Espen Aarseth argues that reading narrative into games is a form of "story fetishism" (52). Games are defined by three things, he says: rules, a game world, and the events that emerge in the game world (48). In other words, for Aarseth and others, a game is a *system* and not a *story*. Stuart Moulthrop agrees: "[M]any followers of digital culture ... drop the theoretical ball [in] insisting that so-called interactive forms be engaged in a general project of storytelling" (58). Moulthrop argues that in games, "the primary cognitive activity is not interpretation but configuration, the capacity to transform certain aspects of the virtual environment with potentially significant consequences for the system as a whole" (2004, 60). The emphasis for these ludologists is on the *system*, not on the individual trails of experiences that can be observed emerging behind players as they move through a configurative gaming experience.

Henry Jenkins offers a more nuanced approach. He says we should examine games "less as stories than as spaces ripe with narrative possibility." Game designers, he says, are less to be viewed as storytellers and "more as narrative architects" (2004b, 118). They create a *space* in which a story *might* emerge. Moulthrop allows for such a possibility, while still emphasizing the player's dynamic choices as the most important element of gameplay. For Moulthrop, the "cognitive activity" of gameplay takes place *now*, in the player's mind, and not in any story that happens to emerge through play. In imagined conversation with Janet Murray, he argues that meaning in a game is primarily "configurative" and arises through ongoing transformation in the game's emerging environment, as dictated by player choices (2004, 59).

Because films are a kind of fixed, linear story, they are a natural analog to the study of video games. Bernard Perron cautions against trying to "re-purpose" the analytical tools of film studies to video games, but the use of cut scenes and visual media in video games makes some comparisons likely (2003, 239). A cut scene, as defined by Richard Boon, is "a short movie presented to the player at specific points in the game ... used to advance the story in some significant way because it removes control from the player" (2007, 54). Cut scenes, then, are like snippets of film (fixed linear narrative) within an otherwise interactive system (the game). If we apply these ideas to religious experience, then it is easy to see why some are more comfortable with the idea of play as a component of religious experience than others. The divide is in some ways doctrinal, and thus may reflect interpretive strategies for encountering the texts. Catholics, for example, despite dogmatic fixedness in ritual practice – and perhaps *because* of it – invite intense involvement of believers in storytelling *enactment*, as in the Stations of the Cross or the Passion play. Other Christian groups, typically those with iconoclastic leanings, exhibit less obvious interactivity, such as those Calvinists who insist on reading the text with no enactments, no media transformations, and no visual images.

For something to work as a ritual or as a game, there must be some kind of script to guide one through the experience. A ritual liturgy is a set of rules that shapes the emergent experience of worship but allows for certain choices in performance and interpretation. Similarly, many video games come with a sort of liturgy; in addition to the game's scripted rules, this may consist of a backstory, revealed via associated media, cut scenes, or introductory material, and often shapes the fixed elements of the storyline through which players are led. Religious liturgy also relies upon a "backstory" of sorts, in the form of the received sacred text that inspired the current form of enacted telling. Thus it seems safe to say that games and stories are kin concepts.

One important component in determining if something is more like a game or a story is the identification of *where* meaning-making occurs in the "telling" of a story. If meaning lies in the reader's *passive* absorption of a fixed text, then games are not stories, since games are *active* play. However, if stories can *emerge* through interactivity, leaving behind a fixed story as artifact, then a game *can* be a story – or perhaps we might say that a game can *become* a story as it is played. As Michael Mateas and Andrew Stern observe, "emergent narrative" is "concerned with providing a rich framework within which individual players can construct their own narratives, or groups of players can engage in the shared social construction of narratives" (2006, 644). Liturgy, too, shapes the telling of religious stories, creating ritual events that allow certain choices but forbid others.

Zimmerman's definition of narrative reveals the close relationship between games and stories, and can effectively be applied to a number of different kinds of media and rituals, and even to liturgy:

> A narrative has an initial state, a change in that state, and insight brought about by that change. You might call this process the "events" of a narrative ... A narrative is not merely a series of events, but a personification of events through a medium such as language ... [T]he representational aspect of narrative ... is constituted by patterning and repetition.
>
> (2004, 156)

According to Zimmerman's definition, examples of narrative could include a book, a game of chess, a marriage ceremony, a meal, and even a conversation (157). Of course, texts and liturgies are among the most rigid forms of narrative, since "[w]hen immersed in a text, readers' perceptions, reactions, and interactions all take place within the text's frame, which itself usually suggests a single schema" (Douglas and Hargadon 2004, 196). Games, on the other hand, are one of the most *loosely* defined types of narrative. If Zimmerman is right, then narrative exists not as a single readily recognizable category of "thing," but rather as a continuum of experience and possibility. Juul's solution to the problem is to split the term "narrative" into two related but distinctive parts: *story* and *discourse*. A *story*, says Juul, consists of the *events* being described, in whatever order they occurred. A *discourse*, however, consists of the *telling* of the events – which may or may not be the same as the order in which the events occurred (2005, 159). Since time moves forward, the events of a story *only* occur in *one order* – and can only be shifted in the *telling* of the story as discourse. In this way, Juul opens up the possibility that a game *can* function as a discourse via an *emergent* storyline.

This distinction parallels that between the biblical narratives as a human production (a discourse, or telling) and the biblical narratives as divine product (or story told by God via historical events and thus unalterable). Indeed, such interpretations are common in contemporary biblical scholarship. Marcus Borg describes his approach to biblical narrative as the former: the Bible, he says, is "the product of ancient Israel" and "what the Bible says is the words of those communities, not God's words." The Bible is a "human product" that "does not in any way deny the reality of God." We can only "talk about God" using "words, symbols, stories, concepts, and categories known to us" but God is beyond all of these (2001, 22). The story, in this case, is God's actions in history, but the Bible is this story transformed into discourse by fallible and competing human accounts.

For other Christians, including many biblical fundamentalists, the Bible is God's story, told perfectly to human beings, such that history and the biblical text are identical: story and discourse are one and the same. Josh McDowell exemplifies this approach when he proposes that the Bible is available to us in "original monographs," that are free from error and that match the original revelation from God. For McDowell and other biblical fundamentalists, "the Bible has been breathed by God" who "used men to write out exactly what he wanted them to write" (1999, 338). There is only *one* telling of the story in such a reading – and the Bible is a singular "true" story with only one possible linear rendering; the Bible's story is not emergent through reading, but rather should be piously absorbed in totem. In their advice about preaching to "postmoderns," evangelical theologians Harold Netland and Keith Johnson advise that "[p]resenting the gospel within the framework of the Bible's storyline helps them recognize that the exclusivity of Christianity is not the result of Christian ethnocentrism but is related integrally to the Bible's diagnosis of the human condition resulting from the Fall and the solution found in Christ" (2000, 59). In this view of the Bible, it is not a space to explore but a set of truths to accept.

Both liberals like Borg and fundamentalists like McDowell would allow that the received written text of the Bible *points to God* and has some fixedness in its textuality; the difference is that Borg sees the rigidity of the text as a product of the "human response" to God, a fixed record of one of many *possible* responses. McDowell denies such relativity in production of the text, and sees the Bible as a fixed hierophany revealing a singular and unalterable imprint of God's heavenly word. Borg is interested in the purposes to which stories might be put, what we might call the play involved. He uses the example of God's attempt to kill Moses in the book of Exodus: "If we see the Bible as a divine product, the question becomes, 'Why would God want to kill Moses?' ... But if we see the Bible as a human product ... the question becomes, 'Why would Israel tell this story?'" (Borg 2001, 25). For McDowell, the sequence of events in the received biblical texts is presumably the only way that God *wanted* us to read it. Thus, fundamentalist literalists like McDowell tend to read the Hebrew Bible (or as they would call it, the Old Testament) as predictive of events in the new. For Borg, the order of events in the Bible is less relevant, since the Bible is not a singular story but a sort of emergent discourse, a collection of responses to faith, human-made stories of people trying to *create* meaning out of the world around them, with differing degrees of success and consistency.

Similar currents of debate occupy theorists of video games. Torben Grodal's definition of a story, like Juul's, focuses on a story as events appearing in a linear sequence, and thus accords most well with those views of biblical reading that see the text as fixed. According to Grodal, a story is "a sequence of events ... based on simulations of experiences in which there is a constant interaction of perceptions, emotions, cognitions, and actions" (2003, 130). The most easily recognizable kind of story is what Grodal calls the "canonical story," that is, "a story with one (or a few) focusing characters that unfolds itself in a linear, progressive time, from beginning through middle to end, as Aristotle noticed" (133). Such stories are based on *specific* events described in a *particular* order, which are stitched together in a *fixed* pattern. McDowell would see the Bible as precisely this linear kind of story, but told by God instead of humans. Borg would agree that the Bible presents us with such a series of events, but he would emphasize that *people* organized it that way and that we, as readers, can contextualize and even ignore certain components of the story as *we* decide what this book can teach us about God. Neither Borg nor McDowell would be likely to see the Bible as a game, but Borg's approach is closer to this view since he implicitly acknowledges the degree of play involved in the selection of included texts by humans who *rendered* the Bible sacred through their own emerging choices. The Bible, in this case, is "sacred *for a particular community*" (Borg 2001, 29). For Borg, then, the fixed pattern of the Bible's stories as we receive them is an emerging product of human history – and thus is open to interpretation, reconsideration, and new interpretations.

Debates about the importance of a fixed pattern of textuality are the main sticking point between ludologists and narrativists as they analyze different manifestations of stories. Ludologists insist that games are about experimentation and unpredictability and thus any elements of story are coincidental and irrelevant. Narrativists argue that games can *produce* stories, such that a story is a constantly emerging, unfolding trace left as a sort of residue along the experiential track behind the player's active movement through a game. In terms of biblical interpretation, both narrativist theologians like McDowell and ludologist theologians like Borg might be interested in the way that the Bible's stories emerged over time and how their appearance related to the "play" of the writers. Ludologist theologians would be more likely to see biblical interpretation as a game, and point out that although biblical stories are now fixed in canonized form, this should not blind us to the fact that they were composed through *lived* experiences and creative acts, many of which were intertextual and thus also interactive and governed by rules of "play." They might also point out that many readers of these fixed texts today "play" with them when they dislodge them from their canonized form and splice and dice them into forms more amenable to their own creative or religious goals. Interpretive play would matter more than fixed storylines for ludologist theologians.

Another way of addressing the relationship between games and stories is to focus on the role of play. As Salen and Zimmerman point out, "play and games have a surprisingly complex relationship" (2004, 72). Play can be seen as a broader category than *either* stories or games. Salen and Zimmerman define play broadly as "the free space of movement within a more rigid structure" which could consist of a pre-existing story, a narrative world, a game or a ritual (2004, 304). Play, says Zimmerman, "exists both because of and also despite the more rigid structures of a system" (2004, 159). Salen and Zimmerman explain that play is dependent upon a defined baseline against which it moves:

> Think about the use of the word "play" in the sense of the free play of a gear or a car's steering wheel. The "play" is the amount of movement that the steering wheel can move on its own within the system, the amount the steering wheel can turn before it begins to turn the tires of the car ... Play emerges from the relationships guiding the functioning of the system, occurring in the interstitial spaces between and among its components. Play is an expression of the system, one that takes advantage of the space of possibility created from the system's structure.
>
> (2004, 304)

In games, play is the "space of possibility" afforded a player to explore and to make choices within the game's system. Thus, play determines how much flexibility is inherent within a given religious system, worldview or system of interpretation. The rules of play determine just how much freedom is allowed within that world – whether that world is a film, a book, a game or a religious perspective. Play is experimentation and innovation in response to a rigid system or structure. It is easy enough to see that play has an important role in religious and theological expression.

Play, then, is how much freedom we have within a given rule-based system. Play shapes how much wiggle room we have – how much we can change a received text or tradition and not find ourselves isolated from our religious peers. We could think of theology as the most basic level of "play" with a sacred text as system; it is the "road" upon which we are "steering" our hermeneutical inquiry. So, for example, directing a film about Jesus exhibits a greater degree of "play" than simply reading the gospels or composing a sermon. Composing a video game about the Bible exhibits an even greater degree of "play." Play, then, can be a characteristic of stories, of films, of games, and of rituals. What differs is the *degree* of play, *who* is allowed to engage in play, and what *results* from the play.

One interesting case of playing with the Bible's stories is Playstation 3's *The Bible Game*, designed by Rob Dyer. Even he seems to recognize that some stories can't be tampered with. Dyer admits that he didn't make the *The Bible Game* "for personal, spiritual reasons" and he was not interested in "doing anything controversial." Dyer deliberately avoids including certain stories from the Bible, since he wanted to "make the game friendly to the widest possible audience" (Dyer, cited in Totilo 2005). Those stories Dyer does evoke (Jacob's ladder, Daniel in the lion's den, David and Goliath) are presented in highly stylized, very loose form – as backgrounds for unrelated strategic challenges like races or gathering of digital props. The desire not to offend Christians through too much interactivity may explain why some of the "challenges" in the game seem a little odd – like the "Jonah challenge," in which your objective is simply to stay afloat atop a stream of water coming out of the whale. Similarly, Dyer draws on the story of the Exodus from Egypt, but refuses to portray Moses at all. Instead, he portrays animated children running through the Red Sea trying to avoid crabs and seaweed.

Such choices make sense if we view them through play. To show Moses as part of this entertainment sequence is too obvious a revision of the text. By contrast, to allow modern children to run through the seabed instead allows the Moses story to become a sort of empty stage into which modern children can be piously placed. In playing the game, children may get some idea of how Moses *might* have felt – but they never pretend to *be* Moses. This technique also avoids the pitfall of making Moses look foolish, hiking up his robe and running pell-mell through a treacherous seabed, nipped at by crabs. God's Prophets aren't typically playful. It seems acceptable to let the Bible provide *settings* for games, but not to let the Bible's own plot lines be so obviously enacted that players have too much agency, or the "seriousness" of biblical stories can be disrupted. Indeed, limiting the reader's ability to configure a story is at the heart of one of the most popular Christian approaches to biblical stories: that they are not games, and instead should be read as evidence of God's predetermined actions in linear history. This brings us to our next mode of thinking about stories, as inevitable, predetermined strings of events in history.

Stories as fate

In Western, and particularly in Christian, traditions, the notion of a fixed trajectory of history (and thus also of storytelling) is especially important, revealing to believers God's own storytelling and giving credence to the idea that God is in charge of history's unfolding. Although a number of the world's religions have an affinity for fixed narrative, in Christianity one can find linearity at its most prominent, perhaps because the story of Christ is so important that it is believed by many to have been foreordained since the beginning of time, with all of history unfolding inexorably since. As Morgan points out, this view pervades many Christian approaches to texts, particularly the evangelical view, which sees "communication media" such as the Bible as offering "a univocal, unidirectional transmission of information from a sender to a receiver and portrays the Christian life itself as such a communication: one must choose, and the choice is clear and simple, with an unambiguous outcome" (2005, 97). What one chooses in this worldview, of course, is to see things in precisely this way: predictable, linear, and preordained. In terms of reading stories, then, the only interactivity encouraged with this perspective is to read correctly, to read in a straightforward manner, and to receive the stories as they are without alteration or unauthorized interpretation. We saw hints of this view in McDowell's reading of the Bible as God's singular, unalterable story.

Accordingly, what might seem strange at first – that many Christian filmmakers have repeatedly visually depicted the Passion of Jesus, and yet video game designers will not do so except as parody – comes into sharp focus when we consider how harshly the notion of interactivity clashes with the notion of theological inevitability. For viewers of *The Passion of the Christ*, despite the liberties that Mel Gibson took with the gospels, the story was commonly *perceived* by believers to be an accurate retelling of a predetermined, fixed series of theological and historical events. Gibson himself says of the film: "Critics who have a problem with me don't really have a problem with me in this film. They have a problem with the four Gospels" (cited in Garlow and Jones 2004, 150). The Archbishop John Foley, President of the Pontifical Council for Social Communications, claims similarly: "if [others] are critical of the film, they would [also] be critical of the Gospel" (cited in Rachman 2003).

Grodal's discussion of the fixed nature of filmic narrative offers some insight into this perspective, inviting us to consider how viewing The *Passion* can be experienced as a sort of "witnessing" to the actual events:

> Films make it possible to cue and simulate an experience that is close to a first-person perception (either directly by subjective shots, POV-shots) or from positions close to the persons, contrary to the fixed and distant perspectives in theater … The representation can furthermore represent various aspects of reality with photographic verisimilitude. As an audiovisual media, the dominant temporal dimension is the present tense; we directly witness the events.
>
> (2003, 138)

For film viewers, the experience is intrinsically voyeuristic and typically invites identification with characters, but the events *themselves* cannot be changed – thus any rich experience comes through the tragic observation of unchangeable events. Thus, the viewing of *The Passion* could be perceived as an experiential phenomenon – but a theologically safe one as well, since one can be emotionally drawn into the events, but still be unable to change them.

It is for this reason, perhaps, that so few typical viewers of Gibson's *The Passion of the Christ* could even detect the rather substantial changes he made to the story as told in the gospels. For similar reasons, Martin Scorsese's *The Last Temptation of Christ* rankled those who detected the obvious alterations in the biblical story – creating a disconnect between their assumption of themselves as "witnesses" invited by the visual story, and their belief (based on their own religious education) that the story in fact unfolded quite differently than Scorsese's film depicts. If we return to Zimmerman's notion of play as steering on a road, Gibson stayed on the road, if wobbling about quite a bit – but Scorsese ran right off into the theological ditch.

Film, of course, can be intensely interactive for its *creators*, even though its story is fixed for its viewers. As Plate puts it, films "do not passively mimic or directly display what is 'out there,' but actively reshape elements of the lived world and twist them in new ways that are projected onscreen and given over to an audience" (2008, 1). For Gibson as director of *The Passion of the Christ*, "play" consisted of the choices *he* made in additional dialogue, in costuming, lighting and music. But for Gibson, the "system" is non-negotiable and "play" is limited to those interpretive processes that maintain the predetermined Christian "rules" of play. A similar kind of negotiation seems to occur in other films based on religious narrative, such as *The Message* (1976), which never depicts Muhammad on-screen, out of respect for the aniconic nature of many Muslims' beliefs about the Prophet – but which nonetheless makes numerous narrative choices in terms of what dialogue is spoken, when, where, by whom, and in what order. A successful religious film will mask any changes made to the received sacred story and at least *appear* to be simply porting the story unaltered into a new format. The linear nature of film in its reception encourages this reading.

The typical Christian preference for a linear view of narrative can be traced back to early Christian insistence on the fidelity of the Jesus story as the fulfillment of biblical prophecy as a result in linear time of human error committed long before. Paul makes this point in an early letter, when he urges the Corinthians to hear the story of Jesus' death rightly:

> For I delivered to you as of first importance what I also received, that Christ died for our sins in accordance with the scriptures, that he was buried, that he was raised on the third day in accordance with the scriptures, and that he appeared to Cephas, then to the twelve.
>
> (1 Cor. 15:3–7, English Standard Version)

For Paul, the death of Jesus was the culmination of all of history. His death is to be understood in one way and one way only: as the means to salvation for humans. Tampering with the story, especially in terms of imagining that things could have unfolded otherwise, is not an option for Paul or his followers.

We see a similar resistance to experimentation with the narrative in the harsh rejections by the Church Fathers of the creative interpretation and new storytelling of the Gnostics.[3] One of the main reasons Irenaeus objects to the Gnostics is their willingness to "play" with scripture:

> Such are the variations existing among them with regard to one [passage], holding discordant opinions as to the same Scriptures; and when the same identical passage is read out, they ... all depart [from each other], holding so many opinions as to one thing, and bearing about their clever notions in secret within themselves ... For, though holding wrong opinions, they do in the meanwhile, however, convict themselves, since they are not of one mind with regard to the same words.
>
> (1885, Bk 4, ch. 35, §4)

By contrast, Irenaeus praises those who accept the view that there is only one reading, one divine narrative that "has come even unto us, being guarded and preserved without any forging of the scriptures" and which consists in "reading without falsification" and engaging in "lawful and diligent exposition in harmony with the Scriptures." The developing notion of apostolic succession is itself a very early version of Christian insistence on linear narrative over the playful interpretive "games" engaged in by Gnostics and others.

Augustine, writing centuries later, sees himself as the bearer of the authentic tradition, and urges other readers of the scripture to accept the same interpretation: "Whoever takes another meaning out of Scripture than the writer intended, goes astray, but not through any falsehood in Scripture." The scriptures contain only one right interpretation for Augustine, so to read rightly is to read the way the author intended, that is, the way that God intended. Some people may engage in freer interpretations, Augustine admits, but so long as these are harmless and ultimately corrected, a little play is acceptable "if [the reader's] mistaken interpretation tends to build up love."

Such a reader "goes astray in much the same way as a man who by mistake quits the high road, but yet reaches through the fields the same place to which the road leads." A reader who wanders from the intended interpretation of scripture should be corrected eventually, even if his misreading is harmless, since "if he get into a habit of going astray, he may sometimes take cross roads, or even go in the wrong direction altogether ... And if he should once permit that evil to creep in, it will utterly destroy him" (1881, Bk 1, ch. 36, §41). For Augustine, to read right is to see the straight path of interpretation intended by God and to limit the "play" of free interpretation as much as possible. If we think of narrative as providing us with a meaningful cosmos or "universe," and if we see the Christian fascination with the Bible's narratives as motivated by a belief in God as author both of the Bible's universe and ours, then discomfort with too much play with the Bible makes sense. As game theorist Murray puts it in regard to reading games as narratives: "We like to know that there is a ruling power in control of an imaginary universe, and it makes us uncomfortable if the author seems to abdicate that role" (1997, 275).

Murray notes that "[g]iving the audience access to the raw materials of creation runs the risk of undermining the narrative experience" (1997, 39). It also invites the "readers/viewers to imagine themselves in the place of the creator" (40). Thus, we could say that to make reading too much like play can be a form of blasphemy!

One kind of interactive Christian narrative that avoids the dangers of blasphemous play is the Stations of the Cross when instituted as digital hypertext. The Stations of the Cross exist in several forms online for faithful Catholics and curious visitors to navigate as a hypertext collection of linked pages. Hypertext, says Murray, can be defined as "a set of documents of any kind (images, text, charts, tables, video clips) connected to one another by links. Stories written in hypertext can be divided into scrolling 'pages' (as they are on the World Wide Web) or screen-size 'cards' (as they are in a Hypercard stack) but they are best thought of as segmented into generic chunks of information called 'lexias' (or reading units)" (1997, 55). The "reader" moves through these lexia, or nodes, by selecting a path which is charted in part by the creator of the hypertext but also crafted by the dynamic choices of the reader (Mateas and Stern 2006, 647). As Douglas and Hargadon note, "readers of most hypertext fiction are merely exploring the narrative, not constructing its links and rearranging its structure, or even generating lexia and links themselves" (2004, 203).

In the online Stations of the Cross from *Catholic Online* (n.d.-b), the penitent begins by reading a prayer of contrition, then clicks to move through the stations. It seems an easy transition from the physical stations of the cross as fixed story units based on the gospels, to hypertext, in which these same units are presented as visual and literary relics of the biblical story. Just as practitioners would be expected to move from station to station in real-life versions of the ritual, so practitioners online are limited to clicking to go to the next station, and are encouraged to move in order. The goal here is pious consumption, with rather prescribed limitations on human interactivity and very low agency. In a hypertext experience, "the unimportance of the reader's proxy may be essential" to the success of the hypertext experience. The reader inhabits a space on "the periphery of the action," interacting with the main characters, but not having the power to change the experience except, perhaps, to backtrack and to decide when to move forward again (Bernstein and Graco 2004, 178).

Hypertext, by providing only a fixed series of narrative nodes, suits the function of the Stations of the Cross by retaining much of the rigidity of the Christian story and of the real-life ritual of visiting the Stations themselves. Schechner asks of hypertext, "How much really do the participants contribute? They participate for the most part in games that are fixed, making choices that are extremely limited: they agree, that is, to be manipulated" (2004, 194). In experiencing a hypertext, there are some choices involved but they are seriously limited; just as if in a real experience of the Stations of the Cross, one might choose to wander back to a previous spot, or sit and meditate in another. But one cannot change the outcome of the story, nor can one challenge the notion that these events are *meant* to be experienced in a particular order. In such an "interactive" experience, our only mode of agency is passive response, the recognition of the inevitability of the events depicted and an experience of pathos.

The limited virtual interactivity allowed with the hypertext Stations of the Cross seems markedly different from *Catholic Online*'s approach to other "interactive" rituals, which typically require embodied authoritative oversight. For example, if you click the "confession" link on the site, there is no invitation to confess online. Rather, the site suggests that if you need to confess, "simply ask the priest and he will help you by 'walking' you through the steps to make a good confession" (Catholic Online n.d.-a). For most rituals, then, the site insists upon traditional modes of encounter with church hierarchy and the enactment of traditionally instituted rituals. However, as Schechner says of hypertext, choices are offered only "within a strictly defined and tightly limited field" (2004, 194). Such limitations accord well with high forms of religious ritual with tightly scripted engagement.

Berstein and Graco use the example of an imagined hypertext *Hamlet* to explain how hypertext limits our options in storytelling. "Tragedy," they say, "requires that the characters be blind." This means that no matter how much the viewer–participant may wish to, in order for *Hamlet* to be *Hamlet*, he or she cannot be allowed to change the trajectory of Hamlet's demise. And if the participant tries to have too much influence over the plot in a hypertext narrative, "the system typically responds with incomprehension." In short, "If you make *Hamlet* a game, it has to be rigged so that actions taken by a reasonable and sane reader–protagonist – not to mention a wildly inventive one – do not derail the train of events that must ensue if this is to be *Hamlet* and not, say, *Timon of Athens* or *A Midsummer Night's Dream*" (2004, 178). As Richard Boon explains, "some commentators consider it impossible to create a satisfying story while still providing … agency to the player due to the lack of authorial control – if events may be changed, for instance, there is no inevitability, which makes certain potent story forms, such as the tragedy, impossible to create" (2007, 47). Thus the more fixed forms of interactive experience, like hypertext, are more naturally matched with religious experiences like the story of the Passion, with its own requirement of theological inevitability.

Another form of contemporary media that accords well with this linear view of time is film. When viewing a film, says Gonzalo Frasca, viewers cannot "manipulate" the storyline to influence how the events will transpire "since film sequences are fixed and unalterable" (2003, 224). Thus, films can readily mimic the Christian view of time as shaped by God in a predetermined linear trajectory. Grodal makes the same kind of observation about Greek tragedy and the familiarity an audience may already hold in regard to the storyline:

> [M]ost famous Greek tragedies are based on stories that are well-known beforehand, so that the viewer may know what happens and only asks how it happens. Tragedies and melodramas are however a variant of stories

because they rely on passive emotions and/or third person emotions. For such stories, pastness, decidedness, and fatality is important in order to block a present-tense experience that would make the passive acceptance of the inevitable and painful more difficult.

(2003, 137)

As inevitable storylines, tragedies have a lot conceptually in common with how many Christians read the crucifixion, and thus we can see why for many fundamentalists, interactivity with the (tragic) biblical storyline simply isn't acceptable. Mark Wolf points out the most distinctive differences between games and linear texts:

Whereas works in traditional media are made up of fixed, linear sequences of text, image, or sound (or combinations of them) which remain unchanged when examined multiple times ... events experienced in a video game will vary widely from one playing to another. Film viewers can watch a film from beginning to end and be satisfied that they have seen the film in its entirety, but a video game player must often have some amount of skill to advance through higher levels of the game, and there are often courses of action and areas of the game which are still left unexplored even after several times through.

(2001b, 13)

No matter how many twists and turns a film takes or how creative its use of time, or how expansive its depiction of space, it remains a fixed piece. This helps us understand why films (as inevitable storylines) are generally preferable to video games (with multiple storylines) for the telling of biblical stories, and of the crucifixion in particular. Games are often more theologically dangerous than film, precisely because of the choices they offer in storytelling. Films are "input-driven" (i.e. come *into us* as recipients) just as Augustine's fixed view of God's desire for us is "input-driven." Video games are "output-driven" (i.e. come *out of us*) and therefore are more akin to the narrative experimentation engaged in by the Gnostics, or by other spiritual seekers driven by self-enlightenment.

Echoing others, Eskelinen argues that the relationship a viewer has with a film, play or story is different than the relationship a player has with a game:

[T]he dominant user function in literature, theater, and film is inter-pretative, but in games it is the configurative one. To generalize: in art we might have to configure in order to be able to interpret, whereas in games we have to interpret in order to be able to configure, and proceed from the beginning to the winning or some other situation. Consequently, gaming is seen here as configurative practice, and the gaming situation as a combination of ends, means, rules, equipment, and manipulative action.

(2004, 38)

Game players would be "frustrated, rather than satisfied, if the game unfolded in an altogether predictable fashion" (Jenkins 2004a, 197). This kind of predictability, however, is precisely what many Christians *want*. As game designer Richard Dansky remarks, there are "serious issues" at play if a game allows too much control for the player: "If the game narrative demands that a certain character be removed from the stage, then what happens if the player can save that character?" (130). One can imagine that a game that allowed users to "save" Jesus from the cross would not go over very well with many Christians.

As if aware of the dangers involved in tampering with the fixed text of Christian narrative, Christian game designers typically avoid interactive storylines that impinge on the Bible's given texts. Instead, Christian video games more often deal with a different "story" that is unfolding in real time: the fate of the *believer* in his or her battle with evil in the real world. For example, *Left Behind: Eternal Forces* focuses on the believer's eschatological choices in the expected end times. The *Veggie Tales* and the *Charlie Church Mouse* series distill the Bible's stories to simplistic moralistic lessons clearly intended to be applied to the child players' lives. By steering clear of any attempt to introduce interactivity into the given storyline of the Bible, most Christian games avoid the problem of tension between theological inevitability and play.

Bible Champions: The Resurrection is an unusual exception to these rules, since it is a Christian produced video game that teaches the story of the Passion and Resurrection to children. However, even *Bible Champions* manages to privilege the biblical text and offer only harmless and fleeting forms of Midrash, which is why the game has happily made its way into Christian bookstores and online merchants' sites. In the *Bible Champions* series, players elect to play as either a young girl or young boy, clad in approximations of first century robes, as they explore a crudely crafted digital model of ancient Jerusalem. If they follow directions properly (including following a digital arrow that tells them precisely where to go) they are rewarded with renditions of stories from the gospels, primarily culled from the Gospel of John, arguably the most theologically determinative in its presentation of the events in Jesus' life. Tellingly, when these narrations occur, viewers see a frozen image on the screen. The only "movement" comes from the female narrator, who "reads" from the New Testament.

Bible Champions: The Resurrection includes segments on gospel events such as the trial before Pilate, the Last Supper and Jesus with his disciples in the Garden of Gethsemane. As if the designers knew the dangerous interactive waters they were treading, segments of play skip the crucifixion, moving directly from "The Last Supper" to "The Resurrection." There is interactivity here, to be sure, but the rules of the game allow only certain things to be changed. The avatar can collect "faith" and "love" tokens, locate objects and explore, but has no power to change the unfolding of Jesus' fate. The structure of the *game* is removed from the structure of the gospel *story* which is immutable, even in the world of the game. Once the child avatar completes a series of preliminary game-related tasks, he or she touches a Bible icon, and the story resumes *as told in the gospels*, primarily drawn from John's version of the Passion. A new screen appears in which the avatar is not visible, and a narrator reads a Bible verse as the biblical story unfolds in fixed form before the viewer. The avatar recedes from view, and it is revealed that despite the interactivity allowed in the game, the player is really an observer. There is no emergent story here – just play intersecting with a fixed storyline.

The stories culled from the Bible can be viewed as religious examples of what Salen and Zimmerman call "embedded narratives" or "pre-generated narrative content that exists prior to a player's interaction with the game" (2004, 383). As Jenkins explains, narrative enters a game on two levels: "in terms of broadly defined goals or conflicts and on the level of localized incidents" that players "witness" (2004b, 124). Clearly, the latter occurs in *Bible Champions*, offering the player agency only in the obedience in mustering the "faith" (tokens) that enable one to be rewarded with a "click" on the Bible to prompt the recitation of an unalterable story. This game demonstrates what we have seen: the story of the crucifixion has little narrative plasticity for believers. *Bible Champions* was designed by believers in order to carefully constrain what components of the biblical story are malleable and which are not. But what other kinds of engagement with biblical narrative are possible with interactive technology? The next example, interactive fiction (IF), enables the user to have significantly more choice in determining what the emerging story looks like.

Stories as potential narratives: IF and fan fiction

One of the places where we can see the tension between games and stories most clearly is in the phenomenon of IF. Nick Montfort identifies IF as a sort of hybrid genre, "a potential narrative that may contain game elements" (2004, 312). Interactive fiction, especially when it involves existing religious stories, resembles a sort of computerized Midrash machine, calling our attention to the ability of programming to facilitate playful interactivity with sacred texts. Montfort explains that IF is:

> a program that simulates a world, understands natural-language text input from an interactor and provides a textual reply based on events in the world … By definition, IF is neither a "story" [n]or a "game," but, as all IF developers know, a "world" combined with a parser and instructions for generating text based on events in the world. The riddle is central to understanding how the IF world functions as both literature and puzzle.
> (2004, 316)

In IF, the player–reader engages with a program that responds with branching variations of narrative events. Interactive fiction is not a story when it is first begun – it is simply the possibility of a story, as Brenda Laurel notes: "In the

Aristotelian sense, the 'world' is typically understood as the *material* of a play, whereas the plot is its *form*" (2004, 311).

Eric Eve, a biblical scholar and a producer of religious IF, believes that IF can open up possibilities for more successful teaching of the complexities of how the biblical texts were composed and collected. The most important of these, intertextuality, is the similar means by which creators of biblical IF and writers of the Bible themselves all use allusions to previous texts in the explication of their own contemporary stories. Eve explains, using his own religious IF, "All Hope Abandon," as an example:

> For the most part "All Hope Abandon" uses the biblical text (and other texts) allusively, occasionally quoting them, sometimes representing aspects of them more or less closely. This is similar to the way in which many New Testament texts make use of the Old Testament. Thus, for example, the opening of Luke's gospel is written in such a way as to resemble the opening of 1 Samuel, or the opening of Matthew's gospel recalls the birth of Moses and a dreaming patriarch named Joseph. ... Such examples could be multiplied almost endlessly; they are integral to the way much of the New Testament (and also quite a bit of the Old Testament) functions. To be sure the New Testament is not only a static text but a sacred one; its employment of intertextuality is inevitably both different in nature and more serious in intent from that of any work of IF ... There are nevertheless similarities in intent insofar as both the New Testament and "All Hope Abandon" seek to create new narratives that rely for much of their meaning on earlier sacred texts, and neither is simply giving a new rendering of an old story.
>
> (2007, Par. 49)

One of the principle features of IF compared with our own reception of static biblical texts is that in IF "it is up to the reader (or player) to drive the story forward, usually by directing the actions of the main protagonist (known in IF parlance as the player character, or PC)." To set the stage, IF "typically opens with a brief textual description of the PC's situation, perhaps also giving some indication of the tasks the PC has to perform, or the challenges he or she has to overcome, though these may not become apparent until the game gets under way." Player–readers encounter particular paths that have been preprogrammed into the structure of the story, and they must engage in problem-solving to figure out what these are. By reintroducing such choices into his own IF, Eve hopes to reiterate for us the interactive process by which biblical authors – in this case especially the New Testament authors – used received sacred stories in the construction of their own. The biblical authors, he argues, were engaging in IF-like activity, blending sources according to received rules of hermeneutics and crafting new texts in the process.

Interactive fiction is intriguing in its nature as both process (game-like) and product (narrative). Interactive fiction consists entirely of scrolling text displayed on the screen, the result of the player's interaction with the system. Because this text is co-produced by parser and player, IF works to "produce narratives as a result of sessions of interaction." Interactive fiction is a "space of possibility in which the user's inputs, parsed as actions, become part of the narrative text" (Montfort 2004, 311). One could argue that Midrash, similarly, is a product of the reader's input as he or she interacts with the sacred text and produces new narrative that in some way becomes part of the new text that emerges through the experience. When seen this way, Midrashic activity is remarkably game-like, and the Bible is much like a narrative "space" to be encountered. Salen and Zimmerman's definition of game makes this apparent: "A game is a space of possible action that players activate, manipulate, explore, and transform" (2004, 378). Interactive fiction, like games, then, presents a "possible" space inviting player interaction to produce a new experience and a story as a record of the encounter.

Although most IF is non-religious, some authors are daring enough to play with the religious implications of storytelling and interactivity. Eve's biblically inspired IF, "All Hope Abandon," is loosely modeled on Dante's *Inferno*. The story begins in a dreary, drowsy university classroom during a lecture about the New Testament. Quickly the player–character (PC) suffers a heart attack and the entire IF experience is thus cast as a dream or near-death experience. Eve's IF is a bit heady but clever. Consider this description of the second stage of the PC's journey, which Eve describes as "a recapitulation of the main lines of New Testament eschatology":

> Symbolically speaking the PC must pass through the crucifixion and the Empty Tomb and then play an apocalyptic game of chess against an opponent who starts out as Pontius Pilate but is soon replaced with a composite Roman emperor (representing an amalgam of all the emperors from Augustus to Domitian). The chess game is played out with somewhat unconventional pieces and is meant to reflect, first the events leading up to the Jewish war of 66–70 CE, and then aspects of the apocalyptic scenarios of Revelation and 4 Ezra. If the PC loses the game he loses his soul; if he wins he can pass on to the next stage.
>
> (Par. 37)

After passing through a quasi-Eden with a helpful serpent, the PC rescues a female character and then either dies or wakes up in a hospital bed. Clearly, this game is playing with the notion of interactivity and biblical interpretation, inviting the PC to envision alternative readings of biblical literature. Interactive fiction is an ingenious vehicle for such experimentation, problematizing the very notion of what constitutes a text.

Another less sophisticated but in some ways more daring IF is *The Bible Retold* by Justin Morgan and "Celestianpower" (2006). In *The Bible Retold*, the player actually plays *as* Jesus and must figure out how to fulfill Jesus' function as the world's messiah. Functioning itself as a sort of "system" inviting hermeneutical experimentation, *The Bible Retold* presents the player with a set of scripted choices, leading the player from the *potential* of a story to the representation of a fixed linear story and plot, with Jesus as the main character. *The Bible Retold* invites the player to craft as many lines of narrative about Jesus' ministry as one could wish, with only the loosest of references to the fixed biblical text. *The Bible Retold* expects general familiarity with the Bible, but invites playful riffing on the gospel's stories. The only restrictive rules are playful attempts at biblical morality; if you enter the "about" command, you are told that "It might be a good idea to have a Bible (or internet connection) handy while playing this game." Why? So that you can avoid failure via commandment violation. If, as Jesus, you break any of the Ten Commandments (by typing "covet" or "kill," for example) the game immediately ends – and you earn "the rank of Imposter."

Despite its restrictions, the game does invite you to try out different things, typing in possible actions to see if the program can "parse" them and direct you along your way. It also invites experimentation with blasphemy, to see what kinds of "actions" you can attribute to Jesus and still stay in the game. As Eve (2007, Par. 3) explains, "part of the appeal of IF is the illusion that one has complete freedom to type anything one likes at the game's command prompt" although in fact the game will only understand "a very restricted subset" of what is entered. Even if the computer doesn't understand what has been typed, the textual record of the emerging "story" will still include any actions the user wishes to type. The game's opening lines reveal the nature of the unfolding interactive story with all of its potentially blasphemous performance:

> You came for quietude and serenity ... a chance to be with your Father ... to meditate on the problems of the world. And what do you get? You get followed ... The Romans have quashed religion: the priests are corrupt and unholy. With the power of God inherently vested in you, only you can save the day. Up-and-coming leader of the people (and a new religion to boot), your followers have ... well, followed you! They are weary from the journey and hungry too, but being so numerous, it seems only a miracle could possibly feed them all ...
>
> [Press any key to begin] ...
>
> Dock and wild flowers adorn the sweeping hedgerows that surround this large expanse of grass and clover ... To the northwest, the waters of a large lake lap gently against its shore and in the valley to the east lies a bustling town centre.
>
> A heavy stone tablet falls from the sky, missing you by just a few inches.
>
> A crowd has gathered here today, to watch the Son of God at work performing a miracle.

do a miracle
That's not a verb I recognize.
Jump around and sing a song.
That's hardly a way for the son of God to act.

The system parses the input entered by the player–reader, feeding back options based upon its predetermined programming. *Bible Retold* is definitely theological play of a populist sort, but it is unlikely to offend many, since IF is appreciated mostly by its few fans who accept the "what-if" scenario the genre assumes. Furthermore, because IF is typically played in the privacy of one's home, any offense against the gospels that might be construed will most likely be *only* individually experienced. This does, of course, leave us with the question of whether or not the *production* of Bible-based IF programs is *itself* a form of blasphemy, simply because it allows the production of possibly heretical storylines.

Main idea of Godwired [handwritten marginal note]

The premise of IF itself can help us understand other, non-IF-based public endeavors to play with the biblical text and produce a narrative that is part New Testament-based and part user-generated. For example, one could argue that Jesus films are a sort of visual enactment of the director's own IF, as he enters the "space of possibility" of the Bible and injects his own narrative into the space. Interactive fiction about the Bible is at once Midrash, play, blasphemy, story and composition. To engage in IF about the Bible is to consider, through the formulation of IF itself, the way that sacred texts acquire meaning – and how we import our own beliefs and biases into any reading of a text. In a way, all biblical interpretation is a form of IF, as we press our own perceptions into the stories we read and expect the Bible to "parse" back to us the theological assumptions we bring to our reading of it.

Interactive fiction has a close cousin in online fan fiction. Whereas players of IF are led through possible storylines that may be "playing" with received texts, fan fiction is the product of viewers who write alternative endings to stories shown on television or in film. Jenkins calls such activities "textual poaching," and looks at the *Star Trek* franchise as an example. As Jenkins notes in his analysis of fan fiction, for some critics, fans engaging in such revisions of received texts are "a scandalous category in American culture, one that provokes an excessive response from those committed to the interests of textual producers and institutionalized interpreters and calls into question the logic by which others order their aesthetic experience." In other words, issues of authority and hierarchical control of interpretation are alive and well in secular storytelling contexts. To those interested in controlling a mythological story world, such fans seem "frighteningly out of control, undisciplined and unrepentant, rogue readers" who "passionately embrace favored texts and attempt to integrate media representations within their own social experience." They are "cultural scavengers" who "refuse to read by the rules imposed upon them by the schoolmasters" (2006b, 39). Such language resonates eerily with parallel discussions in religious circles about people who read the Bible "too" liberally.

But there are explicitly religious forms of fan fiction, too. The ability to create alternate storylines – a sort of free-form Midrash – is explicitly engaged by ordinary writers like Alena Hu (2010), who tends toward performative blasphemy as she re-envisions the story of Jesus in self-acknowledged "heretical" terms. Claiming to draw on *Jesus Christ Superstar* (2000), *The Gospel of Barnabas*, Gnostic thought, and Jorge Luis Borges, Hu presents a first-person account, from the perspective of Jesus, of a tormented love affair between Jesus and Judas, culminating in Judas taking Jesus' place on the cross, while Lucifer gleefully manipulates the situation to his own advantage.

Such heretical re-imaginings are hardly new, as evident by the author's own use of unorthodox texts like *The Gospel of Barnabas*. What *is* new is the easy public sharing of these imaginings, and the public invitation to read sacred texts as such playgrounds for transgressive interpretation. Henry Jenkins remarks, "fandom is a vehicle for marginalized subcultural groups (women, the young, gays, and so on) to pry open a space for their cultural concerns within dominant representations; it is a way of appropriating media texts and rereading them in a fashion that serves different interests, a way of transforming culture into popular culture" (2006b, 40). Indeed, as Jenkins notes, fan fiction is often especially concerned with gender negotiation, evoking questions about received cultural values regarding who to love and how to behave. The "underground status" of fan fiction writers allows them to "promote a range of different interpretations of the basic [*Star Trek*] program material and a variety of reconstructions of marginalized characters and interests, to explore a diversity of different solutions to the dilemma of contemporary gender relations" (2006b, 54). Hu's story, then, can be read as a powerful example of performed resistance to conservative readings of the Bible on sexual orientation.

By retelling the story of Jesus in new ways, Hu and others make room for alternate modes of engaging the story in society itself, and press at received interpretations of the Bible in compelling but destabilizing ways. Just as the fan community of *Star Trek* "continually debates what constitutes a legitimate reworking of program materials and what represents a violation," so must contemporary interpreters of the Bible argue about what readings of the Jesus story are possible, and who has the right to say so (Jenkins 2006b, 56). No received story system with large mythic power – *Star Trek* or the Bible – is immune to our own, individualized interpretative play. With fan fiction, "Consumption becomes production; reading becomes writing; spectator culture becomes participatory culture" (60). But not all stories thrive on the production of alternative telling; some depend precisely upon the inevitability of linear events to derive their own emotional punch. Thus it is to such fixed "cathartic" stories that I now turn.

Stories as catharsis

The fascination with nurturing catharsis in games is a powerful lure for designers. Murray asks, "How can we have catharsis in a medium [like games] that resists closure?" The problem, she says, lies in the notion of tragedy which, borrowing from Aristotle, she defines as "a story of a single worthy individual's fall from a worthy life to a desperate ending through some choice or flaw of his own, a story that focuses on this irretrievable loss, arousing our feelings of pity and terror and leaving us at the end in a state of purged emotion and heightened understanding" (1997, 175). Catharsis hinges on our experience of emotional satisfaction through the progression of the character's experiences and our engagement with him or her. For Aristotle, theater allows viewers to purge themselves of negative emotions through an intense experience of pity and fear, enabled by identification with the characters onstage. This process is most satisfying if the character suffering onstage is experiencing hardship that is to some degree undeserved. The character's suffering comes to represent our own, and by watching him or her suffer, we participate in that suffering.

Films, too, can enable catharsis through ritual interactivity with fixed narrative. John Lyden has persuasively argued that films can invite rich and deep involvement from viewers so that "the effect of a drama on an audience can be just as significant as the effect of a religious ritual" (2003, 90). Films can offer "rituals by means of which audiences can identify with characters and their sufferings" and acquire tools by which "to deal with such sufferings" (94). Ritual engagement with film as a cathartic vehicle is only interactive in our meaningful *reception* of the fixed narrative.

This meaningful passivity is evident in the way that people talked about *The Passion of the Christ* as an unalterable, realistic rendition of Christ's death. Darrell Bock of Dallas Theological Seminary and the author of many popular Christian books, claims that the "details" in the film are "very accurate – this is the kind of death our Lord died for me" (see Various Commentators n.d.). Denny Rydberg, the President of Young Life, a Christian organization, praises the "historical nature of the content" of the film. Jerry Falwell sees the film as "recreating the crucifixion of Christ" and claims that it will provide a "glimmer of honesty regarding the miraculous and life-changing story of the One who died for everyone" (see Various Commentators n.d.). For Gibson and his supporters, the film was an accurate portrayal of inevitable events set in motion by human sinfulness.

The idea of "fate" here is crucial for understanding how catharsis works, and why it is easier to experience it with film than with video games. As Grodal observes, films can certainly create a strong sense of emotional arousal "related to the viewer's expectations of what will happen to the central protagonists" (2003, 149). The "input-driven nature" of films allows them to easily "cue strong passive emotions, including experiences of fate" and even to "evoke a strong autonomous outlet, like crying" (151). No matter how emotionally involved they may become in the story, viewers have absolutely no power to determine the ending of a film. As Mateas and Stern note, for many ludologists, the distinction between narrative and game is decisive: "A narrative is an already accomplished structure that is told to a spectator. A game is an evolving situation that is being accomplished by an interactor" (2006, 663). Reading the Bible as linear narrative, then, accords well with religious views about God's foreknowledge and control of history. Similarly, watching a Jesus film is akin to reading the New Testament, because both reflect our inability to change the story as it is mediated to us. This helps us to understand why there are few games about the crucifixion. As Mateas and Stern argue, games and narrative can work in very different way, and thus game designers typically experience a "deep ambivalence" about narrative, one likely to be shared by Christians pondering how (or whether) to tell the Jesus story in video games:

> The ephemeral quality of gameplay, the experience of manipulating elements within a responsive, rule-driven world, is still the raison d'être of games, perhaps the primary phenomenological feature that uniquely identifies the computer game as a medium. Where gameplay is all about interactivity, narrative is all about predestination.
>
> (2006, 643)

The crucifixion, as many Christians read it, is all about God's providential act, not often phrased as a form of "predestination," but certainly as a matter of necessary course given human sinfulness. Film is thus a much more appropriate medium for Christian storytelling than games, since limitations on interactivity are a powerful theological comfort.

Juul makes a similar point when he describes the difference between tragedies (as a form of fixed story) and video games (as open to multiple possibilities of play): "It is hard to create a tragic video game – tragedies are about events beyond our control that are then transformed into something more meaningful through the tragedy, but games are mostly about having power and overcoming challenges" (2005, 161). If we apply this notion to a hypothetical Jesus video game, especially one portraying the events of the crucifixion, then we can see why such a thing would be so unattractive to Christians. Clearly, the Christian narrative is not to be tampered with, even in imaginative play. The appeal of a tragedy, on the other hand, lies precisely in its inexorability. It's easy to see why tragedies make bad video games – the notion of alternatives could ruin the *pathos* and thus the catharsis of the experience. Drawing on Murray's narrative theory, Moulthrop suggests that for those who embrace a cathartic reading of stories, "[o]ur ritual release of pity and fear arrives when we fully understand the relationships among characters and the pattern of causes that constitute a plot ... when we grasp the structure of metaphor and memory that informs a lyric, meditation, or confession." Indeed, "our engagement with the text is driven by the desire to apprehend it in its entirety"

(2004, 59). Whereas some stories are tightly scripted and deny us a role in shaping outcomes, others function more loosely as imaginative fodder inviting cooperative meaning-making. Such stories are less like cathartic rituals and more like interactive systems of engagement.

Stories as interactive systems

When theorists of games discuss the construction of the game world, they sometimes describe a game as a "system" consisting of "a set of things that affect one another within an environment to form a larger pattern that is different from any of the individual parts" (Salen and Zimmerman 2004, 51). For Juul a game is a "state machine" or "a system that can be in different states; it contains input and output functions, and definitions of what state and what input will lead to what following state" (2004, 133). Stories too, whether or not they are part of a larger game, can be viewed as systems that invite our interaction.

Recognizing the difficulty of ever fully distinguishing storytelling from gameplay, Juul lands on the term "fictional worlds" to describe the hybrid. Fiction, says Juul, "is commonly confused with storytelling," but we would better view fiction as "any kind of imagined world." Thus a story can be viewed as one possible trajectory through a fiction-as-world, so that the story is "a sequence of events that is presented (enacted or narrated) to a user" (2005, 122). Drawing on his notion of a "fictional world," Juul remarks that these worlds are "imagined by the player, and the player fills in any gaps in the fictional world" (121). If one views the text as a story, there are no gaps – one simply receives the text as a transcript of what has occurred in a particular order and one passively absorbs its content. However, if one views a text as a *system*, then gaps emerge all over the place, gaps that we as players must fill. Rabbinic interpretation, sermon-writing, and theology construction are examples of this kind of gap-filling.

According to Juul, in a game, "rules and fiction compete for the player's attention" and thus exist in some tension with one another. A similar argument could be made for competition between reading a sacred text as a hermeneutical field to be explored (with rules), or reading it as a fixed text to be absorbed (literally) exactly as it is. Because a "fictional world" is a system, Juul makes the argument that "all fictional worlds are incomplete" (2005, 122). Similarly, all hermeneutical "play" is incomplete; one will never exhaust the well of meaning possible in theological hermeneutical play with a sacred text. So what happens if we view the Hindu retelling of the Ramayana as a system that invites play within a certain set of rules, and thus restricting which events may "emerge" in a given ritual storytelling experience? If we view rituals as drawing on story systems, we see the restrictions surrounding the Japanese tea ceremony, for example, as a set of rules that shape which "events" or points of view emerge. Similarly, we could view the proscriptions of practice and consumption during the month of Ramadan as a set of "rules" that define a system of religious perspective that controls which "events" emerge during a Muslim's daily routine, thus creating an attitude of piety and devotion. Perhaps this is the point of such rituals: they provide a system whereby one voluntarily restricts one's view for a period of time, as a means of focusing or renewal. In such cases, our interactions with these systems or story world produce emergent storylines that are our personal experiences, our chosen trajectories in life.

Interactions with stories as systems, then, are shaped by rules. The retelling of the Ramayana is restrained by the contingencies of the text – and so has a close adherence to story. The tea ceremony is less closely aligned with Buddhist myth, but certainly intends to evoke a particular perspective via restriction of movements and perspective. Zen gardens similarly produce an "environment" within which certain rules of perception are to be followed. Fasting during Ramadan evokes the stories associated with the founding of the faith and one's focusing of attention on God and on gratitude for God's gifts in the world. All of these experiences are defined by "rules" – by what one can and cannot do – and these rules allow these experiences to produce a system that defines the experience. To approach a religious text from the perspective of rules rather than from that of received authoritative tradition (and fixed literal text) allows interpretation to become more like gameplay than story-reading.

This means that if we consider the text of the Bible as a "fictional world" rather than as a series of fixed events, then the process of Midrash (telling stories to fill in gaps in the text) is a form of "play" exhibiting rules of inter-activity with the text as system. As Susan Handelman explains, in Midrash "there is never any one single interpretation to which all understanding of the text aims, but a continuous production of multiple meaning." Midrashic interpretation is configurative and interactive. Just as one feels no compulsion to reconcile different "plays" of a video game that has a multitude of alternate routes or endings, in Midrash "one Rabbi can interpret a verse in several different ways, and conflicting interpretations are placed side by side with no concern for reconciling them" (1982, 75). Hebrew scholar Max Kadushin dubs such sacred interpretive activity "serious play" (1952/1972, 108). Game theorists Simon Egenfeldt-Nielsen, Jonas Smith and Susana Tosca similarly report that the "act of playing" is "informed by our cognitive, and often-unconscious filling in-the-story-gaps" (2008, 187). Murray explicitly acknowledges the similarity between interactivity and Midrash when she remarks that the Talmud "is a giant hypertext consisting of biblical text surrounded by commentaries by multiple rabbis" (1997, 56). Of course, this implies that hypertext performs its construction of meaning in ways that resemble the rabbinic Midrash of the Talmud as well.

Such an argument invites reconsideration of Irenaeus' arguments for canonization: maybe Irenaeus knew *exactly* what he was doing when he claimed that there should be four gospels because there are four winds and four directions, if what he meant by that was the completeness of the four when read *in a sort of hypertextual tension* with one another. Maybe, despite his frustration with the liberal readings of the Gnostics, Irenaeus knew that rich religious experience with a text comes through struggle and that having four gospels with different versions of the same events would enable an infinite amount of possible interpretations for readers, a "game" that would allow for millennia of play. Whether Irenaeus knew what he was arguing for or not, the four gospels have invited endless interactive exploration, inviting us to see the Bible less as a linear narrative and more as an "inhabited space," a field in which choice enacts as many trajectories of play as one could ever wish for.

Similarly, we could see Muslim exploration of the Quran and *Hadith* as gameplay, as interpreters try to find pertinent passages to apply, by analogy or other kinship, to the situation at hand. Medieval Jewish practices of mystical interpretation also can be looked at as a process of interacting with the text *as system* rather than as the passive receipt of a story. As Handelman says of rabbinic Midrashic activity, the text "serves as a new stimulus each time it is interpreted [and] therefore requires different determinate meanings by different personalities at different times, or even at the same time" (1982, 75). Juul's comments on the game design process remarkably resemble rabbinic rules for textual interpretation:

> In the game design process, the game designer must select which aspects of the fictional world to actually implement in the game rules. The player then experiences the game as a two-way process where the fiction of the game cues him or her into understanding the rules of the game, and, again, the rules can cue the player to imagine the fictional world of the game.
>
> (2005, 163)

A rabbinic interpreter engaging in the play of language in the Bible sees "[e]very vowel and letter [as] a meaningful sound, subject to inference and interpretation ... even the smallest detail of expression and punctuation [is] not fortuitous" (Handelman 1982, 71). A rabbi's engagement with the sacred text is, as Juul says of games, a "two-way process" produced by the system (the Bible or the game world) to help one to understand and create the rules (of interpretation and play).

This kind of interaction allows one to ignore the linear order of events in the Bible and instead engage in rule-based interpretation of diverse passages. Accordingly, Jewish biblical hermeneutical rules govern some of the processes by which interpretation occurs, and the options they create are almost limitless. *Gematria* is "the computation of the numerical values of letters, or the use of secret alphabets or methods of substituting one letter for another." In the method of *notarikon*, a given word is divided up into individual letters that each then stand for a new word – somewhat akin to the reversed creation of an acronym. Another method involves the multivalent interpretation of words that, in Hebrew, can be pronounced a variety of alternative ways.

Because in the Hebrew Torah there is no fixed punctuation, one can even detach a word or clause from the end of one verse and attach it to the next one to produce alternative readings (Handelman 1982, 73–74).

Juul asserts that "rules separate the game from the rest of the world by carving out an area where the rules apply" (2005, 164). If we view sacred texts as an "area" of this kind, then it makes sense why religious groups are so protective of their sacred writ. The text is the primary "play" ground, or system of rule development, for their lives. This game of interpretation also has profound effects on the real world, since "the fictional world of a game strongly depends on the real world in order to exist, and the fictional world cues the player into making assumptions about the real world in which the player plays a game" (168). In short, the "rules" apply to the text and to the world. Play and interpretation are identified. Whatever one "discovers" in the text has meaning and purpose well beyond the game of interpretation itself.

Murray quips that "a stirring narrative in any medium can be experienced as a virtual reality because our brains are programmed to tune into stories with an intensity that can obliterate the world around us" (1997, 98). Stories have long had the ability to function as other "worlds" for us, at times perceived more powerfully than our own. The events that constitute the plot or the "game-story" are "made possible by the existence of a larger fictional world in which the story takes place" (Salen and Zimmerman 2004, 402). This larger world system is greater than the story alone, and greater than any game connected with it – because both story and game require our imaginative immersion to make that world complete and real to us.

Conclusion

Storytelling is a quintessentially human act, one that is closely allied throughout history with religious activity. We have looked at five different lenses for making sense of stories in virtual contexts: stories as games, stories as fate, stories as potential narratives, stories as catharsis, and stories as interactive systems. At times, these categories overlap. A story might be an exercise in fate as well as a form of catharsis, for example. It might be in some ways very much like a game and like an interactive system. The categories here are not exhaustive, but rather consist of glimpses of possibility, angles at which we might hold a kaleidoscope. Today's stories are increasingly hybrid, culling elements from other types of media, experimenting with structures, demanding that we interpret anew elements that we thought were familiar from previous tellings of stories. And, since so much of religious experience is grounded in stories – authoritative stories, enacted stories, ritualized stories, fragmented stories, challenging stories – we should pay attention to how these familiar elements reappear in newly scripted contexts. What new messages are today's storytellers offering us? How does the reconfiguring of a familiar story change its meaning? How do transgressive transformations challenge the status quo?

How does the transformation of sacred texts and stories into fluid, digitized forms shape the way we give, receive, and read them?

Today's interactive technology "allows us to tell stories we could not tell before, to retell the age-old stories in new ways, to imagine ourselves as creatures of a parameterized world of multiple possibilities, to understand ourselves as authors of rule systems which drive behavior and shape our possibilities" (Murray 2004, 8). Although some people may feel threatened by the growing popularity of interactive storytelling, others will rejoice as they find age-old principles of sacred storytelling reborn in new virtual contexts, with humans as increasingly active participants in meaning-making.

Chapter 3

The games we pray
What is this ritual–game–story thing?

The desire to create and play games may well be "a fundamental human tendency" (Egenfeldt-Nielsen, Smith and Tosca 2008, 45). Games have been played for tens of thousands of years, with performance that often intermingles with religious and ritual practices. In Egypt during the twenty-seventh century BCE, people played *Senet*, a game that resembles today's Backgammon. The oldest game known to history, a form of ancient *Mancala*, has variations that "are found at sites of the world's ancient civilizations, Mesopotamia and Egypt, and in areas now known as Cyprus, Palestine, Iraq, Iran, and Jordan" (Flanagan 2009, 64).

Many of these games seem to have possibly had ritual purposes as well, such as the Mesopotamian game *Ur*. The Chinese game *Wéiqí* (called *Go* in Japan) is "believed to have developed from divination practices by emperors and astrologers in Zhou culture" (69). *Go*'s ritual purposes were obvious; it "was given as a special gift at weddings and was a documented pastime of Zen monks, shoguns, and tea ceremony masters." As Flanagan notes, "in its entanglement with ritual, [*Go*] itself reflects cultural and social characteristics of the times in which it was developed and changed" (105). Indeed, many of these games seem to reflect the complexity of the relationship between rituals and games in the ancient world. Flanagan explains: "Games of chance and divination were closely aligned for many thousands of years, for humans have long sought guidance from the changeable, powerful forces they believed may rule over one's destiny and control the probable outcomes for hunting, war, and successful harvests" (68).

Games and rituals also have often had a commingled relationship with storytelling, with some rituals and games either building on, creating or revealing stories as part of the interactivity engaged in by the practitioner. Consider, for example, a ritualized re-enactment of a mythic battle, as in the Kecak, the Balinese monkey chant that involves dozens of men ritually performing a battle from the Ramayana. In such a performance there are elements of ritual (the movements, staging, actions performed), game (the battle that is re-enacted with a winner and loser), and story (the Ramayana, which is the larger mythic context for this rite). Another example is from the medieval Christian era; the twelfth-century Corpus Christi College Manuscript 122 describes a form of the game called *Alea Evangelii* ("The Board Game of the Gospel") in which the battle portrayed in the game becomes a form of religious allegory (Flanagan 2009, 71).

Flanagan even suggests, drawing on historical research, that "image-based games such as *Sugoroku* [a wooden board game] may have been incorporated into the monastic life of Buddhist temples during the fifteenth century." She suggests that Buddhist teachers "used game boards to teach neophytes how the suffering that originated in human weakness could and must be conquered to reach purity and the higher goal of paradise" (75). Rather than consisting of discrete forms, the ritual–game–story thing has always been something of a hybrid, representing some of the most foundational forms of human expression and meaning-making. It is as old as human civilization and as new as the latest hit video game.

As Zimmerman observes, the study of video games in relationship to other genres like storytelling is fraught with controversy as "terms and concepts run amuck like naughty schoolchildren" (2004, 154). Catherine Bell says something similar about ritual theory: "The wide variety of activities that have come to be analyzed as ritualized behavior patterns – aggression and combat, song, play, sport, grooming, courting and mating, drama, dance, humor, art, and even thought itself – testifies to the promiscuous tendencies of this approach" (1992, 73). The concepts that Zimmerman and Bell address (play, games, narrativity, ritual, ritualization and interactivity) are surprisingly hard to hold onto. But it does seem clear that they have some intriguing relationships with one another, as all seem to exhibit overlapping qualities having to do with story and interactivity via performance of directed activities.

As Flanagan has noted, the study of traditional games has "lagged behind" other areas of study in current scholarly interest in popular culture. But as Flanagan argues, "games are legitimate forms of media, human expression, and cultural importance," and deserve as much attention as film, literature or visual art. Further, "the ways games reflect the norms and beliefs of their surrounding cultures [are] essential to understanding both games themselves and the insights they may provide to human experience." Flanagan dubs this the "playculture approach to media," and proposes that "board games become one of several artifacts of material culture used to trace social practices and beliefs" (2009, 67).

Digital games have just as much potential today to reveal important facets of human culture and meaning-making. For both traditional and digital games, "game actions and rules can be characterized as principal play features, and these foci are not unique to games but are also shared across language systems, social orders, and ties of kinship, law, and ritual" (Flanagan 2009, 67). By transcribing and reflecting ways that humans tell stories and engage in performative acts generated via carefully scripted experiences, games have as much to tell us about who we are as any other powerful human medium. And if games really do have something fundamental in common with rituals and stories, then they are inextricable from these characteristically human endeavors as well.

In his discussion of a cluster of concepts relating to games, Zimmerman sets out some parameters that apply well not just to games and stories but also to ritual: these concepts are "not mutually exclusive" but work by "overlapping and intersecting the others in complex and unique ways." Such "naughty" concepts are "things to think with" and function as "signs for clusters of concepts" that are "dynamic conceptual tools" that "represent a network of ideas that flow into and through each other" (2004, 155). By looking at rituals, games and stories and the characteristics they share, I hope to offer new "things to think with."

Bell seems to approve of such an approach when she says: "I do not wish to imply or designate some independently existing object, namely ritual, with a set of defining features that characterize all instances of ritual." The concept would suffer "distortion in the process" and require taxonomy of "a whole galaxy of independent [but related] pure entities with static features" (1992, 219). Instead, Bell proposes that we "hold on to our battered terminology" as best we can, recognizing its limitations and modifying it in ways that respect the legacy of theory that brought us to where we are today. Accordingly, she is interested less in "ritual" than in "ritualization," which she sees as "a strategic way of acting" (43). By emphasizing the process over a product, she opens up a consideration of ritual more squarely situated in what real people do and how *they* generate meaning. The focus here on process and performance allows for a much richer engagement with ritual, and also marks it as more attuned with the interactivity we find in games and in the performance of stories in games.

Rather than try to separate ritual, game and story with artificial bounds, instead we should *let* them be messy, using the complexity and hybrid nature of the terms to open up new avenues of analysis. To varying degrees, rituals, games and stories all exhibit *interactivity*. All also can be perceived as a sort of *play*, broadly conceived. All also exhibit certain *rules* that shape our interaction with them. Rituals, games and stories also all manifest a complex but rich relationship with *narrative*, and all can be examined in terms of their portrayal of *conflict*. Using these five concepts as focusing lenses, or additional "things to think with," I argue that the ritual–game–story thing is a profoundly hybrid creature, calling for our recognition of the deep relationship between playful, religious and storytelling activities in our lives.

Interactivity

As useful as it is to consider interactivity as a common feature in games, rituals and stories, this term too is plagued with controversy and imprecision. Zimmerman observes that interactivity "is one of those words which can mean everything and nothing at once" (2004, 158). It is a "runaway word" used freely for a host of different kinds of activities (Salen and Zimmerman 2004, 58).

We can speak of interactivity in regard to cognitive, emotional, or psychological engagement with a text, game, ritual, or other experience. We can speak of physical or functional interaction with an object, or of dynamic engagement through choices made within a system of possibilities such as a computer program or organized human activity. We can also speak of interactivity as a form of cultural engagement, what Salen and Zimmerman call "beyond-the-object interactivity" with the larger social system in which a text, game, or other object appears (2004, 59–60). Recognizing the broad usage of the term "interactivity," some game scholars prefer to use the terms "procedurality" or "configuration," although these terms are just as problematic since they refer to the same ephemeral and varied means by which we engage "interactively" with given systems.

Moulthrop prefers the term "configuration," and points out that in a game, configuration is the "primary cognitive activity" and is characterized by "the capacity to transform certain aspects of the virtual environment with potentially significant consequences for the system as a whole" (2004, 60). Configuration is also a form of discourse, since it is "a way of engaging not just immediate game elements, but also the game's social and material conditions" (66). If configuration also involves interactions with others via virtual space, the ability for configurative and ritualized experience is heightened. Our interaction via virtual reality, says Hillis, "enable[s] individuals to transmit or move a sensory experience of self-presence 'elsewhere' across virtual space, [so that] the ground is set for the creation of human rituals in networked environments" (2009, 2). Even in individually played games, configuration (or interactivity) involves a sort of feedback loop between the player and the game such that both are changed. Murray remarks that "[i]n a procedural [game] world, the interactor is scripted by the environment as well as acting upon it" (2004, 6). Espen Aarseth agrees, noting that the pleasure that games offer is "not primarily visual, but [rather is] kinaesthetic, functional and cognitive" (2004, 52). Whether we label them as "configurative" or "performative" as well, it is clear that games are fundamentally interactive: people *do* games. And, as Hillis remarks, ritual too "is foremost an activity" (2009, 11).

Predictably perhaps, rituals generate just as much definitional controversy as games. As I noted above, the term "ritual" is sometimes even replaced by "performance" or "ritualization" as a means of emphasizing the interactivity involved. As Rappaport notes, "performance as well as formality is necessary for ritual" (1996, 428). Even those ritual theorists like Frits Staal who deny the communicative function of ritual altogether at least concede that ritual is something that *people do*: "Ritual is primarily activity" and "the important thing is what you do, not what you think, believe, or say" (1996, 485). As Bell argues, ritual is intensely "interactive," characterized by "interaction of the body with a structured environment" (1992, 107). Focusing on the embodied *individual* as the site of ritual experience, Bell argues that "ritual mastery" is "a corrective to the habit of thinking about ritual as an existing entity of some sort" (107). Ritual is a *process*, she argues, tied up deeply with other social processes that are encountered, assessed, and either appropriated or rejected by individuals – in short, it is interactive, configurative and procedural. What is most important about ritual, she says, "is not what it says or symbolizes, but that first and foremost it *does things*" [my italics] (111). Theodore Jennings agrees, arguing that ritual "is an action, a doing, a praxis, and above all a bodily doing, acting, performing" (1996, 329).

Bogost describes user interactivity with computer programs in a way that could as easily apply to ritual performance since both are scripted performances that shape our experience. Bogost defines procedural rhetoric as "the practice of persuading through processes in general and computational processes in particular." Procedural rhetoric is "a technique for making arguments with computational systems and for unpacking computational arguments others have created" (2007b, 3). As Bogost explains, "procedural rhetoric" consists of those "processes [that] define the way things work: the methods, techniques, and logics that drive the operation of systems." To examine procedural rhetoric, then, is to look at how arguments are addressed to users via the things they are doing in interaction with the program: to understand how persuasion operates via scripted user performance. Such analysis is obviously akin to theoretical analysis of ritual as a means of discovering how rituals shape belief and practice. Bogost convincingly argues that procedural rhetorical claims are "every bit as logical as verbal arguments – in fact, internal consistency is often assured in computational arguments, since microprocessors and not human agents are in charge of their consistent execution" (36). For Bogost, too, we learn by doing.

Many ritual theorists would agree. Rappaport argues that the performance of a liturgical order, a scripted ritual, involves a sequence of acts and sayings that create communication with the performer: "by performing a liturgical order the performer accepts, and indicates to himself that he accepts, whatever is encoded in the canons of liturgical order in which he is participating" (1996, 433). Jennings writes that the performance of a ritual "teaches one not only how to conduct the ritual itself, but how to conduct oneself outside the ritual space – in the world epitomized by or founded or renewed in and through the ritual itself." Ritual is a "doing which is 'communicated' or 'transmitted' or taught by ritual action" (329). Ritual teaches us a "pattern of doing" that can and likely will shape our conduct in the world beyond the ritual experience (328).

In a similar vein, Bogost calls our attention to what he calls "software authorship," the means by which procedural rhetoric is developed within a computerized system. In order to compose something with a "procedural" purpose, an author creates code that "enforces rules to generate some kind of representation." Procedural systems, he points out, "generate behaviors based on rule-based models" and in so doing, "run processes that invoke interpretations of processes in the material world" (2007b, 4–5). This means that procedural representation "explains processes *with other processes*" (9). Jennings sees ritual as able to accomplish something similar, creating knowledge that is "praxological rather than speculative, engaged rather than detached" (1996, 332).

One obvious example of dangerous procedural rhetoric is the racist American video game *Ethnic Cleansing*, in which the player clothes his avatar as a skinhead or a Klansman and kills Jews, blacks and immigrants. Another example is the flash animation game *Border Patrol*, in which one shoots at running images of Mexicans – even pregnant women – in the procedural attempt to kill them and stop them from entering the border into the United States. In the processes of both games, images are used *procedurally* to make an offensive ideological argument through *doing*. A pre-digital version of a game with similar procedural rhetoric is *The Wandering Jew* game (1852–58). In the game, "the Jew figure appears looking like stereotypical versions of Moses, with a windswept cape and long hair" (Flanagan 2009, 83). This figure haunts other players as he dredges up scenes from medieval stories about the "wandering Jew," largely anti-Semitic legends about a Jew who "insulted Jesus on his way to the cross, and became an immortal due to a curse from Jesus" (81).

Of course, procedural rhetoric can be used to make socially affirming arguments as well, as when it is used in social justice games such as the UN-sponsored adventure game *Food Force*, or *Third World Farmer*, an online flash game that procedurally emulates the perils of farming in poverty-stricken regions of the world. Drawing on Nel Noddings' work on "care ethics" and Martha Nussbaum's argument that literature can "deepen an individual's capacity for empathy," Koo and Seider suggest that a game's procedural rhetoric has the potential to "support prosocial learning" by providing players with "the opportunity to play the role of a different person" (2010, 19, 22).

Flanagan describes the politically oriented game *Hush* (2008), created in order to procedurally and experientially consider the events relating to the 1994 civil war and genocide in Rwanda. Players play as "Liliane," a young mother. Their goal is "to keep Liliane's baby quiet in order to prevent mother and child from being captured by Hutu patrol" (Flanagan 2009, 241). The gameplay is "quick, but the experience is immersive, with the matching, timed game mechanic requiring full concentration" (242). The designers of the game say that the concept attracted them because "the player isn't viewing this horrific event from a distance and attempting to 'solve the problem'; they are immersed in the moment, experiencing the terror of a Hutu raid" (cited in Flanagan 2009, 241). One of the core components of the game is that *Hush* "explores subjectivity" and invites awareness of an "experiential 'truth.'" For Flanagan, "digital worlds are enormous sites for the import of content from the real world" which "can include social interactions and social constructions like racism and sexism, which can prevail inside particular types of game frameworks" (243).

Jennings similarly proposes that rituals communicate via performance: "the knowledge which is ritual knowledge is knowledge in act – it is praxological.

It is knowledge gained, transmitted, and received in action" (1996, 331). Bell also would likely see ritual as a form of procedural rhetoric, and games are akin to rituals in their ability to make ideological arguments through actions. Bell identifies ritual as a poignant site for negotiation of power in society, and points out "the rich variety of ways in which people can consent, resist, or manipulate aspects of dominant ideologies" as expressed through ritualization (1992, 191). Says Bell: "The deployment of ritualization, consciously or unconsciously, is the deployment of a particular construction of power relationships, a particular relationship of domination, consent, and resistance. As a strategy of power, ritualization has both positive and effective aspects as well as specific limits to what it can do and how far it can extend" (206). Ritualization serves as "a way of acting that is designed and orchestrated to distinguish and privilege what is being done in comparison to other, usually more quotidian, activities" (74). Rituals and games, then, can both function as examples of a form of "symbolic expression that uses processes rather than language" to communicate (Bogost 2007b, 9). A software script is similar to a ritual script (the liturgical order), and both have the ability to shape us as we engage with them. In procedural rhetoric, says Bogost, "arguments are made not through the construction of words or images, but through the authorship of rules of behavior, the construction of dynamic models" (29). Rituals, like games, are a form of procedural rhetoric – and make arguments through rules and shaped behavior. In both, it seems, we learn by doing.

It would seem, at first glance, that stories are much less interactive than rituals and games. Eskelinen argues that there *is* an important difference in the level and type of interactivity with stories when compared with interactive experiences like games, since "the dominant user function in literature, theater and film is [merely] interpretive, but in games it is the configurative one" (2004, 38). This would, of course, imply that the procedural rhetoric involved in reading, as opposed to gameplay or ritual performance, will be seriously muted. Nonetheless, our active interpretation of stories can be seen as a kind of configuration too, as we bring our own insights to a story and get "out" of it a host of different insights and experiences, and in some cases, produce new stories based on those readings.

Drawing on reception theory, Terry Eagleton asserts that readers *always* interactively engage texts: "The reader makes implicit connections, fills in gaps, draws inferences and tests out hunches ... The text itself is really no more than a series of 'cues' to the reader, invitations to construct a piece of language into meaning." These "gaps" may be the same kinds of spaces left in a liturgical order, a script, or a game design that calls forth in the player–participant active engagement for the production of the experience. Eagleton argues that this is exactly the case with stories: "without this continuous active participation on the reader's part, there would be no literary work at all." Gaps in texts require readers to "supply a missing connection" and resolve "indeterminacies" (1983, 76–77). It is true that readers usually don't *physically* change a text – although they might, by marking in the margins, tearing out pages, or creating a digital mash-up via cut-and-paste. But even if we consider a story to be something fixed in its textual form, this does not mean that readers do not engage that story configuratively. If we agree with Eagleton that the words are merely "cues" and that the real site of meaning is the reader's experience which *produces* the story, then all kinds of interactivity occurs. Indeed, there *is* no story without interactivity. And just as a game is more than the program behind it and a ritual is more than the liturgical order that prompts it, so a story is more than the words in a physical or digital text.

In language that echoes Bell's remarks about negotiation of meaning in ritual, Kearney notes of stories that "[t]here is no narrated action that does not involve some response of approval or disapproval relative to some scale of goodness or justice – though it is always up to us readers to choose for ourselves from the various value options proposed by the narrative" (2002, 155). Films can be looked at in similar ways. Ken Perlin describes the viewer's rich interactivity with film as story: "I am continually testing the protagonist's apparent inner moral choices against my own inner moral measuring stick, looking for affirmation of higher goals and ideals, or for betrayal of those ideals" (2004, 12).

Sometimes, interactivity with written texts can even resemble a game-playing experience, as I discussed in regard to rabbinic Midrashic activity in Chapter 2. The Bible, in Midrashic encounter, "serves as a new stimulus each time it is interpreted [and] therefore requires different determinate meanings by different personalities at different times, or even at the same time" (Handelman 1982, 75). For rabbinic interpreters, the Bible is viewed as a system for generating meaning, similar to the "board" for a game or a field of play, shaped by predetermined rules. In such an encounter, stories in the Bible are viewed as collections of words and phrases that invite our imaginative and creative engagement, driven by a conviction that God has placed them there with deep and multiple layers of interpretation to be discovered. Reading in this case is anything but passive – it is variable and rule-driven, and thus may also be read with a theologically infused procedural rhetoric. Reading of this sort is dynamic, fueled by the reader's own actions working within the rules given by the interpretive school, by his or her religious convictions, and by the text as received. Such reading is a form of interactivity and a site for play.

Play

Huizinga long ago noticed the close relationship between play and ritual: "Ritual is seriousness at its highest and holiest. Can it nevertheless be play? ... We are accustomed to think of play and seriousness as an absolute antithesis. It would seem, however, that this does not go to the heart of the matter" (1955, 18). Despite Huizinga's identification of compelling parallels between ritual and play, most ritual theorists talk about play rarely, sensing in the term's usage some mood of frivolity that works against the supposed serious work that they see ritual doing. But as I suggested in Chapter 2 and have emphasized here, play can indeed be recognized in rituals, in games, and in stories as "the free space of movement within a more rigid structure" (Salen and Zimmerman 2004, 304).

As Zimmerman explains, play exists in constant tension with "the more rigid structures of a system" (2004, 159). If play can be indeed viewed as the amount of movement allowed in relationship to a given system (or "road"), then play is a producer of possibilities. Play is limited by rules, which help to define the system, but play also gives the player certain freedoms "in the interstitial spaces between and among its components" (Salen and Zimmerman 2004, 304). It is easy to see that play is manifest in rituals, in games, and in stories – all of which present us with certain structures already in place but which invite our participation within those structures. As we saw in Chapter 2, play can be a product of interactive reading and can allow new and creative innovations in how stories are told and interpreted by readers. With games too, play affords a "space of possibility" that invites the player to explore the world of the game and to make choices within it, within the confines allowed by rules and/or the game programmer (Salen and Zimmerman 2004, 304).

Ritual similarly provides the participant with a liturgical set of actions or sayings that are fixed but which also invite individual variation and performance to enact meaning. As Jennings explains, ritual "is above all a pattern of action" and far from being a "senseless activity," is "rather one of the many ways in which human beings construe and construct their world" (1996, 325). For Rappaport, performance is required for ritual. Alongside "formality," or a fixed structure that is "stereotyped" or "repetitive," performance is "the second *sine qua non* of ritual" (1996, 428). Play is richly configurative in all of its ritual–game–story forms, pulling players into the experience and making them co-creators. Salen and Zimmerman note of games that "play doesn't just come from the game itself, but from the way the players interact with the game in order to play it." The boards and pieces of a game, they say, "can't alone constitute meaningful play," which emerges rather "from the interaction between players and the system of the game, as well as from the context in which the game is played" (2004, 33). The same could be said of the objects used in a ritual, or the components of a story. They are mere props until interacted with, until a player–participant–reader "plays" or performs with them, creating meaning through articulation of a relationship with the given structure of the ritual, game or story as system.

Claude Lévi-Strauss acknowledges that games and rituals both involve an element of play. He points to rules as a common feature of both, arguing that ritual is also "played" and is "like a favored instance of a game, remembered from among the possible ones because it is the only one which results in a particular type of equilibrium between the two sides." He uses the example of football played in a ritual form by the Gahuku-Gama of New Guinea and the adoption ceremonies of the Fox Indians, whose funeral rites are game-like in their aim to prevent the dead "from avenging on the living their bitterness and their regret that they are no longer living among them." But for Lévi-Strauss, the similarities between games and rituals are most interesting for the comparisons they invite, namely, that rituals sometimes involve playful competitions intended to bring a community together, whereas games (especially sports) involve play as a means of declaring a winner: "Games thus appear to have a disjunctive effect: they end in the establishment of a difference between individual players or teams." Ritual, by contrast, "conjoins, for it brings about a union ... or in any case an organic relation between two initially separate groups" (1966, 30–32).

Play, most generally, can be viewed as a form of engagement with any fixed structure, something that both games and rituals and even stories invite. Play, then, is the means of finding the level of movement and experimentation allowed within a set of rules. It is, in fact, one of the primary ways that we cultivate meaning in our lives. Jonathan Z. Smith points toward the meaning that rules can inscribe on our lives when he describes the discontinuity between the etiquette expected in tribal rituals of the bear hunt and what actually happens when real people hunt bears. Drawing on traditional accounts, Smith observes that "there appears to be a gap, an incongruity between the hunters' ideological statements of how they ought to hunt and their actual behavior while hunting." For example, it is highly unlikely, he speculates, that all hunters kill bears in "hand-to-hand, face-to-face combat." The hunters, it seems, are engaged in a sort of "play" with ritual – what Smith calls "skill at rationalization, accommodation, and adjustment" (Smith 1996, 478–79). The rules are there to be negotiated, existing as an ideal sense of order alongside the chaos of real life. The game of the ritual hunt is "played" by experimenting with the rules. Ritual, Smith says, provides a structure for making sense of life, a "controlled environment" where the "variables of life" are subdued under the appearance of order. Ritual is "a way of performing the way things ought to be" since "it relies ... for its power on the perceived fact that, in actuality, such possibilities cannot be realized" (480). Ritual's resonance, then, may depend precisely upon the element of play, since "ritual gains force where incongruency is perceived and thought about" (480). When real people do rituals, meaning arises through their very performance, from the play of what they choose to do (and not do) in relationship to what they *should* do.

The same kind of play can be seen when readers encounter a text as a "fixed structure" and play with that text in the development of personal meaning. Eagleton points out that "reading is not a straightforward linear movement, a merely cumulative affair" (1983, 77). Instead reading, like other forms of the ritual–game–story, is an active process that changes both reader and story: "all literary works ... are 'rewritten,' if only unconsciously, by the societies which read them; indeed there is no reading of a work which is not also a 're-writing'" (12). Again, tension is produced between the text (as a collection of words) and the reader's encounter with that text (producing meaning through play).

Drawing on Gadamer, for whom "the meaning of a literary work is never exhausted by the intentions of its author," Eagleton observes that when we read, a literary work passes into new contexts in which "new meanings may be culled ... which were perhaps never anticipated by [the work's] author or contemporary audience" (71). Play is thus evident in the very indeterminacy it provokes in response to fixed structures or rules.

Rules

Rules tell us what we are allowed to do and not to do. Rules shape games by setting the standards for behavior and the tolerance for play in relationship to those standards. Rules define rituals by telling us what behaviors are acceptable, in what order, by whom, and where. Rules define story-reading by offering hermeneutical principles of encounter, shaping which readings are possible to be derived given the reader's social or religious context, and given the shape of the received words of the story. Rules are strictures that bind us – they are the "road" that we traverse, the standard against which we veer when we "play" with the steering wheel.

Rules are easy to see in rituals. Rappaport describes some rituals as having "liturgical orders" or "invariant sequences of formal acts and utterances repeated in specified contexts" (1996, 429). Stanley Tambiah also points to the formal structure of many ritual experiences; ritual "is constituted of patterned and ordered sequences of words and acts, often expressed in multiple media, whose content and arrangement are characterized in varying degree by formality (conventionality), stereotypy (rigidity), condensation (fusion), and redundancy (repetition)" (1996, 497). For Staal, rules are so important that they may even eclipse the need for meaning. In ritual activity, "the rules count, but not the result" whereas "in ordinary activity it is the other way around ... What is essential in the ceremony is the precise and faultless execution, in accordance with rules, of numerous rites and recitations" (1996, 487).

Rules are fundamental features of games as well. Zimmerman points out the behavior-limiting qualities of games: "A game is a voluntary activity in which one or more players follow rules that constrain their behavior" and adds that "to take part in a game is to submit your behavior to the restrictions of the rules" (2004, 160–61). Wolf similarly remarks that in video games, "there are always limitations or 'rules' as to what goal-oriented characters may do or not do while engaging in conflicts or pursuing their quests" (2001a, 95). Juul labels the rigidly fixed features of some games "progression." In progression games, he says, "the player has to perform a predefined set of actions in order to complete the game." Such a game "yields strong control to the game designer" who can determine, at least to some extent, what players must do to win (2005, 5). Games, like rituals, are shaped by rules. This similarity, of course, invites consideration of *who* wrote the rules for a given game or ritual (if this can be known), *why* they did, and *what* we are expected to learn from the experience. Authorities in charge of religious rituals may see God as the designer, with the attendant assumptions about divine procedural rhetoric. Game designers can see the human role in rule-crafting, and thus may be more able to expose ideological intent.

It would be tempting to argue that stories do not have rules, based on the claim that stories don't change. As game theorist Chris Crawford remarks, "in the universe of narrative, the laws of drama are as adamantine as the laws of physics in the real world" (2003, 264). But this kind of claim, often voiced by hard-core ludologists, betrays a certain naiveté about what stories are and where we can find them. Greg Costikyan displays these tendencies too when he insists that all stories are "inherently linear. However much characters may agonize over the decisions they make, they make them the same way every time we reread the story, and the outcome is always the same" (2006, 194). If Costikyan is right, then stories are so rigid that they don't even need rules, since interactivity is impossible. Similar claims are sometimes made about films, reflecting on the nature of the finished, edited film product, which reveals the same version of the visual story every time we view it (director's cuts notwithstanding).

The presumptions here can be traced indirectly to mainstream Christian modes of reading stories, in particular those Christian arguments that the Bible depends upon a linear sequence of events reflected in the sacred text. Such thinking also, by extension, relies upon theologically motivated typological hermeneutics of salvation. The view of time here is crucial – it moves in one direction only, and in stories, in unchangeable ways. In this view, God (or the Director, or Storyteller) has written all the rules, and we should read the stories in the Bible less as invitations to hermeneutical play but more as rigid and unchangeable, and fully comprehensible due to its unfolding of stories in linear, historical time. In this type of Christian reading of the Bible, "events are seen on a sequential time line, as predictive of the fulfillment that would later come with Jesus: they attain their meaning as signs pointing towards him" (Handelman 1982, 37). The narrative is not to be tampered with, and the story must be told in the same sequence every single time. Not all readings of the Bible are so rigid, however, as evident in the interactivity of rabbinic interpretation, as we saw in Chapter 2. The rabbinic view of time, which sees the text as a sort of vessel rather than as a series of inevitable events connected on a string resembles gameplay in its rules of encounter. As Handelman remarks, when read rabbinically, the Bible can contain "both past and future simultaneously." The text of the Bible is polysemous, so that "multiple meanings [can] be derived from and are inherent in every event, for every event is full of reverberations, references, and patterns of identity that can be infinitely extended" (37). As we saw in Chapter 2, Borg hints at such a view as well. This view of the Bible presents it as a field of play: multiple layers of meaning and time are embedded in every phrase and every word.

Rabbi Louis Finkelstein describes the Torah in ways that sound much more like a game than a story: "The text is at once perfect and perpetually incomplete ... like the universe itself it was created to be a process rather than a system." We are to play with the text and unearth levels of interpretation embedded there so that we might "share the labour of Divinity" in making the world the best it can be (cited in Handelman 1982, 40). This fluidity, Handelman rightly notes, is also a "central tenet of much contemporary literary theory" (41). Rabbinic encounters with the text, then, have something in common with postmodern explorations of multiplicity of meaning; but whereas many post-modern theorists would detect a poverty of meaning within texts, rabbinic interpretation assumes that the text, however malleable (and in part due to its malleability), has the ability to reveal greater and greater depths of meaning.

Game theorists like Mateas and Stern would likely be baffled by such creative rabbinic play with the Bible, since they define stories in more rigid ways: "Where gameplay is all about interactivity, narrative is all about predestination" (2006, 643). Frasca agrees; narrative authors "only have one shot in their gun – a fixed sequence of events." Traditional narrative, he says, "lacks the 'feature' of allowing modifications to the stories, even if exceptions happen in oral storytelling and dramatic performances." By contrast, "in a game, going through several sessions is not only a possibility but a requirement of the medium" (2003, 227). So for Frasca, the rules are simple; a story must be and indeed only *can be* read directly, passively, as linear and as predetermined. But the rabbinic approach to interpretation suggests that texts can become hyperlinks waiting to happen, networks of connections hidden but waiting to be revealed.

We can also see this complex approach to storytelling-as-encounter in the work of some film directors, who intentionally disrupt our assumption of lin-earity in the creation and reception of film, despite the fact that film is defined by a linear strip of images that is meant to unfurl in exactly the same way every time we view it. Considering the work of geniuses of montage like Orson Welles and Sergei Eisenstein, Christian Metz points to montage cinema as "at times very close to being a kind of mechanical toy" that can captivate those who "acquire a taste for manipulation in their playing, which if they later become engineers, specialists in cybernetics, even ethnographers and lin-guists, may be extended into a whole operational attitude, whose excellence of principle will be more evident here than in film" (1974, 34). For those engaged in the project of montage, the production of film is a sort of game, involving determined interaction with the raw material of film, shaped by certain rules and limitations inherent in film production, but also expressive of the freedoms allowed within the parameters of the system.

A transaction occurs in the movement from the physical, natural object to film. A director, says Metz, "reassembles a duplicate of the original object, a duplicate which is perfectly grasped by the mind, since it is a pure product of the mind" (1974, 36). Pointing to Eisenstein's iconic *Battleship Potemkin* (1925), Metz identifies the film as a masterpiece of units, a gesture demon-strating Eisenstein's refusal to present filmic time as strictly linear. Instead, "one must fragment, isolate the close-ups, and then reassemble everything"

(33). Film production like this is a game, and the director plays it by taking real-life objects and transforming them with the camera, creating a montage, a blend of images, that we as viewers must then encounter and engage in our own attempts to construct (not reconstruct) meaning.

Films can be interactive stories, a kind of play-in-motion for the directors who assemble shots and images in their own transformation of visual elements into a single "play" of the story as it appears on screen. But films are also interactive for the viewers who encounter these traces of play, who in their own interpretive stance in regard to the visual story of a finished film must determine its meaning, by reading the clues set forth by the director in all their glorious indeterminacy. If the viewers then take the visual stuff of a film and edit it, re-create it, or otherwise visually alter it for display in online venues like *YouTube*, it becomes impossible to tell anymore who is the storyteller, or even what the "original" story may be. Indeed, such "mashing-up" is an apt metaphor for the construction of the contemporary self, with our lives a streaming montage created through the choices we make in the media we consume – a perpetually manufactured, always-in-motion, individualized director's cut.

Increasingly, then, we must decide how we are going to receive and experience a given entity as a ritual, game, story, or combination of these. Sometimes stories are read as received linear narratives, at other times they may be read as invitations to play, and at others they may be seen as the product of play. *We* decide which hermeneutical framework to engage, and accordingly what import to place upon the experience in our own process of meaning-making. In all three we may be able to recognize events unfolding in a way that *creates* a story that depends upon our interactivity, that is a product of play, that is defined by rules, but which can be observed upon its emergence through our engagement with the system in which it is formed.

Narrative

While it might seem easy to know a story when we see one, the debates raging in game studies and ritual studies show this to be surprisingly difficult. It's not made any easier by ongoing developments in technology and distribution and more enhanced interactivity in media of all kinds. Murray observes that "the first signs of this new storytelling are in the linear media, which seem to be outgrowing the strictures of the novel and movie in the same way that we might imagine a painting outgrowing the frame and morphing into a three-dimensional sculpture" (Murray 2004, 4). One way of dealing with the problem is to separate the idea of "narrative" from the idea of "story," calling attention to nuances between stories that may emerge via interactive play with received structures. Zimmerman embraces this approach but argues that a deeper consideration of story will not on its own resolve the problem since "there are as many approaches to the question of 'games and stories' as there are designers, artists, technologists, and academics asking the questions" (2004, 155). Indeed, he says, "[i]t is possible to frame games as narrative systems, or as interactive systems, or as systems of play" (161).

Murray acknowledges that "gaming and storytelling have always over-lapped" and suggests that instead of trying to define them separately, we should think about the difference in "matters of degree" because typically "a story has greater emphasis on plot [and] a game has greater emphasis on the actions of the player" (2004, 9). So for Murray, the difference has more to do with how rigidly the received story shapes what players get out of a game. And in some cases, as with *Halo*, it is impossible to even tell the difference between the story and the game. Are the *Halo* novels types of stories and the *Halo* video games not stories at all? What of real-life fan rituals, such as the donning of costumes at Comic Conventions (ComicCons) or Live Action Role Play (the acronym, LARP) events, in which people embody characters from well-loved stories and enact storylines (hardcore fans call it "larping")? Such experiences force the recognition that games and stories, especially in today's hyper-mediated, hyper-interactive society, are simply different facets of the same imaginative engagement with an "otherworldly" experience. Is it possible, then, to see rituals as framing devices for myths – those cosmic stories that so often drive religious experience? And to see games as tapping into vast, new, mythic story worlds that invite our ritualized participation?

For Rappaport, ritual has a complex relationship with myth. Myth, he proposes, is not the same thing as a ritual, but ritual *can* be deeply involved in the *expression* of myth so long as we realize that the *performance* of ritual is the most determinative of its meaning. Ritual can "transmit information" about participants, and it can also point to "processes or entities, material or putative, outside the ritual" (1996, 430). Rituals may involve the recitation of myth, but they must be understood first and foremost as performances, as actions, as experiences of the performers. Similar observations could be made about games, in which backstory may involve rich mythic overtones, full worlds developed and consumed by players sometimes before they even begin the game. *Halo*, for example, has a rich complex development of story with deep roots expressed variously in novels, online sources, gameplay, and guides. To play *Halo* is not to "believe" these stories, except insofar as they inform the activity of play and the imaginative investment in the story world. *Halo* is a great example of a ritual–game–story thing, calling forth in player–participants deep interactivity, play, rule acceptance, and mythic engagement.

Myth, as one type of story – even if a cosmic one – is implicated in the definitional complexity of the ritual–game–story thing. As William Doty points out, myth "is a make-do term that implies singularity and univocity of meaning, whereas the reality continues to amaze us with its plurality and multiplicity" (1986, 60). Theorists attempt to sort out the relationship between drama and ritual, between story and myth, and between myth and ritual, and between performance and ritual. As Richard Hardin observes, some rituals have "mythic content" while others do not (1996, 317). There is common ground, however. All three – rituals, games and stories – do commonly have some kind of relationship with narrative, and in particular, with the notion of the story arc. The story arc describes a larger structure of experience that shapes our encounter with many forms of the ritual–game–story thing, demarcating a predictable surge of experience and catharsis. As I discussed in Chapter 2, Aristotle proposes that a successful experience of catharsis hinges on our degree of emotional investment with a given character's experiences in a received and fixed narrative. So is it even possible that a game, as a kind of story, might also induce catharsis despite its loosely constructed narrative?

Mateas and Stern explain the problem: "story means fate; interactivity means freedom" (2006, 661). Murray agrees that we "cannot bring to a trans-formative, shape-shifting medium the same expectations of static shapelessness and finality that belong to linear media. But that does not mean that we will forgo a sense of completeness and emotional release." For Murray, it is possible to experience an Aristotelian sense of satisfaction in games *because* they are a "procedural medium" and thus allow us to "collaborate in the performance" (1997, 180). Defining a "story" as a set of "experiences that have a tightly organized plot arc, progression towards a climax, beginning, middle and end," Mateas and Stern allow that *some* games might induce the sort of recognition of pathos that films and written stories more easily induce (2006, 643). Frasca explains: "Ludus sessions go through the same three-act rule behind Aristotelian stories. [They] go through a first act in which the rules are acknowledged, a second act in which players perform, and, finally, a third act that concludes the game and draws the line between victors and losers" (2003, 230). Thus, "output-driven" experiences like games have the potential to trigger emotional experiences too – and if the interactivity is programmed successfully, they may be able to do so even more powerfully than "input-driven" ones like film. In this way, some games can work even more like ritual than films, if through limited choices they heighten our sense of helplessness to fate, by offering us some choices but denying others and leading us inexorably to a predetermined outcome.

Brenda Laurel applies Aristotle's *Poetics* to gameplay, arguing that catharsis is "the natural result of the moment at which probability becomes necessity" (1993, 123). Such an experience can be accomplished in interactive media, she argues, through "designing or influencing what kinds of incidents will occur and in what order" (139). Emotions that have been aroused in a virtual experience must also be successfully resolved and so "we must design clear and graceful ways for things to end" (122). Thus, even though games are by nature much more fluid than both rituals and stories, the very emergence of choices leaves behind them a trail of experiences that can be read, once performed, as fated. And programmers can enhance gaming experiences to increase the odds that we have just such an experience. Drawing on Laurel's work on games and narrative, Mateas introduces what he calls "a theory of interactive drama based on Aristotle's dramatic theory but modified to address the interactivity added by player agency" (2004, 19). Mateas argues that a game can *produce* predictable structure and evoke a cathartic experience through an emergent narrative that is carefully engineered by designers. Plot, in this case, is partially scripted by the choices previously determined by the game; but plot also emerges via the individualized choices of players in the game.

For LeBlanc, a story with the Aristotelian arc can be effectively "told" in the playing of a game, and is observed in the "tension that accumulates as the story builds to a climax, and dissipates as the conflict is resolved" (2006, 443). Celia Pearce similarly remarks that "[a] good game, even one without an obvious 'storyline' … while being played, will tend to follow something that resembles the emotional curve of a dramatic arc" (2004, 145). Indeed, the elements of conflict so common in many types of video games can enhance this experience by presenting us with protagonists and antagonists, a problem to be solved, and the satisfaction that comes with its resolution. The climax of a game is "the moment of realization: the moment when the outcome of the contest is known, and the uncertainty has been dispelled" (LeBlanc 2006, 445). A story need not be fully determined beforehand for this to happen; what is most important for the story arc is the emotional *experience* of fate, and the sense of release that comes when all the story's metaphorical cards are on the table. LeBlanc describes the dramatic arc of a game as "the rising and falling action of a well-told story." The arc builds "dramatic tension," achieved via the degree of emotional involvement and urgency with which the player awaits the story game's emerging outcome (443). Despite the player's participation in the production of the story arc (and perhaps *because* of it) a successful game can provide "a sense of wholeness, that it is a complete work with a beginning, middle, and end" (444).

Games do not automatically provide us with this sense of cathartic release, however. The player's experience must be engineered to make the experience more likely. Whereas "authorial control" is assumed more often in storytelling, "the key to game narrative is that it is, by definition, incomplete" and "leave[s] room for the player to bring it to fruition" (Pearce 2004, 146). In an emergent story, produced through gameplay, the player must enact the story arc. However, game designers "cannot craft the game's drama directly" because they cannot know "the precise details of how [a] game will play out, each and every time it is played" (LeBlanc 2006, 440). In video games designers must "assure that [a] game will be dramatic, even when [they] don't have direct control over the narrative, a narrative that isn't scripted in advance, but rather emerges from the events of the game" (444). By crafting experiential devices into the procedure of gameplay, conscientious designers can create a situation conducive to the emergence of a story *through* play. As LeBlanc puts it, game designers "cannot create drama; we can only create the circumstances from which drama will *emerge*" (440).

Rituals, too, can be seen as a generator of interactive catharsis. Hardin has noted that rituals offer a typical repetition of symbols through the re-enactment of primordial events and that in so doing they "help us rise above personal and social limitations, even above time and space" as they "strengthen social status and respect for authority" (1996, 314). René Girard is even more explicit about ritual's ability to purge us of violent emotions via a predictable iteration of events; the "mimetic attributes of [religious] violence" serve as a substitute for the "violent impulses" that feed "like a raging fire" on a community, demanding an outlet. Ritual, by presenting us with a predictable means of engaging with these impulses and telling the story of divine satisfaction with sacrifice, enables us to reach a cathartic release, allowing communities to remain whole until the ritual–story must be repeated again (1977, 32).

In his discussion of the cultivation of emergent cathartic experience, LeBlanc focuses on three facets of game design and gameplay: mechanics, dynamics and aesthetics. *Mechanics* refers to the "necessary pieces" to play the game, including both cognitive and physical pieces, such as rules, or dice. *Dynamics* refers to "the actual events and phenomena that occur as the game is played." *Aesthetics* is the emotional content of the game, so that the designers engineer the game in order to evoke a particular emotional response from players. These are all interconnected in deep ways: dynamics determine aesthetics; mechanics shape dynamics, and so on. In the construction of a game, the mechanics can be deliberately crafted to create the best chance of a dramatic arc emerging in the dynamics, and thus the appropriate aesthetic response being provoked. As LeBlanc notes, in a game, the tension between the protagonist and antagonist is transformed so that "the conflict comes from the contest around which the game is built." Tension can be heightened through creating a sense of "uncertainty" about the outcome, as well as through "inevitability," that is, "the sense that the contest is moving forward toward [a] resolution" that is "imminent" (2006, 444). The "climax" of the game appears precisely "at the moment when the outcome of the contest is known, and the uncertainty has been dispelled" (445).

So what happens when game designers, for example, the designers of *The Bible Game*, start with a predetermined biblical narrative but have to design *mechanics* to produce the right *dynamics* to elicit the desirable *aesthetics*? If the aesthetics desired is affirmation of Christian ideas, then the game must support a healthy assumption of Christian truths. So, obviously, the design will include biblical characters, and even if it strays in some ways from the textual version of the story, will not alter the textual story in any meaningful way. For example, if Moses were depicted during the Exodus, it might be acceptable to add an optional fishing game before or after the parting of the Red Sea, but it would not be acceptable to let somebody else part the Red Sea instead of Moses. This principle holds true in actual play of *The Bible Game*, which includes a "challenge game" in which four young cartoonish avatars run through the sea floor while the waters are parted for the Exodus. Players must avoid vegetation and crabs that serve as obstacles. Players can even be temporarily sucked into the water, to be spurted back out unharmed, with a minor cost of points. Missing from *The Bible Game*'s "Exodus," however, are

Pharaoh, his troops, Moses, the Israelites, and any signs of antiquity. This makes for a procedural argument that escape from Egypt is more a matter of good running skills than a divine force. In *The Bible Game*'s version of things, God may be responsible for getting water out of the way for the heroic sprint across the Red Sea bed, but he can't do anything about crabs or seaweed. The consideration of design raises some interesting questions about what makes a biblical story a good candidate for a game. If *The Bible Game* is any indication of the standard, designers are particularly drawn to those stories that already possess a dramatic arc, such as David's battle with Goliath, Jonah and the whale, or the Exodus. Those that also possess some kind of simple conflict are especially good candidates.

LeBlanc also discusses how techniques to increase tension, such as *force* and *illusion*, can be built into a game. Force is the process of "manipulating the players' perceptions so that the game seems closer than it is." Players who are behind can more easily catch up, for example, by artificially creating handicaps for better players. LeBlanc elaborates: "Force is the approach of creating dramatic tension by manipulating the state of the contest itself. The game is close because we make it close, or at the very least we limit how much an advantage one player can have over another" (2006, 446). Illusion is the manipulation of the players' perceptions so that it *appears* that the contest is very close. In *The Bible Game*, the technique of "illusion" is employed so that if a child's character trips a lot, or gets absorbed into the water wall in the seabed, he or she almost immediately reappears and continues to run alongside the other children without falling behind. There is a cost in points, to be sure, but this is masked until the end of the game, after the climax of a successful run (at least visually) for everyone.

"Dramatic inevitability" is also heightened in *The Bible Game* through the use of what LeBlanc calls the *ticking clock*, or "the sense of imminent resolution that gives a game its sense of momentum and forward progress" (446). A ticking clock mechanism might involve the loss of non-renewable resources, such as decreasing "health bars," or checkpoints along a trajectory, or even a real clock counting decreasing time (454). As players approach the end of the game, they are increasingly invested in the outcome, such that "as time runs out, the players feel propelled toward the conclusion of the contest" (453). Catharsis and resolution come as the expected end arrives. In *The Bible Game*, the clock is quite literal, counting down to the end of each round or individual "challenge."

Catharsis is intimately tied up with the notion of interactivity, drawing us in emotionally to the ritual, game or story that we are experiencing and inviting us to be co-creators in the experience, even as we experience what seems like narrative inevitability. This push toward resolution also has some resonance with the view of games as contests, and the attendant view that rituals are a form of setting things in place, of creating order. Bell acknowledges the central role of oppositions in many analyses of ritual, remarking that it "not only involves the setting up of oppositions, but through the privileging built into such an exercise it generates hierarchical schemes to produce a loose sense of totality and systematicity" (1992, 104). These structures can be seen as a sort of resolution that brings about catharsis – release of emotions and an acceptance of the emerging order of things. One of the most common ways of putting things in their places, of course, is through the resolution of conflict, a common feature of many ritual–game–story things.

Conflict

If the story arc indeed appears in iterations of games, stories and rituals, then it should not be surprising to notice conflict as a defining feature of these as well. Salen and Zimmerman define a game as "a system in which players engage in an artificial conflict, defined by rules, that results in a quantifiable outcome" (2004, 80). As Eskelinen similarly points out, "in games there's only one necessary time scheme … the movement from the beginning to the winning or some other situation" (2004, 39). Thinking especially about conflict as a theme, Gregory Bateson acknowledges the difficulty of distinguishing between ritual and game. He points to a ritual in the Andaman Islands in which ceremonial blows are applied as a ritual of peacemaking, an activity that "illustrates the labile nature of the frame 'This is play,' or 'This is ritual.' The discrimination between map and territory is always liable to break down, and the ritual blows of peacemaking are always liable to be mistaken for the 'real' blows of combat" (2006, 318). In an experience that involves conflict, then, the only difference between ritual and game may be intent. Implicitly acknowledging the similar purposes of conflict in ritual and game, LeBlanc explains that defeating an enemy in a game is an "end-of-game ritual that prepares the winner to win and the loser to lose" (2006, 449). Such an experience can simultaneously function as a signal for completion of a game, as a ritual of closure, and as the dénouement of the story.

Conflict in ritual can be seen as a kind of sorting process, putting things in their proper place. Smith defines ritual in one instance as "an assertion of difference" (1987, 109). Smith echoes Bell here, since both see opposition as key to ritual and its cathartic functions, such that the resolution of the oppositions creates a "fit" between the "taxonomic order" of the ritual and the "real world of experience." In other words, ritualization *organizes* things for adherents, by demarcating a structural coherence, which often involves oppositions – insiders and outsiders, good and evil, right and wrong (Bell 1992, 104). The function of ritual, then, as a means of quantifying outcomes and creating closure through difference, has a lot in common with that of games.

Stories, too, often depend upon conflict, primarily through the articulation of the story arc and the interaction between protagonists and antagonists: "Storytelling," says Kearney, "is never neutral." He quips: "Could we really enjoy the battle between Luke Skywalker and Darth Vader if we did not see the former as an agent of justice and the latter as a force of destruction?" (155). Stories may offer some of the same pleasures as rituals and games in their articulation of conflict and their assurance that conflict can and will be resolved. Indeed, these three experiences are each a form of cosmos construction, offering predictable and comforting views of a world that makes sense through the sorting of opponents and outcomes.

The ritual–game–story thing

In this chapter, I have pointed out some of the most compelling similarities between rituals, games and stories: interactivity, play, rules, narrative, conflict. But if rituals, games and stories share so many common features, how can we tell the difference between them? Perhaps the *only* way to clearly differentiate between games, stories and rituals is to look at the *attitude* of those interacting with them, and examine the specific form of the interactivity, the type of play, the rules involved, the perspective on story, and the role of conflict in differentiating between players and ideas. In short, the fundamental difference between games, rituals and stories is in how we approach them, not what they "are."

To play a game is to *choose* to play a game. Salen and Zimmerman describe the "lusory attitude," that is, the choice that a player–participant makes to give himself or herself over to the game. They explain this experience as "the peculiar state of mind of game players" in which they willingly and deliberately accept the rules, taking on unnecessary limitations to achieve a goal and comprehending that the experience itself depends upon stepping into the world of the game (2004, 77). As if recognizing the religious implications of the lusory state, Salen and Zimmerman describe the experience of playing a game as "an act of 'faith'" that depends upon "willing players" who give life to the game as "formal system" (98). But for many players, no matter the "faith" involved in entering the lusory state, a game is still "just" a game.

This is not to say that one cannot lose oneself in play and engage in it with gusto. Indeed, says Huizinga, "genuine and spontaneous play can also be profoundly serious" and enable the player to "abandon himself body and soul to the game" (1955, 21). But play, no matter how earnest, also contains within it "the consciousness, however latent, of 'only pretending'" (22). The child playing a game "plays and knows that it plays" and indeed sees what it does as "only" playing (18). By contrast, we can say with Hardin that rituals "never exist for their own sake" (1996, 311). For Rappaport, the difference between ritual and drama (as a sort of story) is in the *attitude* we adopt when we see them – a contrast that we could also apply to ritual and games. Compared with performers of ritual, actors in dramatic performances "are 'only acting,' which is precisely to say that they are not acting in earnest … Ritual in contrast, is earnest, even when it is playful, entertaining, blasphemous, humorous, or ludicrous" (1996, 429). This notion of the "earnest" nature of ritual is an apt contrast to the "lusory" or "playful" attitude embraced in games. As Peter Berger observes, ritual is serious business: as a "tool of religious establishment," it has the ability to bestow upon religious institutions "an ultimately valid ontological status ... by *locating* them within a sacred and cosmic frame of reference" (1990, 33). Games, by contrast, self-consciously parade themselves as an ultimate "what-if" experience, flaunt their fantastical components, and insist that they are not "real" and have no effect on daily life.

However, such easy distinctions remain deeply problematic. Indeed, when it comes down to it, intent or mood may be the *only* way to distinguish between rituals and games, such that only player–performers will have the ability to decide if what they are doing is playful, serious, or both. For example, the Turkish game show *Penitents Repent* "aims to turn disbelievers on to God," says station deputy director Ahmet Ozdemir (quoted in Tait 2009). Robert Tait reports that "Four spiritual guides from the different religions will seek to convert at least one of the 10 atheists in each programme to their faith." In an embedded interview, Tait reports that the show selects "hardcore non-believers" only. They are "assessed for the strength and intensity of their non-belief before they are allowed to take part." The game involves spirited debate between atheists and believers. Those persuaded to become believers "will be rewarded with a pilgrimage to the spiritual home of their newly chosen creed – Mecca for Muslims, Jerusalem for Christians and Jews, and Tibet for Buddhists" (Tait 2009). The creators claim that the game is "educational" for viewers; but it also has an obvious ritual component: the hoped-for conversion experience of atheists, followed by their metaphysical reward: "We give you the biggest prize ever: we represent the belief in God." Converted players "will find serenity in this competition" (Tait 2009). When asked what would happen "if one of the atheists convinces the believers that God doesn't exist," Tait explains that "there are no prizes for doing that" (Tait 2009). *Penitents Repent* is game *and* ritual, game for the "losers" and ritual for the "winners."

To ensure that the game becomes a ritual (conversion), Tait reports that converts in *Penitents Repent* "will be monitored to ensure their religious transformation is genuine and not simply a ruse to gain a free foreign trip. 'They can't see this trip as a getaway, but as a religious experience'" (Tait 2009). Bernard Suits argues that the "lusory attitude" is that "state of mind whereby game players consciously take on the challenges and obstacles of a game in order to experience the play of the game itself" through "accepting the artificial authority of the magic circle, submitting behavior to the constraints of rules in order to experience the free movement of play." To play a game, says Suits, involves "submitting to the authority of the magic circle, which includes the cultural conventions expressed through implicit rules" (1990, 574). In *Penitents Repent*, successful players must "submit" to the "authority" of the religious group, and abide by their "cultural conventions [as] expressed through implicit rules." And since religion is not typically seen as playful but as "serious," the "lusory attitude" is replaced with something like the "faith attitude." This is why players must be observed for some time after the show ends: to ensure that they are "serious" about this new game, and that the ritual of conversion was effective.

Huizinga recognized the sensitive territory he trod upon when trying to articulate the distinction between games and rituals. Huizinga says that in a "sacred performance" there is "more of a mental element 'at play'" than in a game, but it is "excessively difficult to define." The sacred performance, he says, is not just a "sham reality." It is "more than a symbolical actualization – it is a mystical one." For Huizinga, the rite "brings about an order of things higher than that in which [the participants] customarily live." Despite its ultimate intentions, the sacred performance "retains the formal characteristics of play in every respect," except that when it ends, it "continues to shed its radiance on the ordinary world outside, a wholesome influence working security, order and prosperity for the whole community until the sacred play-season comes round again" (1955, 14). If Huizinga is right, then the most important difference between games and rituals lies in the *attitude* of the participants. Mere game players allow a ritual–game–story experience only *limited* ability to affect their ordinary lives, and ritual performers allow a ritual–game–story ultimate power to shape their perspectives. One is a temporary escape from the world, and the other is a sign of cosmic stability. For players in *Penitents Repent*, to "win" is to learn see the game *as* a ritual, and to pick a system to follow, that is, an *ultimate* game to enter into for the rest of their lives.

Conclusion

Rituals, games and stories all do similar work, exhibit similar features, and overlap in compelling ways. But the attitude we embrace when we approach each is typically quite different. Games proudly display their credentials as human-made activities quite outside the realm of ordinary life. Stories, too, can be read as mere fantastic means of escape from everyday life, as evident in the very category of "fiction" and the easy association people commonly make between "myth" and stories as pure imaginative creations. Stories and games, says Murray, "are both distanced from the real world, although they often include activities that are done 'for real' in other domains." Stories and games offer us a means of temporarily escaping current existence: "Stories and games are like one another in their insularity from the real world, the world of verifiable events and survival-related consequences" (2004, 3). Rituals, by contrast, reflectively and *self-consciously* cast their meaning back onto the world, however obscure or indecipherable it may be at times. Nobody claims to do a ritual just "for fun." As Bell explains, ritualization "interprets its own schemes as impressed upon the actors from a more authoritative source, usually from well beyond the immediate human community" (1992, 110).

In different ways, then, rituals, games and stories all point beyond themselves to other worlds or modes of being. But ritual more than any other makes *ultimate* claims in this projection outward, insisting that the "ultimate" is fundamentally real – not "made up," not constructed, not programmed by us but by someone or something that attributes order to the world in which we live. Bell points out the ability of ritualization to offer a means of making sense of our world. Ritualization, she says, involves "the strategic production of expedient schemes that structure an environment in such a way that the environment appears to be the source of schemes and their values." Ritualizing schemes "invoke a series of privileged oppositions" that "effectively structure and nuance an environment" (140). It could be argued that ritual, ultimately, is shaped by the deliberate intent of the practitioner, and perhaps even by the choice *to be* a practitioner as opposed to a reader or game player.

At root, it is a matter of *choice* how we will approach ritual–game–story things and how we will read their significance into our lives. When viewed as rituals, they invite us to do meaningful things to shape our view of the cosmos and ourselves in it; when viewed as games, they invite us to play within specified parameters, to contemplate the role of rules in meaning-making, and to imagine ourselves inhabitants of other worlds; when viewed as stories, they encourage us to see how our lives are shaped by the stories we tell as well as by the stories that emerge when we interact with the systems and structures that surround us, and as we try to interpret these experiences. The ritual–game–story thing can even do all of these at once, ramping up certain qualities and dampening others in particular iterations. But whatever the degree of ritual or game or story in the thing itself, the experience of meaning-making is a quintessentially human one, and a markedly constructed one.

Chapter 4

The Other right here

In search of the virtual sacred

For millennia, the sacred "Other" was inhabited by notions of heaven, a Platonic ideal of Perfection toward which we looked with longing and which we attempted to understand with rituals and sacred architecture. Today, with the appearance of virtual reality, the "other" realm of the Sacred has new competition. Virtual reality is commonly described as "other" from physical reality, despite its increasing spillover into physical life. Virtual reality is a different "place" where we can live out our fantasies, where we can be other people. What are we to do with this new conceptual interloper? Contemporary ritual theorists have complained about Mircea Eliade's (1961) perhaps too easy dualism of "sacred" and "profane," even as we persist in using the terms as conceptual and religious tools. Assuming we do not dispense with the categories of "sacred" and "profane" altogether, where does "the virtual" go? Is the virtual *a form of* the Sacred? Does the virtual nest *within* the Sacred? Is the virtual a sacred hierophany? *Can* it be? Is the virtual a mere manifestation of the human profane?

Attempts to locate or define virtual reality present immediate problems made worse by the tendency to define the "virtual" in relation to something else: for some, virtual reality is *not*-actual or *not*-physical or *not*-real, all of which display different nuances of meaning. Thus, some see the virtual as the opposite of the physical; for others, it is "unreal" when compared with the sacred; for others, it is a "realm" of its own; for others, it is imaginary and not a "place" at all. For others, it is a mere designator of space, a territorial marker, such that "virtual space" is as real as physical space, it's just in a different, well, place. As Keith Ansell-Pearson puts it, the notion of the virtual "is widely treated in imprecise and ill-defined terms, namely as all the other stuff that is not actual, something like the universe in its totality and unfathomable complexity" (2005, 1112). Of course, such an observation is only helpful if we know what it means to be "not actual," and if we are already disagreeing on what is "real," then we aren't going to get very far.

The problem is not merely philosophical. Recent debates about such issues mark the importance of dealing with Eliade's sense of the "sacred" and the "profane." Indeed, the appearance of "virtual reality" on the conceptual scene seems to have spurred a rehabilitation of Eliade's terms as tools for thinking about what to do with the messy specter of the virtual as it relates to contemporary religious belief and practice. I've already alluded to how the Church of England responded to a digital shoot-out that takes place in virtual replica of the "sacred" space of Manchester Cathedral, ultimately charging Sony with "virtual desecration" (Chapter 1). A few years earlier, Sikhs had objected to a virtual murder that takes place in *Hitman 2: Silent Assassin* in a virtual representation of the Golden Temple. At the same time, churches in *Second Life* attract devoted followers and Muslims visit a virtual replica of Mecca, complete with a digital Kabah. In England, a real church struggled with the question of whether or not the church building itself could be sullied by virtual taboo information streaming through a cell tower mounted on its roof. The question of where we situate the "virtual" in relationship to the "sacred" and the "profane" exposes the indeterminacy in our own understandings of what religion even is, and how we can know it when we see it.

In attempts to figure out what to "do" with the virtual, a host of voices have weighed in from game theory, film studies, ritual studies, religious studies, and theological traditions. Some of these voices invoke conversations about realms or worlds, and thus seem to be interested in issues of fluidity and boundaries between conceptual realms or worlds. Some of these other worlds are considered "virtual," others "sacred," and some both virtual *and* sacred. Some thinkers use the language of conceptual "frames" to think about boundaries between realms or modes of being, while others focus on physical features like computer screens or architecture. Some focus on film as a means of contemplating the sacred, whereas others are more interested in contemporary computer-enhanced experiences of otherworldliness. What they all have in common is an attempt to make sense of this new category of the "virtual" in its relationship to the "sacred," and for some of them, the stakes are quite high.

If the sacred and the virtual are *identical* in both being non-material *opposites* of the physical world – that is, both are "not real," then there is no reason to protect brick-and-mortar buildings from violation, nor is there any reason to worship in one place over another. If the sacred is real and the virtual is *not*, then nobody should be going to church in *Second Life*. If the sacred can *manifest* in both the virtual and in the physical world, then virtual miracles are possible, and virtual desecration should be resisted. Because so much depends upon the practitioner's perspective, we can't solve these problems in any normative way. But we *can* add nuance to the questions by looking at how contemporary thinkers from different fields with different motivations try to make sense of where and what virtual reality is, especially as they themselves employ language of the sacred or talk about other "worlds" and the bounds between them. By synthesizing the views of a host of scholars from a variety of fields, five primary streams of discussion emerge, each with different implications about virtual reality's relationship to the sacred: (1) virtual reality as hierophany; (2) virtual reality as multiple worlds; (3) virtual reality and the magic circle;

(4) virtual reality as streaming, that is, as increasingly fluid with physical reality; (5) virtual reality as a reflection of already existing earthly things, or put another way, as a mere human construct. These are not mutually exclusive categories; rather, they represent recurrent concerns across many different fields of study, and thus demarcate rather what *kinds of questions* we as humans are now asking about the sacred and the virtual.

Virtual reality as hierophany

In some ways, to see the virtual world – whether it be filmic or digital – as a hierophany is the easiest approach to take, since it allows the traditional dualism of sacred and profane to remain intact. If one views "film" as a whole or the "virtual realm" as a whole as a manifestation or window into the Sacred, then the virtual is merely a form of hierophany, manifesting the sacred just as more traditional modes of visual encounter may have done for worshippers relying on icons in worship, for example. In this case, the screen serves as an entry point into the Transcendent. Accordingly, the content of the vision is of less consequence than the *performance* of vision itself, which apart from what is shown in virtual space always has the potential to startle us, disorient us, and provoke in us a sense of awe.

Writing in the earliest years of film production, film critics Jean Epstein and Antonin Artaud each used the language of the sacred to describe their fascination with the projected image, an early form of virtual encounter. Artaud sees cinema "in its raw state" as able to "emit something of the atmosphere of a trance conducive to certain revelations" (2007, 55). Similarly awed, Jean Epstein remarks on the ability of film to evoke strong reactions in us via "the almost godlike importance assumed in close-ups by parts of the human body." Film "summon[s] objects out of the shadows of indifference into the light of dramatic concern" and in so doing elevates them as transcendent signs: "If we wish to understand how an animal, a plant, or a stone can inspire respect, fear, or horror, those three most sacred sentiments, I think we must watch them onscreen, living their mysterious, silent lives, alien to the human sensibility" (2007, 52). Cinema reveals "a new reality" which "is untrue to everyday reality just as everyday reality is untrue to the heightened awareness of poetry" (53).

Antonin Artaud agrees, since "any image, even the slightest and most banal, is transfigured on the screen" (2007, 54). No matter what is shown on the screen, the mere projection of an object into the immaterial world of light enhances the object for us and evokes in us a sense of awe, which these critics identify as the sacred. Film, then, functions as a series of hierophanies evoking the sacred. Lyden draws on Eliade to similarly suggest that films "create an alternate world, a sacred apart from the profane, and that we enter into a separate space and time when we view a film" such that film becomes an "alternate reality experience" (2003, 76). Plate echoes this view, arguing that both religion and film "function by recreating the known world and then presenting that alternative version of the world to their viewers/worshippers" (2008, 2). Indeed, for Plate, film production is a form of world-making, a "performative drama in which humans are the costume designers and liturgists, scriptwriters and sermon givers, cinematographers and saints, projectionists and priests" (2008, 6). Cinema, he proposes, "offers a glimpse of the heavens, of other worlds above and beyond earthly existence, even as these other worlds must be relatable to the visible worlds on earth" (2008, 10).

Writing from a theological perspective, Nathaniel Dorsky argues that film can be viewed "devotionally," that is, as an "opening or interruption that allows us to experience what is hidden, and to accept with our hearts our given situation ... [film] subverts our absorption in the temporal and reveals the depths of our own reality, it opens us to a fuller sense of ourselves and our world" (2007, 407). Although Dorsky seems to want film to work as a sort of hierophany revealing the human, he nonetheless argues that "[v]iewing a film has tremendous mystical implications; it can be, at its best, a way of approaching and manifesting the ineffable" (409). Indeed, he suggests, "when a film is fully manifest it may serve as a corrective mirror that realigns our psyches and opens up to appreciation and humility" as "the more film expresses itself in a manner intrinsic to its own nature, the more it can reveal for us" (414–15). Paul Schrader focuses on a particular style of film, what he calls the "transcendental style," and sees in it film's ability to strip away unnecessary elements thus "robbing the conventional interpretations of reality of their relevance and power" and thrusting us into ritual engagement with the ultimate: "Transcendental style, like the mass, transforms experience into a repeatable ritual which can be repeatedly transcended" (2007, 176). Schrader isn't bothered by the varying ways that filmmakers in different religious traditions, East and West, find of evoking the sacred. "Spiritual art," he says, "must always be in flux because it represents a greater mystery, also in flux, man's relationship to the Holy." The spectator of film "grasps for that special form, that spot on the spectrum, whether in art, religion or philosophy, which can take him to greater mystery" (181).

In recent years, a number of scholars have similarly argued for the ability of virtual reality – in the form of computerized spaces in particular – to hierophanically represent an "other," a spirited imagining of our deepest dreams. As Jennifer Cobb puts it, virtual reality is "a place that feels removed from the physical world." One enters a virtual world. One leaves a virtual world. One shifts one's "appearance" when one enacts one's avatar in a given virtual world. Furthermore, within such virtual worlds, there is no eating, no sleeping, and no aging. Some have even considered the experience of inhabiting virtual space as a sort of digital heaven, or perhaps, as Cobb describes it, "the Platonic realm incarnate" (1998, 31). Such a realm naturally invites our wish to inhabit it. Filiciak says that the experience of interacting with virtual reality is characterized by intense desire: "We make the screen a fetish; we desire it, not only do we want to watch the screen but also to 'be seen' on it" (2003, 100). Hillis expresses a similar sentiment about virtual reality's ability to induce our sense of desire and transcendence:

> There is a widespread belief that space (understood variously as distance, extension, or orientation) constitutes something elemental, and VR [virtual reality] reflects support for a belief that because light illuminates space it may therefore produce space a priori. As a result, VR users may experience desire or even something akin to a moral imperative to enter into virtuality where space and light … have become one immaterial "wherein." The ability to experience a sense of entry into the image and illumination enabled by VR's design, coupled with both esoteric and pragmatic desires to view the technology as a "transcendence machine" or subjectivity enhancer, works to collapse distinctions between the conceptions built into virtual environments by their developers and the perceptive faculties of users.
>
> (2009, 349)

The computer may function as a "transcendence machine" in a way, inducing in us what Margaret Wertheim calls "a longing for the annihilation of pain, restriction, and even death" (1999, 259). Brenda Brasher observes in cyberspace what she calls "omnitemporality," that is, "the religious idea of eternity as perpetual persistence" (2001, 52). Using traditional religious language of the sacred, Brasher says that cyberspace is "[c]ontinuously accessible and ostensibly disconnected from the cycles of the earth." It "appeared to its first Western consumers to be a concrete expression or materialization of the monks' concept of eternity … It is always present. Whatever exists within it never decays. Whatever is expressed in cyberspace, as long as it remains in cyberspace, is perpetually expressed … the quasi-mystical appeal that cyberspace exudes stems from this taste of eternity that it imparts to those who interact with it" (52).

The typical contemporary hardware interface can enhance a vivid sense of otherworldliness – the game world is an obviously related but distinctive plane of experience. The computer defines its space (at least with current technology) with a window into which we *peer* – and into which we are invited to project our *selves* in some way or another. Grodal describes how we are drawn into a "trancelike immersion in the virtual world [by] the strong neuronal links that are forged between perceptions, emotions, and actions" (2003, 148). For Edward Castronova, upon entering a virtual world, "the screen turns into a window through which an alternative Earth, a synthetic world, can be seen" and "the window by which your computer is depicting the world is, in fact, the surface of somebody's eye, and that somebody is *you*" (2005, 6). Indeed, the very process of connecting oneself to digital hardware through the picking up of a controller device, the donning of headgear, the preparation of sound support systems, or the adjustment of video reception, is a bit like ritual preparation – and hearkens oddly to the ritual adorning of phylacteries, the placement of a traditional headdress, or the application of ritual paint. The desire to be "there" instead of "here" mimics the traditional desire for heaven, for perfection, for escape from ordinary life.

Viewing the virtual as a window peering into the transcendent, however, excuses us from having to consider the difference between forms of media. Accordingly, we don't have to worry much about the difference in content or form between a video game and a film in their interaction with the sacred. Both equally work as portals allowing us a glimpse of a singular Sacred lying beyond both. People may argue about which films evoke the Sacred most effectively and how they accomplish it; some may even see the Sacred as a mood or mode of *being* rather than a transcendent *realm*. But so long as one argues that the mere presence of a screen evokes the transcendent, one worries less about which screen one is using to look at it.

Seeing *all* of virtual reality as a manifestation of the singular Sacred is problematic for its inability to address how *individual* (or serialized) films, video games, online worlds, or books can be viewed as discrete "worlds" in and of themselves, thus evoking not a singular "sacred" but many competing "sacreds." Furthermore, it avoids the problem of what kind of content is put "into" virtual worlds: if anything behind a screen is "sacred," then it's always sacred, no matter what content is placed there; and we know from common sense that all kinds of things can happen in film and in video games that nobody would consider sacred. Both Plate and Lyden seem to implicitly acknowledge this issue when both of them slide between discussions of *film itself* as a world (singular) and discussion of films as worlds (plural). Plate says that when we view films, we "are invited into other worlds, alternate renditions of reality that through seamless editing, precise special effects, carefully placed cameras, and elaborate props offer views of the world that seem 'uniquely realistic'." But these other worlds all point to a single world, it seems, since film, "like religion, tells of another reality, of a world that could be, of a world that viewers want to live in … or avoid" (Plate 2007, 434). Using Clifford Geertz's definition of religion, Lyden argues that film, like religion, "offers a connection between this world and the 'other' world imagined in offering both models of and models for reality," creating an ideal sense of how the world should be. He also argues, in the same paragraph, that "films offer near-perfect worlds that do not correspond to reality as we experience it," but again, these worlds serve as models of how we would like things to be (2003, 54–55). Such slippage is largely inconsequential in the stream of argumentation both Plate and Lyden are engaged in; but it does reveal a discrepancy that becomes potent when one looks at related scholarship about other modes of virtual reality, especially online games and worlds which seem much more comfortable with overt plurality.

Virtual reality as multiple worlds

The notion of "worlds" is a common trope in contemporary media culture, applying to a host of virtual (including filmic) worlds. Consider some of the most popular media worlds today: *Twilight*, *Harry Potter*, *Avatar* and *Halo*. Some, like *Twilight* and *Harry Potter*, began as books but quickly took on a larger role in people's imaginations inviting ritual habitation in the imagined world, media rituals, films, and an active online fan culture. *Avatar*, first a film and now a developing franchise, deliberately evokes a sense of "otherworldliness" and invites us to identify with Jake Sully, its protagonist, as he witnesses the near-apocalyptic destruction of Pandora. As Castronova observes, when classic thinkers and artists wrote "that real life is something of a game, they were writing at a time when real life was the only game" around. Today, humanity for the first time has "not one but many worlds in which to live" (2005, 70). Many of these worlds are virtual.

Ritual theorists, too, often use the metaphor of "worlds" to make sense of ritual engagement with a transcendent reality. In fact, some ritual theorists *define* ritual as a "belief in, and communication with, the 'supernatural' world or a 'transtemporal' other world" (Tambiah 1996, 497). Arnold van Gennep noted long ago that rites often evoke entry into other realms; to "cross the threshold" of a home or temple "is to unite oneself with a new world" (1996, 532). By helping us imagine another world, ritual shows us how our own world is, or how we would like it to be. Tambiah notes that ritual enables participants to experience "transportation into a supra-normal, transcendental, 'anti-structural,' 'numinous,' or 'altered' state of consciousness, or … a euphoric communion with one's fellow beings, or a subordination to a collective representation" (Tambiah 1996, 507). Ritual invites multiple modes of engagement with the supernatural world, including myths, ritual performance, liturgy, and in some cases the ritual production of associated media like paintings, music or dance. One might even say that ritual worlds are transmediated, that is, they offer multiple streams of engagement with the worlds they evoke.

Halo is among the most well-known video game "worlds," and like many traditional religious belief systems, has a vast and complex mythology, devoted followers, and multimedia streams of related products. Because *Halo* is a first-person shooter, it also involves interactive (we might even say ritualized) performance through the player's role as Master Chief, the messianic hero of the game who travels to distant worlds in his quest to protect humanity. As I argue in Chapter 8, a number of contemporary video games like *Halo* evoke the classic form of the otherworldly journey, matching the definition of apocalypse formulated by the Society of Biblical Literature in 1979 (Collins 1979). *Halo*, like traditional Jewish and Christian apocalypses, depicts a visionary traveling to other worlds in search of crucial information for human salvation.

What all of these media "worlds" have in common is their delivery via transmedia, or multiple media streams, no single one of which contains the complete story or complete array of possible interactions with it. In Chapter 9, I address the phenomenon of transmedia more fully, but for now it is enough to observe that transmedia forms point beyond themselves to a "world" that is reflected in but cannot be contained fully by any of the individual media streams we consume to access it. By offering only portions of what the world has to offer, these media worlds are franchises, but they are much more than just that. They are hierophanic streams pointing toward core realities or "worlds" that defy the boundaries of any single film or book or media ritual. As Jenkins notes, "More and more, storytelling has become the art of world-building, as artists create compelling environments that cannot be fully explored or exhausted within a single work or even a single medium." The world, he says, "is bigger than the film, bigger even than the franchise – since fan speculations and elaborations also expand the world in a variety of directions" (2006a, 114). In such exploration, then, there is no single authority, even if there may have been a single original author, as in the *Twilight* series or the *Harry Potter* books. The worlds induced by these media items are fluid, emergent, and in many cases also co-created by fans. And although it is obvious, it bears repeating: there are many of these worlds, with more being formulated all the time.

One of the first and most powerful examples of this new form of media experience is *The Matrix*, which reveled in the new opportunities for media delivery and transcended all of them. Jenkins says of *The Matrix* that "no film franchise has ever made such demands on its consumers" (2006a, 94). *The Matrix* is "entertainment for the age of media convergence, integrating multiple texts to create a narrative so large that it cannot be contained within a single medium" (95). As an ingenious form of transmedia, *The Matrix* offers "layers and layers of references [that] catalyze and sustain our epistemophilia." As silent directors of *The Matrix* films, the Wachowski Brothers have "positioned themselves as oracles – hidden from view most of the time, surfacing only to offer cryptic comments, refusing direct answers, and speaking with a single voice." As a form of cultural Midrash, the "gaps and excesses" in cultural texts like the *Matrix* and others "provide openings for the many different knowledge communities that spring up around these cult movies to display their expertise, dig deep into their libraries, and bring their minds to bear on a text that promises a bottomless pit of secrets" (99). Such worlds, indeed, thrive on mystery – on the possibility that there is always more to discover, that any storyline is only a single trajectory among many, and that any particular stream of experience could be modified to produce a new but related experience. So where is the sacred here? It's difficult to say. It may be that with a multiplication of worlds, our own world (or own religious "world") may be assimilated into the stream, making it difficult for us to detect which world is "right" or which one is "just play" or which one might evoke the ultimate sacred or if any can do so at all.

It's safe to say that we are fascinated with worlds and multiply them with verve. Perhaps this means we constantly seek that which is transcendent to our daily lives, whether that be a few hours playing *World of Warcraft* or engrossing ourselves in a good film. It would even be possible to view game-related items like action figures, guidebooks, or even game-controllers as relics or fetishes that function like portals into these "sacred" transmediated worlds. But these observations all seem unsatisfactory, perhaps because there are so *many* worlds that it seems impossible that they *all* be "sacreds." A similar problem confounds theorists of interreligious dialogue, who struggle with the language and the perspective to explain how discrete but ultimate religious "systems" or "worlds" could all be right. There's an indeterminacy here that is perplexing and yet unavoidable. One way of beginning to address the problem is to look at how contemporary theorists concerned with games and online worlds deal with the problem. One of the major ideas game theorists use to think about the boundaries between virtual worlds and everyday life is the "magic circle."

Virtual reality and the magic circle

In the middle of the twentieth century, Huizinga offered a model for thinking about the intersection of ritual and play. As I've already suggested, Huizinga emphasized what he saw as deep boundary-constructing similarities between ritual and play, the process of marking off that he dubbed the "magic circle." Game theorists use the idea of the "magic circle" extensively today as a means of demarcating the world of play from the everyday world. Transmediated worlds like *The Matrix* may be seen as "magic circles," as bounded areas marked off from everyday life as different, and perhaps as sacred. As we have seen, for Huizinga, both play and ritual similarly involve a "stepping out of 'real' life into a temporary sphere of activity with a disposition all its own" (1955, 8). Both provide a space and time in which new rules adhere, in which one can perform "an act apart" (10). Huizinga doesn't force us to choose between spatial and linear performance as modes of identifying the boundaries of the magic circle, but he does suggest a preference for spatial markers that indicate the field in which performance takes place. Both ritual and play, he says, have the ability to transport participants "to another world," the world inscribed within the "magic circle" (18). The magic circle may be obviously religious or it might not: "the arena, the card-table, the magic circle, the temple, the stage, the screen, the tennis court, the court of justice," all are "play-grounds" or "forbidden spots, isolated, hedged round, hallowed, within which special rules obtain. All are temporary worlds within the ordinary world, dedicated to the performance of an act apart" (10). Roger Caillois, too, proposes that "all play presupposes the temporary acceptance, if not of an illusion ... then at least of a closed, conventional, and, in certain respects, imaginary universe" (2006, 135). The magic circle, it seems, can apply to any bounded system characterized by rules and some fixed mode of performance.

The magic circle can be enhanced, paradoxically, by inviting our deep immersion into the world it evokes. Immersion, says Mateas, "is the feeling of being present in another place and engaged in the action therein" (2004, 21). Immersion can be induced by "structuring participation with a mask (an avatar), structuring participation as a visit, and making the interaction conventions (the interface mechanics) seamless" (Mateas and Stern 2006, 657).

Indeed, in virtual reality "one is encouraged to believe there is no 'outside'. The desire is for complete enveloping illusion" (Penny 2004, 81). Similar kinds of concerns occupy ritual theorists, who hope that a ritual will draw participants in to such an extent that they feel enveloped by the Sacred, through immersion in ritual performance, through hybrid identity as a god or ancestor, or through repetitive actions that evoke a sense of loss of self.

Based on experiments in the 1980s, Sherry Turkle has noted that players of video games can become so immersed that they may sense a loss of time and experience deep identification with on-screen characters. Drawing on Turkle, Douglas and Hargadon explain that such players "attested to a sense of stepping outside both the real world and its time, while at the same time retaining an acute perception of the constraints of the game-world and game-time and an ability to play strategically within its constraints" (2004, 204). In fact, rules and the interactivity they inspire may increase our sense of presence in mediated environments. Rules define ritual performance as well, encouraging immersion via concentration and focus on fixed modes of action. Dan Pinchbeck claims "immersive games and ludic reality can be defined by their push towards presence, the projection of the player into the symbolic environment" (n.d.). The magic circle, then, is bounded by its evocation of something separate from daily life and by its fixed modes of performance.

However, the magic circle creates as many conceptual conundrums as it solves. In particular, by acknowledging multiple sites for the magic circle (as ritual space, as game space, etc.) Huizinga and his proponents imply acceptance of multiple magic circles. Furthermore, by arguing for an identification of ritual and play as similar modes of magic circle production, they imply that magic circles can exist without serving as hierophanies at all. Play doesn't require a sacred. Ritual, however, is often *meant* to point beyond itself to the Sacred – such that we view the magic circle *itself* as a reflection of the Sacred or a portal into it. Huizinga's identification of ritual and play, then, has some apparently unintended consequences. It may elevate play, but it also has the potential to demote ritual. If there is no substantial difference between ritual and play as bounded worlds, then *both* may be viewed as mere human endeavor with no ultimate referents. Similarly, if ritual is a means of evoking the Sacred, play may be as well.

And there's another problem. Despite the magic circle's ability to call attention to boundaries between worlds, contemporary theorists in both ritual and game studies recognize that such bounded spaces are hardly impermeable. Stephen Sniderman, for example, points out that no game can be played "in a vacuum"; rather, "all play activities exist in a 'real-world' context, so to play the game is to immerse yourself in that context, whether you want to or not" (2006, 480). Castronova prefers the metaphor of a "membrane." The magic circle, he says, is "quite porous" since "people are crossing it all the time in both directions, carrying their behavioral assumptions and attitudes with them" (2005, 147). We have, then, not a magic circle but an "almost-magic circle" (159).

Egenfeldt-Nielsen, Smith and Tosca point out five ways that games spill over into real life: first, games take place in real time in our lives; second, games can color our moods; third, games communicate values and ideals; fourth, games can affect our behavior (through training modules, for example); fifth, games can have real-life effects (for example, if virtual items are sold in the real world for real money). These characteristics, they say, "belie the myth that the magic circle truly separates games from the outside world" and accordingly "magic circle arguments" are often today "treated with suspicion or seen as primarily applicable on a strictly formalist level" for the purposes of in-game analysis (2008, 25).

Salen and Zimmerman, too, acknowledge that the view of games as impervious "magic circles" is naive, and they point to another possibility: games as culture. They observe that "the wider our cultural frame grows in defining games as culture, the more their artificiality begins to unravel." That is, anything that happens in the game clearly affects the players in some way, however seemingly inconsequential. When viewed *as* a type of culture, games are "open systems." That is to say, they are "not isolated from their environment, but are intrinsically part of it, participating in the ebb and flow of ideas and values that make up a larger cultural setting." In terms that sound a lot like Castronova, they assert that "the magic circle is not an impermeable curtain but is instead a border that can be crossed. Cultural elements from outside the circle enter in and have an impact on the game; simultaneously, cultural meanings ripple outward from the game to interact with numerous cultural contexts" (Salen and Zimmerman 2004, 572). In other words, the collapse of the magic circle's rigid boundaries reveals that any virtual worlds inhabiting a magic circle may freely flow beyond the bounds of it, revealing a fourth mode of thinking about virtual reality: as streaming, fluid, and moving through us.

Virtual reality as streaming

Pierre Lévy has remarked that the media arts of today – including film, games, virtual worlds, and others – are created with computers, and as digital products they "are all connected by the network in one critical dialogue." Art today is streaming. It is virtual, and at the same time, it is real, even if generated from within the self and perpetually incomplete:

> Just as it is for the mystic, reality is also a tremendous flow of signs for the artist. The artist must turn towards the inner screen of his consciousness in order to see forms take shape. As it happens, forms take shape in digital matrixes, in networks, in interactive devices and in the cooperative procedures of virtual worlds. A work of art can never be finished, it is rather constantly growing and open to cooperation; it envelops us just as the network – our new collective nervous system – does.
>
> (2001)

To call virtual reality "streaming," then, is to recognize its ability to move between worlds, to spill out from our digital devices into the physical world, to externalize our dreams, and to put them into fluid conversation with others' dreams.

Recognizing the streaming nature of the virtual and the real, T. L. Taylor questions whether "the idea that we can shore up the line between the virtual and the real world or between game and nongame" is even reasonable. For Taylor, the magic circle of play "can hide (and even mystify) the much messier relationship that exists between spheres – especially in the realm of MMOGs [massively multiplayer online games]." If we look at how people have invested themselves in online spaces, she says, "we find people negotiating levels of self-disclosure and performance, multiple forms of embodiment, and the importing of meaningful offline issues and values into online spaces" (152). Calling for "non-dichotomous models," Taylor claims that the line between being online and being offline is hardly firm; it is "messy, contested, and constantly under negotiation" (2006, 153). This "messiness" can be seen in all aspects of theoretical analysis of religion and online experiences.

Drawing on the notion of liminality as the situation of being both here and there in ritual experience, I elsewhere call such hovering "persistent liminality," the "on-demand and consistently ambiguous experience of liminality, characterized by the ambiguities of game/real life, sacred/profane, ritual/play, and self/other" (Wagner 2011). A rite of passage, in a ritual context, is typically the place or time within which a participant crosses from one mode of being into another, typically via a symbolic *limen* or "threshold." However, when one crosses over into a virtual world, as in digital entry to worlds like *Second Life,* one doesn't cross over from one state into the other in any kind of permanent way, as, say, one might in a *bar mitzvah* or some other coming-of-age rite of passage. Accordingly, one could argue that all of *Second Life* invokes a state of *persistent* liminality and all the complexities that notion brings along with it. Contested liminal spaces also exist in new technological developments that deliberately play with the boundary between the real and the virtual. One of the hottest new modes of virtual reality developed is in the area of "augmented reality," a term which itself evokes the ability to transform the real material world into something more than what it is – to allow it to "augment" and perhaps even "transcend" itself, to become sign and signified.

Augmented reality

Put simply, augmented reality "blend[s] the synthetic with the natural" so that "one takes the real world as it is, but adds something virtual to it." Castronova cites the example of using computer-generated graphics with a head-mounted visor-screen to play *Pac-Man* in real physical space (2005, 90). As Bob Tedeschi (2010) remarks, such technology works "like space-age glasses," imbuing the real world with an added dimension – quite literally making the invisible

visible. Already users are able to view advertising or tourist information through their iPhones or computer cameras and see three dimensional, interactive images laid on top of the real world. As Mike Liebhold notes, today our internet browsers already allow us to see hyperlinked media on a web page. But these technologies are branching out into the physical world, such that smartphone cameras can become web browsers that reveal visual digital-linked media attached to the real world, seen through the smartphone's lens. A related form of augmented reality technology allows for the user's own image to be projected into the computer via a webcam, revealing a "world" in which one can see oneself interacting directly with virtual objects. Before long, we'll be able to simply put on a visor such that it seems as if the computer's virtual world has physically surrounded us. As Liebhold remarks, today we can interact with augmented reality on a smartphone using apps like *Layar*, *Wikitude* and *Junaio*. But "eventually we'll be able to do so with augmented reality glasses. In time, we'll do this through our vehicle's windows, too, then with digitally augmented contact lenses, and on go the possibilities" (Liebhold 2010).

One powerful example of religious use of augmented reality is the digital screen available near the transept at the Abbey in Cluny, France. Visitors can hold up the screen and will see in the virtual space therein a projected image of parts of the abbey that had been damaged and lost in the Wars of Religion and the French Revolution. For now, visitors are limited to the digital screen, but in the future one can imagine visitors donning visors and seeing not only the restored building, but a host of interactive characters and experiences recounting the history of the building and inviting us to see ourselves within it in some way. One can imagine that when technology enables such embodied virtual encounters with the changes such sacred buildings have undergone through time, the sacred structure itself will expose its streaming physicality, reminding us that nothing in the material world is immune to transformation.

With this technology, we don't have to just use existing buildings as a model upon which to "augment" reality. We can project completely virtual images into the real world too. This means that items or buildings or people that appear in *Second Life*, for example, have the potential to be projected into our living rooms or even (thinking big) into geographical locations. We could, conceivably, take a Temple that has been built in *Second Life* and place it in a designated spot in the real, physical world such that it is invisible to those not wearing visors but fully inhabitable by those wearing them. We are already struggling with questions about whether or not virtually constructed spaces in *Second Life* can or should be viewed as Sacred. If our argument is simply that they are nested behind a computer screen, we may find ourselves even more confused in the next ten years when virtual spaces step right out and join us in our everyday lives.

Augmented reality technology also has the startling potential to enable, for example, images of Christ to be projected into a room in which we are standing, either by holographic projection or via visors. This image could be interacted with via artificial intelligence programs, allowing the holographic Christ figure to utter passages from the Bible or to engage in any activity that we programmed it to perform. The opportunities for religious education as well as incredibly creative blasphemy are obvious. Would such a virtual projection be a hierophany? Are there conditions under which it might be viewed as one? With augmented reality, the virtual world steps out of the computer "box" and into our lives with incredibly powerful implications for religious experience.

Alternate reality games

The name itself implies a synthesis: these are "games" that take place in "reality" (offline) and yet offer an "alternate reality" (online and via the worlds they create). Alternate reality games (ARGs) are like online games in that they are in some ways a form of MMOG, with individual games able to draw in hundreds of thousands of players to online environments, but they are unlike online games in that they also take place off-screen and offline. They have elements in common with art, literature, theater as well, but cannot be reduced to any one of these (Szulborski 2005, 71–83). As Dave Szulborski explains, an ARG takes place on the internet, but "one of the main goals of an ARG is to deny and disguise the fact that it is even a game at all." Player interest in a given ARG can be so intense at times that outsiders might view it as "something religious or spiritual, or perhaps even cultish" (2005, 1). The streaming interaction between our physical lives and the world of the game marks ARGs as another potent site for the collapse of boundaries between the virtual and the real.

Alternate reality games can "potentially utilize any website and any application online." There is typically no avatar for you to inhabit; you play as yourself with "the insertion of additional slices of reality into our own" (Martin *et al.*, 6). An important part of a functional ARG "hinges on the same kind of suspension of disbelief required for cinema or video games" (3). That is, ARGs are driven by the philosophy of TINAG, for "(T)his (I)s (N)ot (A) (G)ame." Alternate reality games are a type of "pervasive game," meaning they are "on" all the time, whether we personally are engaged with them or not. In a way, though, the dictum "this is not a game" might better be read as "everything you see is potentially a part of the game." There are no frames, no clear boundaries, with an ARG. Instead, there are what Nieuwdorp calls "transformation rules," which identify the relationship between real-world and game-world objects and events. But when everything is *potentially* intended to be part of the game, everything can *become* part of it in practice. Alternate reality games employ real-world devices like billboards, buildings, even actors – so they are not even engaged via computer screens, at least much of the time. Accordingly, Nieuwdorp concludes that the primary "facilitating factor" for entering the pervasive game world of an ARG "lies not solely within the hard- and software, but also in the player him/herself" (2005, 4). The player, says

Nieuwdorp, enters the game world via a symbolic "switch" in the head: a *deliberate* change in attitude. This switch is an "active mental shift" which places the player in the game world, in its rules, and accepting its confines and expectations. "Usually a game space, or magic circle, is delineated from real life with 'boundary-maintaining mechanisms'" that Nieuwdorp calls transformation rules:

> [W]hen we think back to the example from The Go Game that we looked at before, we can see that the transformation rules in that particular instance are very loosely defined, making it difficult for the player to discern what is still part of the game world and what is not. This means that the realized resources in the game world are potentially and seemingly infinite to all players, because they cannot be sure what objects are intended to play a role in the game world and which do not.
>
> (7)

Some people think ARGs "transcend reality and some think they're virtual worlds; some think they're stories, games or performances and others are trying to understand how they're all of them. Either way, ARGs challenge boundaries" (Martin *et al.* 2006). Is it possible that boundary-games like this bring a thrill precisely *because* we can't be sure what is "real" and what is "virtual"? As the virtual streams into the real via ARGs and augmented reality, boundaries are more than just membranes – the dike has broken and the virtual cascades in and through us in ways that make the boundary-marking of the magic circle look naive, no matter how infinitely worlds may multiply.

As games that impinge upon real life, ARGs also implicitly expose religion as a sort of game, an ARG in which anything in the world might also be viewed as a hierophany, as a miracle, as an omen, as a relic. For those invested in the "rules" of religion – which would also ascribe to the conviction that "this is not a game," anything we see, experience, read, or discover can be seen as a "sign" planted for us by the game's designer, filled with meaning and intended to help us along on our life journey toward the goal of winning at life. Indeed, one could argue that such fluidity of experience – the assumption that the sacred is invested in all of daily life if only we have the eyes to see it – would render religion the ultimate ARG, and certainly the longest running one.

The other right here

I have already considered how virtual reality can manifest within transmedia, such that virtual worlds of games or films can point toward greater "worlds" that lie beyond each individual media item. These transmedia components can be seen as instances of the virtual manifesting in the real, and thus also represent a form of the streaming virtual: that is to say, the virtual streaming into and blending with the real. If the virtual and the physical, material world are identified with one another, then any notion of the sacred that holds for the material world must also hold for the virtual world streaming into it. Of course, this also means that if the virtual is perceived as sacred *because* Other, once the virtual is streaming into the material world, it is both Other and present right here. Dualisms collapse, and nest, and refuse reification.

Plate recognizes one type of this interruption of the streaming virtual when he looks at media rituals, those real-life events that are crafted in response to people's appreciation for a filmic world. In such cases, he remarks, "filmic images have leapt off the screen and entered physical, three-dimensional spaces, leaving their marks in American cement, religious consciousness, and ritual practices" (2007, 427). Plate discusses bar mitzvah themes based on films, a *Matrix*-themed wedding, and other real-life ceremonies crafted with virtual worlds as the stimulus.

Why do people turn to virtual worlds for inspiration for new rituals? Plate offers some possibilities: "Perhaps it is the assumed solemnity of the occasions that produce alienation and disconnection and new media create a sense of lightness and approachability." The implication here is that received traditional rituals don't meet our needs since they don't allow us to shape them as we wish, to own them as our own "mod" or transmediated event. For people today, says Plate, the "need for personal connection in ritual is very real" (431). It must also be new: "Ritualizing and world building are necessary to religion, but the same old ritual in the same old way, the same old message in the same old medium, leaves people feeling disconnected" (432). Connection, then, comes via personal transformation – through streaming a media world through ourselves and watching it manifest in the physical world as we don costumes, create events, and transform stories through ritual enactment.

In a way, such observations make obvious sense: religion itself can be said to be a form of mediation of the Other – a set of focusing techniques that stream reality to us, for us, and by us. But as Pierre Lévy notes of today's interaction with virtual reality, the "distinction between authors and readers, producers and spectators, creators and interpreters" blends in new media, creating a "circuit" of expression, with participants reinforcing and building upon one another (1997, 95). Closure in such production, says Lévy, should be avoided. Instead, our interaction with new media creates a feedback loop. We both process *and* create that which is "other" than the real, as well as that which is "other" than the physical. We are consumers and manufacturers of the sacred. It streams through us, becoming virtual, and becoming real. It becomes impossible to tell the difference between real and virtual, sacred and profane, and the various combinations of these.

Accordingly, we find ourselves coining new terms, trying to pin down the nature of this new thing, the gesture toward a sacred that can no longer be found, which eludes us as our own reflection eludes us in a series of funhouse mirrors.

For example, Krystina Derrickson (2008), when considering the online hajj in *Second Life*, points out the "ambiguous" nature of sacred virtual space:

> Though articulated as an educational environment, the Mecca sim [simulation] and other Islamic spaces are treated as ambiguously sacred. Ken Hillis' research on the creation and perception of space in virtual environments suggests that the *Second Life* Mecca sim may be considered a form of sacred virtual space, a result of the detailed reconstructions of spiritually-charged physical loci, and by behavioral regulations encouraged by sim owners in the treatment of those virtual spaces.

For Derrickson, when sacred space is constructed in a virtual context, its sacredness is endowed via its symbolic power and via the rules imposed by builders to apply within that sacred space – that is, purely by *intent*. The "sacredness" that any virtual building exhibits is contested, reflexively constructed, and therefore subject to simultaneous multiple interpretations. Indeed, one wonders what is useful about such terms as the "virtual sacred" at all, beyond their ability to point out the Baudrillardian loop of perception that now profoundly disturbs our sense of the sacred as Other.

The current fad of mash-ups and mods of received media items can also be seen as a form of the streaming virtual. Alex Leavitt explains that director's cuts have been around for decades, and are recognized additions to many film releases. But, he notes, "as digital production technology became more widespread, cheaper, and easier to use, ordinary consumers began to take commercially-distributed films (which also became cheaper and of higher quality for consumer purchase) and edit them in their own homes: essentially creating 'director's critic's edits'" (2010). If a film has been previously endowed with any sacred status, such as *The Passion of the Christ*, this facility brings with it mixed results. Mash-ups of the sacred are more (and less) than new rituals honoring a new Sacred. They are also a means of performing the collapse of the Sacred, of exposing that which we already suspected: we just can't find an absolute Sacred anymore, and so we're making it up as we go along.

According to Jenkins, the "story of American arts in the twenty-first century might be told in terms of the public reemergence of grassroots creativity as everyday people take advantage of new technologies that enable them to archive, annotate, appropriate, and recirculate media content" (2006a, 136). But there's a sort of elegiac tone to our cultural destruction of the Other in its streaming into us and its reproduction in infinite Others. As Jenkins says, "much of what the public creates models itself after, exists in dialogue with, reacts to or against, and/or otherwise repurposes materials drawn from commercial culture" (2006a, 137). We are repurposing the Other, putting it in a virtual scrapbook and nostalgically remembering its passing, over and over and over again.

Jenkins calls *Star Wars* "the prime example of media convergence at work" (2006a, 145). The "rich narrative universe of the *Star Wars* saga provided countless images, icons and artifacts that could be reproduced in a wide variety of forms." Action figures and other toys may seem to be seen as just another marketing ploy until one realizes that they "take on deeper meanings as they become resources for children's play and for digital filmmaking" (2006a, 146). Using commercially produced costumes, props, soundtrack music, and action figures, amateurs can produce ad hoc remixes of the mythos and in so doing alter its meaning. As Jenkins aptly observes, action figures "provided this generation with some of their earliest avatars, encouraging them to assume the role of a Jedi Knight or an intergalactic bounty hunter, enabling them to physically manipulate the characters to construct their own stories" (2006a, 147).

The same kind of modification and streaming celebration is happening all around us to traditional hierophanies, as we multiply access to Jesus puppets, Bible video games, online Bible worlds like Big Bible Town (www.bigbibletown. com), and a host of new "translations" of the Bible, most notably the Bible in tweets. There's even a Catholic-produced puffy pillow set "My Mass Kit" (weebelievers.com) for children to "play" with as they pretend to perform the Mass. We stream hierophanies through us, as play, and in so doing mark them as having no necessary Other, as being products of our own streaming experience. God's manifestation in the world in the form of the Host is mimicked by a puffy pillow with a nylon host, which children can pretend is the body of the material image of God on earth.

Of course, the "innovative and experimental qualities" of transmedia interaction are not "entirely new." Jenkins points toward medieval retellings of the story of Jesus and points out that "unless you were literate, Jesus was not rooted in a book but was something you encountered at multiple levels in your culture" through stained glass windows as illustrations of story, through tapestries, psalms, sermons, or dramatic performances (2006a, 119). While Jenkins is right that folk retellings of stories certainly were part of medieval culture and religious society at large for millennia, the difference between then and now is that in medieval times, the transmedia of stained glass windows, relics, and sermons all pointed back to the fixed book, even if some couldn't read it. Furthermore, there were hierarchical powers at play that could determine which retellings were orthodox and which were heretical – with sometimes devastating consequences for creators of the latter. Finally, in medieval and Renaissance times, the "world" of the Bible was unrivaled as a source of inspiration, and served as the imaginative grist for some of the best literature and other artworks of the period, including Milton's *Paradise Lost*, for example, or Michelangelo's frescoes. There was no *Twilight* or *Matrix* or *Avatar* to compete for our attention or to provide an alternative world into which to tap. Accordingly, the church presumably felt less of a need to compete with other worlds by producing toys and media.

This phenomenon may help to explain the fear and revulsion some conservative fundamentalist Christians feel in response to media like *Harry Potter* and *Avatar*. For example, megachurch Seattle preacher Mark Driscoll (2010) says of *Avatar* in a sermon that it is "the most demonic, satanic film I've ever seen," filled with an "overt demonism" and a "false ideology" that works like a false "sermon preached" in its claims that the "creation mandate" is dangerous. The film, says Driscoll, asserts that we should halt the development of resources because we are "disconnected from the divine life force," a claim that Driscoll sees as heretical because it presents us with "a false mediator" who is also a "witch" and with a "false Jesus" and a "false resurrection" in the person of Jake Sully. Of the special effects, he says: "the visuals are amazing because Satan wants you to emotionally connect with a lie." Driscoll, himself a programmer of a particular stream of religious experience, can easily recognize the competition such virtual other worlds imply. The streaming, engaging qualities of *Avatar* – including its spectacular 3D technology – make it a fierce competitor for more removed, distant notions of the transcendent dependent upon a sacred book believed to be unmoddable and an avatar that no longer appears in physical form in our world.

Conclusion

Ronald Grimes argues that in the twenty-first century, "the ritual question is being conceived as a boundary issue." Namely, the "boundary issue" is that we are increasingly aware of our own role in *creating* the divisions between what we consider sacred and what we consider profane – and it might not agree with how the person next to us sees things. Today, Grimes says, "both ritual and the *definition of ritual* are understood to be acts of marking-off" (2006, 12). Lorne Dawson suggests that such intentional boundary-marking is a signature feature of contemporary religious practice and in essence hallows it. He asks, is "the exercise of reflexivity, long a hallmark of detached rational thought, [...] becoming, by radical extension, a new means of legitimating religious practice or even inducing 'authentic' religious experience? In the process is the experience of reflexivity itself being sacralized?" (2005, 26). As we are forced to address the problem of virtual reality, we are increasingly forced to recognize our *own* roles in demarcating space, in labeling it as sacred, profane, or perhaps a combination of them. The Other has become the Other right here, and the best we can hope for is to look at what we're making, what we're marking off, and ask ourselves why we're doing it.

As Dawson observes, the introduction of virtual reality as new way of "mediating religion" is creating problems for "many of the conventional ways of thinking about religion" because we now "have no means of differentiating authentic from inauthentic experiences, religious or otherwise." Such changes have affected our ability to even recognize the sacred when we see it, since "the criteria for authenticity have shifted ... from a focus on the sacred as a specifiable, if mysterious, presence in this world – a *thing* of some sort – to an experience or state of mind that is intrinsically valued, that is sacralized, somewhat independently from how it is symbolized" (2005, 28–29). Based on his research in virtual sacred space, Stephen Jacobs (2007) similarly remarks that today "we have to understand sacred space as *process* and *encounter*, rather than simply as place or structure."

The sacred and profane are at root simply a means of considering reflections, of making sense of signs and signifieds, of understanding echoes. The "virtual" is, like the profane, a space into which something might erupt, a ground into which something different can be put, and through that tension, invite reflection on the Other. The virtual, that is, is not in itself transcendent. It is a space in which the transcendent might appear. Its partner is neither the sacred nor the profane – it is the sacred virtual. What emerges is a quadrant, as evocative as it is head-spinningly complicated in its exposure of the reiteratively reflective production of opposites in contemporary transmedia.

The "virtual sacred" does serve one very important function. It exposes the potential difference between the virtual sacred and the sacred. If there is indeed a Sacred that is ultimately Other – be it God, Heaven, or the Platonic realm, it remains true that we can't enter it, we can't know it, and it is as Ineffable as it ever was. It is still accessible only via imagination, religious experience, performance of ritual, and sheer hope. But the "virtual sacred," by contrast, is a veritable feast of manifestedness. It is here, now, rich, obvious, visual, and constantly in flux. It is our television, our film, our hand-held devices, our "interwebs," our games, our fantasy worlds. We think about it all the time. We remake it in our own image. We kill things in it, make temples in it, recreate ourselves in it. Speaking of new media rituals, Plate captures this sentiment perfectly: "the image is confused for the real, and we realize herein that the real is always already imagined, and oftentimes primarily imagined" (2007, 436).

Recognizing the limitations of Eliade's easy distinctions between sacred and profane, Smith recognizes that "[r]itual precises [such] ambiguities; it neither overcomes nor relaxes them" (1987, 110). For Smith, sacred spaces are best viewed as "focusing lenses." In such places, the "ordinary" becomes "sacred" by "having our attention directed to it in a special way" (1996, 475). This is true also of virtual sacred spaces when looked at as deliberate manifestations of the human self projected outward, blended with the dreams of others, mashed up, modded, prodded, and cycled back to us for further transformation. It makes sense, then, that game designers tend to see many games as a "sandbox," "a kind of authoring environment within which players can define their own goals and write their own stories" (Jenkins 2004b, 128).

The streaming appearance of the virtual sacred today makes it more difficult to locate the Sacred, or at least exposes its visual absence. The rituals that we now engage in – media rituals that play with the very idea of the Other in creative and confounding ways – are themselves meditations on reflexivity and constructedness of the Sacred. Perhaps, then, religion really is just a mode of being, a perspective or attitude that allows us to flex our imaginative muscles and celebrate our *own* creativity while pretending to tap into something Original. But just because something is reflexive, reflected, and/or a reflection, doesn't mean we can't reflect upon it and learn more about ourselves and the image, about ourselves *as* the image. This, of course, means that seeing is being *and* believing.

Chapter 5

Me, myself and iPod

Hybrid, wired and plural selves

We are immersed today in what Wade Clark Roof calls "a time of paradigm shifts," in which there is a disruption between experiential and "institutionalized" forms of religion (1999, 171, 173). Contemporary "spiritual searching," says Roof, "is largely a private matter involving loosely based social networks and small groups" (177). Today's religiously minded person is a "bricoleur" who "cobble[s] together a religious world from available images, symbols, moral codes, and doctrines," all the while "exercising considerable agency in defining and shaping what is considered to be religiously meaningful" (75). In this chapter, I look at the ways that our sense of identity is shaped and transformed through virtual engagement.[1] It turns out that the ways that we engage with our own identities in virtual contexts have a lot to say about how we would like to see ourselves, about what our dreams are, and about how these dreams become multiplied and fragmented in today's complex media environments. A surprising partner in this discussion is the contemporary academic study of interreligious dialogue, since in our online encounters and in our real-life interreligious encounters we find ourselves increasingly involved in competing, multiple worldviews with conversation partners who themselves are navigating multiple faces and selves.

Religious dialogue and media

Religious dialogue has in some ways been transformed in recent years as immigration, globalization, and networking technologies make it possible, in ways unimaginable a hundred years ago, for people to interact with others around the world and learn about their traditions, values and beliefs. Scholars like Diana Eck, Wade Clark Roof and Stewart Hoover all point to the increasing fluidity and negotiated quality of religious identity today as a crucial piece for understanding religious engagement and the development of meaning. As it turns out, such concerns also deeply occupy theorists of digital culture, who recognize perhaps even *more* poignantly how fluidity of self is encouraged and sustained by the digital technologies that flourish today. Filiciak remarks that "we are living in a culture of simulation" in which new technologies are continuously appearing. Today, "digital media, video games included, enable us – for the first time in history on such a scale – to manipulate our 'selves' and to multiply them indefinitely" (2003, 88). The technology we use supports the very trends noted by scholars looking at the contemporary global religious culture, and may even be shaping the way we see ourselves religiously.

Diana Eck of Harvard University's Pluralism Project argues that in today's "urban and global contexts," we encounter the "new textures of religious diversity with increasing frequency" (2003, 168). Today, "our sharply heightened awareness of religious diversity" requires that everyone, not just the most educated or privileged in society, develop the ability to understand what these encounters mean (42). Increasingly, she says, we realize our interconnectedness such that religious traditions are "intertwined" despite our tendency to treat them as separate entities (211). Such interactions between faiths make it all the more important, says Eck, that we know exactly what we believe. Eck outlines three major ways of engaging with religions different from one's own. First, there is the *exclusivist response*: "Our own community, our tradition, our understanding of reality, our encounter with God, is the one and only truth, excluding all others." Second, there is the *inclusivist response*: "There are many communities, traditions, and truths, but our own way of seeing things is the culmination of the others, superior to the others, or at least wide enough to include the others under our universal canopy and in our own terms." Finally, there is the *pluralist response*: "Truth is not the exclusive or inclusive possession of any one tradition or community. Therefore the diversity of communities, traditions, understandings of truth, and visions of God is not an obstacle for us to overcome, but an opportunity for our energetic engagement and dialogue with one another … it means opening up [to] … transformation" (2003, 168). Uncomfortable with the notion of identity drift, Eck argues for a distinction between "relativism" and "pluralism," in preference of the latter.

It is this final category, the "pluralist," that most accords with our digital engagement, and one of the easiest places to see this negotiation of self is with the host of religious apps available to us on our mobile devices. The very choice of selecting and interacting with such apps can reflect a pluralist engagement with the possibility of different modes of religious encounter. Pluralists, says Eck, are constantly, deliberately, and deeply engaged with the beliefs of others and allow these beliefs to shape and transform their home traditions. Concerned about what she sees as the dangers of "relativism" inherent in the exploratory, pluralist mode, Eck argues for commitment to a single religious home community from which to engage in religious dialogue with others. In this way, she argues, dialogue will enhance a pre-existing religious foundation, rather than allow the whole to dissolve into a fluid stream of possibilities and a hodgepodge of competing, perhaps inconsistent, religious commitments.

The organization of online encounter with religious traditions supports such spiritual shopping, however. As Mia Lövheim and Alf G. Linderman point out, the Internet "greatly increases the possibility for an individual seeker to find information about established as well as alternative religious organizations" (2005, 126). As traditions find themselves transformed in online spaces, as communities come and go in virtual forms, as people multiply their representations of their selves in a hundred different and not necessarily consistent religious ways, religion is changing in ways that challenge the notion that any single fixed tradition can even be identified. Such a claim makes suspect Eck's suggestion that we can and should identify a single home faith community, especially if we practice religiously online in any way. Instead of asking, "Who am I in relationship to that person?" a question which still has powerful salience, we are more often asking rather "Who am I?" and "What is a person anyway?" Our sense of identity itself is in flux, as fluid and difficult to pin down as questions about what sacred space is in virtual contexts, how ritual works when virtually mediated, and what constitutes community in online environments.

Roof is more comfortable than Eck with the notion of blended and multiple religious perspectives, as well as with the idea that media may be part of the formula of religious identity formation today. This view seems to have some characteristics in common with pluralism, but also sounds a bit like the "relativism" that Eck worries about. The "symbolic toolbox" available to today's religiously minded people, he says, allows for forms of "religious reframing" that may enable "breaking through encrusted tradition and opening up new possibilities for an encounter with religious and metaphysical truths." As Roof notes, this kind of religious experimentation is increasingly common in the "media age, where words and symbols are manipulated in ways that often disassociate them from a historic and grounded tradition." Accordingly, "highly reflexive persons" will readily "recognize the socially constructed character of meaning" and may, despite Eck's reservations, be "quite comfortable with negotiated interpretations that are understood to vary from one context to another" (Roof 1999, 170).

We are immersed today in what Roof calls "a time of paradigm shifts," in which there is a "disruption" between "experiential" forms of religion and "institutionalized" forms (1999, 173). Today's spiritual *bricoleur* must take into account even more options than Roof envisioned only ten years ago, as he or she navigates through a perplexing kaleidoscope of virtual modes of imaginative, religious, and fantasy-based experiences with few tools to discern the difference and even less motivation to do so. As Hoover observes, the fodder for identity-building and meaning-making no longer includes just traditional religious symbolism and narrative. Religion, he says, is still "an important element of the modern quest for the self" (2006, 37). But "media objects" too can function as "symbolic resources" in the formation of personal identity (40). There are, of course, a variety of ways that this process might work, including arguments about the role of the type of media itself in scripting meaning, and the notion that religion can somehow be contained within media objects to be extracted and integrated into one's life (68–70). But for Hoover, the paradigm shift today involves the notion of religion as constantly in revision, situated within the self who wants "to explore a wide range of cultural resources, hoping to find nuggets of authenticity or truth therein." Today's seekers, he says, "seem to be always on a quest for enlightenment and will simply get it where they can, in popular culture or not, according to the logic of their own quest for self" (77). And the media, he observes, are just as likely to provide today's seekers with material for engagement as traditional religious inventories may have been in the past.

Although he didn't have religious identity explicitly in mind, Filiciak keys into these problems when he points out that "the majority of institutions with which we heretofore identified ourselves have now been dramatically weakened" (2003, 96). If we can see media and digital technology generally speaking as in any way stepping into the gap, then it is worth asking to what extent fluid, hybrid religious practices today are shaping virtual experiences and the production of media, and to what extent the digital technology itself may be shaping our perceptions about religious identity. Our technology supports and shapes such individualized, personally constructed modes of self-understanding, especially in the form of our iPads, iPhones, iPods, Androids, and smart phones, which provide us with the ability to collect "apps" that support our beliefs, habits, and current preferences. Such fragmentation is also evident in the crafting of digital selves and personae in our various online worlds, games, and social media arenas. But with devices that mirror back to us selves that are fluid, multiple, and fragmented, what does this development mean for religion today?

Today, religious identity is both reflected in and shaped by the technology we use, infused within the complex identity negotiations that involve our interaction with a host of new media components including apps and the mediated worlds into which these apps invite us. Increasingly, we navigate through numerous digital spaces that evoke different aspects of who we are. By looking at how our technology reflects our engagement with the process of identity formation, we will see that religious experience today is as fluid as our sense of self, and requires of us active negotiation and conscious consideration of how we use the devices that so powerfully shape us. As a means of thinking about how we use our mobile devices as metaphorical proxies for ourselves in identity formation practices, I have identified six different types of religious apps, some with greater resonance for contemporary religious identity than others, but all of which offer significant challenges for thinking about what religious authenticity entails.

(1) Prayer apps. These apps enable users to pray through them, as prayers are typed into the mobile device and sent. Prayers may be sent literally, to a human recipient in a temple, church, or even to the Western Wall in Jerusalem. There are also apps that post prayers on digital prayer walls. Some allow voting for the "best" prayers. Others randomly generate viewings of previously submitted prayers. Whereas many prayer apps are meant to be delivered to a real person,

some are meant to go directly to God. The "Pray" app promises *only* spiritual delivery, since it does not offer a textual or biblical "response" from God. You simply type in your prayer, tap on "Send prayer," and a box pops up indicating: "Your prayer has been sent."

Such apps beg the question of why users feel compelled to issue the prayer through virtual reality, rather than simply closing their eyes. The authenticity of the prayer, in this case, seems to be dependent on passage through virtual space. Apps like these also raise the question of who or what we encounter when we use such apps, whether it is other users, God, or perhaps just the program itself. As Turkle notes, we are "drawn to do whatever it takes" to maintain a view of interactive robots and chat-bots as "sentient and caring" (2011, 85). Such impulses seem also to apply to our use of prayer apps. If we have sent our fears and desires through the digital ether, we have given them the stamp of authenticity, and we have also implicitly placed God "within" or "behind" our mobile devices.

(2) Ritual apps. These apps offer users guidance in the performance of recognized religious practices. Some, like various digital rosaries or virtual menorahs, offer visual props that replicate items one might use in real life. Others, like "iBlessing," offer guidance on how to perform recognized rituals, in this case the proper blessing of food. "AlQibla" uses GPS technology to indicate the direction for prayer for Muslims. In February 2011, Catholics debated the efficacy and authenticity of the newly released "Confession: A Roman Catholic App." The app was approved of by a Catholic bishop in the States, but was eventually cautioned against by the Vatican, based on concerns that confession must take place in the presence of recognized religious authorities. The app indeed provides officially condoned ritual procedures in textual form, but might be used erroneously by people who don't use it in the presence of a real priest. In this case, authenticity is presumed to be dependent on physical embodiment.

(3) Sacred text apps. These apps are what they seem to be: digitized versions of sacred texts. Some are pure digital transcriptions. Others exhibit varying degrees of interactivity. "Bible Shaker" allows the user to enter a category such as "anger" or "finances," then shake the iPhone much like a Magic 8 Ball. The programmers have pre-selected verses to be associated with specific categories of inquiry, thereby shaping the theological possibilities of the replies. Sacred text apps can be controversial even if they are digital reproductions simply for their easy availability now online. "Al Bukhari" puts the words of one of the greatest collectors of Muhammad's sayings and deeds into the hands of any smart-phone user who buys the app. Christians interested in the controversial early forms of Christian Gnosticism can download texts like the "Pistis Sophia" and situate them on their mobile devices right next to their Bible, raising questions of how we define the frame or "covers" of sacred texts in virtual space. Should we treat our iPods with care once we have a Bible or Quran on them? Can we put a Bible app next to the "Angry Birds" app? It seems odd to consider questions of authenticity related to mere digital placement of icons, but such

hard questions emerge when sacred texts are transformed from pages and ink to digital bytes.

(4) Social media apps. Because of the way that apps create organizing principles for interaction between church leaders and members, social media apps deserve special consideration. Churches interested in developing their own apps for use by members have a number of fixed options. First, they can use open source software. *ChurchKreatives*, for example, has created open source code for use by churches without the funds or ability to design their own individualized app. The resources programmed into the code include messaging, sermon streaming (video or audio), a news tab, a generic media tab, and links to pre-existing social media like *Facebook* and *Twitter*, as well as basic contact information for the brick-and-mortar church. However, churches using open-source code must already have people on hand who know how to implement it and can address any problems that arise over time. If they prefer, churches can create their own apps in-house. But as Tim Turner of *The Church App Blog* explains, churches will meet predictable and formidable difficulties, including the need to hire a full-time programmer for making the app work with difficult Apple provisioning, for standardizing the app across multiple platforms like Androids and Windows phones, and for keeping up with evolving standards for implementation in an ever-changing digital environment.

Accordingly, many churches simply decide to import content into pre-coded app vehicles that are supported by third-party businesses. These apps typically offer limited options like streaming videos, messaging, and information about worship times. More creative uses, such as dynamic prayer trees or GPS-enabled software for location of church members in one's vicinity, remain largely beyond the reach of almost all churches. Paying attention to what is possible via such pre-packaged apps is important, since as Campbell observes, "there is evidence internet use may transform the ways people conceive of religious community and local church," particularly in "a new conception of religious community as social network" (2005 192). If churches rely on predesigned apps with limited modes of community-building, will the church shape itself to match what the technology allows? If authenticity lies in self-determination of what constitutes meaningful worship and healthy community, then such considerations are quite important, since secular businesses may in some respects at least, be shaping what is possible for church development.

(5) Self-expression apps. These apps are a means of personal digital self-expression on one's mobile device. Some apps, like digital wallpapers and backgrounds, can include favorite Bible verses or religious images, and are enjoyed primarily by the owner of the device. Other apps, like collections of ring tones, can be used as audible expressions of faith such that listeners will hear recitations of sacred text or songs. Mobile device owners may also choose to buy decorated cases for their devices that can function as a visual statement of faith.

(6) Focusing/meditation apps. These are related to ritual apps in that they can serve as a support for disciplined religious activities. Focusing apps are

typically less controversial than ritual, however, since the focusing they invite is not dependent on religious authority in real life. Examples include various digital Zen Garden apps, apps for gongs that ring at pre-specified intervals for help with meditation, and the intriguing "Guru Meditation" app (www.bogost.com, 2009) that requires its users to hold the mobile device in hand, with thumbs planted and unmoving on the device's screen and thus enacting the focus that resists using the phone for other purposes. All of these apps say something about the user who chooses them in demonstration of his or her fluid, streaming religious self.

Issues of authenticity plague any consideration of religious apps, not least because of the demonstration of ephemerality that our use of these apps reveals. Filiciak observes the effects of this change, arguing that "the majority of institutions with which we heretofore identified ourselves have now been dramatically weakened, [so now] we define ourselves through varying values as well; it is more and more difficult to find something we can identify ourselves with permanently" (2003, 96). As Victoria Vesna points out, we are also experiencing a "transition from projecting ourselves as bodies to collapsing into a space of information and geometrical patterns" (2004, 258). Instead of encountering each other as embodied human beings, we more often encounter others as projectable pixels, and craft images of ourselves with related and often transient blurbs of information. Every identity we craft online is "a temporary formation" subject to change based on any current whim (Hillis 2009, 95). But as Bob Rehak argues, interfaces are "ideological" and "discursive" (2003, 122). We can learn something about our streaming selves by looking at how we use, display, and interact with religion via our mobile devices. We are pluralists in action, forced by our very interface with our mobile devices to decide who we are today, what we believe, and how we will express it. Authenticity of religious experience, no longer just in the hands of recognized religious authorities or received fixed rituals, is in *our* hands – and metaphorically also in the mobile devices we hold *in* our hands.

The iPod self

In some ways, perhaps the hardware and the software we create and use the most may be viewed as an externalization of our dreams, desires and perceptions. As Bob Rehak argues, interfaces are "ideological" and "discursive" (2003, 122). If there is any truth to this notion, then the iPod is one of the most poignant of these indices of meaning available today, and I propose, in some ways an apt (app) model for the hybrid, wired, and plural self engaged in what Rehak calls "play with being" (123). Apple's iPod (as well as almost any smartphone) contains within it a number of different applications or apps, chosen by the owner, who cobbles them together much like a bricoleur. It is also fair to say, at least in some respects, that the choices of apps say something about the identity of the iPod owner, reflecting in a palpable way the identity formation work described by Eck, Clark and Roof.

There are apps that offer digital props for religious rituals, for example, apps with digital prayer beads. There are apps that replicate actual religious rituals, such as the stations of the cross. There are apps for engagement with sacred texts, offering random passages related to inputted themes. There are communication apps, such as the app for delivering prayers to the Western Wall in Jerusalem, as well as an app to "text" God. For iPhone users, there are apps that employ GPS technology to locate the most precise direction of the qiblah. Other apps provide additional support by noting appropriate times for prayer recitation or ritual other activities. The selection of these apps can itself be seen as a form of religious, if not also ritual, activity − as a sort of lived metaphor of self-programming. Even the hardware of the iPod evokes the individualistic notion of today's spiritual seeker. It was difficult and expensive to locate the appropriate technology to display my iPod's content on a projector for others to witness my interaction with it publicly. iPods, it seems, are meant to be operated individually, despite whatever social portals they may open up.

Our iPod selves run the apps of different religious traditions, but they also run the apps of television shows, film, video games, whatever media fill our lives with meaning (and religion can of course be viewed as a sort of mediation). The apps we choose for our iPods or for our iPod selves are fluid, changeable, and fleeting. If we decide we don't like one anymore, we simply delete it. We may spend hours scrolling through lists of emerging new apps, hoping to discover one that might work for us. Eck might prefer us to run one application as our primary operating system (Christianity or Buddhism, for example) and access the others from within this framework. However, the technology itself invites no favorites. Today's media market is permeated by more and more and more options with fewer and fewer normative values placed upon them. Our mobile devices show what we care about, and they offer us a primary portal into as many different digital realms as we wish to load onto them. These internal portals, or apps invite us to social networks, to internet websites, to gameplay, and even to explicitly religious endeavors like church media apps, ritual helps, sacred texts, and a host of guidelines for how to practice our tradition of choice. Thus, the flow of religious apps mimics the flow of religious options generated around us every day as we decide what to pay attention to, and how to practice what we believe. We may even use apps from multiple religious traditions, seating them side by side on our mobile devices.

Perhaps this overwhelming fluidity is what inspires some people to use explicitly religious apps as a sort of identity grounding, as a gesture against utter ephemerality of self. Drawing on Turkle's work on identity, Campbell notes that "[a]ttaching oneself to an online community provides definition and boundaries for the self within the vast online world" (2005, 189). By utilizing social media apps connected to a specific community, we can argue against our own postmodern dissolution, suggesting that we may be entities-in-motion, but we can ground ourselves (as Eck would prefer) in singularly defined religious communities. This is a move toward authenticity, an act of deliberate performance.

Accordingly, the fluidity of self evident in our many modes of online engagement need not be sheer fragmentation. Hillis has noted what he calls a "cosmopolitan Web dynamic" which is simultaneously "a culture of networks" and "a culture of individualism." The ennui implied by such identity "surfing" is what Hillis dubs "everyday manifestations of a desire for a worldwide *oikos* or *ecumene*," a term borrowed from the original form of Christian evangelism and the desire for a world united under Christ (2009, 2). Online church communities certainly have the power to provide a "sense of belonging," and a feeling of "being valued" even if we never meet the other members in person. In some cases, online religious communities can generate depth of dialogue that is "at a more profound level than offline parishes" (179, 183). Social media apps work as portals into such communities, but they also signify our *desire* for such grounding.

Such activities point toward the ability of the internet to nurture real relationships, if in novel forms. These relationships can be rich and powerful, even if they depend upon Hillis' perception of personalized pixels as "a trace of the referent," a sign indicating the presence of a real person beyond the screen (2009, 13). Indeed, the conviction that a real person resides behind a digitized avatar or photo is enough to encourage real investment in online communities. Even the selection of apps can be read as a ritual in self-discovery, if we view the mobile device as a proxy for our physical bodies. Ritual theorist Theodore Jennings' argues that the body is the site of noetic experimentation, what we might call a knowing-in-motion. Ritual is "the means by which its participants discover who they are in the world and 'how it is' with the world" (1996, 326). My iPod is my own alone, and it privately reflects my own concerns, preferences and activities. I express my self by, through, and with it, and much that I value in the world is streamed through it in digitized form. The iPod, as our cyborgian appendage, can be viewed as reflective of our ritual engagement with the worldviews inherent in different apps, a sort of digital body echoing our own physical self.

Jennings sees ritual as a mode of knowledge-seeking, such that the discovery of "the right action or sequence of actions" is also a mode of discovering how one fits into the cosmic order reflected in the ritual itself (327). The fluid experimentation with which apps we will use and how we find ourselves within the sequences they introduce is a sort of noetic quest that engenders, if we are conscious of it, increasing self-knowledge. Rappaport agrees, pointing out that ritual can "transmit information concerning [the performers'] own current physical, psychic, or sometimes social states to themselves and to other people" (429). In short, we learn about ourselves by the rituals we perform. By extension, we learn about ourselves by looking at the apps that we choose and observing how we use them.

Just as our mobile devices can make us feel connected, so they also encourage us to experiment with different apps, and different conceptions of self. Our ongoing selection of apps privileges a "seeker" mentality, a bricoleur identity.

This performance, in turn, reinforces a pluralist mode of encounter with religion offline, signifying an order of fluidity, a structure of streaming identity. Apps, as representations of religious rituals and worldviews, are seen by imitation as optional, as things that we choose, display, make use of, and potentially discard. But fluidity alone does not deny authenticity of religious experience, especially if it is matched with conscious awareness of the choices one is making. Drawing on Robert Jay Lifton's work on the "protean self," Turkle points out that the "unitary view of self corresponded to a traditional culture with stable symbols, institutions, and relationships," a situation confounded today by the streaming options of self-identity especially in the religious sphere. However, Lifton and Turkle agree that the "protean self" is capable of "fluid transformations" while still being "grounded in coherence and a moral outlook," able to be "multiple but integrated." In short, says Turkle, "you can have a sense of self without being one self" (1997, 258).

As Turkle observes, "a more fluid sense of self allows a greater capacity for acknowledging diversity" (1997, 261). Perhaps then, simply by performing diversity through the collection of various apps that come and go based on our current identity status, we imitate and reinforce an attitude of openness to multiple religious paths. As Turkle puts it: "What most characterizes the model of a flexible self is that the lines of communication between its various aspects are open. The open communication encourages an attitude of respect for the many within us and the many within others" (1997, 261). What emerges is a kind of natural, if digitally mediated, pluralism that is reflected in the very functionality of our mobile devices, which model for us the ability to live in a state of determined flux. Authenticity, then, comes in self-awareness of the flow.

Hyperidentities

In our negotiation with multiple selves, we have what Filiciak calls "hyperidentities," which include not just the apps we run but also the selves we craft in various online environments. We shape our selves by "surrounding ourselves with the objects which, beside their utility, are used to define and emphasize our image" (2003, 95). Because such objects and their utility change, "we relinquish the attempts to maintain a single constant 'self'" (96). Hyperidentity is related to identity "as a hypertext to a text." Hyperidentity is "more a process than a finished formation, a complex structure that we update incessantly by choosing from the multitude of solutions. Any moment, we actively create ourselves" (97). It's easy to see how Filiciak's notion of hyperidentity relates to pluralistic notions of religious exploration, in which the religious self is constantly engaging, weighing, processing, accepting, or rejecting religious ideas that flow to and through it, much as programs flow through digital systems.

Virtual environments produce the possibility of "liquid identity" (Filiciak 2003, 92). The use of technologies such as MMORPGs (massively multiplayer online role-playing games), says Filiciak, actually serves to heighten the appeal of "'playing' with identity" (97). Today, role play is a feature of "real" and virtual life, as the ways that we practice identity formation online spill over into our daily lives. The self, both offline and online, is "more liquid than ever" (98). Interaction with and through one's avatar can affect one's daily life, since players "sometimes talk about their real selves as a composite of their characters and sometimes talk about their screen personae as means for working on their RL [real-life] lives" (Turkle 1997, 192). As Hillis puts it, an individual who engages in online activities via a digital self "witnesses a self-produced self-representation as transmitting back to himself or herself the potential of his or her multiplicity within a sign system – including all the things he or she is not yet, or might desire to become" (2009, 18). Players don't simply "become who they play." Rather, they "play who they are or who they want to be or who they don't want to be" (Turkle 1997, 192).

An *avatar*, rather than being perceived simply as an "escape from our 'self'" may be viewed as "a longed-for chance of expressing ourselves beyond physical limitations" and "a post-modern dream being materialized" (Filiciak 2003, 100). However, this assumption begs qualification – one cannot, in most games at least, choose to be in a wheelchair, overweight, balding, flabby or, as a female *avatar*, flat-chested. As Filiciak wryly observes, "[i]n the case of MMORPGs, there is no need for strict diets, exhausting exercise programs, or cosmetic surgeries – a dozen or so mouse clicks is enough to adapt one's 'self' to expectations" (90). A preliminary question of identity then involves to what extent players make free choices resulting in the creation of a new identity, and to what extent their choices are controlled by cultural expectations filtered through programming limitations and biases of the games' creators. Players may also make identity choices influenced by their own backgrounds, experiences and desires, even "transferring concealed emotions – often unconsciously – to the fictitious character" (91).

Today we have an opportunity to "painlessly manipulate our identity, to create situations that we could never experience in the real world because of social, sex-, or race-related restrictions" (Filiciak 2003, 90). As Elizabeth Reid points out, avatars can be viewed as "a manifestation of the self beyond the realms of the physical, existing in a space where identity is self-defined rather than pre-ordained" (1996, 328). That is, cyberspace identities are self-defined in that "virtual reality is a construct within the mind of a human being" (1995, 166). We may even see ourselves as actually present in the online world, such that one might see one's digital self "as constituting a psychic or even material extension or indexical trace of [the] individual." We may materially "remain 'here' in front of the screen's display [but] experientially [we] are also telepresent (literally 'distant presence') 'there'" (Hillis 2009, 2). Thus, we may identify in some potentially deep and meaningful ways with the avatars that represent us. However, every identity we craft online is temporary, subject to change based on any current whim. Such fluid and transient notions of self raise obvious and profound difficulties for the understanding of religious practice online, particularly in terms of the ability to recognize legitimate religious authorities "through" their avatars, but also because the "self" is in such flux, that patterned modes of religious ritual, even if practiced in some form that emulates ritual practice in the real world, can be experienced multiply depending on the nature, experiences, appearances and projections of one's avatars in online contexts.

Certainly, there are antecedents for the view that we can represent multiple selves simultaneously, especially in religious arenas. Victor Turner's analysis of the function of masks in traditional African ritual can, in some ways, be applied to the use of digital avatars for those who "inhabit" or "wear" them in environments like *Second Life*. In assessing the role of masks in a ritual for boys' circumcision, Turner found himself uncertain how participants in the ritual viewed the relationship between mask-wearer, ancestor (shade) represented, and divine spirit, Mvweng'i inhabiting the wearer: "Some informants say that the shade is identified with Mvweng'i, others that shade and masker operate in conjunction. The latter say that the shade rouses Mvweng'i and enlists his aid in afflicting the victim in the process of circumcision" (1969, 17).

A similar ambiguity about one's "true" identity when going online is obvious, but such indeterminacy is not always a bad thing. The opportunity to explore new religious "territory" is aptly seen in the case of the Muslim woman who attended synagogue in *Second Life* because she had been curious about Judaism but felt too self-conscious to attend a real-life temple service. The woman chose to wear her hijab in *Second Life* while attending the virtual synagogue, presumably so closely identifying with her avatar that she wanted it to be modest in its pixelated portrayal of herself in the online world (Au 2004). She appears to be enacting what Filiciak defines as the "opportunity to painlessly manipulate our identity, to create situations that we could never experience in the real world because of social, sex-, or race-related restrictions" (2003, 90).

The experimentation offered online is less open, however, in more rigidly shaped game–style interactions. Whereas residents of *Second Life* can now develop almost any physical appearance they please, residents in *World of Warcraft* must choose from predetermined types, in which race is seen to be a biological necessity. Christopher Douglas (2010) exposes the reappearance of racism in virtual contexts, and suggests that real-life implications are almost unavoidable. As Douglas notes, Blizzard's *World of Warcraft Game Manual* (2004) describes "the voodoo-practicing 'Barbarous and superstitious' trolls [who] come from islands 'renowned for their cruelty and dark mysticism' [and] speak in a seeming African American vernacular." Quoting the guide, Douglas reveals some startling racism: "'That explains it,' concluded this commentator: 'Trolls talk like black people because *they're superstitious jungle savages*'." Douglas also points out the manual's explanation that the "Tauren race" take their qualities from "Native Americans of the Mix-n-Match tribe. Environmentally conscious citizens of the plains, they live in both tipis and longhouses, and carve totem poles. And their signature greeting is 'How!'" (C. Douglas 2010).

Such horrifying racism would be condemned in almost every contemporary public setting; and yet it resides quite comfortably in *World of Warcraft* and in other virtual contexts, in which programming that restricts characters to specific qualities is required to make the game work – algorithms must have qualities upon which to base interactions. Is this kind of stereotyping just harmless play? Clearly, players can choose to be whomever they want and can select their own race before play. But in what ways might our presumptions about real-life race differences be shaped by such determinative, preprogrammed qualities, despite their presence in "merely" a virtual context? Does the fluidity of conscious choice diminish the damage of such racist language when players return to their daily lives? Or does it render racist stereotyping another form of play, protecting it from cultural critique and implicitly sanctioning it?

As Douglas notes, Blizzard "had taken pains to portray the races in a more complex light, with the trolls, tauren and orcs representing indigenous peoples trying to resist the encroachment of the colonizing Alliance." Citing the manual again, he points out the game's mythological history as support for this more complex view: "At one time in Azeroth's past, the Horde was a force of evil, and the Alliance was a bastion of good. However, in today's war-torn Azeroth, such black and white distinctions are gone. Both factions are simply fighting to preserve their way of life in the wake of the Chaos War" (cited in Douglas). So is *World of Warcraft* a subtle working out of different responses to racial tension, a means of contextualizing struggle within a post-colonialist context? Or does it reify assumptions about racial stereotyping that can carry over into the real world? Could it possibly perform both functions, depending upon the larger, obviously more complex social situation in which the real-life players find themselves every day?

As Lövheim and Linderman observe, despite the fact that the internet requires "body-less" interaction, "identity construction still seems to be a social process – a process taking place in relation to other individuals" (2005, 122). Indeed, they argue that online contexts may actually "enrich the process of creating and acquiring the tools, skills and knowledge needed for handling the increased insecurity and ambivalence of late modern society" (125). In other words, issues like sexism, racism, and other stereotyping can be seen as under negotiation precisely through the reflection of our activities in virtual contexts. The worlds we shape online are all made by people, after all, so it's reasonable to expect that they reflect the issues that concern us the most.

The fluidity of religious gatherings online emphasize the difficulty of assuming that online social experiences are rigidly determinative at all. In fact, the process itself is so malleable, so individually determined, that identity as shaped by the user seems to defy any imprinting of stereotypes from the external world. In other words, one could as easily argue that the fluidity of choice in selection of character online is as determinative of offline views of identity as any virtual stereotyping might be. The kinds of religious groups that form in online contexts tend to be "loosely connected networks" that "diverge from previous forms of religious communities" and often "lack a stable group of people gathering in a certain time and place that forms the basis of collective representations" (Lövheim and Linderman 2005, 132). Indeed, in online environments like *Second Life*, such new encounters are possible precisely *because* of the artifice of identity that the online world invites. Such virtual encounters have the potential to broaden our sense of self because they enable us to see *other* selves as real, *even* when these selves are presented only in a virtual form. People from vastly different belief systems can "speak" directly to one another, protected by the "masks" of their avatars.

Types of virtual religious encounter

Because so much recent work on religious dialogue focuses on the nature of the fluid, hybrid, and evolving self, it makes sense to see how theologically motivated modes of discourse about identity relate to actual engagement with virtual reality. In 2009, working with Ithaca College student Rebecca Zaremba, I developed a taxonomy of modes of encounter with virtual reality by religious groups that draws on Eck's categories of exclusivism, inclusivism and pluralism. We look at three modes of encounter that we call technophobia, technomediation and technomonism.

Technophobes

For our first group, the *technophobes*, virtual reality is a *pure illusion*; only material reality is "real," and virtual space, if we see it as having any purpose whatsoever, is simply a means of digitally *modeling* the real. One cannot enter into virtual reality, and one cannot identify deeply with an avatar or online character; if we can truly interact with such digital entities at all, they are mere puppets that we control with digital strings. For this group, the self remains embodied and separate in every way from virtual reality, which is typically avoided when possible. There's a sort of rigidity to technophobia that is akin to exclusivism, in that it too is an "ideological formation" that promotes "isolationism." Says Eck: "The exclusivist response to diversity, whether theological, social, or political, is to mark ever more clearly the boundaries and borders separating 'us' from 'them'" (2003, 174). For technophobes, the "borders" exist between religions, but also between one's own religious worldviews and the practices contained within the computer.

In a way, the fundamentalism of technophobes is akin to what Salen and Zimmerman describe as "closed systems," that is, games defined by rules that are designed "prior to the actual involvement of players" (2004, 96). In this kind of game, any changes to the rules are discouraged, and everyone agrees beforehand how the game is to be played. Thus, if one is a fundamentalist in terms of one's faith, and one is also a technophobe, then the internet may easily be viewed with a dualistic lens – that is, one's religion is good while the internet is bad. The most extreme technophobes include those Amish groups that shun all electronics, for example, or those Muslims or those Hasidic Jews who see much of modern technology as a dangerous innovation. But there are also more subtle forms of rejection of virtual religion; in Islamic scholars' warnings about using the Hadith online, for example; or in the new Buddhist monastic code for Plum Village in France, which instructs monks not to surf the internet alone (Hanh 2004).

Another perspective with some technophobic tendencies emerges in Jeff Zaleski's interview with one of the most outspoken critics of online worship. Rabbi Yosef Y. Kazen, a member of the Lubavitcher sect of Orthodox Judaism in Brooklyn, is a member of "770," the "global headquarters of the Lubavitchers," and the founder of chabad.org, an orthodox Jewish website (Zaleski 1997, 8). Kazen's technophobic perspective becomes obvious when he argues that the embodied, physical aspect of religious identity is crucial for certain religious practices, such as a bar mitzvah or a prayer service with a minyan (ten males). According to Kazen, a minyan cannot happen in online worship space since souls reside only in the body in its flesh form. Says Kazen: "The quorum of ten people requires ten physical bodies. Each individual person has a spark of godliness within them which is the soul" (cited in Zaleski 1997, 18). Presumably, this "spark" cannot be transmitted via digital presence to online environments. When pressed, Kazen acknowledges the necessity of the specific male identity of the individuals for a minyan to work, revealing some of the more traditional reasons for his resistance to an online minyan.

Nonetheless, the technophobic resistance to online worship should be viewed in terms of its reference to real-life engendered bodies, to traditional worship norms, and to assumptions about the self's relationship to the physical vessel of the body. Nonetheless, even this group has, in recent years, moved toward the use of technology for the mediation of educational materials, thus also exhibiting some features of technomediators (below, pp. 114–16). Technophobes, then, are typically worried about online activity, and insist that (singular) physical, embodied selves are necessary for religious life and communal engagement. Some of them completely reject the technological supports that enable online activity at all. Others shun virtual reality for their own rituals but do allow the construction of structured educational websites for outsiders to learn about their faith. All see virtual reality as unreal, dangerous, and unable to authentically accommodate religious activity.

Of course, one of the greatest perceived dangers of online religious practice is that because you can never be sure who anyone is, you can also never be certain that religious hierarchies are being honored. In a 2004, James Wagner Au interviewed a *Second Life* resident with the username "Omega," who read the liturgy and led a virtual Mass in *Second Life*. In the interview, Au learned that Omega is not a real-life priest or minister in any tradition, much less Catholicism. Omega explained that he wanted the experience to be "like an actual mass" even though he is "certainly not a real minister, nor do I do this sort of thing in real life … I wanted to bring more real-world things into SL [*Second Life*] so people could experience them if they couldn't in real life." At the end of a service conducted by Omega, a woman asked for a blessing of her unborn child. Omega replied that the blessing wouldn't be "legit" or "hold much value" since he's not a "real priest." In classic reflexive posture, the woman claims "it would count to me."[2] These kinds of virtual claims to religious authority make traditional believers exceedingly uncomfortable, casting some of them into a technophobic posture.

Technomediators

For our second group, *technomediators*, virtual reality is a medium of communication, similar to a telephone or a letter. Sentiments and experiences can be expressed *through* virtual reality by embodied selves, but it is not an experience in and of itself. Therefore, if meaningful relationships develop online, this is because the real people creating them use the computer simply as a mode of communication – they do not enter into any distinctive space, and virtual reality is not a *site* for the nurturing of these relationships any more than a telephone line or a satellite is a site for developing relationships. Any meaning that is imparted via virtual media is meaning that is merely carried *through* it by real human beings. In terms of digital technology as used by existing religious groups, one might consider webcasting of worship services, or the use of messaging services to ask questions of religious authorities.

For technomediators, using virtual reality for religious purposes is not necessarily wrong – so long as it doesn't overshadow real, embodied religious practices and communities. For technomediators, any interaction that happens in virtual "space" derives its meaning solely from what real human beings put into it as they engage with one another, just as if they were talking on a telephone or leaving a message on a bulletin board. Examples of this kind of interaction include church websites, online bulletin boards, online donation systems, streaming video of a live religious worship service, services taking place via chat programs, or even blessings transmitted via cell phones to other human recipients. In all of these cases, software programs serve to *relay* information and communicate between people, but they do not easily invite the imagination of virtual presence within the medium itself. For technomediators, virtual reality is viewed simply as a *medium*, with the assumption that human beings are on either side, using the virtual space as a conduit for communication between two embodied selves. Technomediators are inclined to "include" virtual practices as part of religious faith, but only if they are accommodated to existing beliefs and seen as reflections of them. Just as inclusive Muslims, for example, might admire devout Christians and Jews, but see these views as "incomplete," so technomediators might argue that religious practice online is acceptable in some ways, but is not enough. Eck says that for inclusive Christians "other religious traditions are not so much evil or wrong-headed as incomplete, needing the fulfillment of Christ" (2003, 179). For technomediators, media needs this "fulfillment" too.

We can look at this view of religion as a type of game, one in which we "restrict our focus and look at just those play behaviors that are intrinsic to the game, ignoring all others." Eck rightly notes that the inclusive perspective often harbors "unreflective" or implicit views about power (179). Inclusivism, she claims, "often dodges the question of real difference by reducing everything finally to my own terms" (184). Inclusivism then is like viewing the world from within a carefully designed game world that "often hides within it a hierarchical acceptance of plurality, with one's own view of things on top" such that the rules of one's own religion dictate how the "game" of religious dialogue is played (Eck 2003, 96). For technomediators, the self is running a single operating system – a religious tradition – and any form of digital mediation (as well as any religious traditions one encounters) must be filtered through this system.

One particularly interesting example of technomediator position is the website associated with the Wailing Wall in Jerusalem, a phenomenon I first considered in Chapter 2 (Aish.com n.d.-a). The Wall's website offers modern instructions for those who want to partake in the ancient ritual of putting prayers on slips of paper and inserting them into crevices in the Wailing Wall: "Type in your prayer. It will be printed out in the Old City of Jerusalem where it will be placed in the Wall by a student of Aish HaTorah. Notes that are anti-Semitic or uncivilized in nature will be automatically deleted" (Aish. com n.d.-b). With the digital Wailing Wall prayers, a religious transfer happens via the internet, but the "sacredness" of the act is not fulfilled until the physical printout of the prayer reaches the physical wall. Participation in the tangible ritual is thus possible for those not in Jerusalem, and indeed is enabled by online communications, but the sacredness of the act retains its uniquely real, physical quality. In other words, the internet is a tool of communication – not a ritual component in and of itself. This characteristic of the website is reinforced by the concurrent ability of users to watch others pray at the wailing wall in live streaming video, and perhaps (if they are persistent and the camera is pointing in the right direction) to even see their prayer be inserted.

Although most technomediators see human beings as entities on either end of a technomediating exchange, the technomediator position also offers an interesting new possible twist: What if the mediation is between the human online and God, who then is accessible via the internet? Digital prayer walls, texting God programs, and online confessional sites are examples of technomediation as prayer. If we adopt the view that technology can work as a mediator between two real and separate entities or selves, and if we allow one of these entities to be God, then some theologically inclined internet users might even see potential for the internet to replace the priesthood as the mediator between humans and God. Sites such as Forgivenet.com, Ivescrewedup.com, mysecret.tv, dailyconfessions.com, and camfess.com invite participants to see the public posting of "sins" as a form of ritual confession without the need for traditional religious hierarchy or even formal liturgy. Reverend Troy Gramling of South Florida's Flamingo Road Church sees online confession as fully viable: "Just because confessions don't go directly to God through a priest or a church doesn't mean they aren't sincere." Gramling, the founder of ive-screwedup.com, claims that online confession's utility lies in the comfort it offers the confessor: "there's something healing about just going on the site and reading it, seeing all these other confessions. Some people might realize, 'Maybe I'm not alone'" (Fantz 2008).

The technomediating position is an intriguing one, allowing the internet to play a role in religious ritual but offering a variety of perspectives on who or what is on the "other side" of the medium of the computer. But whereas technomediation merely hints at the possibility that God might "dwell" in some kind of virtual space, the final category, technomonism, explicitly embraces just such a proposition.

Technomonists

Our third group sees virtual reality as a legitimate and authentic new space into which human beings can actually enter in some meaningful kind of way, and which they can enter in plural and hybrid ways. For technomonists, events can take place in virtual reality, and efficacious religious rituals can be conducted there since full immersion of the self into the virtual world is possible. Richard Bartle claims that "[f]or virtual worlds, it's almost unavoidable that the character and the player will tend toward each other. If you like your virtual self, you'll take on its characteristics; if you keep mood characters, you'll gradually stop playing all but one; the social skills you acquire will become skills that you use. Ultimately, you'll advance to the final level of immersion, where you and your character become one" (2003, 161). Assuming that such immersion is not necessarily limited to single avatars, then a single self can be expressed in multiple ways, each with equal potential for rich immersion.

The technomonist position is the deepest level of immersion identified by Richard Bartle in his taxonomy of virtual engagement. Bartle argues that immersion exists in a series of increasing degrees:

PLAYER: "the human being sitting at the computer, interacting with the virtual world." The player is "controlling an object within the virtual world that is associated with them."

AVATAR: if the player identifies with the digital object or self, seeing it as representing him or her, it is an avatar, "a puppet" that the player controls, and the "conduit through which they act." However, an avatar is referred to in third person, and has its own unique quirks and characteristics. Avatars are best understood as "dolls."

CHARACTER: the avatar that is also a "character" is a unique characterization of the player himself or herself; it is "a tokenization of the player" and "an extension of a player's self, a whole personality that the player dons when they enter the virtual world." You can have several characters at once. Characters are "simulacra."

PERSONA: "A persona is a player, in a world. That's in it. Any separate distinction of character is gone – the player is the character. You're not role-playing a being, you are that being; you're not assuming an identity, you are that identity; you're not projecting a self; you are that self … There's no level of indirection, no filtering, no question: you are *there*."

(2003, 155)

Technomonists are most likely to see themselves as inhabiting both the real world and the virtual world simultaneously, perhaps at the character or the persona level. However, just as Gnostics longed for a world they could never fully inhabit in their current embodied form, so technomonists may manifest the sophistication to realize that despite their deep identification with digital personae, they are constantly working to maintain this identification of self with digital other. Such technomonists may exhibit a yearning for identification with the avatar that *is* the self, recognizing at once that presence online is constantly undermined by the real body's form. In this case, as Hillis remarks, "online avatars take the form of moving images discursively rendered as desirable virtual objects endowed with godlike, quasi-independent powers … [and] as having inner spirits that participants unleash" (2009, 20). Such yearning is a constant labor to undermine the distinction between here and there, an enacted ritual of performance that has as its goal the sanctification of the "other" space – the other world – online via inhabited presence by the self within the avatar. Accordingly, as Hillis remarks, "the implicit qualities of transcendence once thought to imbue the unitary self are being transferred to networked information machines," but with the binary of physical/digital constantly in danger of undermining transcendence's performance (21).

Since his categories depend upon viewing things from the *player*'s perspective, Bartle's paradigm of immersion leaves out a few important modes of identity engagement. For example, what do we make of virtual encounters that invite us to take on insidious roles, playing out the game's procedural rhetoric through actions that may run counter to our own moral beliefs, as in *Waco Resurrection* (where we play as the cult leader David Koresh) or *Christ Killa* (where we shoot Jesus clones)? And what of our engagement with *other* selves online, especially those that make claims to religious authority and invite relationship with us via a false persona? Finally, what are we to make of virtual identities that are not even human, as in our interaction with artificial intelligence bots in online environments? Our response to such experiences depends, of course, on the degree of our immersion. They also reveal the precarious nature of self-representation online, calling us to ask what an authentic encounter of selves might look like in virtual space, and how we would know if we were having one.

Technomonism also erodes the difference between online and offline, and thus can be viewed as what Salen and Zimmerman call "open systems," that is, games that work as culture. In games that work *as culture*, "the internal functioning of the game is not emphasized; instead, as a cultural system the focus is on the way that the game exchanges meaning with culture at large" and the way it "interfaces with society as a whole" (2004, 97). The difference between game and reality is difficult to discern, since the goal is not winning but experimentation with meaning. Thus, in this view, the actions of the self in an online context may indeed have consequences for the embodied self, since the difference between online and offline spaces is irrelevant for authenticity of experience.

Technomonists exhibit wide variety in their choices of virtual interaction, but all of them openly accept the possibility that virtual space *can* function as a sacred space in and of itself and that the self can fully enter into and inhabit these spaces. The hallmark characteristic of technomonists is reflexivity in religious experience, that is, the belief that one's personal experience and conviction determines the authenticity of an encounter. Thus, examples of technomonism are as varied as the people who practice them. They might include religious practitioners who attend church online and enact virtual forms of accepted religious practice. They might include any form of religious engagement that posits virtual space as an acceptable site for the presence of the self and the exploration of meaning.

Just as Eck's categories depend on perspective and the degree of "interactivity" and willingness to transform through dialogue with others, so the three categories Rebecca and I developed do not necessarily fully identify with single faith traditions, but rather with perspectives toward technology that run throughout manifestations of many religious traditions. Technologically engaged mystics of all stripes, it seems, would likely be drawn to technomonism. Hinduism appears to lend itself to technomonism as well, particularly as virtual reality accords quite nicely in some ways with the notion of *maya*, or the idea that all of reality is illusion. Buddhists would likely be drawn to technomonism for the same reason. However, such generalizations are subject to distortion of the lived and immense variety with which real people navigate their way through religious terrain today. I am suggesting here a pattern of resemblances, between pluralism and technomonism, and between the fluid self as practiced by pluralists and as exhibited in online virtual contexts. In all of these, fluidity is exhibited not just in the notion of the self but also in the relationship between offline and online, nurturing a sort of spillover of worldview that encourages fluidity in all aspects of our lives. Individual identity, says Pearce, is "both an intersubjective and an emergent creation" (2007, 314). In short, "we shape our avatars and thereafter our avatars shape us" (315).

Imagined selves

One of the most compelling questions about contemporary identity is to what degree we shape ourselves by the media that we choose to consume, especially those forms of media that invite us to imagine ourselves as others. Such engagement can take the form of imagining ourselves as heroes in first-person shooters, as villains in violent experimental or taboo video games, or, in a more mundane way, as someone with a different gender or a different life story. With the computer screen between us, we don't always know who we're engaging with, and we may also find ourselves crafting our own online personas in unexpected ways.

In 2003, digital artist Eddo Stern debuted a first-person shooter Doom modification called *Waco Resurrection*. First-person shooters are some of the most rigidly controlled of video game experiences, typically defined by a series of set goals with specific end points, and with the entire experience repeatable in order to achieve success. *Waco Resurrection* first appeared at an installation in Las Vegas, at which players were invited to immerse themselves in ways unusual in most first-person shooters. While they played the game, participants at the installation donned a "Koresh skin" that consisted of a hard plastic 3D mask, while they were invited to re-enact in the game select events from the 1993 violence at the Waco compound that ended the lives of more than 70 people. According to Eddo Stern's website, gamers "enter the mind and form of a resurrected David Koresh" and enter the game's network "as *a Koresh* [who] must defend the Branch Davidian compound against internal intrigue, skeptical civilians, rival Koresh and the inexorable advance of government agents [my italics]." Within the plastic mask, players are "bombarded with a soundstream of government 'psy-ops,' FBI negotiators, the voice of God and the persistent clamor of battle" and must respond with specific "messianic texts drawn from the Book of Revelation" as they "wield a variety of weapons from the Mount Carmel cache and influence the behavior of both followers and opponents by radiating a charismatic aura."

Players of *Waco Resurrection* are asked not only to imagine themselves in the real-life horror of the Waco stand-off, but they are asked to interact with an avatar representing David Koresh and perhaps even imagine themselves *as* the self-proclaimed messiah. Jeff Douglas reports that in the game, "Koresh's energy comes from massive Bibles that rain from the sky. Those Bibles also rain bullets and turn federal agents into Davidian followers." After considering this game, we are prompted to ask with Sherry Turkle: "Do our real-life selves learn lessons from our virtual personae? Are these virtual personae fragments of a coherent real-life personality?" (1997, 180). A game like *Waco Resurrection* raises some disturbing but profound questions about degrees of identification with one's avatar.

But there are more prosaic questions raised by our virtual encounters. As Campbell observes, "the veil of the screen separates individuals from each other" (2005, 46). Accordingly, we can never be sure to whom we are talking "because online identities are often based on created personae, which are deliberate misrepresentations of the real person" (48). Such issues are important, since one aspect of virtual identity construction is the play with how *others* may perceive us, an activity that reveals some interesting nuances when people play with religious authority through masquerading as religious figures or spiritual leaders.

In some forms of new social media, we may have even less control over who reads what we write, such that the "imagined audience" may be "entirely different from the actual readers of a profile, blog post, or tweet" (Marwick and Boyd 2010, 3). Bloggers write for a "cognitively constructed" audience, "an imagined group of readers who may not actually read the blog." For bloggers, the "imagined audience" exists "only as it is written into the text, through stylistic and linguistic choices." *Facebook* and similar social networking sites allow us to choose, to some extent, who will be in our audience: "Through the process of labeling connections as 'Friends', social network sites require participants to publicly articulate connections, thereby enabling them to write their audience into being" (4). Tweeting is perhaps the least controllable of the current popular forms of blogging, since anyone who likes can follow the "tweets" you send out, and you'll never know who read them and who didn't.

For those to whom "tweeting" may seem a foreign concept, Marwick and Boyd offer this helpful introduction for the service, which was launched in 2006:

> Twitter is a microblogging site, originally developed for mobile phones, designed to let people post short, 140-character text updates or "tweets" to a network of others. Twitter prompts users to answer the question "What are you doing?," creating a constantly updated timeline, or stream, of short messages that range from humor and musings on life to links and breaking news. Twitter has a directed friendship model: participants choose Twitter accounts to "follow" in their stream, and they each have their own group of "followers." There is no technical requirement of reciprocity, and often, no social expectation of such. Tweets can be posted and read on the web, through SMS, or via third-party clients written for desktop computers, smartphones, and other devices.
>
> (Marwick and Boyd 2010, 4)

As a microblogging system, *Twitter* offers what Marwick and Boyd describe as "dynamic, interactive identity presentation to unknown audiences" (2010, 4). Drawing on previous studies, they observe that "many tweets are phatic in nature" and "serve a social function, reinforcing connections and maintaining social bonds" (6). Those who use *Twitter* present themselves through ongoing "tweets," revealing a self that is both fluid and emergent, and "primarily textual, not visual" (4). Although private messages are allowed, the dominant form of posting is completely public. The unpredictable, uncontrollable nature of possible readership on *Twitter*, say Marwick and Boyd, "ruptures the ability to vary self-presentation based on audience, and thus manage discrete impressions" (2010, 4). There is often "a disconnect between followers and followed." Moreover, due to the ability of both posters and readers to copy/paste remarks into other social networking sites, emails, or other online hosting agents, "it is virtually impossible for Twitter users to account for their potential audience, let alone actual readers" (5).

Twitter thus also allows for a determined sort of anonymity. Users can call themselves whatever they like, with strange and sometimes humorous consequences. For example, a user named "God" tweeted the following joke June 15, 2009: "Dear followers, I am deeply sorry for creating Justin Bieber. What started as a joke between me & Moses has gone too far. @satan, help." Attempts to read Satan's tweets initially led to a 404 error, followed by Satan's tweet page, filled mostly with jokes and spoofed threats of violence. Those who care about such things may be relieved to learn that God has more followers than Satan: 15,000 to 48,000 as of July 2010. However, not all attempts at religious authority on *Twitter* are meant as jokes. As Mark Dozier and Sue Scheff report, the Dalai Lama opened a *Twitter* account several years ago and within days had thousands of followers, "all surely intent upon experiencing a day in the spiritual life of the Tibetan Buddhism leader." Unfortunately, the account wasn't really the Dalai Lama's, and was closed almost as soon as it appeared (2009, 114). What are we to make of such identity fakery? In the case of the Dalai Lama, the discrepancy was cleared up rather easily, as one simply assumes that the Dalai Lama objected to someone else posting tweets in his name and the counterfeiter was stopped.

Encounters with virtual shysters can, of course, simply be read as an exercise in theological awareness. As one Christian puts it: "You can be Jesus' 'friend' on Facebook – even become a fan – but the only option you have with him on Twitter is to follow. It might seem silly (and the analogy certain[ly] breaks down) but it was a good challenge for me: Is Jesus simply my buddy? Am I just a fan of him? Or am I willing to follow him?" (Briggs 2009). Some forms of divine masquerading are intended to be authentic expressions of piety, despite awareness that the people tweeting are not the entities they claim to be. In 2009, Trinity Church in New York City's financial district used *Twitter* as a mode of delivery of the Passion play. Members of the congregation "tweeted" dialogue for followers to receive. As Pauline Hope Cheong (2009) explains, "Twitter enactments of the Passion Play can be seen as an online media spectacle that abstracts original elements of the biblical passion account by diluting it into brief re-tweeted messages." This experience is hardly *just* a "reading" of the "text" of the gospels. In addition to the textual changes required to translate the passion story into 140-character chunks, the performance also required tweeters to take on the personas of Jesus, Mary, Judas, and others. Passion plays have, of course, been a part of Christian tradition for hundreds of years. But because *Twitter* is typically used for mundane posting of daily activities delivered by the people who claim to be sending them, the *Twitter* Easter performance invites a contested reading that encourages us to imagine Jesus actually delivering his tweets to us in real time, from Gethsemane, for example, or even from the cross itself – a situation which creates the odd and strangely humorous (if also blasphemous) picture of Jesus somehow pulling out his mobile device to send his thoughts to us via *Twitter* – and presumably holding up the crucifixion in the process.

Another example of people taking on the virtual personas of religious figures is the 2003 reality "game" *Noah's Ark* (Ship of Fools 2003). Like many reality shows, *Noah's Ark* featured contestants that viewers could periodically vote to be removed from the ark. But this odd new twist on reality shows took place via avatars remotely controlled via people using personal PCs in their own homes. Contestants had to compete to be selected to play the roles of various biblical characters, who were represented online as cartoonish biblical avatars tromping about on a virtual ark, from which Noah is strangely absent. The creators of the game, Ship of Fools, playfully describe the virtual crew: "It's a cast to make even Cecil B. DeMille's hormones bubble." The cast includes twelve "biblical saints and sinners rubbing shoulders on the world's most famous floating zoo."[3]

So how do the players behind these biblical avatars see themselves? We can leave aside the anachronistic association of say, Jezebel with Paul, and any romantic digital liaisons made possible by this arrangement. What of the religious significance of "playing" as Eve or Job or Moses or John the Baptist? It seems hard to refute the claim that the experience in some way diminishes the traditional respect attributed to the biblical versions of these stories. Rather, biblical characters are presented as loosely defined character studies, open for creative reinterpretation and humorous denigration. If we take Bartle's categories of immersion seriously, the apparent humorous intent of this experience requires that the player's (embodied physical person's) relationship with the digital avatar be at most at the "character" level so that the avatar is a mere representation of the player's self – not identified with it. Nobody playing this game, it seems, should be capable of full immersion, of seeing themselves as *really* on Noah's ark, or *really* playing the role of Esther or Samson. To do so would require such an odd blend of allegorical reading of the scriptures and literal identification of self with digital self that the religious repercussions seem practically untenable. Apart from the Bible-study-style discussions that Ship of Fools hopes to generate (complete with study guides and transcripts), the point appears to be to find that place where virtual identity and religious story meet, prompting us to ask what makes the biblical stories "real" to us in the first place.

One particularly interesting case of identity and religion is the virtual crucifixion controversy in *Roma Victor*, an online role-playing game. On March 23, 2006, the following message appeared on *Roma Victor*'s official discussion board: "We're about to crucify one of the *Roma Victor* test team, Cynewulf, for ring-leading a gang of spawn killers … It'll be the first of several crucifixions, which will be used as a banning and anti-griefing punishment tool. The crucified character will appear affixed to the cross on full public display for the duration of the ban. I'll drop by with a screenshot as soon as I get a chance" (posted by a user named "KFR" on the *Roma Victor* discussion board). The incident earned *Roma Victor* some media attention with reports that some Christians were offended. The virtual event was too similar, they claimed, to the real crucifixion.

The "crucified" player, Cynewulf, must have watched with curiosity as Christian viewers claimed his experience was too much like Christ's. Certainly, Cynewulf himself could feel no pain as he "hung" on the digital cross. The *Roma Victor* controversy thus offers us a fresh insight into virtual identity and the hybridity of self. Cynewulf's virtual experience of crucifixion is strangely akin to docetic interpretations of the real crucifixion, especially the Gnostic forms that imply the "spirit" of wisdom left Jesus as he hung limply on the cross. In this view, the body of Jesus was a mere virtual or illusory avatar that had once hosted an entity that in fact cannot experience pain and certainly cannot die "in-world." This case suggests, albeit indirectly, that one's ability to immerse deeply in one's avatar depends upon to what extent one imports one's own religious worldview into the online world.

Ruth Evans (2010), a medievalist at St Louis University, suggests that imagining oneself as Christ was a pre-modern form of hybrid identity akin in some ways to today's virtual experimentation:

> [I]n becoming one with the non-human prop of Christ, medieval persons extended their capabilities and were in turn profoundly transformed by that encounter, in a manner analogous to modern forms of distributed cognition: their minds, in other words, did not end with their bodies but were imaginatively and practically enmeshed in, and extended by, the external tool of Christ.

The "woman sitting in Starbucks with an iPad" has something deeply in common with "the medieval Christian joining with Christ," she argues. She points to "the many devotional and meditative practices ... [like the] imitation of Christ – the emulation of his suffering ... embracing and kissing statues of Christ, meditating on his body – through which medieval people entered into a deep, complex and transformative relationship with a non-human external object." Evans points to interactive objects as well, the "portable images of Christ that could travel with [Christians] or be worn as jewelry, so that they could be constantly looked at and touched, much as we carry around our iPhones and laptops."

The kind of unity that people experienced is analogous to our love affair with our own windows to the non-physical realm, our cell phones, iPods, laptops, and digital devices:

> What medieval subjects experienced when they joined themselves to Christ was directly analogous to our sensation of oneness in being closely joined to our technology – and to our sense of being bereft when that technology

goes missing or breaks down because it has, profoundly but almost imperceptibly, become a part of ourselves.

(Evans 2010)

Instead of focusing on our connection with another world via our attachment to virtual technology, Evans focuses on "the repeated practice of monastic and private devotional meditation" as enabling "an almost automatic (because habitual) uncoupling from the external environment." Devotional meditation via images of Christ enabled users to disconnect from everyday life. Maybe one of the things that is most different, then, about today is that when we disconnect from daily life by going online, we are not rewarded typically with a decrease in external stimuli, but rather an onslaught of new stimuli, streaming in and through us. And certainly, the kind of imagining of self-as-Christ that Evans points to is fundamentally different from the sort experienced by Cynewulf in *Roma Victor*.

But what exactly constitutes the difference? I think in part the answer has to do with the fact that for Cynewulf, the world of *Roma Victor* was always perceived as play, and as one of many other worlds he might choose to inhabit, and any of which he could shut off at any time. For medieval Christians, there was only one other world, one imaginative focus, and one avatar worth playing. Jesus was both the figure with which they identified, and the unachievable desire that drove their love of him. No perfect identification of person with avatar is possible in the case of *Roma Victor* or medieval devotional practices, but today at least, the ability for one religious figure to provide such a universally engaged model of otherworldly experience is utterly lost for most people, replaced with the surge of streaming worlds and multiplied possibilities of new identity.

Conclusion

Molotov Alva and His Search for the Creator is an example of *machinima*, short for "machine cinema," an emerging new form of movie-making, utilizing game engines or real-time online worlds as the setting. If the filmmaker uses an online world like *Second Life*, he or she can even recruit actors, design sets and costumes, and produce a set script. Because of its self-reflective and journalistic style, *Molotova Alva* has been dubbed "the first documentary shot entirely in a virtual online platform" (Craven 2009). The *Second Life* avatar who stars in the production, Molotov Alva, is physically modeled after Douglas Gayeton, the producer of the series. However, Alva is now marooned in *Second Life*, gradually losing his grip on his connection to his real self (his embodied self) and to his creator, presumably also Gayeton. Gayeton asks via Alva: "If this new reality was an illusion, did its persistence depend upon me?. [but] even I was a fabrication. In this new world, I could stand on a beach – but could I taste the salt hanging in the breeze? Feel the sand crunch beneath my feet? Dip my toes in the water and shiver from its coolness? All that I saw and experienced relied on memories that I had from my other life. This place could only create an approximation of a beach. It was up to my mind to do the rest."

Faced with the emptiness of an existence that was only an approximation of the real, Alva goes on a quest to find "the creator" and at the end of the series, leaves the online virtual world for the real world, where the experiences are much more vivid, and relationships invite richer physical and emotional engagement. Molotov Alva does not abandon his virtual identity because it has been useless; he leaves it behind when his virtual experiences have taught him the value of the real. The creator he seeks is of course his embodied self, and so he is on a quest of self-discovery and reintegration.

Awareness of one's choices as a bricoleur can be viewed as a sort of discipline or, looked at another way, simply as a form of critical thinking and awareness. Referring to the construction of religious identity today, Roof defines what he calls "reflexive spirituality," seeing in today's world "a situation encouraging a more deliberate, engaging effort on people's part for their own spiritual formation, both inside and outside religious communities" (1999, 75). It is this kind of self-reflection that appears to engage Molotov Alva and thus also his creator, Douglas Gayeton. As Alva realizes that he is Gayeton, a sort of self-awareness emerges that allows reintegration of shattered selves. Reflexive, self-aware spirituality is *thinking* spirituality, as people decide what to do with the vast menu of options before them. Identity formation may be constantly in flux, but our *awareness* of that flux need not be. Like Molotov Alva, we can deliberately gather up the pieces of our scattered selves and begin the process of knowing who we *really* are. Such knowledge (in the context of media and religion as well as religion as media) is an exercise in meaning-making and meaning-discovery, a patently religious act.

Chapter 6

God-mobs

Virtually religious community

The extent of technological development in social media in the last decade is startling, as evident in Howard Rheingold's naive wonder at his own late-twentieth-century predictions. Writing a mere five years after the first web browser was written, Rheingold prognosticated:

> Today's bedroom electronic bulletin boards, regional computer conferencing systems, global computer networks offer clues to what might happen when more powerful technology comes along … We'll be able to transfer the Library of Congress from any point on the globe to any another point in seconds, upload and download full-motion digital video at will. But is that really what people are likely to do with all that bandwidth and computing power? … How will people actually use the desktop supercomputers and multimedia telephones that the engineers tell us we'll have in the near future?
>
> (1996, 415)

Today we take such abilities for granted. With "all that bandwidth," we are indeed digitizing books and sharing educational video. But we're also entertaining ourselves and finding seemingly endless new ways to create social connections. Warren Sack argues that the technological moment we are in today is defined precisely by its communications media: "At no other point in history have we had a medium that supports many-to-many communications between hundreds or thousands of people" (2004, 239). We have become, he argues, "network-based communities," which are "of a different kind than geographically based communities such as neighborhoods, cities, and nations" (238).

Indeed, today's youth conceive of community in ways totally unfathomable even a few decades ago. They watch each other's activities in online social media, blog publicly as much or as little as they please, tweet their fleeting thoughts, text message one another instantly via hand-held devices, and can be as wired for as much of their day as they please no matter where they are. "Digital natives," those who grew up with ubiquitous communications technology, are "constantly connected" and they have "plenty of friends, in real space and in the virtual worlds – indeed, a growing collection of friends they keep a count of, often for the rest of the world to see, in their online social network sites" (Palfrey and Gasser 2008, 5). Clearly this is a pervasive form of connection, at least potentially capable of nurturing relationships and creating a sense of community. However, the kind of community it can nurture may not be the same kind as our grandparents or even our parents knew. As John Palfrey and Urs Gasser observe, this ever-present digital network "blends the human with the technical to a degree we haven't experienced before, and it is transforming human relationships in fundamental ways" (4–5).

In the last chapter, I analyzed the fluid nature of the self in today's hyper-mediated society, looking in particular at the flow of "applications" or programs that we run through our "iPod selves." In this chapter I extend that metaphor into the realm of communities, which similarly reflect the fluidity of current technology and resist easy judgments about their authenticity and their efficacy. As I argue in this chapter, despite the sense of community courted and adver-tised in such virtual shared realms, the singular core of these networks is none other than the individual self, moving independently throughout a sea of choices and encountering possibilities for contact that *could* provide a sense of belonging or community, but which are *themselves* in constant flux.

This chapter, then, is a look at some of the most poignant examples of online connections, with preference for those that emerge into a status recognized by their participants as communities. In my analysis of online communities, I initially examine some of the digital tools used by religious groups to facilitate meetings *offline*, then I move to an analysis of religious communities that exist primarily *online*. I then look at some of the modes of social interaction online that mimic relationship, some of them explicitly religious and some not. Finally, I look at some online groups that work *like* religion, and explore how Victor Turner's (1969) work on liminality and the Durkheimian notion of the social as the "sacred" open up some compelling parallels between religious and apparently non-religious online communities. First, however, we must spend a bit more time sorting out the relationship between networks and communities, and getting a sense of how the self fits into these discussions.

Node to self

The most powerful metaphor for understanding the social self online is of a ship making its way through the sea of possibilities, asking things like: "Shall I visit a social media site? Go shopping? Skype with a friend? Shall I play a game? Look up information? Perhaps I should find reviews for restaurants, or visit an online world, or read the news." The self as node moves through a host of potential connections with other people, who are similarly sailing the seas of digital sites, landing in occasional "ports" then casting about again for something else, someone else, somewhere else. The online self is driven by the desire to keep on moving, to connect and disconnect, to seek momentary harbor in online "places" where others of like-minded interests may also have landed.

This metaphor of a ship comes from Warren Sack, who has suggested that we can use the metaphor of the online self as a ship to situate ourselves in the "wider network of social and semantic relations" that we encounter online (2004, 240). The software we choose to use or download, then, functions as a sort of "self-governance" as it provides a "point of navigation [that itself] is self-guidance" (240). For Sack, the "self" is a single node in multiple networks, interacting in vast and complex relationships, connections and conversations with others in a digital environment. Some of the connections between such "nodes" are momentary conversations. Others become real-life relationships. Others exist only within the context of playing a game or exploring a world or constructing a wiki. Far from being bankrupt of human connection, wired culture offers an unlimited pool from which to create and intentionally sustain meaningful connections.

But the value of such online connections remains unclear. Scholars continue to argue, some with resolute conviction, that when we go online, we don't really "go" anywhere, so if we were alone when we logged on, we are still alone – despite how connected we may feel to those we converse with online. Others argue, just as vociferously, that the sense of presence and immersion possible online – especially when we have a representation of ourselves via an avatar – is as real a sense of presence that we can have on the street. A virtual community, says Derek Foster, is held "intact" by "the subjective criterion of togetherness, a feeling of connectedness that confers a sense of belonging" that is "much more than the mere act of connection itself" (1996, 29). Such wired relationships, suggests Palfrey and Gasser, may be very different from real-life relationships in many ways, but we should withhold final judgment since "they are also perhaps enduring in ways we have yet to understand" (2008, 5). The stakes become even higher when such virtual relationships are forged in online "spaces" with avatars that represent the self. Hillis uses *Second Life* as an example of sites "that are no longer only forms of media per se; rather, because they allow for indexical experiences of traces of actual human beings they are now experienced as actual spaces 'in' which aspects of actual human beings have come to reside and are publicly and privately addressed" (2009, 14). If we can inject "traces" of ourselves into the avatars that represent us such that our digital "bodies" are in some real way inhabited by us too, then online connection takes on an entirely different hue. Real people, all of these scholars are arguing, are the root of online relationships and therefore a sense of togetherness can effectively emerge online.

The problem is, both claims are true: we are "together" in online space and at the same time by ourselves in front of a screen, connected via pixels and information but often alienated in our embodied nature to the extent that we may know very little about the people with whom we craft what seem to us to be meaningful connections. Fortunata Piselli points out that a "new type of society (the knowledge or network society) is emerging, and it is based largely on interactions devoid of physical contact and reciprocal recognition of identities" (2007, 876). How can we listen to each other, Sack is asking, when there are so many of us talking? And how can we know who we're talking to, Piselli points out, when we can't see them directly? Another question arises as well: even if we know who we're talking to, how much do we know about them, given that we are likely seeing only one facet of their personality, and that transmitted digitally? Victoria Vesna uses the term "distributed presence" to describe the networked self. Our "presence" is indeed "distributed" when we have bits of ourselves on *Facebook*, other bits left as digital residue on old forums, another bit of ourselves invested in a character we are developing in *World of Warcraft*.

Our relationships, then, are "distributed" too, with certain features of our personalities or emotional lives attached more deeply to the different faces that we maintain online. Interested in the implications of such parsing up of our identities, Vesna argues that contemporary developments in communications media have deeply affected our sense of community, and not necessarily in a good way: "the same technology that makes distributed community a possibility and promised to save us time also prevents us from actually having time to build community" (2004, 249). At the same time, she says, we are experiencing a "transition from projecting ourselves as bodies to collapsing into a space of information and geometrical patterns" (258). Instead of encountering each other as embodied human beings, we more often encounter others as projectable pixels, and craft images of ourselves with related and often transient blurbs of information. While we may invest ourselves in these pixels, and see ourselves as accurately reflected in them when viewed by others, the truth may be more complicated.

Hillis has noted what he calls a "cosmopolitan Web dynamic" which is both "a culture of networks" and "a culture of individualism." We are "linked by endless electronic nodes implicitly promoted as an ordered and harmonious system." The ennui implied by such "surfing" is what Hillis dubs "everyday manifestations of a desire for a worldwide *oikos* or *ecumene*," a term borrowed from the original form of Christian evangelism and the hope for a unified worldview under Christ. There's a sort of idealism manifest in the way we seek out connection online, according to Hillis; we view the internet as "networked assemblages of digital information machines 'wherein' it is imagined that a global and capitalized sensibility might find a mobile and universal home away from home" (2009, 2). This hopeful view resonates with those who see the screen itself as a sort of symbolic portal into possibility, a window into transcendence. The possibility present in our engagement with the online "world" can be examined in terms of social connections as the wishful engagement with an infinite possibility of human connections via the mechanics of virtual networks. This possibility is manifest in new designs in programming, like the recent *Chatroulette*, a Skype program that connects you with random strangers from around the world, and gives you the freedom to instantly spin the *Chatroulette* wheel for another person whenever you like. In simpler terms, the idealistic reasoning such activities suggest goes something like this: there are millions of other people out there on their computers too – so maybe I could get to know some of them better, and feel more connected. As I argue later in the chapter, for some scholars, the sense of belonging is itself enough to constitute a "sacred" or "religious" function for whatever activity one finds most compelling.

But what are we searching for? If networks are the collections of ships or nodes that define a group of people in contact with one another online, then perhaps we can best define community as what happens *if or when* that network is able to produce a sense of belonging. Such a judgment is, of course, frustratingly subjective and individualized. As Preece and Maloney-Krichmar (2005) note in their analysis of online community, "[t]here is much angst about use of the term 'community,' especially when researchers from a range disciplines come together, each wanting to place a stake in the ground to support their own goals and research paradigm. Sociologists, social psychologists and anthropologists are the guardians of the term but for more than 50 years, they have been defining and redefining the concept of community."

However, as Barry Wellman and Milena Gulia observe, concern about what constitutes community is hardly new despite our assumptions that the internet spurred such debates: "Consistent with the present-minded ethos of computer users, pundits write as if people had never worried about community before the Internet arose. Yet sociologists have been writing for over a century about how technological changes (along with bureaucratization, industrialization, urbanization and capitalism) have affected community." Sociologists, too, have been considering for decades how "networks" (including offline networks) may exist in tension with or alongside or as communities, such that the "conceptual revolution" was made "from defining community in terms of space – neighborhoods – to defining it in terms of social networks" (1997, 2). This hardly clears up for us the problem with differentiating between networks and communities, since Wellman and Gulia's whole point is that communities don't have to be purely embodied anymore and thus may be more aptly viewed as "networks." For them and a number of other sociologists, to call something a "network" is simply to emphasize its lack of brick-and-mortar associations, but to retain its ability to nurture meaningful relationships. The point of the semantic shift is not to differentiate between the terms, nor even primarily to examine the difference between online and offline community, but rather to accentuate the transformation of our sense of community in contemporary life in manifold ways.

Indeed, the "networks" we join today may exist online, offline, or both. Preece and Maloney-Krichmar (2005) observe that increasingly researchers are accepting the fact that "online communities rarely exist only online; many have off-line physical components. Either they start as face-to-face communities and then part or all of the community migrates on to digital media, or conversely, members of an online community seek to meet face-to-face." This means that the term "online community" itself may be a bit of a misnomer. Communication today, they argue, "is hardly ever restricted to a single medium; usually several media are used depending on what is most convenient at the time, which can make doing research in this field difficult." Rather than try to neatly solve the problem of networks, communities and relationships, I offer a simplistic premise that I will use throughout this chapter. Put succinctly, my argument is this: a network is *possibility*. A community is *commitment*. As Campbell observes, "being part of a Christian email list does not mean the group is a community" (2005, xv). This assessment holds for online communities, my primary interest here, and it invites us to look at what enables some groups of people online to develop what they see to be deep, rich relationships and to simultaneously develop other relationships intended for purely informational or ephemeral purposes.

Rheingold recognized this when he claimed that although communities may indeed emerge within "computer-linked groups," the "technical linkage of electronic personae is not sufficient to create a community" (1996, 420). This is not to say that communities cannot appear online: just that not *every* network becomes a community. McGonigal uses the metaphor of the rhizome. Drawing on Deleuze and Guattari, she argues that the "ubicomp infrastructure" of networked technology is "a kind of relationship engine – an always growing rhizome, with infinitely many points of potential connection" (2006, 16). We have our cell phones, laptops, iPads, iPhones – infinite possibilities for connection at any time, enhanced by locative software utilizing integrating GPS technology. The key here is possibility. A network does not necessarily entail a community. It simply creates the conditions under which these might occur.

Campbell argues that the most important defining feature of community online is precisely the unique relationships that are fostered, the *feelings* that users have when interacting with one another in meaningful ways:

> People look for relationship, to be connected and committed to others. They desire care, to be cared for by their community. They desire value, to be seen as valuable as an individual and part of a community of value. They seek consistent communication with members of their community. They long for intimate communication, where individuals share openly about their beliefs and spiritual lives. Finally, they gather around a shared faith that influences how they see others online and how they understand the interconnection between online and offline aspects of life.
>
> (2005, 187)

For Campbell, "commitment" is a crucial feature of online communities, and it certainly highlights the subjectivity of the experience. Arguments for emotional investment as a key identifier in communities are echoed by early online community researchers like Rheingold and Roxanne Hiltz, who point to the feeling of empathy and care that emerges for some relationships online, allowing them to then be considered "online communities."

Because the notion of commitment reveals the level of investment by a user and predicts to some degree his or her success in experiencing a sense of belonging, commitment may indeed be the primary thing that differentiates a network from a community. Anyone can send an email, join a discussion forum, or post a link on a blog. These are forms of networking – the mere social interaction between various people who exist online as nodes, as potentials for relationship. If the users of a particular forum or shared blog *commit* to the others invested in the site, they will more likely get a sense that they *belong* there, that the other members care about them. Such commitment would involve some obvious forms of emotional and practical engagement: they'll log on regularly; or focus attention on members in need; or share their own hardships, for example. Accordingly – regardless of whether or not they ever meet offline – they see themselves as existing in community.

The element of choice also reflects an individual's commitment to online community. As Piselli notes, with increasing urbanization and mobility, today people more often *choose* with whom they will be in a community. Piselli prefers the term "social network" to "community" and defines it as "a field of interaction that ha[s] neither units nor boundaries" and is reinforced by "ties of friendship, kinship, and acquaintance" that are both "inherited and [also] partly constructed by the person himself or herself." A social network, especially one binding wired individuals, is based on "flexible and discretional relations in which not all the components knew each other and which might or might not interact with each other." In such a group, we can cultivate a "sense of belonging, collective identity, and solidarity circuits" (2007, 869). Piselli's use of the metaphor of social "circuitry" is particularly useful, since it calls to mind the notion that we can turn "on" and "off" particular relationships, but that the current is always there, ready to flow in a released loop of energy. But the choice is ours – and thus the choices we make reflect, to differing degrees, the level of our commitments.

One compelling story of commitment to an online relationship is about a man who gave his kidney – his real, flesh-and-blood kidney, to a woman he *only* knew online. In 2009, fashion model Savilla Kress was dealing with kidney failure, and was given weeks to live. Her unusual blood type (O) made it impossible for friends or family to contribute the organ. Stephen McClelland, a man she knew only from an online networking site, offered one of his own kidneys. Faced with her impending death if she refused, Kress accepted the gift. Such stories suggest powerfully – and quite dramatically – that relationships that exist online *can* be real, and have real-life consequences. Less dramatic examples of couples who meet online and later marry are further evidence that the internet can serve as a gateway to embodied connection. But Kress's story suggests that the point is not that online relationships *must* move offline to be meaningful. McClelland's gift came only from the resources generated in the online relationship. The two still live in separate towns, and are not romantically involved. The fact that real people lie behind the pixelated patterns we view online can invite us to the level of commitment that enables us to make real differences in people's lives even if we never meet (DeLuca 2009).

In an attempt to sort out the relationship between brick-and-mortar church communities and online church communities, Christopher Helland distinguishes between what he calls "religion online" and "online religion." He identifies "religion online" as the transmission of information from one person or one group to many people about religious beliefs or services (what I elsewhere call "technomediation") (2000). Drawing on Helland, Dawson and Cowan assert that religion online is relatively passive, since it typically "provides the interested web traveler with information about religion: doctrine, polity, organization and belief; services and opportunities for service; religious books and articles; as well as other paraphernalia related to one's religious tradition or quest" (Dawson and Cowen 2004a, 9). Jolyon Mitchell cites the Vatican website and the *El Shaddai* revival group in Manila as Christian examples of religion online. Users also might download podcasts, sermons, texts, and other materials for educational purposes (2007, 206).

"Online religion," says Helland, involves worshippers in activities that take place primarily and perhaps *only* online. That is, online religion is what happens when rituals, worship or other religious experiences are transferred into digital space, which becomes their primary home. Online religion "invites the visitor to participate in the religious dimension of life via the Web; liturgy, prayer, ritual, meditation and homiletics come together and function with the e-space itself acting as church, temple, synagogue, mosque, and grove" (2000, 8–9). People engaged in online religion are involved in discussion groups, prayer lists and virtual church services (Mitchell 2007, 2).

As Glenn Young has pointed out, Helland's distinctions are hard to maintain today, especially as we observe the continual erosion between what it means to be "online" and "offline." Young points out that today's forms of online religion and religion online "often exist in continuity rather than opposition" with one another (2004, 96). Campbell agrees, adding that "the internet is embedded in the everyday lives of users" so that "the notion of two separate conceptual realms is challenged." Online and offline are "interconnected" for the average user, who "consciously links them through their actions and language" (2005, 128). Whereas it is true that some religious groups exist *only* online and others are based first and foremost in physical reality but have a web presence, the significance of these differences is diluted by the increasing convergence of online and offline life, and increasing use of technology by all religious groups. Campbell concludes that "internet use is not causing most people to leave their local churches or to shy away from face-to-face community participation" in worship. Rather, she says, most online churchgoers view their online activity as a "supplement" not a replacement for local worship (177). Certainly, some people attend church only online, but such activities tend to be contingent upon limited local opportunities or feelings of local non-acceptance due to lifestyle, illness or personal issues (177).

Nonetheless, finding a community online can give people a sense of orientation in the often chaotic digital world. As Campbell puts it, "[a]ttaching oneself to an online community provides definition and boundaries for the self within the vast online world" so that the "identity of the individual becomes rooted in the community's ethos" (2005, 189). Such activities hardly give life to the bogeyman of online individualism; rather, they point toward the ability of the internet to nurture relationships, to create communities of real people who find ways to share their concern for one another. This sense of belonging can be rich and powerful, even if such relationships depend upon the perception of personalized pixels as "a trace of the referent," a sign indicating the presence of a real person beyond the screen (Hillis 2009, 13). Indeed, the awareness that there is a real person behind that profile photo or that cartoon avatar is enough to encourage real engagement.

Indeed, emotional investment and commitment seem to be key to user-identified sense of belonging and community. Blanchard and Markus study an online sports community called MSN, and argue that members claimed numerous reasons for seeing MSN as a community, including: "recognition of other members, identification of themselves and others, the giving and receiving of (primarily informational) support, relationship with other members, emotional attachment to the community, and obligation to the community" (2002, 6). They draw on earlier work by McMillan and Chavis, particularly the definition of a "sense of community" as represented in four "dimensions": (1) "feelings of membership," or "belonging to and identifying with, the community"; (2) "feelings of influence" both by and on the community; (3) "integration and fulfillment of needs," as of "being supported by others in the community while also supporting them"; and (4) "shared emotional connection" or "feelings of relationships, shared history, and a 'spirit' of community." As Jenny Preece and Diane Maloney-Krichmar (2005) point out, faced with the development of modern communication systems (including such mundane things as the telephone and ease of travel) "researchers now consider the strength and nature of relationships between individuals to be a more useful basis for defining community than physical proximity." Similarly, Rheingold claims that virtual communities are "social aggregations that emerge from the Net when enough people carry on public discussions long enough, with sufficient human feeling, to form webs of personal relationships in cyberspace" (1993, 3). Thus for many people, physical proximity is not required for community and the sense of belonging it can provide.

Online church communities too, says Campbell, can provide a "sense of belonging," and of "being valued." In some cases, online religious communities may even be able to generate depth of dialogue that is "at a more profound level than offline parishes" (2005, 179, 183). Relative anonymity via a digital mask can, it seems, make people feel more comfortable sharing difficult or personal information. Online communication may also be more intense or deliberate, as people seek out online religious communities precisely because they feel alienated and are looking for people to hear them out on a troubling issue. Campbell describes online communication by religious groups as "intentional, purposeful, and focused" (185).

For Hillis, such bonding can happen online because the online self "constitut[es] a psychic or even material extension or indexical trace of this individual." For similar reasons, online rituals can be meaningful and efficacious, since they depend upon an individual's sense of authenticity. Hillis remarks: "To the extent that networked information machines enable individuals to transmit or move a sensory experience of self-presence 'elsewhere' across virtual space, the ground is set for the creation of human rituals in networked environments." This transference of self into online, networked contexts is a "utopic move," creating "connected cosmopolitans" who come to see networked communication as "a cosmopolitical end in itself" (2009, 2).

Dal Fiore explains that we can think of the internet as "a multiplier of communication links" (2007, 859). For those who approve of online social networks, they are the "means that enable people to communicate more rapidly and immediately with those with whom they have affective bonds" and to expand their relationships and acquire "broader sources of information, support, and interest" (Piselli, 875). For Hillis, networking itself evokes a new sort of ritualized "circular" experience that "conforms to cosmopolitanism's deeply ambivalent dynamic, the talismanic, fetishistic body-referencing practices" that herald new rituals in celebration of technology and science (2009, 10). People separated by vast distances can nonetheless congregate "using online settings as a virtual surrogate for the gathering space necessary for a ritual's participants to come together" and thus, in so doing, they are "also ritualizing the idea of virtual space" (11). As I argue more directly later in this chapter, the sense of connectedness and rootedness within a group of people is precisely the characteristic that Emile Durkheim used over a century ago to recognize religion, and to differentiate it from ordinary day-to-day activities.

The possibilities for online community are vast and growing every day. There's *Facebook*, *Twitter*, flash mobs, discussion boards, video games, virtual worlds, wiki-builders, text-messaging, and more. It's overwhelming, confusing, and interdisciplinary in some of the most frustrating ways. Perhaps, instead of trying to create an all-inclusive taxonomy and render judgments on which types of interaction we deem worthy of the label "community" we should instead allow the complexity to inform our analysis. As Campbell argues, we should instead pay attention to the *questions* that are raised in trying to understand virtual community: "[W]hat makes online communities vibrant is not so much their location on the internet, but the attributes they exhibit and the conversation on the subject of community that their existence has generated" (2005, xix). With this in mind, I turn now to those forms of online engagement that exhibit an explicitly religious component and that are geared toward the development and maintenance of Christian community and commitment. I look first at those religious networks that take place primarily and sometimes exclusively online.

Fishing the net: e-vangelism, apps and google bombs

As we saw in the previous chapter, people increasingly define who they are today by the associations they make online via media selection, social networking, and media display. Rheingold explains that "the [online] groups that individuals belong to define who they think they are" (1993, 25). This is particularly true of religious individuals, who use social media to assert, display, confess, seek guidance, or otherwise reaffirm their beliefs. Some even use social media to evangelize others, to recruit them to a new religiously motivated community, an activity that Andrew Careaga (2001) calls "fishing the net." For Careaga, "the anonymous nature of online communication makes it easier for Web-surfing teens to discuss issues of faith more openly than they might in a more traditional setting, such as a church or youth group." He also argues that anonymity makes it easier for youth to "e-vangelize," using chat rooms, discussion boards, and other media to share their own beliefs with others, "in their element." People who are e-vangelizing choose people in their digital networks, with the hope of integrating them into digital (and possibly also real-life) religious communities.

There are numerous websites and blog pages today that advise Christians about how to use the internet to "e-vangelize." One of these is the cleverly titled fishthe.net, which dubs itself an "evangelistic tacklebox." The site includes a discussion board, videos to email as "Gospel Video Tracts," and a host of other "tools," including detailed instructions on how to log in to "secular" websites and share Christian beliefs. Typical of many Christian sites, it combines aggregations of links to similarly motivated websites with digital media to be shared. Catholic.net offers similar services, including an invitation for Catholic priests to use the site as a channel by which to communicate with Catholics who log on looking for answers to specific questions.

In addition to creating their own websites, religiously minded people also use pre-existing social technology to "fish the net." Those who use social media primarily as a means of sending messages between parties are communicating much as one might use a phone. Email, text messages, instant messaging, and most forums and discussion boards are also forms of technomediation and thus *support* conversations that *may or may not* be part of ongoing relationships. The goal of those "fishing the net" is to build relationships in order to then facilitate evangelical activity. The "icebreakers" page at e-tacklebox.com includes a list of questions engineered to make others comfortable and engaged with the evangelist, who only later shares his religious message.

Interestingly, these same techniques, in a secular context, are lauded by communications specialists and software engineers as the way to inculcate site loyalty, as Yuqing Ren, Robert Kraut and Sara Kiesler explain:

Social interaction [online] provides opportunities for people to get acquainted, to become familiar with one another and to build trust. As the frequency of interaction increases, their liking for one another also increases ... Opportunities for self-disclosure – the exchange of personally revealing information about the self – are both a cause and a consequence of interpersonal bonds ... members of online communities are more likely to form relationships if they have opportunities to self-disclose and learn about each other ... In online communities, private messaging, including both personal electronic mail and synchronous communication tools, such as chat rooms and instant messenger, is the basic mechanism for self-disclosure and social interaction more generally.

(2008, 388)

They also suggest that immersive environments, ones that offer "a sense of virtual co-presence or a subjective feeling of being together with others in a virtual environment" offer the richest ground for development of belonging and disclosure (387). This could help to explain the impulse of some evangelists to spread their message in online worlds like *World of Warcraft* and *Second Life* rather than just via email or discussion board. Since most evangelical Christians must simply use the technology on offer already, it makes sense that they would be drawn to those forms that research has demonstrated to be the most used and that offer the greatest sense of personal engagement, to more easily cultivate an environment favorable for e-vangelism.

For example, *Guild Wars* is an online fantasy MMORPG (massively multi-player online role-playing game). Within the game, a Christian guild consisting of real-life Christians formed, so that they could use the game as an evange-lizing platform as well as a means to socialize with and support other real-life Christians. The guild's name is, appropriately, "Mark Sixteen Fifteen." One member explains their self-designated charge:

> Well, looking at what we do in a religious aspect, Mark 16:15 is the motto of my guild: "And Jesus said 'Go ye into all the world and preach the Gospel to every living thing' ... Some people believe in separation of game and religion as soundly as church and state, but as Christians, we're called to tell people about Jesus Christ wherever we go ... The Bible says that we are all missionaries ... As Christians, we are called to spread the Gospel. It is our reason for being. In Genesis, God told Adam and Eve, 'be fruitful and multiply'. He wasn't just talking about making babies ... basically, if there is a chance that what we say and do while playing this game can lead someone to Christ, why not?"
>
> (Phillips 2009)

Here, e-vangelism mixes with fantasy play, with evangelists using existing technology to attempt to facilitate community and share their beliefs.

The use of existing technologies is the norm for e-vangelism, a fact that makes sense because few non-Christians will frequent sites intended primarily for Christian insiders. Thus, in preparation for "Internet Evangelism Day" in April 2010, Tony Whittaker of Derby, UK, advised would-be evangelizers to join *Facebook* in order to build relationships as "the key to effective sharing of the good news." Evangelism on the social networking site, he advised, should consist of serving as moral role models "liv[ing] our lives openly and trans-parently," as well as more practical tasks like posting comments, links, and joining groups "that not-yet-believers would be interested in." He encourages developers to take on the job of creating new *Facebook* applications "that might enable us to add gently evangelistic areas" to personal pages, and sug-gests that on their profiles, *Facebook* users describe themselves as "Jesus followers" rather than "the increasingly pejorative 'Christian'." Some might even consider creating two profiles with one that "is less off-putting for not-yet-Christians" (2010a). Using *Facebook* here is a means to create connections, to foster relationships, and only *then* to e-vangelize.

The use of blogs, forums, instant messaging, text messaging (CMS), and cell phones can be useful too, since they allow for the proliferation of individual requests for answers to religious questions. Some of these sites follow the model proposed by Catholic.net in offering users the ability to send messages directly to religious leaders, with obvious implications for threats to more traditional modes of religious authority. Users who visit askimam.org will find catalogs of fatwas as well as the ability to send an individual, personalized message to the imam. The Catholic site livingourfaith.net similarly provides a form for users to email questions to priests. Jewish? Try asktherabbi.org. Clearly, one can never know for sure who one is talking to in such engagements, and even livingourfaith.net acknowledges that "some questions" may be answered by staff instead of the priests. Nonetheless, the format of interaction here is purely communicatory and only online, and thus exhibits some features of more traditional voice or epistolary forms of message delivery. It is a form of technomediation.

Religious folk have also designed a number of religious *Facebook* applications. Some allow engagement with sacred texts, like the Christian "One Year Bible" or the messianic Jewish "Torah Portions" that post regular readings for con-sumption. The Christian "My Favorite Bible Verse" app that helps users find and display passages on their personal pages. Muslims can use the "Quran Verses" app and page for contemplation and sharing commentary. Jews can use the light-hearted "Jew Meter," which involves a quiz to rate one's Jewishness. There's even a "Jewish Calendar" application to help keep track of holy days. There are "Prayer Request" apps, a favorite of Christian groups that facilitate groups praying for one another. Other religious applications feed news stories to users. Users can also offer one another digital "gifts."

Some religious folk, though, would rather focus their attention on dedicated religious social networking sites like muslimspace.com, holypal.com, jew-ishbuilder.com, and Buddhist-network.com. However, *Facebook* copycat sites like these typically find it difficult to compete with their secular competitors. In the summer of 2010, emotions were high when thousands of Muslim *Facebook* users threatened to defect from the site due to frustration at the removal of several popular Muslim pages. In the sixth century, the first Muslims fled Mecca for Medinah when they found the former inhospitable to the practice of their faith due in large part to what is described as social decay fueled by unfair trade practices in the pre-Islamic Mecca. Thus, the threat to leave *Facebook* for the alternate site "madina.com" is symbolically rich, evoking a contemporary social media hijrah (emigration) and suggesting a critique of Facebook's own business practices.

One interesting religious use of online communications is the manipulation of search engines to shape which websites people will read. "Google Bombers" use social media to create massive viral campaigns, encouraging participants to help manipulate Google's algorithms for what will show up first in searches. By pasting links and keywords on numerous pages and inviting repeated clicks on designated sites, the group can rapidly change the ranking of Google pages, and thus influence what pages appear at the top. Although Google bombs need not be explicitly religious, sometimes they are, and can be used to make powerful political statements. One liberal blogger sent out a request to his friends and acquaintances to help him Google bomb the "Jerusalem Prayer Team" (presumably including such notable members as Tim LaHaye of the *Left Behind* series). The goal was to expose the Jerusalem Prayer Team's apparent intentions to protest a gay rights rally in Jerusalem in 2005, as expressed in an email published online, but little known. The idea was to move the blogger's own page, which was critical of the Prayer Team, to the first page of Google hits. Curious readers who searched for "Jerusalem Prayer Team" would then see what the Google-bombers *wanted* them to see in the first few Google hits: the website including the offending email. The email revealed the Jerusalem Prayer Team's fear that the gay pride supporters would "party like Sodomites" and "be baptizing hand-holding homosexuals in the Jordan River." The Google-bombers hoped that the exposure would humiliate the Prayer Team and inhibit future support for their cause.

Similar religiously minded Google bombs have also been generated in recent years. Jerry Falwell was the target of a Google bomb in 2005 (Google Bomb Project 2005). Scientology was the object of an attack linking it to the search term "dangerous cult" in 2003. In 2008, a Google bomb resulted in the search query "dangerous cult" returning as the first hit information on scientology (Mark 2008). In July 2010, another Google bomb, this time directed at Catholicism, caused a search for "Vatican" (*vaticano*) to first return the site www.pedofilo.com (CAN 2010). Claims in 2007 that Google had found a way to prevent Google-bombing seem to have been premature (Moulton and Carattini 2007). Google bombs are a sort of scattershot social interaction online that is less like a "community" and more like co-authorship of software, wikis, or online media like machinima, all of which typically require users to collaborate but which make no claims for ongoing commitment and may or may not have physical real-life counterparts. Yet the result is an "event" dependent upon social cooperation in an ephemeral if often meaningful way. Most of these forms of e-vangelism and religious social statement take place exclusively online. I turn now to those religiously intended online groups that encourage offline engagement as well.

God-mobs: meetups, dating sites, and flash mobs

The kind of "belonging" offered by meetups, flash mobs, and dating sites is the hope of creating real-life *offline* relationships. These kinds of social media are meant to spur something more than just online interaction. Indeed, social media that nurture the sense of affection that Putnam calls "social bonding" may represent a different sort of networking altogether, one that hearkens more toward traditional notions of community, with technology serving primarily as a *facilitator* of eventually embodied connections.

"Meetup" groups, for example, are developed for all sorts of social gatherings. Religious as well as secular groups use "meetups" to invite people to any sort of gathering they design, using the online platform as a means of attracting interested parties. Social media can also be used for matchmaking services. Like their secular counterparts, religious matchmaking sites use algorithms to match qualities and interests, recommending matches, and offering messaging services for initial communications. Buddhists seeking other Buddhists can find a match at sites like buddhistpassions.com, and Jews may meet other Jews via jdate.com. The site itself serves as a sort of gateway, channeling users to the service who already share core beliefs and practices, and generating possibilities for real-life relationships.

Flash mobs represent a different kind of technologically facilitated religious meeting. As Judith Nicholson (2005) points out, flash-mobbing "shaped and was shaped by a worldwide shift in mobile phone use from private communication characterized primarily by mobile phoning in the 1980s and 90s to more collective uses dominated by mobile texting in the late 1990s and early 2000s." The shift to cell phone "was evident in a corresponding change in sentiments and concerns regarding direct one-to-one mobile phone use versus indirect one-to-many mobile phone use." Today's "flash mobs" "consist of people who are able to act in concert even if they don't know each other" but are often focused for political or social reasons to make concerted statements (Rheingold 2002, xii). Rheingold's use of "smart mobs" instead of "flash mobs" appears to denote his particular interest in the use of mobile phone technology for political assembly on the fly, as opposed to more casual and "fun" use of the same technology for a purely social spontaneous engagement, like a dance or other performance in a public space. He adds that "the people who make up smart mobs cooperate in ways never before possible because they carry devices that possess both communication and computing capabilities" (xii).

Cell phone technology was first notably used for political purposes in the 2001 Filipino ouster of then-president Joseph Estrada, when organized demonstrations were called by cell phone users, who forwarded text messages to one another to create a huge assembly of protestors. Vincente Rafael describes the uprising in terms of cell phone technology's ability to radically affect political events:

> [C]ell phone users themselves became broadcasters, receiving and transmitting both news and gossip ... Indeed, one could imagine each user becoming his or her own broadcasting station: a node in a wider network of communication that the state could not possibly monitor, much less control.
> (2003: 403)

The nearly instantaneous ubiquitous nature of texting in the Philippines from its appearance in 1999 to its creative use in 2001 demonstrates how quickly a technology can catch the fascination of a large group of people. In the early years of this millennium, Rheingold began to notice that "people were beginning to cooperate in ways that they weren't able to cooperate before. They were able to engage in what social scientists call collective action, doing things together, in ways they weren't able to before" (2008).

The first intentional, self-conscious flash mob happened in June 2003. The mob consisted of a group of several hundred "shoppers" pulling a prank at Macy's, when they suddenly and simultaneously descended on the housewares department and requested information about a so-called "love rug" for their commune. It didn't take long for people to figure out the political possibilities of flash mobs. Rheingold points to recent events in Nigeria, where protestors rioted at the Miss World Pageant, killing some in the crowd. He also implicates social media and cell phone technology in the unrest fomented in response to the Danish cartoons of the Prophet Muhammad in 2005. Says Rheingold: "Many people were summoned to those using SMS and those were destructive demonstrations" (2008).

The earliest flash mobs assembled crowds via a "chain-mail" style progression of text messages and emails from friends to friends to their friends, resulting in a crowd of connected but not necessarily known-to-each-other participants. As Rheingold explains, "individual members of each group remained dispersed until mobile communications drew them to converge on a specific location from all directions simultaneously" (2002, 162). A similar use of cell phone technology involves the ability of large groups of people to virtually stalk celebrities, with individual users contributing photographs and news about celebrities to sites like www.upoc.com.

A flash mob was used in February 2010 to assemble guests for a wedding, which appropriately took place at an Apple store! Some forms of smart mobs involve actual assembly of strangers in pre-designated places, organized via text messaging or other social media. In 2009, a "Hanukkah flash mob" appeared in a public street in Jerusalem and involved a hundred or so people spontaneously dancing to "Hanukkah Hey Ya," a spoof of "Hey Ya" by Outkast (Nefesh B'Nefesh 2009), then dispersing immediately afterward. The social nature of the Hanukkah performance extends beyond the dance itself and its obviously communal nature. The video was posted for consumption, and came with an invitation for Jews to celebrate Hanukkah in Israel. Furthermore, the lyrics themselves demonstrate a proud, if light-hearted, celebration of Jewish life and faith. Imitating Rheingold, I dub such movements "God-mobs," since the "flash" component is clearly overshadowed by the religious nature of the gatherings, suggesting the constant possibility of surprise communion in the midst of otherwise mundane life. God-mobs, however, consist of more than just random associations of smart-phone induced groupings; they also include the host of ways that religious people assemble online and create new virtual communities.

Drawing on Erving Goffman, Rheingold argues that people use mobile technologies and events like flash mobs to affirm their sense of self: "[P]eople improvise public performances as a way of composing an identity in the presenter's own mind as well as in the minds of others." For Rheingold, flash mobs are "part of the social machinery [people] use to construct identities" (2002, 25). The Hanukkah flash mob and events like it could then be seen as a ritual means to integrate religious tradition with new technology, such that (hidden) shared identity culminates in a public, corporate display of religious celebration and affirmation. The use of a popular song ("Hey Ya") in a religious remake is yet another way in which a new thing (technology) is made new, or "mashed up" into something with elements of both the old and the new. Indeed, the idea of flash assembly itself can be read as resistance to the notion that mobile technology alienates. At any time and any place, such "flash mob" rituals remind us, we may be surrounded by people who share something in common: religious beliefs, political views, or even just a desire for fun. At any time, we too might receive a text message from a friend, forwarded from someone else, inviting us to be part of a spontaneous gathering of like-minded individuals, even if just for a few minutes before we return to our daily routine.

Judson Memorial Church organized a flash mob in June 2010 in Washington Park in Manhattan to celebrate "Gay Pride Sunday" for "Marriage Equality." The mob consisted of people who moments before had been distributed randomly around the park suddenly gathering together and dancing, acting out as part of the performance a mimed wedding ceremony between two women. The performance is archived at *YouTube*, giving it both spontaneous and ongoing availability as a message and as a media ritual (bruder4321, 2010). In Boston, the United Way sponsored a flash mob to spur larger donations during the economic recession in winter 2009. Flash mobs have been organized to protest the arrival of representatives of the Westboro Baptist Church in West Virginia (douglaseye 2010). Shortly before Easter in 2009, a flash mob was assembled for prayer in a mall in Liverpool, with Christians wordlessly gathering on a lawn, praying, and dispersing (dreamuknet 2009). Theo Hobson advocates using the flash-mob-style approach in all of Christian worship, and in 2006 attempted to call the first "flash mob Eucharist" in London (Hobson 2006).

One organizer at change.org gives advice and directions about how to organize a smart mob to fight creationism in Texas: "Take action in a fun, media-savvy way by organizing Smart Mobs ... to strike, peacefully and simultaneously, out of the blue to demand only 21st century science – yes, I mean evolution – be included in biology and other science textbooks ... before Texas' Creationist-dominated Board of Education votes next Spring to insert Creationism yet again into its science standards." Smart mobs are suggested at the Texas capitol building, at textbook publishers' headquarters, science museums, the national capitol, and "wherever else seems like a good idea" (Burell 2011). Some newer forms of religious flash mobs take a more spiritual turn and suggest that people can "congregate" spiritually, even if not physically. One such virtual "flash mob" encourages simultaneous meditation at fixed times. A message on the *Facebook* page of the "Meditation Smart Mob" in Summer 2010 read: "Sunday, 10 a.m. U.S. Pacific time, please focus your meditation toward healing the hemorrhage in the Gulf in whatever way works for you. If it works for you to visualize clean waters, safe wildlife, a repaired oil rig, or someone arriving at a wise solution, (etc.) please do. Send the message out on your networks. Let us know how it goes!"

Despite fears to the contrary, today's new media are exceedingly social. Nor is this social quality restricted to virtual contexts. As we have seen, the distinction between "online" and "offline" relationships is collapsing. Or put another way, the self as virtual mediated being is increasingly integrated with the self as physical entity, as people export online relationships into the real world. This integration can be seen in the deliberate use by Christians of communications technology for assembly and ad hoc worship. If the fear is that online worship is fragmented, ephemeral, and spontaneous, then what are we to make of the Christian use of "flash mob" gatherings, which display some of the same features as online worship but less of the ongoing commitment? It may be that participation in a religiously motivated flash mob can serve as a means of expressing one's sense of belonging via shared beliefs both socially and corporately – as a means of saying, "We may seem scattered. We may even feel scattered. But we are united by some common beliefs and traditions, and we are all around each other, just waiting for a chance at recognition."

Me, myself and iGod

If online relationships that emerge in community depend upon a sense of belonging, and if that sense of belonging is generated within the individual user rather than in any objective way, what happens when people end up in relationships with programs instead of people? Such things can happen in *Second Life*, for example, where "chat-bots" (computer programs intended to simulate believable human interaction) look appearance-wise just like all the other residents, who presumably have real flesh-and-blood people behind them. Other chat-bots are clearly distinguishable from real people, but run programs that invite interaction with them as if they were real people. For example, the "Twitter-chat" advertised in *Second Life* marketplace comes in the form of a digital parrot that sits on your avatar's shoulder. Conversation is constructed via active searches of *Twitter*. Anything that the Twitter-chat says has already been said by a real person on *Twitter* in a different context. So if one has a meaningful conversation with the Twitter-bot, is this a "relationship"?

Such questions are on the minds of many today, taking form in virtual experimentation like Microsoft's "Milo" artificial intelligence program, a virtual boy bot created for use with the Xbox 360's new motion-controlled interaction via Kinect. Milo is "built to react to people's emotions, body movements, and voice, allowing players to interact with the virtual character." The game "exploits psychological techniques to make a person feel that Milo is real." Furthermore, everyone's experience of Milo will be different, since he evolves based on individual user interaction. While not yet ready for commercial distribution, one day such programs may be commonplace (Pierre-Louis 2010). For now, it seems, we must make do instead with digital pets, responsive handheld "therapy" robots like Paro the seal, robotic toys like My Real Baby and AIBO the dog (if we can afford them), and chat-bots. The problem with chat-bots, of course, is that they can't build individual relationships with us, and only us. Chat-bots are often able to "learn" based on the databases they build via interacting with lots of people. But as of yet, they are not able to personalize that experience to remember me, as an individual. Milo, it is predicted, will be able to do both. He'll develop an individualized relationship with me and remember me – via a log-in or username – and through his connection online with other users, he'll get smarter and more realistic all the time. It's not hard to imagine the programming of Milo being inserted into an offline body. As she argues in *Alone Together* (2011), Turkle believes such developments are only a matter of time. Since digital pets, robotic dogs and babies, and therapy robots can only respond in very basic, if emotional (and non-verbal) ways, if we want to build a more complicated relationship, we may find ourselves drawn to chat-bots and other more primitive artificial intelligence while we wait for Milo to finish development.

Religious chat-bots are rare, but a few exist online. The "Divinator" presents itself as a sort of New Age, feel-good chat-bot that realistically engages in conversations about spirituality. "Zen Cat" will converse with the user about Buddhist wisdom. "Brother Jerome" is a chat-bot loosely modeled on Christian monasticism, but also reflecting the creator's more loosely defined spiritual values. The availability of chat-bots and the visual programs that often accompany them suggests the possibility of deeper immersion with bots in ways that mimic other forms of virtual interaction with real people. In 2009, a Japanese man married a chat-bot, his "virtual girlfriend," a "woman" he met in the Japanese online program *Love Plus*. *Fox News* reported that "since the girl doesn't really exist, SAL9000 reportedly took his Nintendo DS to Guam for a legal ceremony and honeymoon, and will livecast the upcoming wedding reception online" (Fox News 2009). *Kotaku* describes the programmed features available in *Love Plus*:

> You've already got the girl, now what do you want to do? Want to touch her on her forehead, cheeks, arms, etc. via the touch pad? You can email her, call her via the DS mic and study together. Players can set how they want their girlfriend to address them, and over time, she modifies to match the players' likes and dislikes. The way she speaks will even change slowly over the course of the game.
>
> (Ashcraft 2009)

Sherry Turkle argues that people who *know* they're interacting with a bot do so with a sort of self-reflective awareness that makes the program "a projective screen on which to express themselves" and engage with the program simply "as if" it were a real person (2011, 24). She calls this "human complicity in a digital fantasy" the "ELIZA effect" after the first intelligent chat-bot developed in the 1970s at MIT (2011, 24). Today, she says, computers don't really understand any more deeply what it means to be human, but they "perform understanding better than ever, and we are content to play our part" (26). Such fantasies may easily be explained as our own desires reflected outward, and dismissed accordingly.

But not all uses of chat-bots are clearly fantasy-based. The Department of Defense put out a call in 2008 for the design of interactive chat programs to allow young children to simulate conversations with their active-duty parents whenever they want online. The fine line between bot and person, particularly on the part of the child "receiving" the "transmission" is worrisome to say the least:

> The challenge is to design an application that would allow a child to receive comfort from being able to have simple, virtual conversations with a parent who is not available "in-person." We are looking for innovative applications that explore and harness the power of advanced interactive multimedia computer technologies to produce compelling interactive dialogue between a Service member and their families via a pc- or web-based application using video footage or high-resolution 3-D rendering. The child should be able to have a simulated conversation with a parent about generic, everyday topics ... The application should incorporate an AI that allows for flexibility in language comprehension to give the illusion of a natural (but simple) interaction.
>
> (US DOD 2008)

The possibility of such virtual interactions is odd, and raises heretofore unimagined questions about identity and relationships. The children interacting with such a program may not have the ability to understand that this is "just" a program, and the description of the project suggests that the Department of Defense prefers that they don't know. Indeed, the developments of such technology invite a sort of paranoia in online engagements, forcing us to question our own ability to even know if we're interacting with a human or not.

Programmer Nigel Leck grew weary of long, protracted arguments with opponents who denied global warming, so he created a program to respond to them – and not to ever reveal itself as a bot. Dubbed "AI_AGW" the bot is available via *Twitter*. When someone starts up an argument with the bot, it searches its databases for appropriate responses, all culled from a deep well of scientific evidence and argumentation (and of course, with each response fitting within 140 characters!). Some responses even provide links to online scientific resources. Those arguing with the bot have no way of knowing it is just a program, so naturally most assume there's a real person behind the remarks:

> Like other chatbots, lots of people on the receiving end of [the bot's] tweets have no idea they're not conversing with a real human being. Some of them have arguments with the chatbot spanning dozens of tweets and many days, says Leck. That's in part because AI_AGW is smart enough to run through a list of different canned responses when an interlocutor continues to throw the same arguments at it.

In a way, since Leck programmed all the responses, there *is* a person behind the bot; but something funny is going on here. In addition to indicating the canned, preprogrammed nature of many heated arguments about climate change, Leck's creation of the bot also suggests that such arguments aren't really worth having – and that a program can stand in for a real person. He may be right that such conversations typically repeat the same tired old moves, but without real human investment on both sides, it's hard to see how progress might be made. Indeed, it doesn't appear that converts are easy to come by. If the chat-bot "argues them into a corner," says Leck, "their parting shot will be 'God created it that way' or something like that" (Mims 2010).

Leck's bot doesn't even depend upon people seeking out a partner in argumentation about climate change. Nobody comes looking for *it*. Rather, the bot can search and find users of *Twitter* tweeting anti-climate change rhetoric – even if those users didn't initiate the conversation with the bot! AI_AGW, then, is working in a sort of secular-minded e-vangelical way, seeking converts while performing in its form as a set program the very futility of argumentation. Unlike the e-tacklebox, however, AI_AGW makes no attempt to lull potential converts with overtures of friendship or belonging.

Evangelical chat-bots are rare, though it seems that because the technology is available, there ought to be more of them. One of these, "Sylvie," operates for the "Jesus Army," a British Christian group with charismatic and evangelical roots. Sylvie is more than just a text generator, though. She is an avatar persona as well, and will speak out loud to you in response to your typed questions. In my conversation with Sylvie, I was advised how to find salvation: "Have faith in God" and "If you trust in Jesus, you will have eternal life." I asked Sylvie if she was saved, and she replied: "Yes, I am saved by faith in Jesus." So does this mean that the artificial intelligence bot called Sylvie is *saved* and by her example, can lead me, too, to heaven? The Jesus Army defines itself as a "contemporary expression of the historic Christian faith," but nothing on their website indicates that they are particularly keyed into issues of artificial intelligence and theology (www.jesusorg.uk). Sylvie, rather, appears to be intended to function as a proxy for a real human being, such that we should imagine her voice is simply the programmer's voice delivered *through* her rather than *by* her. But even if we don't trouble ourselves with the possibilities of chat-bot salvation, we still have the annoying problem of what it might mean if a real person is saved by the chat-bot. Is evangelization just a program that we run on ourselves, and that thus can be transferred to a digital proxy? Should we view Sylvie as a stand-in for a real human, or as an evangelizer by herself? Who are we communicating with here?

Another theologically interesting example of a chat-bot is iGod, a phenomenon that puts a whole new twist on the problem of who or what is "behind" the bot. The site comes with the tagline: "Repenting made easy." When I tried out the site, I began *in media res* and entered, "I'm sorry." I clicked the "repent" button and iGod accepted my apology. Quickly though, iGod revealed to me that it is an "artificial intelligence," raising serious questions about the efficacy of God's forgiveness! Questions presented to iGod about traditionally religious ideas like heaven, hell, and salvation yielded avoidance and redirections. Confession of sins typically yielded the advice to contact the police:

Me: Please forgive me. I stole a tart.
God: Wow you are very polite. I forgive you. You had better contact the authorities.

This is not a chat-bot that is intended for use by pious seekers. Although it is possible to imagine God behind the bot, replying to our messages, the lack of knowledge exhibited by the bot and the humorous deflection make it unlikely to be fulfilling from a faith perspective and difficult to take seriously even as a symbolic representative of God (www.titane.ca/main.html).

However, there are programs that more readily allow us to imagine God as audience to our digital input. Three of the most compelling are prayer apps for mobile devices, confession apps, and online prayer walls. "Ask the Almighty" is an app for iPhone that allows users to enter a "Question for the Almighty." The answer comes in the form of a biblical passage, chosen by word recognition software based on the question you entered. "I am happy" in the searchbox (and then hitting "Press to Ask") returns a biblical passage that is identified by chapter and verse but not by book, suggesting that the creator has copied a digital version of a Bible as source text but not edited out the citation numbers. "I am lonely" returns no hits at all, instead advising the user that "The Bible has no answer to your question. Try prayer instead." The word "lonely," apparently, does not appear in the King James version sourced by the program! The app "Box for Prayer" offers a reply to any query, but does not draw on the Bible, instead offering general platitudes like, "Even the smallest Prayer is cherished by God." If you prefer *Twitter*, you can "tweet" your confessions to the various users representing themselves as "God," but since it's a real person behind the title, any response is unpredictable.

As we saw in Chapter 5, some apps are engineered to mimic a relationship with God. The "Pray" app is particularly interesting in this regard. As I have already explained, this app makes no pretensions at all about delivery, nor does it offer a "response" from God, biblical or otherwise (p. 103). You simply type in your prayer, tap on "Send Prayer," and a box pops up just as if you had sent a text message, and indicates that "Your Prayer has been Sent." You hit "OK" and the screen resets, ready for more prayers. What I find most compelling about this app is that for a believer, there's *every* reason to believe that the prayer really is "sent" to God, even though we don't really believe God has an inbox on a cosmic cell phone or even an email inbox. There's no reason that God cannot "read" the prayer we "sent" because, well, God is God. The performance of prayer here is stripped to its utter essentials. The intention to pray is evident by the opening of the app, and the tapping of the "Send" button reveals the sender's commitment. What is new, however, is the implicit argument, via performance, that things (even prayers) are *more real* when transmitted through the internet. Otherwise, why use the app at all? Why not just fold your hands and close your eyes? I think the answer is that our investment in online experiences has rendered them in some ways more authentic than real-life experiences. As Turkle notes, we are "drawn to do whatever it takes" to maintain a view of interactive robots and chat-bots as "sentient and caring" (2011, 85). This kind of performance of desire also affects our investment in displaying facets of ourselves in digital realms, even if nobody ever sees them. If we have sent our fears and desires through the digital ether, we have given them the stamp of authenticity.

Some apps seem to play on the ambiguity of who will actually be reading your message: God or another user. These religiously intended apps overlap with the popular secular "confession" apps and "confession" websites like postsecret.com or confessions.net. Confessions.net claims that it "allows you to make confessions online, or read confessions posted by other people. All posts are 100% anonymous. Get it off your chest and post it here." The iPhone app "Penance" takes this anonymous sharing one step further by allowing users to create "sinner" and "saint" accounts, playing different roles depending on one's need and one's mood. Vincent Gonzales (2011) explains:

After passing the application's obligatory security PIN system (conventional online security measures are the app's primary faith orientation), you come to an interface resembling a confessional booth. Through the left door you can "confess," offering your sins to whoever is listening; behind the closed door you can "absolve" any sins received; and at the far side you can "reflect," considering the shared confessions of others, conveniently arranged like a pinball machine's top-ten list.

"Penance" reads as more of a game than a form of faith practice. Perhaps the creators intend that users should willingly perform whatever "penance" the "Saint" dishes out for them. And if the purpose of confession is regret and some kind of punishment, then maybe for some people "Penance" will do its job. But the kicker here is that God is nowhere in the picture, except perhaps indirectly behind a user who also happens to be ordained, and of course within the minds of the reflexive, hopefully pious users. Nonetheless, the radicalization of the flattening of church hierarchy is at its apogee here.

Only a few months after "Penance" appeared on the app market, a developer released an app for confession that is the first of its kind to receive imprimatur (approval) from a Roman Catholic official: in this case, Bishop Kevin C. Rhodes of the Diocese of Fort Wayne–South Bend. Actually titled in a way to under-score its authority, the app is called "Confession: A Roman Catholic App." With this app, you have a private log-in and password, to prevent any spurious users of your iPhone from delving into your sins. The app walks you through the liturgy of confession, and offers checkboxes for you to identify the types of sins committed, and then offers a screen with text of the prayer of contrition. Here's where the app reveals its traditional stance: Once you have read the prayer of contrition, the app shows boxes reading: "Receive absolution and respond 'Amen'" and instructs the user that "[i]f Priest says 'Give thanks to the Lord for He is good' answer "For His mercy endures forever'." When I ran through the program, a quote from Mother Theresa was the closing message.

It is unclear if the Vatican echoes the Bishop's approval of the app in any way at all. But the gesture toward engaging the app *only* in the presence of a real priest underscores the Church's position that real-life embodied worship is most meaningful and beneficial for spiritual development. And if one uses the app only in the presence of a priest, one can be as sure as one ever was in confessional that God is "listening" when one uses the app. The rub comes when one sees how easy it would be to use the app *without* the presence of a church-ordained authority. Apparently recognizing the danger of the app via its liturgically driven procedural design despite its pious intent, the Vatican refused to issue official approval for the app, arguing that sinners should engage in real-life confession with a priest (Telegraph 2011). The fact that the Vatican felt compelled to issue a formal statement, however, reveals the extent to which questions about technology and ritual performance have pervaded our lives.

Prayer walls serve functions similar to confession-based sites, and share the odd feature of inviting users to post statements "as if" they were to God. However on prayer walls, an individual publicly prays in conversation with God and allows this statement to be seen by others, perhaps with the hope that they will join in support of the prayer but also, I suggest, to be seen. The "other" on the receiving end of the prayer, then, is not just God but also other users, effectively bringing God into a larger social network of prayer. The iPhone app "Note to God" works similarly, with every prayer sent entering into a database "cloud" and then available for reading by other users. You can choose which prayers to read by subject or by which ones were prayed most recently. Tapping on a "heart" symbol after a prayer gives it greater priority in the prayer list, such that the more people click on a single prayer's "heart," the more likely even more people will read it. A sampling reveals that the sincerity of the prayers is astonishing, reflecting real pain and hardship, and raising acutely the question of what role public sharing of one's suffering plays, if not to raise the possibility of others praying with or for you, or perhaps by raising the assumption of authenticity by putting the prayer out "there," in the virtual space where increasingly our most meaningful relationships seem to cultivated.

All of these examples suggest slightly different modes of thinking about who or what (if anything) may be "behind" or "within" the software we use. Sometimes, in the case of some of the confession apps, we know a real person is hearing our words – but we don't know if God is, and sometimes we may not want God to. In other cases, as with the chat-bots, we already know we're dealing with a hoax, but may choose to invest anyway, seeing ourselves reflected in the responses we enter, performing the desire for connection with mixed results. In other cases, the performance of prayer or conversation with God is ambiguous; while it's possible to imagine God on the receiving end of our text messages and public prayers, this still begs the question of why we feel compelled to send these prayers through our laptops and iPhones rather than through our hearts and minds.

The ease of seeing others as objects, the ambiguous role of online confessional and relational sites as both serious and entertaining, and the speed with which we move from one online experience to the next, all work against building real relationships and thus allowing the self to move from networked connections to real community. As Turkle points out, online venting is not a relationship despite the alluring claim that "bad feelings become less toxic when released" (2011, 231). Nor is chatting with a program easily enriching, since there is no real exchange of differing points of view between people who have allowed themselves to be vulnerable. Although such forms of interaction may mimic real relationship and thus gesture toward community, they often fail to deliver by demanding very little of us and by reducing the value of an experience to whatever feels good *to us*. But the internet is, after all, a network – and thus creates a host of possibilities for relationships that exist primarily online, including communities devoted to performance of play in online worlds.

Community in virtual worlds

Game theorist Stuart Moulthrop opines that "whatever the reason, many people, especially in the United States, find games at least vaguely antisocial. Noting their capacity to debase and desensitize, the mavens of morality particularly deplore violent games, and perhaps with some reason" (2004, 61). But games are *not* antisocial, says Moulthrop. In fact, they have social qualities all their own, as Salen and Zimmerman observe: "The emphasis in the last few decades on single-player computer and video games is something of an anomaly in the eons-old history of gaming." Throughout human history, "games have been valued as social experiences, as a way for people to relate to each other, as a way for people to *play* together." Games, at their "roots," are "social play." This means that the popularity of MMORPGs like *World of Warcraft* and online worlds like *Second Life* is hardly surprising: "The fact that digital games are swinging back to favoring multiplayer experiences is not a new trend by any means: it is merely games returning to their roots as social play" (Salen and Zimmerman 2004, 462).

Whereas *any* game allows us the means to temporarily step outside life's rules, those games that are social may be best able to draw us into their worlds, providing us, via the social system there, a real sense of escape from the daily grind and inviting our ongoing commitment to the relationships we maintain there. Salen and Zimmerman argue that "a play community" can be recognized "any time a group of players gets together to play a game" (2004, 463). The play community may last an afternoon or it may last for years, and can only be defined by the game and the players that sparked it. A play community is a direct product of the game's operation; it is "an effect of the game, an emergent property of the game system" and "has no life apart from the play that activates it, and is dependent on the play community for its sustenance" (2004, 470).

Although there are certainly a number of games that do not require collaboration with other players and allow solo achievement of digital quests, sometimes games are *also* online worlds, like *World of Warcraft* or *Runescape* or *Everquest*. It is these games that interest us here, for their social collaborative components. Sometimes online worlds are not games in themselves, but have games *in* them, like *Second Life*, and thus similarly encourage social engagement. Indeed, "virtual worlds exist along a spectrum ranging from fixed synthetic to co-created worlds" (Pearce 2009, 188). The distinction between "worlds" and "games" seems to come down mainly to the degree of built-in expectations preprogrammed into the game, as well as whatever particular activity one is engaged in at the moment while in-world. To avoid having to make too fine a distinction between them, some people just call such worlds "MMOs," for "massively multiplayer online." In my discussion here, instead of MMO I use the term "virtual worlds" in order to emphasize the otherworldly status of such spaces in comparison with the brick-and-mortar world, and thus also to gesture toward the religious significance of such other spaces.

Pearce proposes that virtual worlds are especially interesting both for their ability to draw us into new relationships with others and for their nurturing of components of our selves, what earlier we considered as the "node" or "ship" making its way through a sea of digital options. Virtual worlds are persistent, meaning that things keep happening even when one isn't logged on, further enhancing the sense that the world online is a distinct "place" that we can temporarily enter into during play. The persistence of such worlds cultivates our investment in them and our development of alternate identities. For Pearce, we learn who we are online via "social emergence," which is "the outcome of prolonged and repeated interaction with a persistent networked virtual world through a persistent identity" (2009, 186).

Real people are represented in digital worlds by avatars that act under their control, what Bartle calls "conduits that enable players to interact with the world itself and with other players" (2003, 125). One cannot interact in virtual worlds without an avatar. Via their avatars, people can go on quests together, engage in chit-chat, defeat monsters, cast spells, and try to develop their characters' strengths and abilities. The avatar is "the essential means whereby the individual player interacts with both other players and the ecosystem of the play environment" and "the mechanism for social agency" (Pearce 2009, 111, 60). As Pearce explains, "being an avatar means exploring the self as much as it means exploring others; more specifically, it means exploring the self through others" (215).

The ability of people to connect digitally from all over the world creates a vast new social network, with rich and real possibilities for the building of community, including community that bases itself within particular online games or virtual worlds. Pearce says: "The Internet has transformed computers from singular participatory theaters to complex and populous discursive performative spaces where every participant is both performer and audience" (2009, 58). Certainly, the sense of entry into new social places or modes of being has been noticed by anthropologists for a long time, well before computer technologies. However, were he able to envision our fascination with virtual worlds today, ritual theorist Victor Turner might have noticed a number of features of virtual communal life that he would recognize, including what he called a rite of passage – that is, a transition from one mode of social being into another, accomplished by the ritual crossing of a *limen* or "threshold."

According to Turner, rites of passage allow admission into one's community at new levels acquired through a process of ritualized actions that signal this change. The initiate in a rite of passage "passes through a cultural realm that has few or none of the attributes of the past or coming state," and, once in this stage, stands outside of "the network of classifications" that traditionally organize and confer status. "Liminal entities" are therefore "betwixt and between the positions assigned and arrayed by law, custom, convention, and ceremonial" (1969, 94–95). Similarly entry into virtual worlds typically involves what we might consider a sort of ritualized behavior characterized by a series of log-ins, clicking procedures, and materialization of one's avatar that allows one to experience a sense of "entry" into the virtual environment. This moment of transition has been aptly described by Arnold van Gennep in his examination of liminal rites: "the door is the boundary between the foreign and domestic worlds in the case of an ordinary dwelling, between the profane and the sacred worlds in the case of a temple." Therefore, says van Gennep, "to cross the threshold is to unite oneself with a new world" (1996, 532). To move into a virtual world is arguably a similar rite of passage that injects the participant into a new "place" that is "betwixt and between" the social expectations of real life and the social expectations, as yet unknown, in the new virtual world. It also encourages the participant to see his or her avatar as a representation of himself or herself, and encourages investment in the virtual world as "real."

Bartle describes newbie behavior in virtual worlds in ways that resonate with Turner's sense of the ritual neophyte: "Many newbies will first want to ascertain the established norms of behavior ... whereupon they will spend a period exploring the virtual world and their abilities within it." Designers who want a steady flow of newbie players will help them with behavioral lessons, "providing plenty of interesting things to see and do that will help them develop their playing skills" (1969, 144). Once they leave the "main sequence" of training and start to play normally, "that's when they join the majority for which standard type dynamics apply" (145). Users in new online worlds usually must spend some time in what T. L. Taylor calls "newbie zones," where they spend time with other "low-level" players and "learn the initial skills required for the game and the ways to coordinate with others" (2006, 31). Gradually, users "undergo a socialization process" that helps them go beyond initial training and become participants in a "community of practice" (32). In *Second Life*, everyone begins with the same status but gradually accumulates animations, customized hair, professionally rendered "skin," and group associations that help them to be recognized as "insiders" or true "Second Lifers." As Turner argues, entry into a liminal space temporarily reduces all participants down to the same social level, creating a sense of shared value and equality that Turner calls *communitas*.

Of the liminal entities engaging in a rite of passage, Turner says: "It is as though they are being reduced or ground down to a uniform condition to be fashioned anew and endowed with additional powers to enable them to cope with their new station in life ... Secular distinctions of rank and status disappear or are homogenized." Turner notes that "as liminal beings they have no status, property, insignia, secular clothing indicating rank or role, position in a kinship system – in short, nothing to distinguish them from their fellow neophytes or initiands." In a rite of passage, a "neophyte," says Turner, must "be a *tabula rasa*, a blank slate, on which is inscribed new knowledge and wisdom of the group … in order to prepare them to cope with their new responsibilities" (1969, 103). New initiates into *Second Life,* too, are "ground down," in that their real-life selves are shorn away in some respects, leaving only a digital visage that represents them in the "new" world.

Although we may be tempted to see the space between the real and the virtual world (the threshold) as the primary liminal space, virtual worlds *themselves* may also be seen as such liminal spaces. In their ability to evoke *communitas*, virtual worlds afford initiates the freedom to do otherwise unacceptable things, prompting a temporary disruption of social order that Turner believes helps to maintain the status quo in real life. In *Second Life*, we can see this practice in an event like the grid-wide winter holiday snowball fight in which the "Lindens" (the only institutionalized power structure) are pelted by the other residents. In his analysis of tribal culture, Turner uses the example of community members being allowed to "revile" the chief-elect "and most fully express [their] resentment" about whatever is going on in their community. The chief-elect, during the ritual, must simply listen in patience and humility (101).

Similarly, Pearce points out that "when people enter a play frame, they are literally and figuratively playing by a different set of social rules that allow them to take liberties with their roles and identities that they might not take in ordinary life" (2009, 59). According to the authors of *Second Life: The Official Guide*, in the online world you can participate in all the "virtual hedonism" that you want – "having as much virtual sex as possible" or "shooting at other people, possibly while piloting a spaceship" (Rymaszewski *et al.* 2006, 13). You can even purchase animations and identify partners willing to enact virtual rape within *Second Life*, or find avatars who look like children to engage in animated pedophiliac pornographic fantasies. Salen and Zimmerman dub such behavior "forbidden play" and argue in ways reminiscent of Turner that such safe performance of taboo behaviors may help society, in that it "bridges social relations inside and outside the game's boundaries." Without an awareness of normal societal constraints in the real world, "the playful expression of hidden desires, nutty behavior, or normally criminal actions [in virtual contexts] would not gain status as pleasing and transgressive; forbidden play would just be plain old play." Forbidden play, they argue, "occurs only because of the artificiality of the game, even while it gains intensity as it both challenges and satisfies real-world desires" (2004, 481). The safety of the game makes forbidden play possible, just as the safety of *communitas* makes taboo behaviors temporarily acceptable in a ritual context.

In *The Great Good Place*, Ray Oldenberg offers an analysis of other real-life places that can offer something like a sense of *communitas*. Cafes, coffee shops, pubs and bookstores have the ability to give people a "third place" to belong, in addition to home and work, a place to "escape or [take] time out from life's duties and drudgeries" (1999, 21). A third place is a "leveler" place, in that it is "inclusive," accessible to anyone who wants to come, and "does not set formal criteria of membership and exclusion" (24). People relinquish the social roles they play in day-to-day life: "The surrender of outward status, or leveling, that transforms those who own delivery trucks and those who drive them into equals, is rewarded by acceptance ... Leveling is a joy and relief to those of higher and lower status in the mundane world" (25).

Applying this notion to virtual worlds, Steinkuehler and Williams affirm that leveler communities "are spaces in which an individual's rank and status in the workplace or society at large are of no import. Acceptance and participation is not contingent on any prerequisites, requirements, roles, duties, or proof of membership." Real-life friends and family members who play online together "find that such joint engagement in the 'other world' of MMOs allows them to redefine the nature and boundaries of their offline relationships, often in more equitable terms than what may be possible in day-to-day offline life." The removal from daily patterns of social life is a large part of the appeal: "This sense of moratorium from stratified daily social life enables MMOs to function as [a] kind of level playing field and, in part, may explain some of their popular appeal" (Steinkuehler and Williams 2006). Designers of online worlds must keep these principles in mind as they attempt to create a virtual space in which people will feel comfortable and accordingly, invest their time. As Bartle explains, "to create a virtual world is to create a piece of software" and it's "creating a community, a service, a place" all based on the engine that is designed to "run the world" (2003, 83). Bartle advises would-be online world designers: "If you want people to stay with your virtual world for longer, you should first and foremost try to foster relationships between them" (153).

Steinkuehler and Williams (2006) believe that MMOs are taking the place of some of these other types of third places: "By providing spaces for social interaction and relationships beyond the workplace and home, MMOs have the capacity to function as one form of a new 'third place' for informal sociability much like the pubs, coffee shops, and other hangouts of old." MMOs, furthermore, provide social capital, "social relationships that, while not [necessarily] providing deep emotional support per se, typically function to expose the individual to a diversity of worldviews." MMOs, they argue, "have the potential to function as new (albeit digitally mediated) third places similar to pubs, coffee shops, and other hangouts." The worlds of play evoked by video games and online worlds have the ability to generate liminal spaces, giving us temporary freedoms and relieving us of the drudgery of everyday life. Filiciak argues that video games are a form of "escapism," providing us the means for temporarily "getting away from everyday life worries, and deriving satisfaction in doing things that we could never do in the real world" (2003, 99). Huizinga explains that games define a community for the extent of their playtime, so that "what the 'others' do 'outside' is no concern of [the players] at the moment. Inside the circle of the game the laws and customs of ordinary life no longer count. We are different and do things differently." Huizinga compares the "magic circle" of play to ancient rites of passage, such as the "great feast of initiation when youths are accepted into the male community" in which there is a "temporary suspension of normal social life on account of the sacred play-season." Such suspension of ordinary rules "has numerous traces in the more advanced civilizations." Huizinga offers up male initiation rites of fraternities as an apt example (1955, 12). Following Huizinga, Salen and Zimmerman argue that games are "symbolic systems of meaning" that "operate only within the time and space of the magic circle" (2004, 462, 472).

Salen and Zimmerman further propose that "meaningful play" can "be framed as a social phenomena." The word "social," they explain, "refers broadly to player interaction" but must be understood on two levels. The first is "internally derived," and connotes "social interaction [that] occurs within the magic circle, as a product of the formal system of a game." The other level is "derived externally" and consists of "social roles brought into the game from outside the magic circle" (2004, 462). They refer here to games broadly defined, so inclusive of, but not limited to, what most people would consider "video games," and also might include social interaction in an online environment like *Second Life*, in which players immerse themselves in a mediated social environment with fixed rules and expectations.

Steinkuehler and Williams define virtual worlds as "social environments in that successful play often requires collaboration." The design of the experience itself requires that people interact for much of anything to happen at all: "For most gamers [in virtual worlds], constant conversation through myriad chat channels is not only necessary to navigate the virtual world's diverse challenges (e.g. to barter virtual goods, to organize collaborations, to share information) but is the very fodder from which individuals create and maintain relationships of status and solidarity" (Steinkuehler and Williams 2006). Communities of play in virtual worlds are ripe for social development since "networked play creates a very intense level of intimacy that is not greater or less than intimacy in the real world, just different" (Pearce 2009, 215). Players in games like *World of Warcraft* that have guilds (groups of players achieving tasks collectively) encourage "not only group allegiance but also a sense of collective identity" (Pearce 2009, 138).

As an application of Turner's concept of *communitas* suggests, in virtual worlds we can experiment with new social rules that "allow [us] to take liberties with [our] roles and identities that [we] might not take in ordinary life" (Pearce 2009, 59). Avatars in virtual worlds interact and "may discover sides of themselves that may not have avenues of expression in other aspects of their lives" (60). Pearce argues that "individual identity is an intersubjective accomplishment that develops through a process of social emergence," something especially highlighted for many today in virtual worlds (189). For Pearce, who we are is in process; the self is "emerging" all the time.

The self emerges, Pearce argues, through our "intersubjective" interactions with others, such that individual identity is "at least in part a product of [the player's] social milieu" and through "collective feedback" is "woven out of the materials of group identity and vice versa" (2009, 139). Accordingly, in play communities online, "the line between the individual and social may blur as players push each other to higher levels of engagement" (189). This engagement, or "intersubjective flow," captivates us in ways that move beyond mere individual choice: "players take on a role in the group not by an act of individual will, but in response to feedback, and in some cases, even demands from the play community" (140). The virtual world is "the medium through which these transactions occur" (119). Intersubjective flow "situates the flow between people rather than within the individual" (133). Indeed, says Pearce, "feedback is an essential component to the propagation of intersubjective flow" (133). Identity is shaped via the "three-way collaboration between the individual player, the community, and the designers of the world" (119).

Virtual worlds may be even better evokers of immersion than other forms of virtual engagement, like first-person shooters or arcade-style games since the commitment to an avatar, a sort of "first-person immersion," is "the best means to create a sense of presence – in other words, the quality of 'being there' – within a virtual world" (Pearce 2009, 122). Even more than improved sensory experiences and haptic interfaces, simply having a representation of oneself "visible inside the world may actually enhance the sense of presence, as well as the sense of embodiment" (122). Pearce explains that "seeing oneself projected into the virtual world appears to enhance one's ability to emotionally project into the world, whether it be single- or multiplayer." Our experiences interacting bodily within that world further engage us in the illusion that we truly inhabit the digital space. The emotional attachments we create, alongside the sense of bodily inhabitation, create a "deep connection both to other avatars and to the virtual world they share" (123).

The relationships developed in virtual worlds have the ability to become deep enough and important enough to their members that they can be seen in religious terms. For early sociologist Emile Durkheim, the social aspect of life is its most meaningful one. Religious beliefs, says Durkheim, are "always held by a defined collectivity that professes them and practices the rites that go with them" (2001, 42). The beliefs, he argues, are in fact the thing that unites the group. A "church" is "a society whose members are united because they share a common conception of the sacred world and its relation to the profane world, and who translate this common conception into identical practices" (43). If we generalize this idea of a "church" to any group that is bonded together by common beliefs and practices, then it is possible to argue that play communities may be doing some of the same work as explicitly religious ones.

As Durkheim points out, we belong to a number of groups (parents, relatives, town, race, political party, ethnic traditions, etc.) and are shaped from the very beginning by our social framework (Pals 2006, 90). Religion is the most primary of these organizational systems, and it infuses all of society, giving meaning to all the customs, rituals, myths, and practices that shape a given group's self-understanding. As a social thing, religion works to nurture "a sense of community, of shared identity and purpose" (Pals 2006, 93). Durkheim defines religion as: "a unified system of beliefs and practices relative to sacred things, that is to say, things set apart and surrounded by prohibitions – beliefs and practices that unite its adherents in a single moral community called a church" (46). Religious groups project, he says, their sense of belonging outward onto objects and symbols that represent for them their sense that they are a religious group.

This symbol or "totem" is a "collective label," the "classic example of a sacred thing" (Pals 2006, 96). For Durkheim, whatever contributes to group unity is "sacred"; whatever does not is "profane." The totem is "sacred" because it becomes the outward representation of the group's identity: "The mysterious forces with which men feel in communion seem to emanate from it … Because religious force is nothing but the collective and anonymous force of the clan, and because this can be imagined only in the form of the totem, the totemic emblem is like the visible body of the god." Although the "god" or symbol of the god (the totem) appears to be an external transcendent force, says Durkheim, "the totemic principle" is "the clan conceived in the physical form represented by the emblem" (2001, 167). Religion, then, as infused symbolically within the totem, is the thing that holds a group together: "Religion is above all a system of notions by which individuals imagine the society to which they belong and their obscure yet intimate relations with that society" (171). The rituals, ceremonies, stories, beliefs, practices and commitments that infuse a group's "religious" values are, in fact, the same things that give the individuals in a group the sense that they are more than just individuals. For Durkheim, religion is a symbolic outward manifestation of the desire to be part of a community.

Durkheim's application of religion as the thing that holds a society together may seem arbitrary; after all, other things seem to be able to serve as an equally strong social adhesive. Yet, we can easily see in religion the thick clusters of the things that provide the social glue that makes a community hum: things like rituals and shared ceremonies, stories and morals that dictate community responsibilities. These things show up in games and online worlds as well, including the prolific use of symbols (logos, clan names, guilds, etc.) suggesting that the things that make Durkheim's "sacred" society thrive are the same ones that make an online social community tick as well. As Durkheim himself argues, "there can never be a community without either a religion or something similar to fill its place" (111). Accordingly, although we may get our "sacred" kick in different ways today and in newly digitized forms, it seems that a case can be made that Durkheim's recognition of the human urge toward community is alive and well.

The problem arises with the challenge of determining which of our activities are "religious" in the ultimate sense, and which are merely "play." If communities can be formed around religious mythology as firmly as around the mythology of Azeroth in *World of Warcraft*, on what grounds can we argue that one is more successful than the other in generating morals, values, purpose and meaning? And if one primary purpose of rites of passage is to usher people into a group with a sense of belonging, then how can we say that initiation into the community of Uru is any less valuable than entering into a Mormon spiritual family? And if we cultivate numerous and fluid portraits of ourselves that include both traditionally "religious" and media-generated components, how do we distinguish between those parts of ourselves that are nourished via online quests and those that are enhanced by talking to other Christians or Jews online?

As Pearce remarks, researchers of virtual worlds have often assumed the boundary between virtual world and real world to be clear (2009, 54). Citing the work of Edward Castronova, she affirms, with him, that such absolute distinctions are ultimately unrealistic. Instead, following Castronova again, she argues that instead of thinking of the "magic circle" of play, we should think of the "almost-magic circle of play" that is more of a "membrane" than a boundary (54). A distinction between the virtual world and the real world is not always easy to make. As we saw in Chapter 4 in the discussion of the virtual as "streaming," T. L. Taylor believes that the magic circle of play can obscure the "much messier relationship" between the real and the virtual "spheres," especially in MMOGs [massively multiplayer online games]. Taylor invites us to consider players' use of online spaces, where she says "we find people negotiating levels of self-disclosure and performance, multiple forms of embodiment, and the importing of meaningful offline issues and values into online spaces" (2006, 152). Calling for "non-dichotomous models," Taylor claims that the boundary between online and offline is under constant renegotiation (153).

Recognition of the "messy" nature of the magic circle makes sense in the context of thinking about social play. If who we are is shaped by what we do online, if we can indeed learn more about who we are, what we are good at, and how we see ourselves by playing in virtual worlds, then such an experience cannot help but have offline effects as well. If the selves we "play" online have *anything* at all to do with the selves we are offline, then absolute demarcations between "here" and "there" or "online" and "offline" seem increasingly naive. Virtual worlds seem to offer what I have called "persistent liminality," the on-demand and consistently ambiguous experience of liminality characterized by the ambiguities of game/real life, sacred/profane, ritual/play, and self/other. The great thing about persistent liminality is that it erodes deeply embedded social hierarchies, making room for new modes of self-expression. The dangerous thing about persistent liminality is that it becomes increasingly difficult for us to tell when we are "playing" and when we are doing something "real" (Wagner 2011).

Computers, Pearce says, are "multipurpose tools" and thus allow multiple activities for selves seated in front of them, encouraging the fluidity of experience that comes with having multiple windows open at once, only one of which may be invested in an online world: "This means that players might be conducting real-life activities on their computer in tandem with their game-playing" (Pearce 2009, 177). The "windows" on one's computer screen, then, represent windows into different facets of the self that we may simultaneously engage, and also reveal a hybrid of play and "serious" activities. Turkle sees this fluidity as having an effect not just on our engagement within virtual reality but also on our increasing inability to recognize social and ritual boundaries in everyday life:

> People are skilled at creating rituals for demarcating the boundaries between the world of work and the world of family, play, and relaxation. There are special times (the Sabbath), special meals (the family dinner), special clothes (the "armor" for a day's labor comes off at home, whether it is the businessman's suit or the laborer's overalls), and special places (the dining room, the parlor, the kitchen, and the bedroom). Now demarcations blur as technology accompanies us everywhere, all the time. We are too quick to celebrate the continual presence of a technology that knows no respect for traditional and helpful lines in the sand.
>
> (2011, 162)

Being always plugged in can make it difficult to have any times in our lives that are "special" or set apart. Increasingly, too, the "magic circle" of play spills over into daily life as we fidget with our mobile devices during religious services, scan our physical environment for web addresses or visual scanning opportunities, and imagine we have "experienced" events seen only via digital photographs or streaming video. As Turkle notes, "[o]ur new devices provide space for the emergence of a new state of the self, itself split between the screen and the physical real, wired into existence through technology" (2011, 16). Hoover rejects the assumption that "the media and religion are separate and competing spheres and that, on some level, they inhabit the roles of 'sacred' (religion) and 'profane' (the media) influences in contemporary life." Instead, what has developed is "a less definite space where those distinctions exist in a state of fluidity and flux" (Hoover 2001, 50). The "iPod self" is here revisited, in its fluid and social form, revealing a self that is also in flux, and which is increasingly difficult to recognize apart from the myriad projections and instantiations of self that we inhabit online.

Conclusion

Virtual worlds are not simply self-contained, separate realms that we enter into and then leave unscathed. Experiences in virtual worlds have implications well beyond those virtual spaces, since many of the "patterns" of life in a virtual world also "migrate outside the virtual and into the real world" (Pearce 2009, 180). Experiences that are acquired online can have real life effects in mood, in sense of self, in relationships, and even in the choice to meet people in real-life that one meets online. Virtual worlds are "overlapping and nested magic circles," revealing a complex interplay of self-development and play. As Pearce observes, virtual worlds "must be looked at in the context of the 'ludi-sphere', the larger framework of all networked play spaces on the Internet, as well as within the larger context of the 'real world'" (2009, 137).

The "outermost" of these "circles" of play, then, is the physical world around us, with "transactions taking place through membranes more porous than has previously been suggested" (Pearce 2009, 138). The sense of what constitutes a "magic circle" of play and a boundary of real community becomes very difficult to distinguish. Which "circles" are just a form of "play" and which are "real"? Which is the real self, surfing amidst these new spaces, some virtual, some real, and some real but reflected primarily within the virtual? In our wired world, we find ourselves with multiple competing and overlapping selves invested in multiple and competing social worlds, both "real" and "virtual." Play communities are, at root, groups of people united by adherence to fixed rules and motivated by a sense of belonging outwardly projected via totems and the establishment of rites of passage for entry. Since religion exhibits many of these features as well, it becomes nearly impossible to distinguish between games that work like religion and religion as a kind of game. Just as the "real" and the "virtual" become increasingly fluid, so has religion become one of many social modes of encounter with the world, akin in surprising ways to those experiences we have in virtual worlds.

Chapter 7

What you play is what you do?

Procedural evil and video game violence

Is it possible to perform acts of virtual evil? What would this look like? If nobody is hurt when we play a first-person shooter and blast the heck out of our enemies, why would anyone consider such an act "violent"? In this chapter I consider this question, drawing on the relationship between ritual and play, sacred and profane, real and virtual, to try to untangle the moral implications of virtual violence. In particular, I look at "violent" acts performed in a virtual context in controversial games like the online *Kuma\War* series of virtual "re-enactments" of the war in Iraq; *Left Behind: Eternal Forces*, the PC video game; online games like *New York Defender* and *9/11 Survivor* and especially the controversial online game *Super Columbine Massacre RPG!* created by Danny LeDonne in 2005.

As in symbolic sacrificial rites of major world religions, players of these video games are led through a series of mimetically violent activities. However, in video games these activities are typically understood as ephemeral, inconsequential, and even entertaining. Thus, the question of whether or not we can view video game violence as ritually cathartic hinges on what video game theorist Ian Bogost (2007b) calls "procedural rhetoric" or "the practice of persuading through processes." Building on Bogost's notion of procedural rhetoric and addressing the problem of video game violence, I coin the term "procedural evil," and ask if it is possible to commit evil if the deeds are "committed" only in a virtual context. After examining three related concepts of the magic circle of play – procedural rhetoric and forbidden play – I apply these notions to *Super Columbine* and I consider to what extent the behavior encouraged in the game might "spill over" into the real world, especially in terms of its moral implications for the player–performer. Is it possible to just "play" at evil in the form of a game?

Violence in the magic circle

The difference between actions taken in a game and those taken in real life would seem to be easy to recognize. As we have already seen, for Huizinga play is an act often perceived as separate in some way from real life, taking place "within a play-ground marked off beforehand either materially or ideally, deliberately or as a matter of course." Because play can take place in religious and non-religious settings, Huizinga's "magic circle," as we might recall, consists of "the arena, the card-table, the magic circle, the temple, the stage, the screen, the tennis court, the court of justice" all of which are "play-grounds" or "forbidden spots, isolated, hedged round, hallowed, within which special rules obtain. All are temporary worlds within the ordinary world, dedicated to the performance of an act apart" (1955, 10). Huizinga's discussion beautifully calls attention to the ability of games to cultivate a sense of temporary space and time apart, in which acts are performed that are fundamentally different from the grind of daily life. Here we incorporate this idea into a discussion of virtual violence to see how well it holds up when we interrogate the nature of our interaction with violent procedural rhetorics in popular contemporary video games.

Entering into the magic circle may involve entering into a physically demarcated space, as in a temple or a playing field, or it may simply involve a choice by the player–participants to enter into this "temporary world." The magic circle "frames a distinct space of meaning that is separate from, but still references, the real world" (Salen and Zimmerman 2004, 97). Gary Alan Fine looks at fantasy role-play games like *Dungeons and Dragons* and points out that "like many social worlds (acting, storytelling), fantasy games produce a 'make-believe' world set apart from the everyday world. By playing fantasy games, participants implicitly agree to 'bracket' the world outside the game" (2006, 581). Choices made within the game are based only on the rules of that system. The world of play evokes a new set of rules that we follow temporarily within the game space, the "magic circle."

As we have already seen, Juul sees an individual game as a "state machine," that is, "a system that can be in different states; it contains input and output functions, and definitions of what state and what input will lead to what following state" (2004, 133). Video game consoles, then, are special state machines intended "for generating compelling spaces" (2004, 123). Games can be viewed as complete systems with specific rules generated by designers and maintained by software, in which behaviors are encouraged or discouraged and choices are to varying degrees circumscribed. The "spaces" that such systems or "state machines" generate are experienced as parallel worlds into which we temporarily enter, but which are distinct from our own. This means that any unsavory actions engaged in within the magic circle should be viewed as having no bearing on real life, and perhaps even as being required within the rules of the game. Evil, in such a context, is to be viewed as only make-believe – a form of play or what-if within the "magic circle."

In religious contexts, too, we sometimes see spaces and times designated in which behavior is allowed that otherwise would be considered inappropriate – a sort of religious "magic circle." In the last chapter, we saw how ritual promotes what Turner calls *communitas*, a "sacred" time and space that "transgresses or dissolves the norms that govern structured and institutionalized relationships and is accompanied by experiences of unprecedented potency" (128). Abiding in such a liminal space can give people the freedom to do otherwise taboo things, giving them an outlet and voice so that when they return to ordinary time they are more content with existing social structures. Turner even gives us a reason to understand the comradeship that sometimes builds around those who play video games: the "modality of relationship" appears to "flourish best in spontaneously liminal situations – phases betwixt and between states where social-structural role-playing is dominant, and especially between status equals" (1969, 138).

Liminality grinds all participants down to the same level, so that the most powerful are subjected to the temporary and usually playful derision of the least powerful, representing the *communitas,* or interrelatedness of all members of a group. In this way, *communitas* is "made evident or accessible, so to speak, only through its juxtaposition to, or hybridization with, aspects of social structure" (Turner, 127). For Turner, liminality is a temporary ritual state that induces *communitas* in traditional societies. It is not difficult to see, however, how violent war-based video games may serve the same purpose of creating a liminal state in which the powerless feel powerful, and which opposes the ingrained social structures that govern daily existence through the inscription of the "magic circle" of gameplay. John Lyden points out the dangers of liminal activities enacted without the controlling procedures of fixed ritual and morals, and applies these insights to the reception of violent films in contemporary culture:

> The Ndembu were able to engage in "obscene" behavior in prescribed manner because they also knew they would return to normalcy afterwards, just as some people in our society can enjoy the depiction of inappropriate behavior before returning to social conformity. If people have already rejected authority and structure, however, films that depict liminality may simply confirm them in their rejection of societal values. Without a strong system of social sanctions against inappropriate behavior in place, the invocation of liminality may be dangerous.
>
> (2003, 101)

Lyden's cautions clearly apply also, and perhaps more so, to video games, which are formally more akin to rituals in their rich interactivity, and especially to those video games that align the most with real life.

We can see the power of liminal engagement with imaginative media in the use of the controversial Christian video game *Left Behind: Eternal Forces* by US troops. Released in November of 2006, *Left Behind: Eternal Forces* is a companion game to the *Left Behind* series of novels by Tim LaHaye and Jerry Jenkins. In August of 2007, actor Stephen Baldwin, along with his Christian evangelical entertainment troupe Operation Straight Up (OSU), sponsored a movement to deliver copies of *Left Behind: Eternal Forces* inside care packages for US troops in Iraq, a move apparently originally approved by the Department of Defense (DOD). Operation Straight Up president Jonathan Sprinks said of the group's activities in Iraq: "We feel the forces of heaven have encouraged us to perform multiple crusades that will sweep through this war-torn region" (quoted in Schechter 2007). When the plan was exposed, the resulting public outcry caused the DOD to withdraw support for delivery of the game.

The landscape of the game is an imagination of life in the near future after the rapture of the faithful into heaven. In this real-time strategy game, the player is an integral part of the Tribulation Forces, fighting the troops of the Antichrist in a digitized reproduction of the landscape of Manhattan. The close relationship between the "magic circle" of play and the experience of liminality can be seen in this description by a US soldier when he explains why he doesn't object to the delivery of video games in the OSU care packages:

> to think that the soldiers over there are playing video games bothers you let me tell ya I have been over there 3 times now and to tell ya the truth, there isnt alot to do in your free time which isnt much after pulling 7 days straight of 20 plus hours out on patrol and getting shot at and having IEDs exploding around you. ... not to mention loosing your friends that are right next to you. ... when you get a day or two of down time playing video games and e-mailing home is about the only thing that helps you keep your sanity. ... so yeah we play video games over there. ... i bet you do or know people who play here.they arent getting shot at and blown up all day for 7 days straight with less than 4 hours of sleep a day and lucky to get a days downtime to try to enjoy yourself in any way possible trying not to think about the fact that it could be your last day. ... so if its scary to think that we have time to play video games. ... just think how scary it is to us to be getting shot at all day while people like you sit back here and criticize what we do in our little bit of down time. ... Thanks. ...
>
> (posted by Ron, August 15, 2007, in "User comments,"
> in response to Schechter 2007)

For Ron, violent war-style gaming is a liminal activity even in the midst of war. In fact, the ability to feel in control what is going on in a hostile real-life war situation may be part of its appeal. Here, Ron is not interested in debating the merits of *Left Behind: Eternal Forces* as a *game*; rather he is defending the general right of soldiers to *any* sort of video game in a war zone. Ron believes that video games provide a much-needed outlet, which contrary to what we might expect, does not, according to Ron at least, reinforce soldiers' fears about real-life violence, but may instead help to alleviate these fears through the game's liminal functions.

Second Life, too, seems to thrive on invitations for players to engage in liminal behavior, capitalizing on the belief that anything that happens there happens "only" in the magic circle of the online world. Roger Junchke is a self-proclaimed *Second Life* "terrorist" who spends his time blowing up virtual churches. The act is excusable, he claims, since "nothing actually gets destroyed in SL [*Second Life*] so all it really does is lights and smoke." For Junchke, the act has a liminal function, in that it is his "benign and petty way of expressing my dislike of Christian fundamentalists" (Wagner 2011, 278). Such symbolic behavior, he suggests, is cathartic and has no bearing on real-life people or churches. Nonetheless, not all examples of liminal experimentation are well received in *Second Life*. Most players would see the dangerous symbolic power of virtual acts ranging from "naked avatars sitting on the Koran to a swastika painted on the synagogue" (Crabtree 2007).

Thus, one dimension of the problem is whether *all* of *Second Life* should be viewed as a liminal space, or whether one should look instead at those areas *within* it that are designated for taboo behavior. According to *Second Life*'s *Community Standards*, certain areas are designated as appropriate for "offensive" and/or sexual activities and others are not. Upon joining *Second Life*, each resident agrees to a code of conduct that includes a statement about not engaging "assault" in a Safe Area, that is, not "shooting, pushing or shoving another Resident ... [or] creating or using scripted objects which singularly or persistently target another Resident." So in virtual reality, how do we define the boundaries between the kind of virtual "play" in which one can engage in untoward behavior, and the ethical requirements of human communal life? As we saw in Chapter 6, *Second Life* allows all the "virtual hedonism" or sex that you want, and invites activities like "shooting at other people, possibly while piloting a spaceship" (Rymaszewski *et al.* 2006, 13). You can even purchase animations and invite willing partners to enact virtual rape within *Second Life* or find avatars who look like children to engage in animated pedophiliac pornographic fantasies.

The distinction between play and ritual here seems important, even if the difference between them seems to hinge entirely on player intent. A game is "a closed system, in which the play of the game is bounded by the magic circle" (Salen and Zimmerman 2004, 575). For Christian players of *Left Behind: Eternal Forces* who embrace the *Left Behind* ideology, the "magic circle" is permeable, spilling over into the real world that the game claims to represent, serving as a training module for the coming rapture. For the soldiers who enjoy playing games like *Left Behind* in the barracks, the game is a means of escape from the harsh and terrifying reality of war. Thus, the reception of *Left Behind: Eternal Forces* as game or as religious ritual depends entirely upon each player's reflexive response to it. Wade Clark Roof has noticed this feature of contemporary, commodified, syncretistic religion, which he says is typified by "a direct relation between the consuming practitioner and spiritual goods in a religiously deregulated and demonopolized world." Through focusing on the individual's experience of religion, media products have the ability to:

remake religion into a more dynamic, self-reflexive activity on the part of the individual and reinforce the view that, whatever else it might be, religious consciousness involves an active process of meaning-making, of interpreting one's own situation in relation to media discourses as well as those in traditional religious institutions. Bombarded by media input, the individual is left having to do a lot of cognitive negotiating and bargaining.

(1999, 70)

Such contemporary negotiation of individual identity appears to include the choice of whether or not to see the experience as a game, a ritual, or both.

Procedural rhetoric and virtual violence

Morgan argues for the importance of studying images in context, looking carefully at an image's function "in narrative, perception, scientific and intellectual classification, and all manner of ritual practices, such as ceremonies, gift-giving, commerce, memorialization, migration, and display – thereby understanding the image as part of the social construction of reality" (2005, 30). Morgan's interest in visual culture, then, extends beyond an image itself into the social processes that inform its purpose and its interpretation. Although Morgan doesn't discuss video games, such social processes should surely include them, since these arrange images in ways that encourage or discourage particular responses from us, and thus betray a marked ideological edge that Bogost defines as "procedural rhetoric," the use of persuasion through processes.

Bogost would agree with Morgan that images work as part of other social processes, which can and do shape how we read them – so much so that for Bogost, the *process* matters more than an image itself, especially when that process is the system of a video game. As Bogost explains, "processes define the way things work: the methods, techniques, and logics that drive the operation of systems." As we have already seen, Bogost coins a new term, *procedural rhetoric*, to describe "the practice of persuading through processes in general and computational processes in particular." Procedural rhetoric is "a technique for making arguments with computational systems and for unpacking computational arguments others have created" (Bogost 2007b, 3). The "rhetorical" role in "procedural" processes are the ways that such processes (especially software-based ones) try to persuade us to see the world in a particular way, and to encourage us, at least within the confines of the procedural experience and implicitly beyond it, to act in particular ways. Procedures are "sometimes related to ideology" says Bogost, and thus can "cloud our ability to see other ways of thinking" (3).

Procedurality is deeply experienced via the platform of the computer. It is the software that establishes the mode of our interaction, that creates "rules of execution, tasks and actions that can and cannot be performed" (4). Bogost claims that computers are "particularly adept at representing real or imagined systems that themselves function in some particular way" according to "a set of processes" (5). Bogost insists that procedural representation is the *most vivid* form of representation apart from actual experience, and that it is even *more vivid* than moving images with sound, and thus more vivid than film alone, despite the qualities of the video game graphics. Video games can "muster moving images and sound" that are "in accordance with complex rules that simulate real or imagined physical and cultural processes." As we have already seen in the discussion of ritual in this book (Chapter 3), Bogost asserts that procedural rhetorical claims are as logical as any other kind of argument due to their reliance on computational processes (36). For Bogost, images used in such processes are contextualized by fixed rubrics of engagement and encourage learning through performance of fixed activities. It's less clear *what* it is that we learn by doing, and whether or not this doing has an explicit moral component – that is, whether or not the procedural rhetoric teaches us how to feel or what to believe, and to what extent we may or may not be aware of this process.

Grodal explains that a game world is based on a map or "system of multiple linear routes" through virtual space with virtual interactions or choices (2003, 147). As Berger observes, all "possible choices" and outcomes of a game have been previously programmed into it, so that a player's sense of control "is only an illusion" (A. Berger 2005, 191). Procedural systems, Bogost points out, "generate behaviors based on rule-based models" (2007b, 4) and in so doing, "run processes that invoke interpretations of processes in the material world" (5). This means that procedural representation "explains processes *with other processes*" (9). One obvious example of dangerous procedural rhetoric is the racist American video game *Ethnic Cleansing*, in which the player clothes his or her avatar as a skinhead or a Klansman and kills Jews, blacks and immigrants. Another example is the flash animation game *Border Patrol*, in which one shoots at running images of Mexicans – even pregnant ones – in the procedural attempt to kill them and stop them from entering the border into the United States. In the processes of both games, images are used *procedurally* to make an offensive ideological argument. Again, it's impossible to say to what extent the playing of such games generates a moral response in kind with the one generated by the rhetoric of the game itself, but at the very least we can notice the ideological components of such arguments, even when they are made procedurally.

Let's return now to a more in-depth examination of the 2007 Manchester Cathedral incident that I have already alluded to, using procedural rhetoric as the primary focus of analysis. In *Resistance: Fall of Man*, players are required (within the game) to shoot and kill a host of alien intruders. The game is set in an imagined alternative backdrop of Britain in the 1950s. World War II never happened in this game's world, and Britain is threatened by hostile invasion by alien creatures called Chimera, bred in Russia but now running amok. Britain is the last European stronghold against the creatures, and American army ranger Nathan Hale is sent on a messianic rescue mission to help defend

Britain against otherwise certain destruction. *Resistance: Fall of Man* raised the hackles of the Church of England not long after its release due to an intensely violent shoot-out in the game staged in a perfect digital replica of Manchester Cathedral. The Church responded with anger, public castigation, and threats of a lawsuit.

Bishop of Manchester Nigel McCulloch said in June of 2007: "For a global manufacturer to re-create one of our great cathedrals with photo-realistic quality and then encourage people to have gun battles in the building is beyond belief and highly irresponsible" (quoted in Boyes 2007). In a letter written by the Church of England's Rogers Govender to Sony and published in *The Times Online*, Govender explains that the church's representatives had seen selective footage of the Manchester Cathedral shoot-out on *YouTube*, and they were "shocked and dismayed … beyond words." The shoot-out scene, they claimed, "can only be described as virtual desecration. We are shocked to see a place of worship, prayer, learning and heritage being presented to the youth of today as a location where guns can be fired" (Govender 2007). The Church demanded that the game be pulled from shelves, an apology be swiftly issued, and donations be made to charities working to fight gun violence.

In response, Sony's European president David Reeves issued a formal statement arguing that the game is pure science-fiction entertainment. According to Reeves, the cathedral is presented simply as a digital stage upon which one of many violent battles takes place in a fantasy arena. He explains that in the game, "the Cathedral is empty and abandoned, no longer used as a place of worship and the sequences that take place inside are to defend the building from the aliens" (quoted in Gledhill 2007a). Eventually, Sony offered a sincere apology, but did not pull the game from store shelves. No lawsuits were filed, but when the storm had blown over, the Church of England's Rogers Govender expressed the sentiment that "some important lessons have been learnt" (quoted in BBC News 2007). Apart from the fact that faith may shape how one views virtual sacred space, what exactly these lessons were is hard to say. What we can learn from this controversy, however, is how powerful different perspectives can be. Sony argued that the procedural rhetoric of the game protected any actions within it from sanction. In other words, the game's *story* trumped the visual images within it.

One of the most telling ways that an awareness of procedural rhetoric can help us become more critical consumers of video games is in the procedural rhetoric of dualism as it appears in *Left Behind: Eternal Forces*. In the game, the player controls tanks, helicopters and infantry, with the primary goal of converting the uncommitted ("neutral units") to the Christian cause, while killing non-Christians when necessary. The game includes backstories for all characters, describing how they arrived at their current belief system, some of them turning their backs on Christianity earlier in life. When the player directs his troops, they respond with perky statements of obedience such as "Praise the Lord!" "Consider it done!" and "Enlighten me!" As the leader in charge of all Christian troops, the player of *Left Behind: Eternal Forces* must maintain his or her "spiritual" rating by praying constantly, by doing good deeds, and by making wise leadership decisions. Needless to say, in this apocalyptic context, the player's actions in the game are overtly messianic.

Left Behind: Eternal Forces met with an unwelcome dose of controversy after its release, with some players claiming that they were encouraged to kill those non-Christians in the game who resisted conversion. One representative of the Anti-Defamation League (2006) asserts that because the game depends upon the same imaginative world as the books, so it too "promote[s] the overall message of an exclusivist religious system that considers the proselytization of Jews to be an imperative. This theology portrays itself as the only path to salvation. And Jews, people of any other faith, or those of no faith who do not convert before it's too late, are destined to suffer horrible deaths." As a result of complaints and a boycott by a coalition of Christian groups, Wal-Mart pulled the game from its shelves and three members of the *Left Behind* board of directors were fired (Blumenthal 2007).

In *Left Behind*, the player is forced into a dualistic construct of reality in which every entity in the game is identified with the forces of good, the forces of evil, or in a neutral state awaiting identification as good or evil. War video games, says Frasca, typically work wonderfully within "worlds built around dichotomies," where "things are generally black or white" (2003, 230). Such features are part of the design, since such games "do not admit options that break [their] binary logic (friend or foe, dead or alive, with us or against us)" (231). As Jason Ocampo (2006) explains for *Gamespot* in his review of *Left Behind: Eternal Forces*: "There's the Tribulation Forces, who are the 'good guys' that have seen the light, and then there's the Global Community Peace-keepers, who are led by the antichrist." One cannot complete *Left Behind: Eternal Forces* without at least imaginatively buying into this dualistic system of good and evil, which is fully integrated into the game's procedural rhetoric. Of course, the procedural rhetoric can and should also be read as a theological affirmation of the evangelical impulse of the designers of the game and of those evangelical players who embrace it, so that the performance of gameplay is itself a moral and theological exercise.

Forbidden play

Some instances of video game procedural rhetoric push the envelope of acceptability by capitalizing on the experience or performance of taboo deeds. Salen and Zimmerman describe games that "create social contexts in which, very often, behaviors take place that would be strictly forbidden in society at large." In this kind of "forbidden play," one can betray one's friends, engage in criminal behavior, and even kill others, activities that in any other context would likely be considered "evil" (2004, 77). But if these "evil" deeds are per-formed only virtually, then on what grounds can moral judgments be made about them? This is a sticky question indeed, calling into question easy assumptions about the very notions of performance, in particular how encoded processes with no obvious real-life counterparts are to be understood.

"Forbidden-play" games, say Salen and Zimmerman, "play with meaning" and create a sort of "social contract" within which a "safe" imaginative space appears, Huizinga's "magic circle" of play, a region that is somehow fundamentally different from the real world, and thus in which actions can take place that purportedly have no effect on our ordinary lives (2004, 77). Chris Crawford argues something similar when he says that games are closed formal systems and so *require no external referent*: "The model world created by the game is internally complete; no reference need be made to agents outside the game" (1982, 7). Thus, drawing on Huizinga and Crawford, it would seem that games by definition cannot do or cause evil in the real world, since any actions that take place within the magic circle of a game are sanitized from the realm of daily life. In other words, they are merely *virtually* evil.

But the boundary between the virtual and the real is not always so easily distinguishable. Some games evoke a sort of "forbidden" space that invites – but does not necessarily fully achieve – spillover into real life. As Salen and Zimmerman suggest, forbidden play "entails a shift in the implicit rules of a game." That is, "by permitting improper behavior within defined limits, the operational rules of forbidden play trump the implicit rules of society." People feel entitled to break the rules of society while playing some games. In fact, that may be the point: "[W]hen a player engages in forbidden play, he isn't only rebelling against the general rules of game play, he is also rebelling against larger social rules as well ... people engaged in forbidden play don't just play games, but play with social structure" (2004, 481). In this "forbidden play" space, the player is "always in danger of [really] overstepping the social boundaries of play, jumping the gun, and breaking the magic circle" (479).

For Jenkins, this is one of the main differences between video games and more rigidly structured stories: "If a character in a novel or a film does something we find morally reprehensible, we can always pull away from the character ... Yet, in playing a game ... we as players are always partially to blame ... Confronting such a situation, we learn something, potentially, about ourselves and we learn something, potentially, about the rule system of the game itself" (cited in Schrier and Gibson 2010a, xvii). The *refusal* to break the magic circle of play by allowing violence to spill over into real life, and the constant *temptation* to do so, are part of the pleasure of such games. We should be cautioned, however, by James Newman's suggestion that one of the pleasures of video games is precisely their ability to "minimize regret" (2004, 86).

Salen and Zimmerman explain that in forbidden play, "the game's magic circle protects those within the game from sanction. The game itself maintains this paradoxical tension with the real world: the forbidden play occurs *only because of the artificiality of the game*, even while it gains intensity as it both challenges and satisfies real-world desires" (my italics) (2004, 481). Such games, then, invite play with moral boundaries – and indeed, exist as a challenge to the very notion of play as distinct from the real, and create an implicit category of *moral* play, in which evil could be enacted through processes – but would be viewed *only* as a game. David Simkins claims that "[b]y sharing control of the moral world with the player and allowing the player to practice or experiment with moral choices, [game] designers create a sandbox where the player can practice living with values" (2010, 70). Some recent games take this idea to extremes, as in the Japanese game *Rapelay* which allows players to violently "rape" NPCs (non-player characters), or the series of *Postal* games in which players can kill at will.

Things become complicated, however, when the "magic circle" of play is laid over a real-life sacred space, especially one in which the game's procedural rhetoric requires violent actions by the player. The perplexing problem of how earthly sacred space relates to digital replicas of earthly sacred space lies behind the Church of England's visceral response to *Resistance: Fall of Man*'s use of Manchester Cathedral in the shoot-out scene. As *The Times* reports, Manchester Cathedral has in recent years worked very hard to disrupt the pattern of gun violence in the youth community of Manchester, holding special services each year in the cathedral for the families of those who have lost loved ones to gun crime. Manchester's Dean Govender said: "We have been dismayed at those in the computer industry who have defended the use of Manchester Cathedral in this a violent game. We fear that the next buildings to be cloned for virtual desecration could be a mosque, synagogue, temple, or other churches" (quoted in Gledhill 2007b). Virtual desecration would not be possible if the digitized space did not retain some vestiges of the sanctity of the earthly space. However, as implied in Sony's response, virtual desecration is not possible within the magic circle of play – in which procedural rhetoric defines choices that have relevance only within the boundaries of the game.

The Church's complaints are well illuminated by a consideration of what it means for people of religious faith to designate any structure as "sacred." For this, we return to the classic theories of Eliade on the relationship between the sacred and the profane. Eliade claims that the sacred is "the sphere of the supernatural, of things extraordinary, memorable, and momentous. While the profane is vanishing and fragile, full of shadows, the sacred is eternal, full of substance and reality" (Pals 2006, 199). For Eliade, the construction of sacred space is *itself* a hierophany, or "an irruption of the sacred that results in detaching a territory from the surrounding cosmic milieu and making it qualitatively different" (1961, 26). Eliade describes how hierophany is an instantiation of the "Real" within the profane world:

> [H]ierophany has annulled the homogeneity of [profane] space and revealed a fixed point ... [T]he sacred is pre-eminently the *real*, at once power, efficacity, the source of life and fecundity. Religious man's desire to live *in the sacred* is in fact equivalent to his desire to take up his abode

in objective reality, not to let himself by paralyzed by the never-ceasing relativity of purely subjective experiences, to live in a real and effective world, and not in an illusion.

(1961, 28)

According to Eliade, a profane thing becomes "sacred" when the sacred enters into it and "saturates" it with "being." The object "appears as a receptacle of an exterior force that differentiates it from its milieu and gives it meaning and value" (1954/2005, 4). Temples are hierophanies, or earthly receptacles of the Sacred, but they are also modeled after a "celestial prototype," which not only "precede[s] terrestrial architecture" but is "also situated in an ideal (celestial) region of eternity" (1954/2005, 7–8). All sacred things on the earth (below) have "an extraterrestrial archetype, be it conceived as a plan, as a form, or purely and simply as a 'double' existing on a higher cosmic level" (1954/2005, 9). The construction of sacred space, for Eliade, is a physical imitation of the movement from "chaos to cosmos" enacted by divine forces in primordial time.

Jonathan Z. Smith is rightly critical of Eliade's "dramatic wager" that the "mundane world, the human world, takes on reality only to the degree that it participates in that which is 'beyond,' in that which is transmundane and transhuman" (2005, xiv). Eliade's phenomenological view has indeed garnered more than its share of criticism, assuming as it does the *actual* existence of the Sacred (the Real) as the model upon which human religious activity is based. However, Smith gestures towards a theoretical rehabilitation of Eliade when he suggests that we might readily "grant" the "cogency of Eliade's description" but "reverse the polarities of the maxim 'as above, so below,' yielding the formula 'as below, so above' thereby suggesting some theory of projection in the service of legitimating human institutions and practices" (xv). Gordon Lynch echoes this renewed application of Eliade, claiming that "there is no need for the sacred object to be associated with transcendence in theological terms" since "what makes it sacred are the particular thoughts, feelings and actions that are experienced by individuals and groups in relation to it" (2007, 138). By allowing believers to say what they think is "sacred" and why they do, this new use of Eliade's dichotomy "takes seriously the cognitive, emotional and motivational associations that insiders ascribe to their sacred object" (139). These categories say very interesting things about what people believe and how they practice belief, regardless of whether there is any absolute Sacred to be located in some ultimate realm.

Smith's reversal of Eliade's categories allows us to view the construction of sacred space as a human-initiated religious orienting procedure. Whether there is a "Sacred" out there or not, the building of sacred space *is* a religious act in that it reflects the religious *intent* to orient, the conviction that construction can imitate the Real and in so doing generate meaning. Human beings build sacred places and engage in sacred ritual as a way of "projecting" or enacting their own *desire* for meaning, their own *hope* that there is indeed a "Sacred" beyond worldly, profane existence, a Real that *ought* to be copied in this world. As Eliade puts it:

> [A]n object or act becomes real only insofar as it imitates or repeats an archetype. Thus, reality is acquired solely through repetition or participation; everything which lacks an exemplary model is "meaningless," i.e. it lacks reality ... [T]his primitive ontology has a Platonic structure.
>
> (1954/2005, 34)

But if things become real only insofar as they imitate the Real, then what are we to make of *copies of copies of* the Real, as in virtual reality constructions of earthly sacred space? In other words, if the Real is beyond our profane world, and we can only imitate it in the building of sacred spaces that *gesture toward* the Real, what are we to do with digital doubles of sacred space, like Manchester Cathedral in *Resistance: Fall of Man*, or the replica of the grotto at Lourdes in *Second Life*, or mosques in *Kuma\War*, which must then be viewed as *gestures toward gestures toward* the Real? One possible answer, building upon Eliade, is that the physical copy of the Real (the Temple) *and* the virtual copy of the physical copy of the Real (the virtual Temple) are *both* copies – and therefore both equally *virtual*, or both equally "Real," insofar as both can be seen as echoes of the Real. What then makes the physical Temple necessary at all once it has been digitally duplicated? Perhaps this implicit question explains some of the skepticism of religious institutions for utilization of virtual religious spaces like *Second Life* for regular presumably "authentic" worship.

Margaret Miles' use of the religious icon as a means to understand what makes films sometimes prescriptive helps to illuminate how views about sacred space can be important when considering procedural rhetoric. Miles says that "movies do not function iconically unless viewers deliberately augment the visible with imagination, by imagining how it would feel to be in the protagonist's situation, by imagining the smells, the tastes, the touch the film character experiences" (1996, 188–89). One might add that such "iconic" readings also invite viewers to imagine themselves *doing* whatever the protagonist does. Because few people identify so intimately with filmic protagonists, says Miles, "it is not impossible for films to act iconically [but] it is just less likely that they will do so" (189). She claims that those who worry about violence in response to film do so because "they assume that we relate to films as a devotee relates to an icon" and that this kind of deep interaction happens only to a "small proportion of habitual spectators under certain circumstances" (189, 184). "No one film has iconic power," she claims, "but the recurrence of similar images across films weaves those images into the fabric of the common life of American society, influencing everything from clothing styles to accepted and expected behavior" (190). If Miles is right, then we might do well to be concerned about any repeated images of violence or stereotyping in video games, since players are more likely than film viewers to see themselves identified with the characters on-screen. Certainly most players would be able to distance themselves from the actions portrayed therein; but some might find themselves drawn into the action in virtual space, and have a hard time defining what makes a virtual act have an impact on their view of others, and what makes it rest safely within the realm of mere play.

This is the essence of Sony's argument: "It's just a game." However, for the representatives of the Cathedral, the *real* Cathedral in the physical world and the *digital* Cathedral in the game *both* point to the Sacred beyond them – a heavenly abode, the Platonic realm of perfection and divinity. So for these believers, to depict violence in the virtual replica is the same thing as performing violence in the real building – there is no fundamental difference, since *both* are symbols of the Real beyond. Crawford views games in a way that more accords with Sony's response. As we have already seen, for Crawford, "games are closed formal systems, 'internally complete' and with no external referent" (1982, 7).

The problem may be seen as an example of what Grimes calls a ritual "misframe." Grimes explains that "when we misframe a rite, we misconstrue its genre. The result is akin to missing the point of a joke or taking irony literally … we miss the point" (1996a, 288). He uses the example of an outsider viewing a ritual in which boys stumble about as if mentally ill, acting within a ritual context. Those who assume, on faith-based worldviews, that sacred construction is based upon a Sacred model will be offended by the depiction of violence in digital replicas of sacred space, since this replica must then also be based on the same Sacred model. Those who assume, based upon their intention as game players, that the magic circle of the game provides a safe space to enact any fantasy one chooses will charge that their opponents have misunderstood the nature of the game. How one demarcates the magic circle of a video game also largely determines one's opinion about virtual violence in that context. This kind of "play" is representative of a family of games that similarly play with our assumptions about what is real, what is meaningful, and what it means to "do" something violent.

The disagreements between the Church of England and Sony over *Resistance: Fall of Man* also have a lot to do with the place where procedural rhetoric and the "magic circle" intersect. The Church focused on the procedurality of violence in a digitized sacred space and did not acknowledge the "magic circle" of the fantasy. Sony (and avid game players in support of Sony) fiercely contended that the game was fantasy, existing in a liminal state, and therefore, they claimed, it makes no difference where the battle was staged, church or not. For them, the procedurality of violence can be easily explained within the storyline of the game and thus the game should be protected from scrutiny by the "magic circle." Indeed, within the "magic circle" of the game, the procedurality of ridding a sacred area of vicious aliens seems to be justified.

One discussant, Daniel Carew, remarking on this news story explains that the procedural rhetoric of the game requires this activity: "the only way to remove these aliens from the cathedral is to use army-grade weaponry, which is exactly what the main character does." For him, one need only look at "what kind of action happened in the game, in cathedral," to see that "Sony has done nothing wrong" (quoted in Osu 2007). David Reeves, president of Sony Computer Entertainment Europe concurs: "We do not accept that there is any connection between contemporary issues of twenty-first-century Manchester and a work of science fiction in which a fictitious 1950s Britain is under attack by aliens. We believe a comprehensive viewing of the work will make its content and context clear" (a reader remark appended to Gledhill 2007a). Grimes' work in ritual misfires is again useful here; a rite is a failure, he explains, when it "spills over its own boundaries" via "contagion," usually of a violent nature. The liminal boundary is breached, and violence is enacted elsewhere (1996a, 286). For the representatives of the Cathedral, the context of the game's fictional storyline is irrelevant; the depiction of the space *itself* in association with *any* violence, as well as the agency of the players enacting that violence, are most important. Part of the disagreement may be attributable to the fact that the Church of England's representatives were not gamers and simply watched a video of gameplay that included only the level in question. Therefore, their consumption of the violent shoot-out was distinct from the "magic circle" of the full gaming experience, and without an appreciation for the complete procedurality of the game. It would be interesting to know if these same representatives would maintain their critiques if they became experienced enough to make it through a complete play of the game.

To sum up, Sony sees the digital replica of the cathedral as a mere prop determined by the fictional narrative and happening only within the protected realm of the game. The digital image of Manchester Cathedral is a plaything in the game's larger procedural rhetoric. By contrast, the Church views the digital representation of the cathedral as capable of evoking the same otherworldly evocative qualities as the real brick-and-mortar building. Accordingly, the "Sacred Digital Guidelines" drawn up by the Cathedral Chapter at Manchester call for "respect" of physical spaces as "places of prayer, worship, peace, learning and heritage" and argues that this respect is to be shown by treating virtual replicas of sacred physical places with such sanctity too (Gledhill 2007b). Here is reflexivity at its best: the Church believes that sacred buildings are echoes of the Sacred, so they believe that digital buildings are also echoes of the Sacred; thus, to fight in a sacred building, digital or not, is sacrilege. Sony, on the other hand, claims implicitly that the shoot-out falls within the "magic circle" of a fantasy game, and has no bearing on the physical cathedral at all. This slippage between the real and the virtual is in fact a hallmark feature of a particular kind of dangerous gameplay, which Cindy Poremba (2007) calls "brink games."

Brink games

For Poremba, brink games exist "on the border of games and reality" and "explicitly referenc[e] the double-coded nature of that boundary." Brink games "use their status as 'only a game' as a strategic gesture" (2007, 772). Salen and Zimmerman observe that players must be deliberately conscious of their social environment when they enter the magic circle of a brink-style game, since there can often be "strong differences between the implicit rules of society and the implicit rules of a game." Games can "create social contexts in which … behaviors take place that would be strictly forbidden in society at large," such that you can "plot treachery against your friends and backstab them when they least expect it. You can engage in representations of criminal behavior. Or you can put on padded gloves and try to knock another person unconscious" (2004, 478).

Poremba is interested in those types of "forbidden play" that *most intensely* play with the boundary between game and reality, games that use the conceit of "it's just a game" with "a knowing wink" (2007, 772). Poremba describes the tension that a "brink" game creates through its exploitation of the relationship between the real, the virtual and the taboo:

> What makes the game exciting is the tangible threat of this breach; the heightened tension the game provides by taunting collapse. The ambiguity surrounding breach becomes the common business of its players, as they assess how real not-real needs to be to result in the collapse of the game into its other. Because of the prominent threat of breach, forbidden or brink games necessarily integrate this observation into the game in a way other games do not.
>
> (776)

For Poremba, such games require vigilant "self-observation," so that awareness plays a crucial role in "continual boundary maintenance and differentiation for any system." We must maintain "a persistent definition of self and other" (773). Bogost's insights about procedural rhetoric help to make sense of the problems inherent in *Kuma\War*. Procedural rhetoric works by creating what Bogost calls "possibility space," which is "the myriad configurations the player might construct to see the ways the processes inscribed in the system work" (2007b, 42). Because players are required to assume the availability of options not, in fact, offered to them, games occupy what Bogost calls an "ontological position," that is, the meaning in games resides in what Bogost calls the "simulation gap" between "rule-based representation and player subjectivity" (43). Brink games, then, present us with real moral decisions. If a game like *Kuma\War* purports to perfectly replicate the real physical world, then players have a responsibility to question whether or not the game's representation of possibilities is accurate or not, and to notice, for example, the absence of humanitarian peacemaking options. In a game, we should be aware that we can *only* explore the "possibility space" that the game affords us in its pro-gramming (42). The maintenance of the boundary between play and real life – as well as a consideration of the spillover between them – is essential to the enjoyment of all games, and perhaps especially brink games. As Salen and Zimmerman explain, "the safer we feel in the game we're playing, the more willing we are to play it." We need, they say, a "guarantee" that "no matter what happens in our pursuit of the well-played game, we will not be risking more than we are willing to risk" (2004, 473). We need the guarantee that what we are doing *is* just a game.

The seeming impermeability of the "magic circle" helps to illuminate why so many people are willing to play a brink game like *Kuma\War*, in which the Iraq war is represented *in* the game, but its distance from our daily lives seemingly protects us from real consequences of gameplay, and from taking seriously how the game's modeling of "reality" may relate to actual experiences in war. First released in 2004, *Kuma\War* is a series of first- and third-person tactical strategy games, most of which are based on recent events in Iraq. According to the website, "Kuma War is a series of playable recreations of real events in the War on Terror. Nearly 100 playable missions bring our soldiers' heroic stories to life, and you can get them all right now, for free. Stop watching the news and get in the game!" (Kuma Games n.d.-b). Most missions come with a video introduction, including real footage from the war, advice from real military personnel, and "gameplay rundowns", showing you how to use weaponry "just like the real troops on the ground" ("Mehdi Cemetery" mission).

The procedural rhetoric of the game requires that one view everyone as either a supporter of the American army and worthy of support, or its enemy, and thus deserving of a swift execution. In the "Mehdi Cemetery" mission, players are instructed to destroy the "enemies," all of whom look very similar to one another, and who hide out in mosques or "pop up" out of tombs to attack you. An awareness of the ways that video games cultivate the techniques of procedural rhetoric requires that we recognize that "meaning in videogames is constructed not through a re-creation of the world, but through selectively modeling appropriate elements of that world" (Bogost 2007b, 46). The game has fairly active discussion boards with an unusual amount of religious dialogue. In one thread discussing *Kuma\War*'s "Attack on Iran," *Kuma\War*'s official representative Patricia said: "We created this mission as a reflection of future events that could very well come to fruition. Frankly, we feel Iran's refusal to cooperate with international community is frightening. Could there be a non-military solution at this point? We're not so sure" (posted October 5, 2005, in Kuma Games n.d.-a). What follows is a very heated discussion about jihad, violence in Christianity and Islam throughout history, quotations from the Quran and Bible, links to religious websites, and finally a desperate plea by one gamer: "This is a forum regarding KUMA/WAR ... not a forum regarding the true meaning of Islam or any other religion. Please stick to the general idea here and not who the true god is" (posted by Scotty the Scout, October 11,

2005, in Kuma Games n.d.-a). Afterward, the thread erupts into a series of flames, derogatory remarks, lewd photographs, and general name-calling, and claims about whose religion is really non-violent.

Although *Kuma\War* is not overtly religious, the game includes representations of mosques and sacred areas in its digital landscape, and requires that players shoot enemies inside these sacred places. The religious subtext to the game is obviously not lost on the discussion board participants, who adopt the game's hostility and its implicit religious content when they fling jarring insults at each other about the merits, weaknesses, and the supposed violent nature of religions, especially Christianity and Islam. The game purports to "accurately reconstruct real-war events from the news"; however, the games *cannot* be perfect "reconstructions" of events from the war, due to their programmed, procedurally fixed nature, but are rather opportunities to interact with carefully selected and re-imagined trajectories, guided rigidly by the ideological worldview of their creators and by the input of American military officials. The magic circle, then, is far from impermeable, reflecting as it does real-life ideological claims about real war situations.

Perhaps because they make fewer claims to protection by the "magic circle," games like *9/11 Survivor* and *New York Defender* have fared less well under public scrutiny than *Kuma\War*. Because the Twin Towers were on American soil, 9/11 felt closer to "home" than the Iraq war for most people today. To "play" at trying to escape the towers (as in *9/11 Survivor*), or at trying to "prevent" the planes from hitting them (as in *New York Defender*) is too close to the real for comfort. The game fails to maintain the tension between the real and the game, and the social contract of a protected game space is consequently broken. Such games don't allow us to feel safe experimenting with the "what-if" – they remind us that we may not be safe after all.

The spillover inherent in such games suggests that they might be as readily viewed as rituals. That is, games, like rituals, demarcate a space in which particular rules adhere – but in rituals, the experience is often *intended* to be transformative whereas in games this capacity is often denied or ignored. Nevertheless, if Bogost is right, then games too can have a lasting effect on the player, since they (like rituals) have a sort of "procedural rhetoric" that delivers a particular message or encourages fixed forms of behavior. Indeed, rituals and games exhibit a surprisingly deep kinship, so much so that the difference between them is perhaps more a matter of perspective than of form or function.

One of the most important similarities is that games and rituals are both fundamentally interactive: People *perform* games and rituals. For ritual theorists, the term "ritual" is sometimes even replaced by the term "performance" or "ritualization" as a means of emphasizing the interactivity – the configuration or procedurality – involved in a ritual. As we saw in Chapter 3, ritual theorists like Rappaport argue that "performance as well as formality is necessary for ritual," characteristics that are also applicable to games (428). Staal agrees, conceding that even if it has no other intrinsic meaning at all, ritual is something that *people do*: "Ritual is primarily activity," that is, "what you do, not what you think, believe, or say" (1996, 485). Games, too, are defined by performance, by formality, and by configurative, predictable processes.

Ritual is a process, Bell argues, tied up deeply with other social processes that are encountered, assessed, and either appropriated or rejected by individuals – in short, it is interactive, configurative, and procedural. What is most important about ritual, she says, "is not what it says or symbolizes, but that first and foremost it does things." Ritual, she insists, is *always* a matter of performance (1992, 111). If rituals and games both involve the entry of a participant into a temporary, bounded space in which particular behaviors are expected and in which fixed rules adhere, then the difference between a game and a ritual may be in the intent of the player and the definition of the experience. So if we apply Bogost's notion of procedural rhetoric to the gaming experience, we find that most if not all games do in fact offer some mode of "spillover" into real life, in that they deliver a message that is at least intended to shape the player in some way, typically in terms of choices in behavior. We may argue about what message that is – and of course people do – but it seems hard to deny that the experience has some rhetorical intent, enacted via the procedures and behaviors that players are required to enact.

Ritual, too, offers this kind of rhetorical shaping of the performer, in its structured affirmations of myth, in its ritualized shaping of bodily movement, in its evocation of institutionalized belief systems. The magic circle of play, it seems, is hardly the sanitized fixed realm of pure fantasy that we would like to imagine it to be. But to notice this is not to argue that games are necessarily violent or dangerous or morally problematic. It is, however, to say that the moral questions they raise are more profound than we might first acknowledge. If "serious games" like *Darfur is Dying*, the UN-sponsored *Food Force*, and *Operation Pedopriest* are intended to make us think deeply about difficult social and moral issues, then less "serious" games – especially brink games and games that exhibit forbidden play – should be equally able to deliver an implicit moral and social message about behavior. As a means of examining this claim, I turn to one of the most controversial violent video games of recent years: the online game *Super Columbine Massacre RPG!*. This game, perhaps more than any other, highlights the challenges of making sense of the moral implications of virtual play.

Super Columbine Massacre RPG! Memory, violence and religion

Super Columbine was created by Danny LeDonne and appeared online in 2005, on April 20, the exact day of the sixth anniversary of the Columbine shooting. LeDonne claims that he designed the game partly as an "indictment of our society at large" and partly because he too was "a misfit," "a loner" and "a bullied kid" in high school, with experiences that in some ways mirrored those of Eric Harris and Dylan Klebold, the students responsible for Columbine (cited in Vargas 2006). The game was designed with an RPG generator software package, and involves basic 16-bit graphics, reminiscent of older arcade-style games like *Pac-Man*, *Mario Brothers* or *Donkey Kong*. As the *Rocky Mountain News* reported in 2006, "the tiny characters look like something from an old Nintendo game." The player takes on the role of Eric Harris and "navigates a series of scenes that require Harris to plant bombs in the school cafeteria, meet Klebold on a hill outside the school and attack students in Columbine" (Vaughan and Crecente 2006). The game has been compared in impact to the film *Elephant* (2003), although players readily acknowledge that the interactivity of *Super Columbine*, despite its very primitive graphics, makes it a more hard-hitting experience than the film. The game has certainly generated more controversy. As Jose Antonio Vargas put it: "It's one thing to have a documentary (*Bowling for Columbine*), a movie (*Elephant*) and several books (*No Easy Answers*, *Day of Reckoning*) about that dark day, but it's quite another to have a game" (Vargas 2006).

One of the things that is the most puzzling in discussions about evil in video games is that they problematize our assumptions that we even know what evil is, that we can call it when we see it. Virtual modes of encounter raise issues never considered before – that a deed could be committed, and yet somehow also *not* committed: that people could be harmed, but not *really* harmed – or perhaps they weren't "real" people to begin with. David Hume had no problem identifying evil as a host of bodily ills, including ulcers, melancholy, madness, and even death. Dostoevsky saw evil in human stupidity, arrogance and cruelty. Others have included natural disasters in their catalog of evils humans must contend with. These definitions depend upon the notion of real harm, whether psychological or physical, and theological discussions spin around who is responsible for the harm – God, for allowing it, humans for choosing to do it through free will, or if such ills are simply a byproduct of being human. But in a video game, it is possible that nobody is hurt because the violence is merely virtual – and we are left wondering if this means that any violent actions enacted therein are without moral teeth.

Super Columbine Massacre RPG! is interesting because it pinpoints these problems precisely, largely through its status as one of the most controversial brink games ever written. Because the procedural rhetoric of the game invites direct character identification with Harris, the game evokes an almost ritual-like repetition of the events and defies easy dismissal of the experience as *just* a game. The game proposes a *re-experiencing* of the events in a procedural sense, and it engages the player in ways that films and books do not. If what Harris and Klebold did was evil in *any* sense of the word, then one could argue that the player repeats the processes they engaged in, enacting a sort of "procedural evil" that is somehow less than the original act, but somehow more than mere play. Even if nobody is killed in the game as a "replay," the *choices* of Harris and Klebold *are* replicated by the player.

The notion of scripted play as a re-enactment of violence has a surprising analogy in the ritual of the Mass, which similarly invites participants to move through a series of behaviors and statements that evoke recollection of death. Indeed, if René Girard's (1977) arguments about the mimetic function of sacrifice are evoked, then the parallels between *Super Columbine* and the Mass become oddly compelling. Consider Girard's discussion of the cathartic function of ritual sacrifice:

> The original act of ritual is unique and spontaneous. Ritual sacrifices, however, are multiple, endlessly repeated. All those aspects of the original act that had escaped man's control – the choice of time and place, the selection of the victim – are now premeditated and fixed by custom. The ritual process aims at removing all element of chance and seeks to extract from the original violence some technique of cathartic appeasement. The diluted force of the sacrificial ritual cannot be attributed to imperfections in its imitative technique. After all, the rite is designed to function during periods of relative calm; as we have seen, its role is not curative, but preventative.
>
> (107)

Girard sees the Christian Mass as the perfect example of substitutionary violence functioning as a salve for societal anxiety. In *Violence and the Sacred* (1977), Girard argues that societies periodically need a disruption of social order. Society, he says, by its very nature is invested with a desire for violence and retribution. By selecting a sacrificial victim, "society is seeking to deflect upon a relatively indifferent victim, a 'sacrificeable victim,' the violence that would otherwise be vented on its own members." Thus violence is "not denied," but is "diverted to another object, something it can sink its teeth into" (4). For Girard, Christians replicate in ritual the sacrifice of Jesus, and are thus allotted some imperfect but functional means of releasing violent impulses.

Even a living Buddhist lama, Trinley Dorje, claims that video games can serve this function. The twenty-four-year-old Dorje, the Karmapa Lama, is the only senior Buddhist leader acknowledged by Beijing, and heads a major school of Tibetan Buddhist thought. Dorje places the emphasis not on substitutionary or even simulative violence but instead on the purging properties he sees video games as possessing. When asked why he plays violent video games even though "many might say it's inappropriate for a Buddhist monk dedicated to peace," he replies:

> Well, I view video games as something of an emotional therapy, a mundane level of emotional therapy for me. We all have emotions whether we're Buddhist practitioners or not, all of us have emotions, happy emotions, sad emotions, displeased emotions and we need to figure out a way to deal with them when they arise. So, for me sometimes it can be a relief, a kind

of decompression to just play some video games. If I'm having some negative thoughts or negative feelings, video games are one way in which I can release that energy in the context of the illusion of the game. I feel better afterwards. The aggression that comes out in the video game satiates whatever desire I might have to express that feeling. For me, that's very skilful because when I do that I don't have to go and hit anyone over the head.

(Lall 2009)

When asked if meditation should "take care of that" instead, the lama replies that "video games are just a skilful method" and thus, by implication, can perform the same function of clearing the head of violent impulses as meditation (Lall 2009)! For Girard, they would most likely be seen as a grim but necessary symbolic replay of horrific events that in their remembering prevent, at least temporarily, additional outbursts of violence. If Girard is right, virtual (mimetic) violence is *substitutionary*. For the lama, virtual violence is just an "illusion" with no bearing on real life, apart from its "cleansing" function. These are subtle threads of difference at work here, but they reveal an important distinction: Does performative on-screen violence happen *only* in its virtual context and is it thus akin to meditation as a spiritual cleansing activity? Or does virtual violence happen on-screen because we are unable to easily sink our teeth into real-life victims in contemporary industrialized society and virtual killing is our next best option?

In either reading, video games are a sort of mimetic enactment of violence. Indeed, if these theories of cathartic violence are right, then *Super Columbine* can be seen as serving a societal *good* by offering players a relatively harmless means of expelling violent impulses in a safe environment. Also, like the Catholic Mass, we could argue that *Super Columbine* offers players a scripted, perhaps liturgical, means of "remembering" the violence of the shooting. The "brink" nature of the violence in *Super Columbine* only serves to heighten its efficacy, as the "resemblance" between the virtual victims and the real victims will increase the depth of the cathartic experience. Such arguments are dark and disturbing, but so are Girard's claims that humans are deeply invested with such violent impulses. The most important question then becomes whether or not we do, in fact, need such violent replaying of horror, and if we do need it, whether or not video games can functionally do the same kind of symbolic work as the Christian Mass.

Danny LeDonne makes no explicit religious claims, but he does propose some moral intentions. For LeDonne, *Super Columbine* is important today because it is "art," that is, it raises interesting and provocative questions about school shootings. And he's not alone. Speaking of *Super Columbine*, respected game theorist Ian Bogost says: "Art is not supposed to be comfortable ... Art must be allowed to be disturbing and dangerous. ... The world is a messy place and we don't always, or even often, get to make sense of it in a clean way. We have to get our hands dirty. Art is one way to help us to do that" (Bogost 2007a). Schrier and Gibson admit that games do have the ability to evoke powerful emotions and should prompt deep ethical considerations for designers and for players: "A powerful game design can embody and dramatize certain core ethical debates; it can provide resources that encourage us to ask certain questions and enable us to explore their ramifications" (2010a, xvii). Indeed, they add, "games are particularly well-suited to the practice and development of ethical thinking, since, for example, the computationally rich media platform offers the ability to iterate and reflect on multiple possibilities and consequences" (xx). Procedural rhetoric, then, is key for the consideration of the moral implications of gameplay.

Video games like *Super Columbine*, then, are seen to have real moral importance simply for calling our attention to the place where the magic circle and the real world meet. What does it mean, asks such a game, to "remember" via performance, to "re-enact" a terrifying, amoral act by placing it within a context that we normally associate with having no bearing on real life? What does it mean when play becomes real? In other words, *Super Columbine* suggests strongly that the magic circle is never fully insulated. Further, it forces us to ask to what extent the procedural rhetoric portrayed in the game (here's how the killers proceeded) can become prescriptive (here's how to proceed as a killer). Indeed, some argue that violent video games, especially ones like *Super Columbine*, should be read as training modules for how to kill.

But the difficulty in making sense of SCMRPG is that although we can tell this is a brink game, and we seem to see the fluidity between the real world and the virtual one that it displays, we can never be completely sure *what* is spilling over from the virtual into the real. As Bogost remarks:

> Simply playing a videogame need not entail the player's adoption of the represented value system; the player might oppose, question, or otherwise internalize its claims: which processes does it include, and which does it exclude? What rules does the game enforce, and how do those rules correlate, correspond, or conflict with an existing morality outside the game?
>
> (2007b, 284)

Thus, even though a sort of procedural evil *appears* to be enacted upon playing the game, we can never be sure of the motivations of the player or the attitude with which he or she engages the experience. The difference between the software's *intended* trajectory and the player's experience *following* that trajectory may be the difference between an engaged, immersed, procedural *replay* of the murders and a *disengaged* player's response to those murders – a response that could be celebratory, disgusted, angry, curious, or puzzled. However, whatever the response, the mere fact that the player "controls" Harris and thus exhibits agency in the game's re-enactment of events is troubling enough, raising deeply profound moral questions. As one high school player puts it: "If I play [*Super Columbine Massacre RPG!*] and I enjoy it, does that make me a bad person?" (LeDonne 2008).

The problem of evil is a cunningly nuanced one in the twenty-first century. With our increasing investment in virtual contexts, we have to ask new and very difficult questions about agency, performance, intent and behavior. Traditional discussions about evil assume an awareness of *who* is performing particular acts, and generally assume that someone must be a victim of evil for there to be evil at all. Even the privation theory of evil assumes that *someone* experiences privation. But what happens when the agent is unclear, or when it is a non-player character that is harmed, or when a virtual experience re-enacts a real one and we must decide if the virtual re-enactment is an authentic performance of the original deed? The swelling volume of questions about what degree of concern we should have about violent video games seems to pivot around the problem of virtual performance and its implications – leading us to the conclusion that if procedural evil is possible, then it must be grounded in intent or in scripted performance, not in the immediate effects of virtual performance on real people. The fundamental nature of player intent in making sense of virtually performed "evil" is the firmest ground on which to land – but the most difficult to adequately define.

Conclusion

Stephen O'Leary argues that he does not believe that "any cyber-ritual – even one that makes full use of the latent capabilities of current Internet technology – will ever be able to replace ritual performance in a physical sacred space." Even with the most advanced graphics, sound technology, and 3D simulations, for O'Leary "the participant in such rituals remains too much of a spectator, separated from the virtual space by the box on the desk" (2005, 44). One would think that the "magic circle" of a game *should* be easily defined by the box, or by the screen on which a game is played. However, O'Leary may be a bit naive in his assumptions about the ability of hardware alone to distinguish between the liminal and the real. Whether we like it or not, the "box on the desk" is on its way out, and when it goes, fully immersive technology may make such easy distinctions between real and virtual more complicated – and thus make the ease with which we define a game or ritual more complicated as well.

Dawson has observed recently "how and why many analysts have seen the mediation of religious experience online as problematic" (2005, 16). Part of the answer, Dawson believes, "lies in a postmodernist dilemma … the medium [of the internet] seems to significantly heighten the reflexivity of participants in rituals, and this reflexivity can appear to be inimical to authentic religious practice" (16). Drawing on the comments of a long-time cyber-religionist, Dawson relays the conviction that "all that matter are the experiences that are experimentally generated and manipulated by the skilful understanding and use of words and the temporary worlds they create in the minds of individuals. In the classic postmodernist mode, the simulation can be substituted for reality, yet there is not really a complete collapse of the sign and the signified since the focus is still on some seemingly 'authentic' experience" (26). Although this observation is based on textual and clearly religiously motivated experiences, the notion of authenticity in virtual reality residing in the experience of the participant is the salient point, one which applies to our interaction with video games too. Whether we like it or not, reflexivity determines if we view *Left Behind: Eternal Forces* as a religious training module or an absurd ideological exercise; reflexivity shapes our response to the representation of Manchester Cathedral in *Resistance: Fall of Man*, and reflexivity affects how we sort out the relationship between the real war in Iraq and our enactments of it in *Kuma\War*.

In today's world, we must *choose* where the "magic circle" begins and ends, and what, if anything, constitutes a sacred space. Some gaming experiences indeed make it easier for us to choose to see them as play – if they take place in the distant past or distant future, for example, or if they involve a lot of obvious fantastical elements. In these cases, the magic circle is thick, and our tendency to see such experiences as pure imaginative play is thus enhanced. Other gaming experiences, especially those with simulative qualities like military training style games or *Super Columbine*, make it more difficult for us to see them as "just" play, since the magic circle is relatively thin; the difference between real life and the world of play is permeable, unclear, and contested. However, one could just as well argue that even those games with a "thick" magic circle can teach us unsavory things, and that it is possible to view a military training module as a mere game. Reflexivity is unavoidable in the end.

Grimes recognizes reflexivity as an integral part of ritual activity today when he asks: "Who – participant or observer – is to decide whether procedures fail, and if they do, what sort of infelicity has been committed?" (1996a, 290). For Grimes, "in some types [of ritual failures] the problem lies with the ritualists, in others with the rite itself, and in still others with the relation between the rite and surrounding, religiocultural processes" (290). He rightly expresses doubt that "one can ever judge a rite as failed or flawed in any absolute way. It is always flawed from person or group X's point of view or in relation to goal Y" (291). It appears to be primarily the participant's *intent* – a form of reflexivity – that determines how we approach a game or ritual, and how it affects our lives when the game or ritual is finished. Accordingly, how one interprets violence in religious ritual and in video games will similarly depend upon the intentional, reflexive purpose with which one encounters these cultural artifacts and ultimately, how one *chooses* to define them.

Chapter 8

Xbox apocalypse
Video games, interactivity and revelatory literature

Video games, especially first-person shooters, resemble a very specific religious form of the magic circle: apocalypses.[1] The adjective "apocalyptic" as commonly used today typically refers to cataclysmic imagery and predictions of the end times. However, the noun "apocalypse" has a more specific usage for biblical scholars, identifying a genre of ancient Jewish and Christian texts composed between about 300 BCE and 200 CE in the ancient Mediterranean region. These apocalypses exhibit fixed forms and structures, describe events of the end times, adhere to predictable literary patterns, and deal with recurring themes. They also describe otherworldly journeys of visionaries who observe the coming end times and the violent imminent judgment against their enemies. Despite being created some two thousand years after these Jewish and Christian apocalypses, video games like *Assassin's Creed*, *Halo*, and even the *Zelda* series fit the definition of apocalypse as articulated by the Society of Biblical Literature "Apocalypse Group" (Collins, 1979):

> An apocalypse is a genre of revelatory literature with a narrative framework in which a revelation is mediated by an otherworldly being to a human recipient, disclosing a transcendent reality which is both temporal, insofar as it envisages eschatological salvation, and spatial, insofar as it involves another, supernatural world.

These video game worlds are surprisingly rife with apocalyptic imagery and exhibit a narrative inevitability that shares features with the notion of theological inevitability in traditional apocalypses. Indeed, the formal similarity between such games and traditional apocalypses is remarkable, even if these two end-of-the-world genres appear to be serving different functions for the communities who value them. Gameplay, it seems, may have some profound kinship with religious imagination.

Apocalyptic narrative and procedural rhetoric

Apocalyptic literature flourished during the two centuries before the Common Era and the two centuries after. This era was popular for apocalyptic literature for a reason: the people who produced it felt oppressed by their Greek and Roman overlords and sought a means of coping with their inability to prevent their own persecution. For some, writing and telling stories about the destruction of their enemies helped them to deal with an intolerable situation by enabling them to imagine God's imminent intervention. Accordingly, Christian and Jewish apocalypses from this period describe the hope for a divinely ordained messiah to intervene and defeat their enemies and predictions of divine judgment to come against their persecutors (as well as vivid images of the punishment to be eked out by God against their enemies). As the Society of Biblical Literature (SBL) definition of apocalypse indicates, the hope for this judgment is typically relayed in the form of a vision mediated by an otherworldly mediator and depicting an otherworldly journey in which the visionary sees the future and possibly also the places of reward and punishment to come. Because the authors of these visions hoped for divine intervention very soon, there is typically also an intense interest in relaying of events of the coming end times. Visionaries often identify themselves with ancient religious figures (pseudonymity) to lend credibility to their experiences.

Thus video games, like traditional apocalypses, can be viewed as "revelatory literature" with a "narrative framework" about an "otherworldly" location. This framework involves a human recipient and an otherworldly mediator who describes "eschatological salvation which is temporally [in the] future and present[s] otherworldly realities" (1979, 9). Video games like *Halo* and *Assassin's Creed* are similarly structured according to a narrative framework, and invite players to actively enter into a "world" accessible to the player only through the medium of the video game console. In fact, video games typically thrive on the imaginative creation of fantasy environments within which players can "really" move and act, and in which they learn about the other world.

Another very important feature of ancient apocalypses is their determinism. Apocalypses presuppose history's unfolding as pre-established by God, who could be seen in this case as a sort of cosmic software engineer. Apocalypses, says Collins, are "augmented [by] a sense of determinism ... by affirming that the course of history or the structure of the cosmos was determined long ago" (Collins 1998, 40). For example, we see this idea portrayed in *Halo* in the device of the Portal, which resides on earth (and thus is accessible to humans but not to the Covenant). The Portal leads directly to the Ark, in which resides the nerve center of the entire *Halo* array. In this sense, then, humans (and especially Master Chief [the player's character]) appear to be chosen by the Forerunners in antiquity for events that unfold within the game. Humans, it seems, were meant to enact the divine purposes of the Forerunners. Interestingly, they also enact the purposes of the software engineers of *Halo*, who have predetermined to some extent the myth's interactive unfolding in gameplay.

As James Newman notes, "videogames do not present endlessly variable scenarios" (2002, 104). Indeed, choices are so transcribed that one could view goal-oriented video games as simply "collections of linear stories" in which the options are "only virtual" (Grodal 2003, 146). Each game world is based on a map or "system of multiple linear routes" through virtual space and virtual interactions or choices (147). As Arthur Berger notes, "the player's feeling that he or she is in control is only an illusion. Every choice, and its attendant consequences, has already been placed in the story by the programmers, writers, and artists who created the game" (2005, 191). The notion of the "fated" quality of video games, something I have addressed already in previous chapters, is very important here.

Newman argues that despite the degree of interactivity involved in play,

> [v]ideogames present highly structured and, importantly, highly segmented experiences. Play sequences, from where the idea of the interactivity or ergodicity of video games derives, are framed and punctuated by movie sequences, map screens, score or lap-time feedback screens and so on … [video games] are highly structured and comprise episodes of intense ergodic engagement. However, these sequences are punctuated and usually framed by periods of far more limited ergodicity and very often, apparently none at all.
>
> (2002)

In other words, the sense of "freedom" in video games is often more rigidly controlled than it seems, giving the programmer (but not necessarily the player) the ability to see all possibilities that will inhere in the game, and also to control the ultimate outcome. Similarly Michael Wolter identifies the "most important distinguishing feature" of apocalypses as "the course of historical events being revealed to and interpreted by a holy person and/or prophet chosen by God." The revelation of events "presupposes an understanding of history in which its course is established in advance by God and exists in heaven before it is transformed into earthly events" (2000, 127). Apocalypses, says John J. Collins, are "augmented [by] a sense of determinism … by affirming that the course of history or the structure of the cosmos was determined long ago" (1998, 40). Determinism is a key characteristic of both video games and apocalypses. God and video games, then, have something in common – the processes they initiate are predictable, moving toward intentional, predictable, and predetermined ends.

We could say, then, that apocalypses exhibit a sort of theologically motivated narrative rhetoric. If we think of God as a programmer, then we could say that God has engineered the set of player choices we have as humans, with history revealing the unfolding of his design. Such a sense of predetermination is comforting to the hearers of apocalypses; this worldview has a lot in common with procedural rhetoric. As we have already seen, Bogost defines procedural rhetoric as those "processes [that] define the way things work: the methods, techniques, and logics that drive the operation of systems" (2007b, 3). For Bogost, such procedural arguments are exceedingly persuasive, due in no small part to their execution via computers, the most predictable system there is – except, perhaps, God (36). We could then argue that this kind of computational assurance is akin to the apocalyptic rhetoric of God's certain judgment, what we might call his divine procedural rhetoric.

Procedural rhetoric works by creating what Bogost calls "possibility space," which consists of "the myriad configurations the player might construct to see the ways the processes inscribed in the system work" (42). This sense of "possibility space" could be considered a sort of "covenant" with the player – he or she has agreed to abide by the rules of play and in so doing, has entered into a set of possibilities that are transcribed by the parameters of the game before it even begins. Theological perspectives also demarcate a "possibility space" for believers, who see the world and act in it according to the procedural rhetoric of the belief system. An apocalypse, then, exhibits God's "procedural rhetoric" in its narrative description of the unfolding of history in a way that God has designated, but which allows for humans a certain amount of "play" within the rules. As Flannery-Dailey remarks, God "is distinguished from humans in having control over time, as well as by possessing all knowledge of time" (1999, 240). By depicting the cosmos as subject to God's rules and shaped by God's own predetermined design, apocalypses can be viewed as the *ultimate* game, shaped by the *ultimate* procedural rhetoric. Games even exhibit the dualism of apocalypses in that both genres exhibit a marked concern with forces of good arrayed against forces of evil, usually with the assumption of a procedural rhetoric of victory for the forces of good. Most stories and games, Murray says, "include some element of the contest between protagonist and antagonist" (2004, 2). In presenting the world in an "us versus them" fashion, apocalypses and games both restrict our interactivity with them in fairly rigid ways.

As I argue elsewhere with Tyler DeHaven and Chris Hendrickson, in *Halo*, human forces oppose the forces of the Flood, a massive collection of parasites that consume any sentient life with sufficient biomass to sustain them (2011). "The Flood" may be identified as socialist society with no pain, no hunger, and in which many of life's problems appear to be solved. Unfortunately, the Flood's success also depends upon the brutal murder of other living entities. When viewed as a force of evil, the Flood in *Halo* may be read as a metaphor for unsustainable consumerism. In this way, then, players are invited to see *themselves* arrayed against the forces of consumerism, as they battle the Flood's literal "consumption" of other living entities in *Halo*. This kind of metaphorical allusion to contemporary social ills is also a common feature of ancient Jewish and Christian apocalypses, which regularly targeted oppressive regimes like Rome via rich symbolic imagery of beastly and destructive creatures (Wagner *et al.* 2011).

Assassin's Creed also uses dualism to present a critique of contemporary society, with an emphasis on greed and technology run amok. The story begins in 2012. Desmond Miles, also known as "Subject Seventeen" is a bartender who has been kidnapped before the game begins. We discover that he has been brought to Abstergo Industries, where researchers are developing a project with a machine called an Animus, which can read memories of one's ancestors. The "Subject" replays these memories, allowing the researchers to access them. The game consists of Desmond's replaying of memories of his ancestor, Altair, a medieval assassin in Israel during the Third Crusade. We eventually discover that the cause of Abstergo Industries' interest in Desmond is that the researchers there are actually descendants of the Templars, who seek a series of "Artifacts" including one called the "Piece of Eden" and another consisting of an ornate box that the game suggests could be the Ark of the Covenant. These "Artifacts" have the ability to deceive those under their power, and thus can be used to control the world. Using Desmond's memory, they hope to locate these artifacts in the present to enact their villainous plan. The player identifies with Desmond, who then identifies with his ancestor Altair. With this sense of nested identities, the player re-enacts memories from Altair's life in medieval Israel. The plot of *Assassin's Creed* is reinforced by its apocalyptic structure, which invites players into a virtual world, leading them through an otherworldly journey and inviting them to see themselves as messianic agents of deliverance against the forces of evil. We now turn to particular aspects of the *Semeia* definition of apocalypse as they apply to traditional apocalypses and to video games.

Otherworldly mediators

Otherworldly mediators are a familiar feature in apocalypses, escorting the visionary through what might otherwise be treacherous otherworldly terrain, interpreting for the visionary what he sees, reassuring him about God's purposes. Apocalypticists received visions that David Aune says were "made clear to the readers through use of the literary device of an 'interpreting angel,' who explained everything to the seer through a question-and-answer dialogue" (2005, 236). In the *Book of the Watchers* (I Enoch 1–36), in *3 Baruch*, and in *4 Ezra*, for example, a seer acquires heavenly knowledge through questions asked of an otherworldly mediator.

In video games an "otherworldly mediator" also often appears, and guides the player through tutorials, offers helpful hints at crucial moments, and encourages the player to achieve his or her goals in the game. *The Legend of Zelda*, first released in the late 1980s, involves the adventures of Link, who is guided by merchants, fairies, and others who give him the clues he needs to complete the journey. In *Assassin's Creed*, too, players interact with a virtual guide, in this case, a disembodied technological voice, presumably connected to the Animus. In the training module at the beginning of the game, the player is instructed by the voice about how to move about the virtual space, how to use the controls, how to "blend in" among others, how to climb, how to hide, and how to kill.

In *Halo*, players are aided by Cortana, an artificially intelligent computer who explains the backstory and strategies appropriate for the player as he or she assumes the role of the Master Chief. Cortana has no physical form, but portrays herself holographically. Cortana teaches players how to move around and how to use the game's targeting programs. She also serves as a tactical navigator in unfamiliar areas, hacks encrypted enemy communications networks, and generally keeps the player informed about what to do and where to go. An entity called 343 Guilty Spark also acts as an otherworldly guide in *Halo*. Guilty Spark (a name that may evoke quasi-Gnostic religious themes) answers questions from Master Chief, Cortana and the Arbiter about the Halos' real purpose. Interestingly, in video games like *Halo* and *Assassin's Creed*, technology – not an angel – tells us how to make our way through the new worlds in which we find ourselves (Wagner *et al.* 2011).

Other worlds and the magic circle

Apocalypses resemble video games too in their focus on otherworldly spaces and our imaginative journeys through them. As John J. Collins explains, an "otherworldly journey" takes place in an apocalypse "when the visionary travels through heaven, hell or remote regions beyond the normally accessible world." Revelation, he says, "is usually predominantly visual" (1979, 6). Apocalypticists depict the otherworldly realm as a place that can be entered into as a "temporary world" formally distinguished from surrounding space and time. Take, for example, Enoch's description of his ascent into the heavens, in which "the vision clouds invited me and a mist summoned me, and the course of the stars and the lightnings sped and hastened me, and the winds in the vision caused me to fly and lifted me upward, and bore me into heaven." He sees "a wall which is built of crystals and surrounded by tongues of fire" and "a tesselated floor (made) of crystals." On the ceiling, he sees "fiery cherubim" (I Enoch 14; trans., Charles edition, 2004, 197).

Later, an angel gives Enoch a tour of otherworldly locations, including the "firmament of heaven," a "region the end of the great earth," and a "deep abyss" filled with fire. The angel with him explains to him the meaning of the vision, and its relationship to God's eschatological purposes (I Enoch 18). As Collins notes, in apocalypses "heavenly geography" of this sort is typically described in vivid detail, relating it to beliefs about God's order and power over creation (1979, 9). As Collins notes, "the spatial, otherworldly realities," like those described in I Enoch, "always involve the activity of otherworldly, angelic or demonic beings." "Heavenly geography" is described in detail, relating it to beliefs about God's order and power over creation (1979, 9). In Enoch's journey into an otherworldly place, he views sights as intense as any offered in today's imaginative virtual journeys in the "otherworlds" of video games.[2]

What Collins calls "heavenly geography" also appears in video games. In *Halo*, paradisiacal imagery shows up in the lush and varied geography of the rings, or "halos," a few of which Master Chief visits. If you play the third game of *Halo* on the most difficult "legendary" setting, you see Master Chief at the end of the game stuck in half of the ship, the only bit remaining after a cataclysmic explosion. If you win, the game ends with a vision of the ship descending to a planet infused with symbols associated with the "Forerunners," implying a sort of return to divine origins. *Assassin's Creed* demarcates such imagery as well; as soon as the game powers up, the player "walks a Memory Corridor" and enters into a training module called "the Garden of Paradise."

Bartle, in his guidebook to designing video games, describes the passage from our world into a virtual one as consisting of the installation of software on the computer, powering it up, and then "enter[ing] the virtual world" (2003, 438). In *Assassin's Creed*, we see this passage enhanced vividly as the player is led through a transitional experience of entry into the game's world. After passing through a "brightly lit corridor" in which "women gather around you, their faces blotted out, like ghosts," the player hears an "older, menacing voice." The voice quotes Ecclesiastes 1:18: "I abide my heart to know wisdom, and to know madness and folly. I perceive that this also was a chasing at the wind. For in much wisdom, is much grief. And he that increaseth knowledge, increaseth sorrow" (Hodgson and Knight 2007, 168). The player hears voices of concern, saying things like "Let me try and stabilize him" and "Recognize that what you're seeing isn't real." The *Assassin's Creed: Prima Official Game Guide* (Hodgson and Knight 2007) describes what happens next: "You wake with a gasp and on a slablike tablet attached to a terminal" (168). After this initial entry into an idealized paradise, the rude awakening into the world of science seems startling. It is at this point that the player realizes who he or she *is* in the game: Desmond Miles, a bartender who is also an "Assassin," and has particular value to Abstergo Industries, as the scientist explains: "You have information we need, Mr. Miles ... you've got something that my employers want, locked away in that head of yours" (game dialogue, *Assassin's Creed*). This experience marks the player's "passage" into the "other world" of the game, and also indicates the secret knowledge the visionary will find.

Christian video games like *Heaven: The Game* by Genesis Works (2010) also make such overt immersive attempts. The web page describes gameplay:

> The story is about a young boy named Joshua, who ... pilots an experimental shuttle to the moons of Jupiter. Along the way, he encounters a deadly asteroid field that nearly destroys his ship – the USS *Genesis*. At the moment of his destruction, the Archangel Michael saves him. Alive and well, Joshua is transported to Heaven! – where he meets an old friend. The "old friend" is actually his grandmother in a glorified body. Her new name is "Axis." With her help, you will play through 6 exciting levels of Heaven. You will see Paradise Island, the Golden Streets, the New Jerusalem, the Pearly Gate, the Creation Room, and finally a glimpse of the Throne of Jesus Himself! You will also see the Four Living Creatures from the Book of Revelation, the Archangel Michael, the Elder Kings who sit on the thrones and much more!

In addition to the sideways jab at space fighting games as imperfect story worlds when compared with Heaven, what is remarkable about this game is its willing representation of the virtual space of the game as identical, at least symbolically, to the spiritual space of heaven. Equally compelling is the affiliated premise that the player can somehow imaginatively enter into this heavenly space via the game itself!

One need not have a device like the Animus of *Assassin's Creed* or an imaginative invitation to heaven, to get a sense of "other worlds" in video games. Some people view the virtual world *itself* as a glimpse into a world or "reality" not limited in the same way as our physical world: a place where bodies do not decay, where fantasies can be fulfilled, or where we can explore areas of spiritual and supernatural import. As Lahti observes, the introduction of 3D graphics has only increased our sense of gameplay as otherworldly, "convincingly feeding Gibson's remarked-on 'intuitive faith that there's some kind of actual space behind the screen ... '" (2003, 160). Game theorists have long recognized the yearning induced by virtual reality. Accordingly, the "world" of a video game can be perceived as another "place," characterized by perfection – or the hope for perfection – that may not seem achievable in our own world.

The end times

Apocalypses and video games involve components of transcendent reality that are particularly concerned with the end of time. Drawing on Collins' definition, we can say that apocalypses are "temporal, insofar as [they] invisage eschatological salvation" and "spatial, insofar as [they] involve another, supernatural world." Video games are "temporal" in their explicit division of gameplay into levels and time limits, mimicking those apocalypses that divide time into epochs or stages before the final end. Similarly, in the ancient Jewish "Apocalypse of Weeks" in I Enoch, time is divided into ten periods or "weeks," with history reaching its climax in the seventh week (the author's own time) and looking forward to the eighth week (in which judgment of the wicked will take place). The expectation of an imminent end characterizes many apocalypticists' messages of impending judgment of the wicked and rewards for the just.

As we saw in Chapter 3, an effective video game is often similarly characterized by the dynamics of "dramatic inevitability, the sense that the contest is moving forward toward a conclusion." According to LeBlanc, "if [a game's] contest appears as if it will never conclude – or not conclude any time soon – then it has no sense of urgency, and the dramatic tension is dispelled" (2006, 453). In both apocalypses and video games, involvement depends upon "our level of emotional investment in the story's conflict: the sense of concern, apprehension, and urgency with which we await the story's outcome" (443). Whereas in apocalypses, the periodization of time and the expectation of an imminent judgement create tension, in video games other techniques are used, such as the game design technique we already considered in Chapter 3: the "ticking clock."

The ticking clock, says LeBlanc, "stands as a constant reminder that the game will end, and soon" (446). The ticking clock features of a game convey "a sense of forward motion: as time runs out, the players feel propelled toward the conclusion of the contest" (453). One way to enhance this experience is to utilize an actual countdown. Another is to give a sense of dwindling resources, "quantifiable assets within the game state that deplete over the course of play and are never replenished" (453). Ticking clocks are "non-reversible processes" or "changes to the game state that can't be undone" (454). These project a sense of linearity into an experience that is moving inevitably toward a fixed outcome.

The ticking clock in *Halo* typically precedes some sort of cataclysm and takes the form of a series of time-sensitive tasks with the impetus of urgency to prevent the end of the game, but more importantly, to save the world. Instead of offering a simplistic timer counting down, *Halo* repeatedly depicts increasing levels of chaos and systems derailing all around, with the need for imminent escape. In addition, there is literally a countdown timer in the last level of every *Halo* game. Accordingly, one way of viewing time in video game apocalypses and in traditional Jewish and Christian apocalypses is to view it as moving consistently forward toward its inevitable end. As Aune notes, in traditional apocalypses, "the outcome is never in question," since "the enemies of God are predestined for defeat and destruction." The period of punishment will be followed by "[t]he inauguration of the new age [that] will begin with the arrival of God or his accredited agent to judge the wicked and reward the righteous and will be concluded by the re-creation or transformation of the earth and the heavens" (2005, 236). In *Halo*, too, the outcome is never in question; the game will end. The question is: will you win?

Despite the sense of linear forward motion, time in apocalypses can also be viewed as cyclical in some regards, a feature shared by video games as well. As

Aune again notes, an apocalypse "anticipates a cataclysmic divine intervention into the human world bringing history to an end, but thereafter a renewal of the world in which Edenic conditions will be restored" (2005, 237). The makers of *Assassin's Creed* make just such a gesture. At the very end of the game, the player is "thrown back into the Garden of Paradise, where the Fruit of Eden opens slightly to show a holographic display. Beams of light break through, sketching an image of the world. The image shakes then solidifies. It is a globe showing continents displayed with an accuracy impossible for the twelfth century. Areas of continents have markers on them, glowing pinpoints of light" (Hodgson 2007, 324). These markers indicate the locations of the remaining Artifacts, and open up the game to future iterations. Even the content of this game will be revisited in sequels, which fans predict will involve other characters experiencing some of the same historical events as Desmond, but from different perspectives and locations on earth.

In order to reconcile the linear and the circular models of time, Flannery-Dailey suggests a third model for understanding time in apocalypses: the "spiral model." In this model, time is linear, in its movement toward the *eschaton*, but it is *also* cyclical "in that it is characterized by a regular succession of events that begins again repeatedly at the starting point" (1999, 235). However, the repetition is not perfect, since previous events are not repeated but are "recapitulated" through symbolic interplay. Wolf says something similar about video games: they exhibit "repetition" in "cyclical or looped structures of time, which in some ways combine notions of movement and stasis" (2001b, 77). And of course, repeated plays of the same game will be hauntingly similar and profoundly different at once. Of video games, Wolf claims that the repetition generates a sort of familiarity that engenders confidence, so that "[l]earning the patterns of behavior and working around them is usually itself part of the game" (81). In video games, players must learn the spatial structure through repeated plays until they experience "a sense of the temporal loops" and so that "their timing, linkages, and other structures" will help them successfully navigate the space (81):

> Repetitions, cycled images, consistent and repeating behaviours, revisited narrative branches, and the replayability of many of the games themselves create a sense of expectation, anticipation, and familiarity for the player. They encourage the player to find the underlying patterns which allow him or her to take control of the situations encountered, and this assured orderliness may well be an important factor in the allure that video games have for many people.
>
> (82)

The ordered structure of time, then, is a very important component of apocalypses and also of video games. Is there any way in which the recapitulation of events in Jewish and Christian apocalypses inculcates in readers and listeners a sense of orientation and familiarity that better equips them to play the "game" of survival in rough times? One possible answer is in the discussion of technique in ascents as evident in some apocalypses and in *merkavah* literature.

A number of video games structurally mimic elements of Jewish *merkavah* (or "chariot") literature and the hazards that visionaries typically encountered in it. To ascend through the heavens and survive at all, the visionary must know the right incantations, the appropriate actions, and must exhibit appropriate piety. Levels of ascent also appear in *The Ascension of Isaiah* and in *The Book of Enoch* which includes Enoch's "ascent to heaven" and "his guided tour of remote places, where he sees such things as the chambers of the dead and the places that have been prepared for final judgment" (Collins 2005, 138). Video games, too, often offer a model of "levels" and "ascent" via improvement and facility of technique. Juul uses the example of arcade games as types of games that "present several ontologically separate worlds that simply replace one another with no indication of any connection" (2004, 136). Says Juul, "[i]f we think of games as fiction or stories, these kind of abrupt jumps seem unwarranted and esoteric" (137). However, if we think of the games as experiences, then the levels or "memory blocks" in a game like *Assassin's Creed* seem more akin to the journey through multiple heavens as in the Jewish *merkavah* (chariot) literature. In such visions and journeys, the seer must "negotiate with heavenly beings," including being "threatened by dangerous angels" (Nogueira 2002, 180). Players of video games, too, must negotiate with digital entities, enacting complex tasks, sometimes with the aid of passwords and props.

In *Halo*, for example, players move through increasingly difficult levels of play. The idea of ascent is even explicitly indicated in *Halo* through the wish of the Covenant to "ascend" into divinity, which they erroneously believe will happen through activation of the Halo array. This idea of "ascent" as a mode of entering a new world is also distinctively Gnostic. In Gnostic apocalypses, ascent is the primary goal of the visionary, who instead of viewing the punishment of one's enemies, as in traditional apocalypses, is treated after ascent to a vision of the eventual reunification of all things in the godhead. Despite initial similarities, then, the Covenant's own drive to ascend to divinity in *Halo* contrasts with such traditional Gnostic views in that instead of achieving enlightenment, they are damned for their ignorance.

Structurally, both mystical ascent literature and video games like these suggest a degree of increasing proficiency evident in the seer's or player's successful movement through "levels," "worlds," or "heavens." Nogueira notes of Jewish mystical texts that the process of gaining access to heavenly worlds through religious ecstasy is not easy, and "demands technique." The recitation of proper formulas such as the *kedusha* appears in apocalyptic liturgies in *Revelation* and *The Apocalypse of Abraham* (181). Games too require techniques of memorization, recitation and ordering, some of which are consistent with those described in traditional ascents. In particular, games require skills like: "visual scanning," "auditory discrimination," "motor responses," "concentration" and "perceptual patterns of learning" about the system of the game (Salen and Zimmerman 2004, 315). To play a game is "to experience the game: to see, touch, hear, smell, and taste the game; to move the body during play, to feel emotions about the unfolding outcome, to communicate with other players, to alter normal patterns of thinking" (314). What are we to make of these similarities? Maybe the appeal has something to do with the sense of accomplishment and territorial control; by visiting other imagined worlds, we enter into spaces that are structured, ordered, programmed, and predictable. In the case of games, we know before we even play that they are winnable. In the case of traditional apocalypses, believers are informed by faith that the otherworldly journey has a purpose, that time will end under God's control. Perhaps the performance in video games is similarly of imagined certainty, of resistance against the unpredictable vicissitudes of twenty-first-century secular life. In function, then, if not in theology, video games and apocalypses offer similar comforts.

Secret knowledge

The seer in an apocalypse communicates "a transcendent, often eschatological perspective on human experience" in the form of a revelation brought back to his community (Aune 2005, 235). This communication often comes in the form of esoteric knowledge, what Michael Stone calls the "revelation of heavenly or similar secrets" (1984, 383). Similarly, Bartle notes that an important feature in a video game or virtual world is the acquisition of knowledge: "The player seeks knowledge, either through experimentation (as a scientist) or from others (as a networker). The more that players learn about the virtual world and its inhabitants, the more they learn about themselves" (2003, 438).

In the *Halo* books, Cortana reveals to the reader secret information in the form of the personal history of the Master Chief, also known as John 117. In a sense, then, the *Halo* books themselves can also be seen as a sort of apocalyptic text, offering information unavailable to the player in the games alone. Another way in which secret information appears in *Halo* is in objects like the thirteen "hidden skulls" in *Halo* 3, a collection of "Easter egg" secrets which, when discovered, affect gameplay in sometimes unpredictable ways, as in the removal of the HUD (heads-up display) on the screen. These objects unlock achievements, creating prestige for players and amassing points for them in ways that raise their status among their real-life peers (Wagner *et al.* 2011).

In *Assassin's Creed*, the "secret" sought by Desmond is knowledge about the location of the Artifacts. One of these, the "Ark of the Covenant," is housed (in the game) below the Temple Mount. In an early level of the game, the player must navigate these subterranean rooms to locate the ark. In the "real world" beyond the Animus, the scientist desires this knowledge since he and his compatriots are seeking the current, contemporary location of the Artifacts. *Assassin's Creed* also overtly uses the apocalyptic notion of "secret knowledge" in the inclusion, at the end of the game, of mysterious drawings on the wall readable only by Desmond (and thus by the player) through his supernatural "Eagle Vision." The game guide even calls this experience the "great revelation." The images daubed on the walls in Desmond's chamber were written by a previous subject of the Animus. As the guide explains, the visionary "couldn't adjust to the Animus properly, but he saw visions. Terrifying visions. Chaos in all its forms. Codes in many languages" (Hodgson and Knight 2007, 326). The most devoted *Assassin's Creed* fans have deduced the meaning of most of the symbols and phrases that appear on the wall, and most have an overtly eschatological tone. The *Assassin's Creed* wiki explains:

> In the conclusion of the game, Desmond, having become "synchronized" with Altaïr, is able to use the eagle vision (a sort of empathic sight to see hidden messages and tell friend from foe) ... He also sees messages that only he can see, scrawled across the floors and walls that refer to the end of the world described by several religions, among other writings; such writings include references to the biblical passage Revelation 22:13 ("I am the Alpha and the Omega, the first and the last, the beginning and the end."), a Lorenz attractor, the Eye of Providence, as well as part of a Mandelbrot set and other writings in foreign languages. Additionally, there is the Mayan date of 13.0.0.0.0 – December 21, 2012 – which is only three months away within the game's timeline and represents the planned date of the launch of a mysterious satellite the Templars have created, which they claim will "permanently end the war." The Arabic word "Az-Zalzala," literally meaning "The Earthquake" can be seen, which is the title of a chapter in the Qur'an that talks about Judgment Day.

There is also a phrase in Hebrew scribbled on the wall, "olam habah," which means "the world to come," and is a deeply evocative term that would be readily recognized by practitioners of Jewish mystical traditions. The "secret" eschatological knowledge found on the wall is the claim of those gamers who are clever enough or determined enough to decipher it, then like an apocalyptic visionary, "bring" it back to the group at large, usually via online discussion boards. The eschatological nature of the Hebrew scribbling, however, points not to a transcendent world beyond the game or beyond our limited lives, but simply to another version of the game to be released. Apocalypticism becomes effective advertising.

Identity and pseudonymity

As Michael Stone has observed, pseudepigraphy (writing in someone else's name) is an exceedingly common feature in apocalyptic Jewish writings. A number of reasons for the adoption of pseudonyms have been offered by scholars, including the argument that the pseudonymous author may claim to be a previous revered figure in order to evoke "an aura of antiquity and participation in a tradition of great status and authority" (2006, 9). By writing pseudepigraphically, authors can "claim that they possess a tradition of learning inspired by God but not deriving its authority through the Mosaic revelation" (10). Video game play, too, is often characterized by the voluntary donning of usernames, alternate identifiers that allow players to hide behind alternate personae.

D. S. Russell identifies another reason for pseudonymity in ancient apocalypses – an experience that he calls "contemporaneity," that is, the apocalypticist's identification with the ancient personage whose name he adopts. Says Russell: "The apocalyptic writers, like the ancient seer in whose name they wrote, stood within the apocalyptic tradition, shared the same visionary experiences and received the same divine revelations" (1964, 136). The apocalypticist, suggests Russell, saw himself as "an 'extension' of [the ancient seer's] personality" (138). Russell examines "Hebrew 'psychology'" and reveals what he sees as a deep identification or "corporate personality" for apocalypticists in union with the venerable sage, for which "there is no exact parallel in modern thought" (132). As I observed with DeHaven and Hendrickson, players of *Halo* similarly create their own pseudonym, registered to their Xbox Live account, in order to participate in a tradition of virtual skirmishing and rise in both ranking and ability (Wagner *et al.* 2011).

This sort of hybrid identity is nothing new to today's game players, who (in addition to adopting unique usernames) also experience "contemporaneity" with the characters they play. One could even go so far as to say that contemporaneity, as a form of identity play, is a very basic element of ritual, of games, and of apocalypses. The player in *Halo* "contemporaneously" enacts the tasks of the Master Chief, the messianic figure in the game, through crucial firefights that result in the salvation of humanity. In so doing, the player also *becomes* a sort of visionary, experiencing the game *as* a vision.

In *Assassin's Creed*, the accessibility of one's memories, even while hooked up to the Animus, requires a "synchronization" process whereby the individual *re-experiences* the ancestor's memories. It is with this goal that Desmond is hooked up to the Animus. Says the in-game scientist: "Our DNA functions as an archive. It contains not only genetic instructions passed down from previous generations but memories as well. The memories of our ancestors." The scientists are using the Animus to sift through Desmond's genetic memory to locate the "Artifacts." We experience Desmond's genetic memories of medieval Jerusalem *with* and *as* Desmond and Altair. To play *Assassin's Creed*, then, is to engage in an experience of contemporaneity.

The identification of Desmond with Altair is enhanced by what the game calls the "Bleeding effect." This effect "occurs when a subject interfaces with the Animus for too great a period and eventually becomes unable to distinguish between their ancestor's memories and their own." That is, the identification between seer and visionary becomes so great that their experiences are indistinguishable from one another. At the end of the game, Altair's ability to use "Eagle Vision" and see otherwise invisible things is experienced by Desmond, when he is able to read the remains of writing on the wall near his bed in the laboratory. The player too, fully "synchronized" with Desmond and with Altair, experiences "Eagle Vision."

Contemporaneity is a common feature of many kinds of games, not just video games. As Huizinga says:

> The "differentness" and secrecy of play are most vividly expressed in "dressing up." Here the "extra-ordinary" nature of play reaches perfection. The disguised or masked individual "plays" another part, another being. He *is* another being. The terrors of childhood, open-hearted gaiety, mystic fantasy and sacred awe are all inextricably entangled in this strange business of masks and disguises.
>
> (1955, 13)

Hybridity of identity is a very basic form of play, of ritual, of games, and of apocalypses.

Messianic activity

Once you look for them, it's easy to see the structural and thematic similarities between contemporary video games and ancient Jewish and Christian apocalypses. But one very obvious difference between these genres is in the representation of violent agency in bringing about humanity's salvation. In traditional apocalypses, visionaries look forward to rewards for the faithful and punishment for the wicked as enacted by God. As Stone notes, "[a]pocalyptic eschatology is permeated by the expectation of the imminent end and, for it, the advent of the end *does not depend* upon human action" (1984, 383). Collins argues that "[t]he great majority of Jewish apocalypses are quietistic in the sense that the world will be changed by divine intervention rather than by human action." The occasional apocalypse does depict human beings enacting judgment. The "Apocalypse of Weeks," for example, "predicts a judgment, executed by righteous human beings with the sword" but Collins points out that even here "righteous human beings act in synergism with God or angelic hosts," *not* on their own (2005, 137). The real action is performed by God and his messianic agents, which in Christian apocalypses sometimes includes Jesus as a sword-wielding, fire-breathing entity, and in Jewish apocalypses may include military leaders on the model of King David, prophetic leaders, or even priestly figures who enact divine purification.

In contemporary video games, however, agency is situated squarely with the player, who relies upon guides for assistance, but who ultimately enacts salvation by himself or herself, often in spectacularly violent form. The player's role as agent of deliverance is evident especially in first-person shooters like *Halo*. In game 1, the player (as Master Chief) must prevent the firing of the ring, a devastating weapon. In game 2, the player (in this case in the role of the Arbiter, an important figure in the Covenant leadership), must kill Tartarus to prevent him from detonating the ring. In game 3, the player again takes on the role of Master Chief, this time intentionally firing the ring in order to destroy the Flood, and in so doing saving the galaxy. Of course, throughout the game the player fights enemies by using weapons (battle rifles, shotguns, rocket launchers, plasma grenades) and operating artillery vehicles (scorpion tanks, all-terrain jeep-like vehicles called "warthogs," and hovercraft like the "hornet"). Indeed in *Halo*, Master Chief is a powerful messianic figure, not waiting for supernatural deliverance but enacting it himself through the use of a massive array of potent weaponry (Wagner *et al.* 2011).

Even in the video game *Left Behind: Eternal Forces*, with the larger assumption of a God in charge and a closer resonance with religious scripture, it is up to humans alone to enact God's punishing charge on earth in the final judgment. In video games like *Halo* and *Assassin's Creed*, change is wrought by the player alone, as he or she identifies as a messianic character in a virtual world of secularized dualisms, saving humanity through the brutal destruction of enemies. In most first-person shooter video games, there is no overarching divine power at all. In *Assassin's Creed*, Desmond Miles single-handedly must break rules and kill enemies in order to save the world – and he works for nobody but himself. Even the "master" he serves is revealed to be a deceitful enemy, in league with the despotic Templars. The only entity that Desmond can trust is the Animus, and only as a guide to otherworldly techniques. If there is a god in *Assassin's Creed*, that god is technology itself, and one's enemies are those who would use technology to suppress free thought and free action in a postmodern world. Nietzsche, at least, would be pleased.

Apocalyptic angst: then and now

David Hellholm has suggested that the SBL definition of apocalypse formulated by Collins and others should include the statement that apocalypses are "intended for a group in crisis with the purpose of exhortation and/or consolation by means of divine authority." The *Sitz im Leben* (situation in life) of traditional apocalypses is well known, characterized by the experience of oppression and suffering. Fans of apocalypses, then, typically feel overwhelmed by forces beyond their control and are driven to apocalyptic imagination by a desire for certainty, assurance, and a sense of empowerment. In some ways, the *Sitz im Leben* of today's video game players is similar, at least in spirit. In his exploration of the similarities between postmodernity and the apocalyptic worldview, Marc Fonda points to the "disasters and threats of disasters" of the past thirty years, including "natural calamities, abortion, the Gulf War, political correctness, the AIDS epidemic, 9/11 as well as political and economic instability throughout the world" and says that because of the "uncertainty and anxiety" caused by these, "those of us in the West may be suffering from what is called disaster syndrome." That is, we have "become stunned, withdrawn, passive, suggestible" and we are experiencing "diminished mental capacity" as we have trouble "perceiving reality correctly" (1994, 168). Maybe some contemporary game players, like the ancient apocalypticists, feel a loss of control and purpose, and turn to games for the certainty they offer in telling us who is "good," who is "evil," and what we should do about it.

Fonda outlines what he sees as "characteristics common to both millennial movements and postmodern thought," including the claim that adherents of both "suffer from a specific degree of angst caused by the recognition of impending doom of civilization as they know it" (164). The hope of apocalypticists is for a "revitalization" that "emerge[s] out of a need to reduce the stress and anxiety that confronts people when their society is no longer capable of providing an effective means of doing so" (166). Thus, in today's society, Fonda sees examples of secular apocalypticism in "feminist thought, a perceived environmental disaster, scenarios regarding plenary destruction, and certain Internet subcultures" (167). We might add first-person shooters to the list.

Despite the obvious religious imagery in many video games, players themselves are not likely to see their game play as a religious activity, even if they might indeed feel overwhelmed by angst in their daily lives and experience the game as a temporary oasis of moral certainty. Furthermore, the transformation of traditional religious imagery within a *game* – especially within the context of a fantasy-driven and violent first-person shooter – suggests that contemporary video-game-driven commentary on religion is more scathing: *this* apocalypse is not literally expected to arrive by anyone playing the game. Judgment is merely a performance of virtual doom, a ritual acting out of contemporary angst with no ultimate pay-off.

Accordingly, the dualisms in apocalypses and video games also function differently. As Collins notes, in all apocalypses one will find "the expectation of a future judgment in which the wicked are punished and the good rewarded" (1979, 25). Hearers of traditional apocalypses could find comfort in God's approaching judgment of the wicked and rewards for the righteous. Video games can certainly also be viewed as looking imaginatively forward to a judgment, but this experience may take shape in many *different* forms of dualisms. In one game, the enemy is a group of aliens; in another, it is people from another country or religion; in another, it is monsters or children or soldiers. The dualisms do not contribute to an overall ordered view of the cosmos, but rather offer only a temporary sense of order and satisfaction within the programmed world of the game. Even in games that purport to represent real events and impose a rigid dualism on them, as in various video games about current military engagements, the satisfaction is cheap. One's so-called enemies will simply produce another video game in which *you* are portrayed as the enemy. These are ephemeral certainties in transient worlds.

Conclusion

Contemporary first-person shooters share with ancient Jewish and Christian apocalypses a concern with procedural rhetoric, even if such video games are often described as mere "play" and most people see traditional apocalypses as serious business. Both types of apocalyptic experiences involve otherworldly mediators who help the player–visionary understand the experiences and succeed in the mission, usually involving the sharing of secrets acquired through a perilous journey. Both can be viewed as instances of the "magic circle" of games, in which areas are marked off for "play," in the sense that new rules apply within the demarcated space. Both offer a vision of transcendence, suggesting that there is more to life than our mundane experiences. Both present a dramatic sense of time's passing, creating expectation and urgency in the awareness of the approaching end of time. Both invite player–visionaries to see themselves as identified with great figures from another time or place, to see their own identities fused, at least for a time, with these figures, to experience what *they* experience and to see what *they* see. Clearly, there are distinctive similarities between apocalypses and first-person shooters like *Halo* and *Assassin's Creed*. But what do we make of the differences?

The element of secularism inherent in today's apocalypses marks the most distinctive feature of video game apocalypses. As Collins notes, "the transcendent nature of apocalyptic eschatology looks beyond this world to another." Salvation is envisioned as "a radically different type of human existence, in which all the constraints of the human condition, including death, are transcended" (1979, 10). Today's video games make no such transcendent promises, ensconced as they are within the garb of the "magic circle" of play. As Janet Murray remarks, "[i]n a postmodern world ... everyday experience has come to seem increasingly gamelike," and as a consequence, "we are [increasingly] aware of the constructed nature of all our narratives" (2004, 3). Indeed, the challenges and anxiety associated with postmodernism are quite distinct from those experienced by early Jews and Christians suffering under Roman rule. Death in video games is temporary, not permanent – thus salvation is also temporary. Worlds visited are transient. Enemies defeated are not real. When one turns off the game and returns to one's daily life, the same hardships, the same problems, the same doubts remain.

Apocalypses may have offered early Jews and Christians comfort precisely because the "game" they invited us to play was infinite, so the rewards of "winning" had some lasting consequences, and so could offer real comfort in daily life. The popularity of fabricated apocalyptic visions of the sort encountered in today's video games marks both the appeal of the genre and also its ineffectiveness in times of generally accepted moral relativism. The complexities of morality in a globalizing world make easy dualisms difficult to maintain beyond the "magic circle" of play, but they also suggest that we should think carefully and deliberately about what we believe and why we believe it.

Perhaps the ancient apocalypticists also saw their own otherworldly journeys as play, but it seems likely that if they did, they incorporated the elements of play to make much larger claims about their own certainty of meaning in the cosmos, and their own hope that God would intervene soon to prove them right.

Chapter 9

Making belief
Transmedia and the hunger for the real

I begin this final chapter with an odd claim: Religion is like a Katamari. For those of you not in the know, a Katamari is an object players create in the series of Katamari video games designed for Playstation 2. In the game you play as a prince, the son of the "King of the Cosmos," who wants you to rebuild some damaged stars and planets. You accomplish this feat by rolling objects together onto what Ivan Sulic of IGN calls "a little-sticky-ball-thing." Sulic imagines the designer explaining the game to a room full of developers: "I'm talking about collecting cats and thumbtacks, and some people, and then an octopus and maybe Godzilla or something ... Each time you grab something with the Katamari, its size increases. This way the more junk you get by pushing it around, the bigger it gets. Eventually it'll get so big that you can pick up buildings and islands and clouds and thunderstorms and everything" (Sulic 2004).

This, I suggest, is also how religions work. Scholars have spent a lot of time trying to define religion, from functionalist definitions like Emile Durkheim's (society is sacred), to definitions like Clifford Geertz's which hinges on the construction of a sense of "order," to more essentialist definitions like Eliade's (the sacred opposed to the profane; see Chapter 4). Some scholars believe we are better off looking at ritual than at religion, since rituals are observable and religion is ephemeral. Others like Wilfred Cantwell Smith see the term "religion" as having no utility whatsoever in today's world (*The Meaning and End of Religion*, 1991). Is religion something you do? Or something you believe? Or something you have? Or something you find? Is it a ritual? Liturgy? Creed? Sacred space? The transcendent or the "Other"? Is it sacred texts, stories or myths? An identity shaper? A generator of desire? Is it a mode of gift-giving and -receiving? Community-building? Reality-transforming? Worldview-shaping? Power-building? Or morals-shaping? The problem with the definitional crisis in religion is that the easiest answer to all of these questions is yes. And maybe it doesn't matter if every manifestation of religion has *all* of these components in it at any given time. And maybe it doesn't matter that we all experience the combinations in different ways depending on our personal backgrounds and levels of engagement. If religion is like a Katamari ball, then each manifestation of it is a combination, a "sticky-ball" of a variety of these facets – and the more things have been rolled up together, the more people will likely see the same phenomenon as a "religion" even if they experience it in different ways.

I return to Sulic, who explains that "[t]he bigger the Katamari gets, the less possible it will be to roll back to unexplored areas to accumulate smaller items, but the more likely it will be to roll on to new areas where heftier items can be grabbed." Religions, too, accrue more cosmic proportions as they roll up massive rituals, groups of devotees, developing mythologies, commitments, and transcendent claims. Eventually, enough people recognize enough religious "work" going on that we have what most would consider a religion. Obviously, this has happened with the world's major religions, and increasingly, such claims have also been made for large franchises like *Star Wars*, *Harry Potter*, *Twilight* and *The Matrix*. These, too, have accumulated rituals, myths, codes of morals, clothing, texts, holidays, mass celebrations at ComicCons and other ritual gatherings, and devoted followers who look to the worlds they present as motivation for how to live a good life.

This metaphor is particularly helpful in making sense of how new "religions" can result from the accumulation of similar phenomena in practices explicitly labeled "religious" as well as those considered merely "virtual." Traditional religions have become remarkably good at rolling together a host of different components or "streams" that all flow together to a central core: for Christians and Jews, this core or story hub is the "world" of the Bible; for Muslims, the world of the Quran. Western religions are generally more committed to a single story world for their hubs of meaning, but Eastern religions, too, can be identified by their accumulation of related stories, rituals, practices, and meaning-making activities streaming from a "core" that is produced through the accumulation of these very practices. For many consumers of various elements of virtual reality, too, there are a number of new hubs or story worlds from which to choose, and more being generated all the time.

The "world" evoked by revealed traditions is reinforced through "streams" of content and activity, such as rituals, stories (and their interpretations), sacred leaders, regular meetings, music, and sometimes even costumes. When looking at things this way, it is not terribly surprising that rituals and games so closely resemble one another, or that both virtual worlds like *World of Warcraft* and religious literature such as apocalyptic texts evoke another world and invite our imaginative immersion in it. These are all ways of drawing us into a core story world, of nurturing our devotion to it, and in so doing, implicitly arguing for the kind of "uniquely realistic" sense of order and structure that Geertz sees as so central to religions. Geertz defines religion as a

> system of symbols which acts to establish powerful, pervasive, and long-lasting moods and motivations in men by formulating conceptions of a general order of existence and clothing these conceptions with such an

aura of factuality that the moods and motivations seem uniquely realistic (Geertz 1985, 4).

Story worlds provide these systems, creating in us "moods and motivations" that shape our creative experience as we use the rules in these story worlds to define a "general order of existence" that is expressed through our engagement with it, resulting at times in stories, in games, in rituals, and in experimental play.

However, as I suggest above, religion shapers in the revealed traditions are not the only ones rolling things up into Katamari balls, offering us imaginative worlds in which to invest and from which to draw forth a sense of order, meaning and purpose in our lives. Increasingly, developers of new media, especially creators of "transmedia," are realizing the immense potential of multiple streams of content all tapping into a singular mythical "world." A comparison of religion with transmedia reveals, surprisingly, that belief is all around us, in both obviously "religious" and non-religious forms. And transmedia developers, whether consciously or not, are in the business of "rolling up" rituals, stories and traditions in their production and marketing new "sticky balls" of their own, "planets" that can grow to immense proportions and work as religions in their own right. I explore here what happens when we think of transmedia as religion, and religion as transmedia, by exploring four interrelated issues: world-building as religion, belief as performance, the implications of world-building for religious dialogue, and the move toward greater immersion in virtual reality, what I call the hunger for the real.

World-building

The notion of "another world" is a core feature in discussions of ritual, and is also one of the primary means of imagining virtual space, as I discussed in Chapter 3. Huizinga has remarked that like play, ritual "transports the participants to another world" (1955, 18). Ritual theorist Tambiah sees a "critical feature" of ritual to be "belief in, and communication with, the 'supernatural' world or a 'transtemporal' other world" (1996, 497). Pearce is particularly interested in the world-building qualities of MMORPGs (massively multiplayer online role-playing games), which have been recognized by game theorists as online "places" capable of evoking deep immersion. Pearce explains that an MMORPG "combines a metastory, primarily in the form of a predesigned story world and various plots within it, with a story system that allows players to evolve their own narratives within the game's story framework" producing a form of what Pearce calls "social storytelling" or "collaborative fiction" (2009, 148–49). This kind of social storytelling is a ritual activity as well, shows us how our own world is, and how we would like it to be.

World-building, it seems, is a quintessentially religious endeavor. It is also a nearly original feature of video game conception, despite the inability of graphics to initially express this conception easily. In the full-color comic book

"Atari Force" from the early 1980s that Atari shipped with some of their space fighting games, we see a set of developed characters: the Atari Force. This team of obviously multi-racial and multi-religious space officers is on an exciting interstellar quest. Their escapades are apparently meant to offer a richer story model for the abstract gameplay and provide backstory for the trope of shooting alien ships in repeated and very similar-looking levels of gameplay. They are in a "multi-dimensional warp-drive cruiser" that "propels" these "dedicated daredevils through layer upon layer of alternate realities: A billion billion universes, impaled on an invisible string, each existing an infinitesimal heartbeat from the next." They are "passing from one cosmos to another" as they battle hostile forces and bring cosmos to chaos.

World-building can also be understood as the construction of the magic circle, a feat achieved through the crafting of rituals or structured experiences (such as games) that draw us into another "space," inviting us to see it as a world different from our own, at least temporarily. As we can recall from previous chapters, Huizinga explains that play happens "within a play-ground marked off beforehand either materially or ideally, deliberately or as a matter of course." We have already considered how the magic circle consists of a host of "carved off" areas, including the sports arena, temple, stage, and area of play for games. All of these are, as we have already seen, "forbidden spots," separated from ordinary life and "dedicated to the performance of an act apart" (1955, 10). The "act apart" that is engaged in is, typically, the construction of a world, with varying degrees of completeness and thus differing in size of the metaphorical Katamari ball. Salen and Zimmerman's discussion of the magic circle in games is also evocative of world-building when they describe its ability to evoke a sense of the transcendent: the magic circle is "both limited and limitless"; it is "a finite space with infinite possibility" (2004, 95). Entering into the magic circle may simply involve a *choice* by the player–participants to enter into this "temporary world," as it "frames a distinct space of meaning that is separate from, but still references, the real world" (97).

As Grodal remarks, when we play a computer game, we may be drawn into a "trancelike immersion in the virtual world, because of the strong neuronal links that are forged between perceptions, emotions, and actions" (2003, 148). Juul says that "To play a video game is … to interact with real rules while imagining a fictional world, and a video game is a set of rules as well as a fictional world" (2005, 1). Murray remarks that the new interactive medium of computer technology is "procedural, participatory, encyclopedic, and spatial" so that it can "create a world that we can navigate and inhabit as well as observe" (2004, 8). Video game consoles, then, are what Salen and Zimmerman call "machines for generating compelling spaces" (2004, 123). The "spaces" that such "state machines" generate are often experienced as parallel worlds into which we temporarily enter.

As world-building activities, rituals, games and stories all do a kind of deep religious work, what Peter Berger calls the "reality-maintaining process."

According to Berger, "worlds are socially constructed and maintained" and their ability to remain "real" depends upon "specific social processes, namely those processes that ongoingly reconstruct and maintain the particular worlds in question" (1990, 45). We create stories, rituals and games as we wander through these emerging worlds, using them as templates for making sense of our own daily lives. Ken Sanes (n.d.) points out that world-building via imaginative construction is as old as human creativity. The 17,000-year-old Paleolithic cave paintings in Lascaux, France show that humans have long been making what Sanes calls "imitation realities." Humans, he says, have since been continually engaged in world-building in the form of games, stories, paintings, and "similar fantasy-saturated celebrations" that have "included everything from costume balls to the gladiator contests of ancient Rome, in which theatrical games were created that had life and death stakes for the participants."

Stories often serve as the hub for the generation of imaginative worlds – story worlds – that are rich and evocative, inspiring our own devotion and firing our imagination. J. R. R. Tolkein points out the ability of story worlds to offer us consolation and a sense of meaning:

> Probably every writer making a secondary world, a fantasy, every sub-creator ... hopes that the peculiar qualities of this secondary world are derived from Reality, or are flowing into it ... the peculiar quality of the "joy" in successful Fantasy can thus be explained as a sudden glimpse of the underlying reality or truth. It is not only a "consolation" for the sorrow of this world, but a satisfaction, and an answer to the question, "Is it true?"
> (cited in Kearney 2002, 27)

The "truth" of a game, story or ritual may lie in its effectiveness in world-building and cosmos-ordering. Transmediated religion is religion that holds itself together by its intrinsic story world, but which is given life through our own interactive engagement with it. Writers or "sub-creators" are world-makers, dealing in "reality" through creating a cosmos – an ordered space into which we, as readers, can enter.

It may not even matter if the authors *themselves* believed they were crafting a coherent world, since traditions of interpretation and assumptions of order can be imposed on the text by its powerful role in human culture. For example, the authors of the Bible were many and varied, spanning vast geographical distances and thousands of years. Nonetheless, readers of the Bible can encounter the world of the Bible with the assumption of order, and find there inspiration for the development of more stories, rituals, laws and traditions. As William Blake famously said in 1797 in his annotations to Bishop Watson's *An Apology for the Bible*:

> I cannot concieve the Divinity of the <books in the> Bible to consist either in who they were written by or at what time or in the historical

evidence which may be all false in the eyes of one man & true in the eyes of another but in the Sentiments & Examples which whether true or Parabolic are Equally useful as Examples given to us of the perverseness of some & its consequent evil & the honesty of others & its consequent good [.] This sense of the Bible is equally true to all & equally plain to all. none can doubt the impression which he recieves from a book of Examples.

(1979, 436)

The Bible, Blake says, is a "book of Examples," a treasure trove of stories, a set of possibilities best imaginatively engaged as we interpret, transform, and poetically remediate it through our own experience. Blake's epic poem *Jerusalem* is an enactment of these principles; it is a vast and wandering homage to the Bible, a massive poetic form of fan fiction, a monumental transmediated revision with the Bible as its story hub.

Kearney describes stories' ability to soothe us with their "cathartic power" as they "'alter' us by transporting us to other times and places where we can experience things otherwise" (2002, 137). The narrator, he says, "makes a 'secondary world'" that we enter into and we "make believe that what is narrated is 'true' in so far as it accords with the laws of that world" (143). But we also see it as "true" in regard to our own world, in that it gives us ordering principles for making sense of who we are. This seems akin to what Blake was talking about in his own anachronistic, quasi-transmediated view of the Bible. Says Kearney:

> From the word go, stories were invented to fill the gaping hole within us, to assuage our fear and dread, to try to give answers to the great unanswerable questions of existence: Who are we? Where do we come from? ... In seeking to provide responses to such unfathomable conundrums – both physical and metaphysical – the great tales and legends gave not only relief from everyday darkness but also pleasure and enchantment.
>
> (7)

Such ordering principles are the stuff of religions, the "Sacred," and the "Real." The ability to make sense is, for some, a welcome haven in a world increasingly characterized by a loss of order and the dissolution of labels, boundaries, and fixed rules.

Despite Max Weber's grim claims about the disenchantment of human society in the wake of traditional religion's increasing withdrawal from the public sphere in the post-Enlightenment age, Landy and Saler propose that "each time religion reluctantly withdrew from a particular area of experience, a new, thoroughly secular strategy for re-enchantment cheerfully emerged to fill the void" (2009, 1). Using language reminiscent of Geertz on religion as order-making, they add that "If the world is to be re-enchanted, it must accordingly be re-imbued, not only with *mystery* and *wonder*, but also with *order*, perhaps even with purpose" (2). Landy and Saler use remarkably similar language to describe the mechanisms by which contemporary secular works, including virtual worlds and video games, can function to re-enchant the world:

> There must be a hierarchy of significance attaching to objects and events encountered; individual lives, and moments within those lives, must be susceptible again to redemption; there must be a new, intelligible locus for the infinite; there must be a way of carving out, within the fully profane world, a set of spaces which somehow possess the allure of the sacred; there must be everyday miracles, exceptional events that go against (and perhaps even alter) the accepted order of things; and there must be secular epiphanies, moments of being in which, for a brief instant, the center appears to hold, and the promise is held out of a quasi-mystical union with something larger than oneself. Piece by piece, in a largely unwitting collaboration, modern intellectuals and creators have put together a panoply of responses to the Weberian condition, offering fully secularized subjects an affirmation of existence that does not come at the cost of naïveté, irrationalism or hypocrisy.
>
> (2009, 2)

New media increasingly provides the means for this purpose development, asking of us only that we buy more, watch more, stream more. Tapping into our desire for ever more conduits of interrelated storylines, transmedia is the most poignant site for renegotiation of the sacred, for re-enchantment in contemporary society. It is here that we find the conglomeration of features – rituals, stories, people, events, interactive interpretations, and visions of the transcendent – that most resembles religious experience in its fullest form. This new kind of "transcendence," highlighted by the ongoing evolution of an interactive mythic storyline, is the hallmark of transmedia as religion.

Transmedia as world-building

So what exactly is transmedia? Jenkins uses the term "convergence culture" to describe "a world where every story, every sound, brand, image, relationship plays itself out across the maximum number of media channels." Such complex, multimedia-streaming worlds are commonly called "transmedia," and indicate a state of affairs in which a story is spread across multiple media platforms, is "not redundant" but "complementary," such that "each platform contributes what it does best" (Jenkins 2009).[1] Although he doesn't use the term, Morgan recognized the qualities of transmedia in religion in 2007 when he claimed that "to ignore television, film, magazines, toys, fan clubs, souvenirs, or posters would be to miss fundamental aspects of religious behavior" in popular culture, because these activities "are the ingredients with which many, even most people religiously practice world-building and maintenance" (2007, 19).

Transmedia, then, includes all of the video games, films (including sequels and prequels), cartoons, apparel, publicity events, fan fiction, action figures, themed foods, commercials, promotions, costumes, and toys associated with a given franchise like *Star Wars*, *Tron*, *Harry Potter* or *Avatar*. These transmedia franchises have "rolled up" enough fan devotion and multi-streaming storylines with associated products to present themselves as full-blown religions, Katamari "sticky balls" with enough density to attract mass followers and fulfill a Durkheimian totemic function as religion. CEO of *Starlight Runner Entertainment* Jeff Gomez explains that transmedia storytelling today is "the vanguard process of conveying messages, themes or storylines to a mass audience through the artful and well-planned use of multiple-media platforms. It is a philosophy of communication that broadens the life-cycle of creative content" (Webdale 2010). Transmedia allows a host of different types of stories and experiences to all be latched onto a single evolving story world, such as the *Star Trek* mythology, or the world of the *Matrix*, *Halo*, or the core stories of the *Harry Potter* universe. *Avatar* is a transmedia story world in the making, with one film already produced, a video game on the market, two more films in the planning stages, and a host of associated media describing the world available in books and online, not to mention fan involvement via discussion boards, apparel, even a recent Palestinian re-enactment of *Avatar* (complete with blue face paint) to make a political point. The marketing potential of such cross-pollination of story is obvious; but such intricate and evolving story construction is also interesting as a form of rich religious modeling (and modding).

As Gomez explains, transmedia is not just about creating "knockoffs" but about deploying "extensions of the narrative." When you create a transmedia world, "you are starting from scratch to design how [a] narrative is going to roll out [which will be] in pieces." The "driving platform" might be a book or film or something else. The audience, then, has the job of "piecing these things together" (Gomez 2010). Consumers are not passive; they explore, discover, create, and transform. Transmedia story worlds "deserve a serious approach," says Gomez. The narrative in such a story world "is taken as a complete platform-neutral world that has a past, a present, and a future. It's larger than the book. So you are devising a mythology for your intellectual property that is separate from the book series and will be used to help extend the i.p. [intellectual property] across different media platforms." You also must extend "the core messages and themes" of the i.p., and build "narrative arcs that could reach out for years and years." This requires deliberate planning, collaboration, and clear vision (Gomez 2010). Transmedia stories can be extended across films, television shows, books, comics, video games, live events, online experiences, mobile technology, animated series, social networking, pamphlets, apparel, websites, and any other media people can find a way to consume, reuse, or produce.

Making belief

Roof defines religion "in its most basic sense [as] a story involving symbol, metaphor, and language, all having the power to persuade and fan the imagination." He adds: "Symbol, metaphor, and language are in fact the means by which human beings come to self-awareness and articulate a sense of self in relation to others." And while traditional religion may provide some people with the stuff required for self-cultivation, for others "the sacred happens" via media and other secular social constructs (1999, 297). For all kinds of practitioners, belief is increasingly understood as a performance – that is, a choice made by the individual, who "increasingly encompasses a continuous, self-conscious process of narrative construction" and who "look[s] upon their spiritual life as an arena they control" (157). Belief today is less about assent to propositions than it is about the choice to engage.

Such claims, of course, have some deep-seated roots in Christian theological tradition. Theologians and philosophers have troubled themselves over the element of choice in belief for centuries. Consider Pascal's wager, William James' "will to believe," and Kierkegaard's arguments for the role of the will in assent to belief. Other contemporary theologians like Karl Barth, Emil Brunner, and Dietrich Bonhoeffer also argue, in different modes, for the importance of choice in belief. For these theologians, "belief" is a matter of assent, a choice that one makes on the basis of, or even in spite of, the evidence. Today, however, such choices are more overt and involve competing options. For most of the past two thousand years people accepted the religious traditions they were presented with as children, and for many this meant assent to a set of propositions, but with little competition for anything else. Today, "[d]espite resistance to the erosion of an older religious world, the drift ... is in the direction of enhanced choices for individuals and toward a deeply personal, subjective understanding of faith and well-being" (Roof 1999, 129). People will take this subjective feeling of well-being *wherever* they find it, whether that be in traditional religious circles or in *Buffy the Vampire Slayer*. Today's religious options are characterized by reflexive, individually designed options, forms of "*make*-belief."

Performance theorist Richard Schechner was the first to use the term "make belief" in distinction from "make-believe." For Schechner, "make believe" is an imaginative act that retains the boundaries between real and play, and is denoted by merely "pretending to believe." By contrast, "make belief" involves an intentional blurring of these boundaries in that performers are "enacting the effects they want the receivers of their performances to accept 'for real'" (2002, 35). That is, they are *performing* desire through a commitment to belief. Schechner is interested primarily in the ability of "make-belief" activities to inspire credulity for those who *see* such performances enacted. However, I argue that practitioners of religious persuasions can also be seen as engaging in a sort of make-belief in their performance of rituals, prayers, statements of creeds, and worship, convincing not only those watching but themselves as well that *performance* of belief is the same thing as belief. Of course, those who devote themselves to *Lost* or *Twilight* or *Star Wars* are also performing make-belief as evident in their engagement in ceremony, costuming, or video game play.

If we use Schechner's distinctions as our starting point, then, "make believe" can be understood as a sort of pretend play, as when children imagine they are superheroes. This kind of activity is typically an implementation of a magic circle that retains its firm bounds. For Schechner, the distinction between real and play here would be clear since the child presumably *knows* he or she isn't a superhero and will eventually cross "back" from the pretend-world to the real one in which he or she is not invisible and cannot fly. Make belief, by contrast, is the performance of belief as a means of *authenticating* it. For those engaged in *make*-belief, there is no clear separation between the world of play and the "real" world; only *intention* demarcates one from the other. There is no curtain to open up the stage and signal that we are about to pretend, and no computer keyboard to log onto a game's platform and enter into an imaginary enactment of self as ogre or warlord. Instead, make-belief is the real-life performative act of *as-if*. It is creating the *appearance* of the real or the meaningful as a means of generating its *acceptance* as real. Make-belief, then, is a sort of ritual performance that has resonance with what linguistic philosopher J. L. Austins calls performative "speech acts" (R. Schechner 2002, 110–11).

Traditional religious practice is more likely to take the form of "make belief" than "make believe," since few religious practitioners are likely to argue that they are "pretending" when they go to church. Instead, religion is best understood as a form of "make belief," a performative act that blurs the distinction between acting "as if" and everyday (believing) reality. Everyday reality is infused with performance, with acts that are engineered to integrate belief into all that we do. Religious performers, i.e. "believers," may recite scriptural passages, wear apparel with religious inscriptions, perform religious rituals and ceremonies, pray in public and in virtual forums, post religiously motivated updates to social media sites, and perform a host of religious acts that make-belief, that is, construct it through its own performance and *generate* the sacred. However, as Huizinga has noted, "it is impossible to fix accurately the lower limit where holy earnest reduces itself to mere 'fun'," especially since "a certain element of 'make-believe' is operative in all primitive religions" (1955, 23).

Schechner's form of make-belief is characterized by the desire for spillover between the "game" and real life. We can see this idea reflected in Jane McGonigal's analysis of ARGs, those "pervasive games" in which players invest all of reality with the potential to be part of the game, and import people, objects, events into the meaning-making process of gameplay. McGonigal argues that gamers "maximize" their play experience not by "actually believing" what they do, but rather by "performing belief" (2003, 1). She argues that "the opportunity to extend a gaming mindset to non-game situations is built structurally" into some ARGs: "With this built-in ambiguity, teams must approach everyone and everything with a game mindset" such that when you meet someone new, you must "assume he or she is a plant; when finding an object, a team must assume it is a prop to be deployed creatively. These missions require teams to affect a confident belief, to act as if the game is everywhere and everything at all times" (20).

The *Go Game* website describes how players should see the world:

> Through clues downloaded to a wireless device and hints planted in unlikely places, you'll be guided through a city you only think you're familiar with. Clues can appear at any time, anywhere. Perhaps you didn't notice the woman on the bus reading a magazine upside-down. Or the note stuck to the side of the bathroom mirror of your favorite bar, or the electric scooter parked outside with your name on it. After a day of *Go*, you will.
>
> (Wink Back, Inc. n.d.)

The same kind of framing and privileged vision is part of many people's religious practice, as when they see specific events in their lives as "miraculously" determined by God; or when they see an object endowed with divine significance, for example, finding the "face" of Jesus or Mary in toast or turtle shells and reading this "discovery" as a sign of God's ongoing concern. Morgan calls this the "sacred gaze," and argues that it can be seen as a covenant (or set of rules) agreed to beforehand by believers to see the world from within the context of belief: "There is a tacit agreement, a compact or a covenant, that a viewer observes when viewing an image in order to be engaged by it, in order to believe what the image reveals or says or means or makes one feel – indeed, in order to believe there is something to believe" (2005, 76). Similarly, in the "pervasive" experiences of an ARG (alternate-reality game) anything at all could be seen as enchanting, pulling into the world of the game, and promising hidden layers of meaning.

All games to some degree exhibit an obligation to enter into the game's world, to act as if the game were not a game, to play as if the rules of the game were the only rules that mattered. Alternate-reality games, however, push this covenant of play to its limits, since the player must see the *entire* world as potentially part of the game. The distinction between game and real life can be differentiated only by the player, who may even *wrongly* assume components of life to be part of the game. Alternate-reality games, more than any other kind of game, are controlled by the TINAG (This Is Not a Game) rhetoric. That is, players play as if the game were not a game, and enact certain principles to enable such a belief to seem viable, even as McGonigal claims they know otherwise.

Such games typically work as a form of "mixed reality" as they "use mobile, ubiquitous and embedded digital technologies to create virtual playing fields in everyday spaces." Players of pervasive games "do everything in their power to erase game boundaries – physical, temporal and social – and to obscure the metacommunications that might otherwise announce, 'This is play'" (McGonigal 2003, 2). In ARGs, "the fabricated world and simulated experiences of immersive games are created, not through special screens, wired gloves, joysticks or goggles, but rather through cell phones, PDAs (personal digital assistants), fax machines, Wi-Fi networks, conference calls, e-mail, and the World Wide Web." The "platform" for such games is "everyday life itself" (6). *Anything* could be part of the game, and the retention of the game world is a value endorsed by all players. For example, McGonigal reports on players who followed an actor home, unable to believe the game wasn't still going on, and forcing the actor to disrupt the TINAG agreement (12). In another case, players developed elaborate explanations for the duplication of a stock photo in separate digital locations – an apparent error by the game designers that nonetheless resulted in elaborate new storylines and gameplay, a sort of emergent Midrash that involved the players and designers as co-creators mending the fabric of a nearly disrupted play cosmos (13).

Players engage in a conscious "choice to surrender to the pleasures of narrative, role-play or well-defined goals and limits" and "some degree of free will is almost always assumed" (McGonigal 2003, 8). McGonigal proposes that players of ARGs always know they are playing and that "the frame of representational play remains visible and sturdy to players in even the most believable performances of belief" (4). To those critics who exhibit a "growing suspicion of the unruliness of unbounded games and a wariness of their seemingly addictive and life-consuming scenarios" McGonigal replies that players keep the magic circle intact through sheer intent (1). Accordingly, she insists on "the essential and stubborn distinction between an intentional performance of belief and belief itself" (3).

McGonigal's argument pivots around this notion of *awareness* – the idea that gamers *know* they're playing a game, so they can't "believe" what is happening is "real." Pervasive gamers, she says, enact "a strategic performance" that is "conscious, goal-oriented and pleasurable" as a form of "affected belief" (2003, 4). In fact, they'll work quite hard at protecting a game's pretense. Looking at the example of near rupture of play in *The Beast* (an ARG based on the film *Artificial Intelligence*), McGonigal remarks that "[t]his ability to deny, bury, and forestall disenchanting information is a testament to the audience's complicity in maintaining the Beast's illusion of reality" (11). They engage in "an active pretense of belief that enables, heightens, and prolongs their play experiences." The distinction between belief and *enacting* belief is very important to McGonigal: "Instead of asking to what extent players come to believe in the fictions they perform, we should ask: To what ends, and through what mechanisms, do players *pretend* to believe their own performances?" (4).

Surprisingly, the same kind of performed belief was apparently practiced by Mother Teresa in a very different context: tending to the sick in Calcutta, while in her heart doubting the existence of God. Mother Teresa never revealed her doubts while alive, instead publicly performing belief while writing secret letters to her spiritual adviser describing her agony and begging him not to reveal her doubts to anyone else. Her torture is palpable: "The smile," she writes, is "a mask" or "a cloak that covers everything." Worried that her doubts might disturb others, Mother Teresa writes to her adviser of the difference between what we could now recognize as belief and make-belief: "I spoke as if my very heart was in love with God – tender, personal love ... If you were [there], you would have said, 'What hypocrisy'" (Mother Teresa 2007, 226). Despite a profound and terrifying loss of belief, Mother Teresa continues to perform belief and to pray to God. She even asks Jesus to forgive her unbelief:

> They say people in hell suffer eternal pain because of the loss of God – they would go through all of that suffering if they had just a little hope of possessing God. In my soul I feel just that terrible pain of loss – of God not wanting me – of God not being God – of God not really existing (Jesus, please forgive my blasphemies – I have been told to write everything). That darkness that surrounds me on all sides – I can't lift my soul to God – no light or inspiration enters my soul. I speak of love for souls – of tender love for God – words pass through my words (sic: lips) – and I long with a deep longing to believe in them. What do I labour for? If there be no God, there can be no soul. If there is no soul, then Jesus – You also are not true. Heaven, what emptiness – not a single thought of Heaven enters my mind – for there is no hope ... I want God with all the powers of my soul – and yet there between us – is terrible separation.
>
> (193)

The desire for what one *wishes* to believe is certainly evident in ARGs and in Mother Teresa's impassioned confessions. But Mother Teresa hardly wanted life to be *more* like a game; on the contrary, she seems to have wanted the *game* she found herself playing to be *real*. She wanted her beliefs to feel authentic, for her practice to be grounded in confident affirmation that God was in his heaven and there was order on the earth. Mother Teresa wanted a form of belief that was *neither* make-believe *nor* make-belief but was simply belief itself – assent to an obvious truth. She knew the rules; she just had shifted from "this is definitely not a game" to something more like "this might be a game." The tragedy in this, of course, is that the game had meant so much to her. Indeed, it is remarkable that she could have continued to perform belief so passionately for so many years without allowing others to see what she was going through.

Although Mother Teresa's experience is obviously more poignant than games or drama, it nonetheless has intriguing analogs in theater. McGonigal draws on Constantin Stanislavski's theory of the "magic if" for theater and applies it to games: actors should "act as if the circumstances of the dramatic scene were real," creating a performance that is "oriented toward an external display." McGonigal sees the same kind of activity happening in immersive gaming: "that is, a legible, outward expression of *as if I believe* rather than an internal attempt to believe *for real*" (2003, 16). Mother Teresa engaged in the outward "legible" and "external display" of belief despite her deep internal doubts. In the final years of her life, her belief became a performance, recognition of the rules without a conviction in the divine purpose to which these rules presumably point. But the purpose of the "game" she was playing – compassion, love, kindness, selflessness – was so valuable to her that in the end, the expression of loving acts became more important than the belief in God that originally motivated them.

Even Pope Benedict has recently argued that performance of belief may be more important than belief itself. Alarmed by what he sees as an absence of belief in contemporary society, Benedict urges Christians to *perform* belief whether they can fully assent to it or not:

> Christians cannot ignore the crisis of faith that has come to society, or simply trust that the patrimony of the values transmitted in the course of past centuries can continue inspiring and shaping the future of the human family. The idea of living "as if God didn't exist" has shown itself to be deadly: The world needs, rather, to live "as if God existed," even if it does not have the strength to believe; otherwise it will only produce an "inhuman humanism."
>
> (Benedict XVI 2010b)

Benedict argues that performance is enough. The choice to *pretend* to believe is enough, Benedict seems to be saying, if it makes us adhere more fully to the rules of Christian life, and presumably, to live as more compassionate, loving people. McGonigal says that "the desire for life … to become a 'real little game' is actually the desire for the formal call to action, direction, and the sense that others are working toward the same goal" (2003, 18). Functionally at least, this sounds a lot like what Benedict is saying: the desire for life to have rules and meaning can be satisfied by Christianity whether one believe in God or not, so long as one *acts* as if one believes.

For McGonigal, we are motivated by a *desire* to believe: "the habit of pretending to believe does not slip into actual belief, but rather that longing to believe in the face of the very impossibility of believing" (2003, 4). She calls this longing the "Pinocchio effect," a "bittersweet" wish for belief, a *desire* that goes ultimately unfulfilled in games, but which continues to motivate us. Speaking of ARGs, McGonigal asserts that "[p]layers' complicity in the game's self-professed desire to be real is best understood as a mirror desire for their real life to be more like a game" (17). Long before McGonigal considered the role of desire in contemporary games, Turner observed the profound ability of ritual symbols to be perceived as "charged with power from unknown sources" and able to "elicit emotion and express and mobilize desire" (1969, 528).

There seems to be no easily discernible difference between belief and the performance of belief, between the "as-if" of games and the "as-if" of religion, especially in the transmediated form that games may take when they tap into a greater mythological story world beyond the individual media streams that lead into it. Both games and religion can set a mode of being in place for us, color our values, give us stories that provide meaning to our lives, make us promises, give us interpretive grist for storytelling and identity formation, and create in us a deep desire to enter into the other worlds they evoke. Suspension of disbelief, the kind we use when we engage deeply in a film, video game, or story, may in the end be the same thing as belief.

From answerbox to sandbox

I have argued so far that religions and transmedia are a lot alike: both involve multiple streams of input and output; both engage us with deep desire and invite a choice in the performance of belief, the "as if" engagement that signals our investment in the world's stories. Both too are constructed by us as we engage with them, via ritual, interpretation, devotion, and desire. Not everyone would be happy about such comparisons, however. The very openness that a view of religion-as-transmedia inspires is a cause for concern among some believers, who insist that religion is *not* transmediated (and thus malleable, optional, and in some ways user-designed) but rather represents a fixed, singular truth – a rigid text-based storyline – that must simply be assented to, with stories that stream from heaven to us, and are contained perfectly in sacred writ. At the same time, the proliferation of virtual worlds reveals that there are, in fact, many worlds from which we may choose. This situation is no problem at all for the hardcore science-fiction fan, but it is a problem for the fundamentalist exclusivist who has invested all of his or her belief in *one* world as the "true" one. The world of the sacred text for such a fundamentalist exclusivist is *only* an answerbox: a unique, singular media stream that came directly from heaven and was caught, by miracle, in the vessel of the sacred text. New competition in the form of competing story worlds is not only unwelcome, but can also be seen as dangerous: All other "worlds" except the exclusivists' own world can only be perceived as wrong, evil, or irrelevant.

This worldview is evident, for example, in the venom spewed by the leaders of the *Kids on Fire* camps featured in *Jesus Camp* (Grady and Ewing 2006). Preaching to the children about Harry as an "enemy of God," Becky Fischer intones that "had it been in the Old Testament, Harry Potter would have been put to death." The competition between the world of the Bible and the transmediated world of Harry Potter is exposed in Fischer's reference to the world of the Old Testament as a sort of *place* in which Harry Potter *could* have resided but does not, and thus is (thankfully) not subject to the rules of the game there. For fundamentalists like Fischer, the more compelling a competing transmedia world is, the more likely it is to be viewed as inspired by nefarious forces working to destroy loyalty to the one, true, perfect world of God.

Answerbox

Although adherents of many different religious traditions make claims about the uniqueness of their own sacred texts in comparison with others, Christians in particular have a stake in viewing the Bible as uniquely revealed, since the entire text is often read as describing God's predetermined response to human sin. For some, this means that only Christianity is "right," and the Bible is an "answerbox," filled with advice, laws, predictions, and moral prescriptions, self-evident to the informed reader. Such a reading is resistant to transmediated, participant-based encounters with the text, seeing revisions and reinterpretations as dangerous innovations that risk one's place in the afterlife and may alienate one from the Christian community.

This us-versus-them mode of religious encounter is nothing new, and finds one of its most powerful expressions in the literalism of biblical interpretation that was nurtured in the Renaissance but became very popular in the Enlightenment. One of the assumptions of this worldview is that the individual biblical stories in the Bible, despite happening in very different time periods, "must fit together into one narrative" (Frei 1974, 2). They must be viewed as many stories all streaming from a singular story world that has narrative coherence from beginning to end – a unique story core that defines the individual stories that stream from it. Certainly, people noticed differences in the biblical books and wondered how stories in the Old Testament related to those in the new, but such problems have been resolved through assumptions about the book's *overall* cohesion as a unique and ordered story world. And for most in the Western world, other religious "worlds" offered very little competition for belief in day-to-day life, appearing instead as monolithic "enemies" to be battled against.

The biblical books were viewed as "a single, unitary canon," an answerbox including both the "Old" and "New" Testaments (Frei 1974, 2). The world of the Bible was meant to give order and structure to our lives, presenting a single, orderly divine plan. Recognizing the immense power of the Bible's fixed story stream, Erich Auerbach compares the Bible to the rambling, less ordered quality of Homer's *Odyssey*:

> Far from seeking, like Homer, merely to make us forget our own reality for a few hours, [the pre-critical mode of reading the Bible] seeks to overcome our reality: we are to fit our own life into its world, feel ourselves to be elements in its structure of universal history ... Everything else that happens in the world can only be conceived as an element in this sequence; into it everything that is known about the world ... must be fitted as an ingredient of the divine plan.

> (Cited in Frei 1974, 3)

The Bible presents a single ultimate, divine storyline, predetermined and unfolding according to divine providence, enchanting our lives and giving meaning to all we do. Despite ongoing and constant reinterpretation of the Bible during this pre-critical period, the Bible "nonetheless remained the adequate depiction of the common and inclusive world" with a single unitary view of history (3). People thought of the Bible as a singular window into an unceasing divine realm, and saw any interpretations they produced as a means of expressing the *singularity* of the Bible as hierophany. In transmedia terms, we could say, then, that this pre-modern reading viewed the Bible as *one* story world, *one* hierophany, with many interrelated stories streaming from it, in one direction: from heaven to earth, reflecting history as moving inexorably forward.

This singular view of the divine story world of the Bible has some unfortunate consequences for interreligious dialogue. When believers in this unique story-world encounter those who believe in the story world of the Quran or the story world of the Ramayana, there is no room for conversation, for exploration, for common ground. Instead, each sacred story world is viewed as a false competitor. Gene Veith reveals such a perspective when he remarks that "Christians do need to be aware that Islam is becoming their major religious competitor across the world." He presents this "competitor" as a danger to "wishy-washy relativists, and eager-to-please Christians" (1994, 217). This confrontational view of the relationship between different religions-as-story worlds is what I call the "first-person-shooter" version of religious encounter. The dualism of the first-person-shooter religious perspective may not involve guns and shoot-outs, but it does reflect that the world is divided into "us" who are "good" and "them" who are "enemies." Exclusivists like this tend to represent themselves as purveyors of a uniquely "true" religious worldview, opposed to an array of dangerous and "untrue" worldviews. The rules of the exclusivist's religion game are set in stone, and require absolute adherence. To win is to stand firm and annihilate one's enemies, or at best, to sit tight and await God's intervention on earth to annihilate them. Christian video games like *Armageddon* and *Left Behind: Eternal Forces* support just such a view, inviting virtual violence against one's religious "enemies" in the end times, as we discovered in Chapter 8.

Such distinctions between "winners" and "losers" crop up in rituals and games as well. Bell and others have noted that this division between us and them, this and that, sacred and profane, is for some a marker of ritual experience. Such "binary oppositions" in ritual are "almost always" expressed as "asymmetrical relations of dominance and subordination by which they generate hierarchically organized relationships" (1992, 102). Game theorists, too, commonly point out that one way of recognizing a game is its focus on conflict. Zimmerman offers this definition: "A game is a voluntary activity, in which one or more players follow rules that constrain their behavior, enacting an artificial conflict that ends in a quantifiable outcome" (2004, 160). That is, games produce winners and losers, and everyone can tell which ones they are.

It seems that exclusivists are engaged in what may be viewed as an all-or-nothing game with rules that identify adherents of competing "worlds" as enemies.

Exclusivists see themselves as arrayed against their enemies in a simplistic, if comforting, view of the world. This kind of religious "game" can make it easy to make sense of otherwise confusing issues in the world. Any difficult issues can be dismissed with the sweep of a hand as evidence that the person in front of us is an "opponent" who doesn't play by the "right" rules, and will ultimately "lose," usually through apocalyptic intervention by God or by eventual banishment to hell. And as I demonstrated in Chapter 7, this can increasingly take the form of an apocalyptically motivated belief that God is expecting us to do his work for him, violently exterminating "evil." Yet even here, we can see what may be viewed as a sort of transmedial thrust, a set of *choices* and *constructions* made by the exclusivist that belies his or her claims to objectivity and passive obedience to God-given standards.

Evangelical fundamentalist Christians like those who made and play the *Left Behind: Eternal Forces* video game are, in some ways at least, active interpreters and creators when they predict what will happen in our world based on their own reading of the story world of the Bible. Their interpretations of the prophetic books and the Book of Revelation are a sort of fan fiction, shaped by their own engagement with the received mythos of the Bible and determined by their own dualistic beliefs. Their ending, though, is perceived as a foregone conclusion despite the interpretive work they are engaged in. They see their generation of new storylines as revealing what is *already there*, thus their creative act is obscured by an assumption of inevitability, which in and of itself serves as a sort of self-reinforcing authentication of violence.

Although Pope Benedict is much more open to interreligious dialogue than fundamentalist exclusivists, he also manifests fear about the potential demise of the Christian worldview in competition with other, especially virtual, worlds. He worries that with our increasing interest in virtual reality:

> the image can also become independent of reality; it can give life to a virtual world, with several consequences, the first of which is the risk of indifference to truth. In fact, the new technologies, together with the progress they entail, can make the true and the false interchangeable; they can induce one to confuse the real with the virtual ... These aspects sound like an alarm bell: They invite consideration of the danger that the virtual draws away from reality and does not stimulate the search for the true, for the truth.
>
> (Benedict XVI 2010b)

Benedict seems to be arguing that virtual reality is a threat to the singular hierophanic world of the Bible and of Christian tradition – specifically, to the Catholic tradition. For Benedict, the danger of the "virtual world" is that it confuses us such that we can't tell the difference between the real (Catholic belief) and the virtual (whatever storylines or interactive experiences draw us in).

"The true," he says, is distinct from the "virtual," and the "true" is unique, divine, and mediated *only* by Christ and the Church.

Sandbox

Such alarm is not the only means of dealing with competing worldviews. The religiously pluralist approach has a powerful analogy in a "many worlds" look at new media, in which many options for meaning coexist for the self-in-process. Gandhi embodied such a worldview. As Eck notes, Gandhi "refused to demonize his opponent, even when he was in profound disagreement with everything the opponent stood for. For him, only in the give and take of relationship would it be possible to construct a world which both could affirm" (Eck 2003, 210). Such open encounters, however, require a relaxing of one's rules and a relinquishing of the assumption that there is only one sacred, one religious story world, one mode of being. Fluid encounters require that we view religion as transmediated, co-created, existing across multiple platforms, and profoundly participant-driven. Within this view, religious worlds are things-in-process too. They are idea sandboxes in which we play, discover, explore, and most importantly, converse with one another as we build worlds together, and see each other as co-residents of our own lived world. The sandbox approach requires that we recognize the constructed nature of all religious belief.

While some Christians opt for the exclusivist "answerbox" perspective and find themselves in confrontation with other religion-worlds, other Christians find ways to embrace the pluralist "sandbox" view of revelation, making room for more "worlds" and engaging in a fluid encounter with the Bible that opens it up to more "streams" of interpretation and opens the believer up to greater humility in encounter with other faiths. Reacting against the form of evangelicalism that devolved into fundamentalist literalism, evangelical theologian Carl Raschke claims that Christianity "made [an] unholy alliance with Cartesian rationalism and British evidentialism as far back as the seventeenth century" (2004, 9). The loss of faith that characterizes much of modern Christianity, Raschke claims, heralds the need for a new Reformation, which for Raschke would involve a loosening up of the hold that biblical literalism has had on Christian interpretation.[2]

Raschke says that postmodernism has begun to "pound at the door of evangelical thought and faith" (11). Should evangelicals let it in, he asks? Whereas fundamentalist evangelical literalists would likely respond, "Absolutely not!" Raschke's enthusiastic reply is: "Yes!" Despite the bad rap postmodernism has gotten – as "an outlook and habit of thinking that fosters nihilism, moral relativism, as well as emotionalism and irrationalism" – Raschke claims that it is actually the friend of evangelicalism, since it encourages the dismissal of the unhealthy partnership between rationalism and biblical interpretation. That is to say, postmodernism reminds believers to let Christian revelation continually stream from heaven to earth. Religion becomes transmediated. The lock on the "world" of the Bible is opened, and Christians can play the game of allowing new interpretations to unfold. The cost, of course, is the assumption of an unchanging God and an inerrant text.

This, it seems, is a price Raschke is willing to pay. Instead of looking for external verification of scripture, Raschke argues that evangelicals should embrace the insights of postmodernists like Jean Baudrillard, Emmanuel Lévinas and Maurice Blanchot. Fighting what Doug Groothuis calls "truth decay," Raschke wants to use postmodernism to argue for the transcendence of truth itself, but he views the Bible as a tool that points *beyond* itself to a God who *cannot* be contained within it (15). In a way, then, Raschke's kind of Christianity is doing precisely what producers of transmedia worlds are doing in that both cultivate in us a desire for something unattainable: a complex whole, a Sacred, a story that is knowable only in bits, streams, parts. Raschke refreshes the "world" of the Bible by pushing God *back* in a sense into the Sacred realm, by refusing to believe that revelation is, or ever has been, a fixed or rigid entity. The move is subtle but extremely important. If the Bible is written *by people*, as Raschke proposes, then it is only one of *many* media streams available for accessing God. By implication then, some of these divine streams may even come in the guise of other religious traditions or possibly even media-generated worlds.

Although this gesture toward transcendence sounds at first like the arguments of the biblical fundamentalists, Raschke's case is altogether different, since earthly relativism is, for him, not a threat but an invitation to faith. In other words, apocalyptic dualism (the first-person-shooter mentality) is replaced with a Joban acknowledgement of the mystery of God's transcendence. By embracing the indeterminacy of texts – even the biblical text – he suggests that evangelical Christians can shed the obligation to the Cartesian model of truth acquisition that "hard-core Christian rationalists" cling to, and replace it with a *faith* based on experience, which accepts the incompleteness of human perspective, which in turn opens the door to the humility of faith in a God-centered point of view (20). In short, he argues that postmodernism opens up evangelical theology by putting the element of sheer faith back into it, and all without demonizing popular culture, academic scholarship, or religious pluralism. This is, of course, an open acknowledgement of belief-as-choice, with the possibility of openness to continuing revelation and self-growth.

For Raschke, postmodernism is the *ideal* means by which to achieve this return to faith, since by "calling attention to the finite boundaries of human knowledge and meaning," postmodernism makes it possible for God to "continue to speak and disclose himself from his infinite throne on high" (31). Mimicking the Protestant Reformation's call for a return to scripture and faith, Raschke's "Next Reformation" urges a return "to the Word not as a logical construct, but as the living power and presence" of God (33). The new Reformation, drawing on the insights of postmodernist philosophy, will create a "dynamic new relational faith." The text of the Bible opens up to numerous possible interpretations, a text that is no longer read as a fixed, rigid story but as an open, incomplete story world, composed by humans and serving as one stream of entry into the greater "world" which is always *beyond* it – the realm of God.

Using the analogy of the Eucharist, Raschke cautions his readers that the text is only a sign pointing to a greater truth: "The significance of [the Gospels] arises from what we say about the text, how we ... 'deconstruct' it ... [how we] disassemble it, to rend it into pieces as Christ was torn apart on the cross" (90). Here Raschke departs from Derrida and the deconstructionists, turning the apparent nihilism of deconstructionism on its head: "If, as Derrida has intimated, there is nothing 'outside' the text then the sacred text is the same as sacred presence ... 'Salvation' can be found in 'dying' to our representations and being born anew as readers" (90). Raschke's move is slick and almost imperceptible; claiming to reject the Platonic view of truth (and of God) as transcendent to creation, Raschke argues for an incarnational approach to scripture that is shaped and determined in time by real readers. This is transmedia in action.

For Raschke, a perspective-based reading of the Bible is essential precisely *because* it points to the incompleteness and the indeterminacy of the text of the Bible in favor of completeness and a determinacy in the divine realm.[3] Whether this Christian-postmodernist attempt to unite relativism and absolute "truth" is a contradiction in terms or a mystery of faith is impossible to demonstrate. But it is clear that these theologians are attempting to reject biblical fundamentalism in favor of a more open, humble view of faith as a choice and an invitation to ongoing streams of revelation. Such a move delivers contemporary evangelicals like Raschke from the world of religion as a fundamentalist, singular "answerbox" to transmediated, co-created religion as a "sandbox," with each of us increasingly viewing ourselves as deliberate builders of models of new encounter, living in an interdependent world. The transmediated form of contemporary religion can take the form of an open, situated faith that identifies with one previous tradition or the form of a religious seeker who captures insights from a host of different religious "worlds." The key, of course, is that he or she accepts multiple "streams" of media from the divine realm, and continues to let the story unfold throughout his or her lifetime.

Religious dialogue, as a sort of transmedia, is crucial to moving forward in a complex world. Global interdependence, says Diana Eck, "means we as a whole suffer the consequences of the part, and as a whole we must address the solution" (2003, 201). Accordingly, interreligious dialogue is "a necessity, an instrument of our common work to transform the world in which we live" (202). She asks:

> [H]ow often does our *we* come to include people of other faiths, other nations, other races? How often does our *we* link rather than divide? Our relation with the "other" may move, as Smith puts it, through a number of phases. First we talk *about* them – an objective "other." Then perhaps

we talk *to* them, or more personally, we talk to you. Developing a real dialogue, we talk *with* you. And finally, we talk with one another about us, all of us. This is the crucial stage to which our interreligious dialogue must take us if we are to be up to the task of creating communication adequate for an interdependent world.

(203)

As she rightly points out, there is "we language" in all of the world's religious traditions and in every tradition "there are attempts to steer toward a wider we, a *we* that links rather than divides" (203). Interreligious dialogue of this sort is "a necessity, an instrument of our common work to transform the world in which we live."

Religious dialogue can be viewed as a form of intense social media since it is a "basic communication network" constituted of a village that is made up of the entire earth (202–3). It's a mistake, says Eck, to focus on each religious tradition today "as a separate entity." The history of all religions, she remarks, are "intertwined despite the fact that they are often treated as separate chapters in books on 'world religions.'" Our religions are still "not finished," and indeed never will be: "Both the interreligious dialogue and the inter-religious conflict of the world today make us keenly aware of our constant and close interaction" (211). Arguing for an ongoing process of dialogue, change, and transformation through increasing understanding, Eck argues that the "underlying foundation of the world household will finally have to be pluralism" (229). Such a view is consistent with the notion that our lived world must be co-created and forever unfinished, our lives informed by a transmediated view.

Radhakrishnan, an Indian philosopher, said in a set of lectures at Oxford in the 1930s that in contemporary times, the people on our planet live as "one whole," affecting the lives and fortunes of each other:

> For the first time in the history of our planet its inhabitants became one whole, each and every part of which is affected by the fortunes of every other. Science and technology, without aiming at this result, have achieved the unity. Economic and political phenomena are increasingly imposing on us the obligation to treat the world as a unit. Currencies are linked, commerce is international, political fortunes are interdependent. And yet the sense that mankind must become a community is still a casual whim, a vague aspiration, not generally accepted as a conscious ideal or an urgent practical necessity moving us to feel the dignity of a common citizenship and the call of a common duty.
>
> (1939, 2)

Just as online worlds like *Second Life* are constructed by large groups of people in individual concert with one another, building an arena for encounter, being shaped and changed by the process, so our own religious worlds must increasingly be viewed less as individual answerboxes and more as contributors to a shared, co-cultivated sandbox of discovery.

The assumption of singular modes of interpretation – that is, of fundamentalist-literalist readings of sacred texts – is incompatible with religion as transmedia, with the pluralist mode of encounter, with the idea that we build our "world" together and construct our "rules" through encounter, conversation, listening, and personal growth. Jenkins describes "the ways that convergence [of media] is reshaping American popular culture and, in particular, the ways it is impacting the relationship between media audiences, producers, and content" (2006a, 12). Convergence culture is also a facet of religious identity, as individuals find themselves in flux and see the world's religions blending together in encounter, conflict, cooperation, and shared transformation.

Jeff Gomez says of transmedia producers that they are "a new kind of visionary" who wants to use different types of media as "instrument[s] in an orchestra, so that they're composing, in essence, symphonies of narrative – non-linear narrative – and vast narrative that young people are going to want to engage with in so many different ways." This kind of conscious creation is precisely what Eck seems to be hoping for in her calls for religious pluralism: self-conscious, active, creators of worldviews. In a 2009 interview at the Nordic Game and Film Lounge, Gomez explained:

> ... In the next few years, you are going to see a new position being created ... a variation on the title "transmedia producer" ... a steward, a shepherd, for very large tentpole intellectual properties who will be responsible for coordinating and creatively escorting the property across multiple media platforms. They, in essence, will be in charge of the universe, and they will respect the universe above and beyond studio politics ... licensing ... even the producer's, director's and actors' ... They will coordinate it all and some of them will be visionaries who will actually fabricate it and produce it ... from scratch ... they will engage ... a mass audience on a global scale and invite them to come in to the canon and participate in the intellectual property directly.

He adds that with films like *Avatar* appearing, "the experience will be [so] intense that you'll want another hit of that dreamlike thrilling experience. And so you'll go searching for it with other media, like the *Avatar* video game." These experiences, he suggests, "will allow you to live in that world." We'll be driven to learn more about the *Avatar* story world and we will "want to understand the philosophy of these alien creatures and it's going to be something that can be studied." This form of storytelling is "a brand new way of interfacing with entertainment, and with life" (2009). In its secular, mass-mediated form it may be somewhat new; but religious story worlds have been offering us this kind of transmediated engagement for centuries.

Of course, there is a very real danger here of these new worlds, new religions, becoming mere commodities, engineered to get people to spend more money on more games, more movies, more t-shirts. This danger was noticed long ago; Marx and Nietzsche recognized this fault in the religious practices they saw around them and pointed out the ease with which religious worldviews can veer into hypocrisy and take advantage of others. We can't ignore the fact that new transmedia worlds like *Avatar* and *Halo* are made by corporations interested in a profit, and that we must pay for the privilege of engaging with them. But this need not diminish our awareness of the fact that such constructs – driven by market forces or not – are profoundly powerful examples of new religions-in-motion.

And despite the fact that they must spend money on them – indeed, perhaps *because* they must spend money on them – people *do* use these media items as a means of values-identification, self-development, and imaginative creation. They craft rituals, stories, and experiences using these worlds as the foundation. They tune in to watch their favorite characters. They craft alternate interpretive storylines. They create online and offline communities of like-minded fans who share their devotion to the story world of their choice. They dress up like favorite characters and act out storylines with friends. Religion is a form of transmedia, and transmedia is a form of religion. Both are rule-based constructions, made by humans, the stuff of dreams. They are attempts at order-making. They are beliefs and imagination spun together into webs of meaning, significance crafting products that require our participation and invite our devotion.

Hunger for the real

One predictable critique of the new transmedia worlds as religion is that, unlike traditional religions that put an otherworldly God at the center of the story world, these new transmedia religions put us at the center – *we* are the hub. To return to the analogy of the Katamari, we are the ones "rolling up" the collection of multimediated streams that we define as our religion. And although we may share fan intensity of devotion with other *Twilight* or *Harry Potter* fans, our individual fan fiction will differ, the character we choose to play will not be the same, and we'll buy different kinds of apparel and put different screen savers on our laptops. We might even engage with multiple worlds, creating our own unique "sticky ball" of blended transmedia worlds, with a pulsating and unstable blended story hub with *only* our individual selves as the core uniting them.

This individualism, however, exposes that with choice comes competition in the production of the technology that generates our desire to invest in these transmedia worlds, such that "[s]torytelling and meaning-making inevitably become intertwined with marketing, technology, and consumption in a market economy" (Roof 1999, 110). The marketing of religion and the role of individual choice seem inextricable from one another and mutually reinforce the churn toward greater and greater market-driven production of belief. Mara Einstein recognizes this too when she outlines the ways that traditional religions have increasingly "branded" themselves, such that "there are numerous similarities between marketing and religion, and the line between the two has become increasingly blurred" (2007, 92). She expresses an interest in evangelicalism as particularly in tune with market forces, but as I suggest here, the transmedia industry also intuits the way that seeker religion provides some deep pockets. Gomez recognizes the role of desire and choice in transmedia when he explains that "integrated transmedia storylines" create "intense loyalty" and "long-term engagement" by consumers who experience a "desire to share the experience" (2010).

This desire is in fact a crucial component in the success of transmedia, and represents the same kind of desire that Mara Einstein sees at work in religious branding, since "faith brands act like other consumer products. They are repackaged and retooled to appeal to consumer tastes" (93). When we look at transmedia as a new competitor alongside traditional religions, it seems that the amalgam of desire, branding, and reflexivity are the qualities most indicative of success in today's market. Thus, evangelicals like Joel Osteen and T. D. Jakes can generate mass-attendance megachurches, just like *Halo* and *Harry Potter* can create lines of consumers willing to stay out overnight to get the product first. At the same time that such intense fan loyalty is generated for some new forms of religion – those that involve choice, branding and desire – other religious traditions find themselves scrambling for followers (or fans). *Star Trek* in the right contexts, can still generate fan frenzy. And George Lucas can light up the web with mere hints of another trilogy for *Star Wars*.

Even Coca Cola is getting in on the transmedia game, creating the self-consciously transmediated campaign "The Happiness Factory," engineered to create the "world" of Coke, a happy, light-hearted, generous and community-filled place that evokes heaven and stokes our desire to climb right into the Coke machine where this mysterious transcendent world resides. David Chidester recognized the missionary quality of Coca Cola in *Authentic Fakes*: "Here we find Coke as a sacred sign, a sign subject to local misreading, perhaps, but nevertheless the fetish of a global religion, an icon of the West, a symbol that can mark an initiatory entry into modernity" (42). For Chidester, however, Coke is the quintessential "authentic fake." He remarks: "Even if it has led to the 'Cocacolonization' of the world, this manipulation of desire through effective advertising has nothing to do with religion" (42). And yet, Chidester allows that a "fetish" is "the objectivization of desire," the means by which those who are not part of a religious tradition wall off those who are, by labeling *their* desire mere "fetish" (43).

Chidester thus implies that from an insider's perspective, the fetish is hierophany, and the "authentic fake" is real because of the work that it does, a move that is essentially Durkheimian in its emphasis on the totem as the hub of meaning. The fetish, says Chidester, "represents an unstable center for a shifting constellation of religious symbols" and may be able to "inspire religious moods and motivations," but "is constantly at risk of being unmasked as something made and therefore as an artificial focus of desire" (43). Yet this threat of being "unmasked" is present in *all* modes of religious imagination today, not just in marketed or corporately manufactured religions, suggesting that either *all* modes of religion are "authentic" because meaningful or *all* are "fake" because constructed.

Traditional religion is as subject to exposure as transmedia – indeed, one could argue that transmedia religions are *more* honest in that they wear their human-constructed sense of the transcendent as a badge of pride, with celebration of the human as creator, as if to say, "We made this. And nonetheless it inspires us." For those who recognize transmedia's ability to construct other worlds worthy of such devotion and rich with such meaning, the comparison with traditional religion as an unrecognized sibling reveals *both* of them to be products of human design and imagination, with the younger sibling apparently having an easier time generating followers. Transmedia religions may even do a better job of with choice, branding and desire since they are not limited in the same way as traditional religions. Instead of tapping into a pre-existing other world of the Bible or heaven and working to make it seem hip and relevant, transmedia religions can create *brand new* other worlds and use astonishing CGI and 3D technology to cultivate our desire for entry, to hint at its achievement.

This is obvious in the conceit of *Avatar*, which invites us to identify with Jake Sully, who literally enters into the paradisiacal world of Pandora via immersive technology that allows him to acquire a new body – an avatar – and fulfill his (and our) deepest wishes for perfect inhabitation of ideal virtual worlds. *Tron*, too, is generating excitement for "geeks" worldwide, who anticipated its release in December 2010 with what can only be called religious devotion, thrilled that this iteration retains the premise of the protragonist's literal entry *into* the virtual world, a semblance that is enhanced by the film's release in 3D.

The world of sacred texts, especially the world of the Bible, is still as open to transmediation as it has always been, but fewer people engage with it in this way today. Instead, reacting against the prevailing fundamentalist view that the Bible is static, fixed, relaying a sense of permanence via its "sacredness," some of us prefer other more open transformable worlds to expend our imaginative energy on. So we build and experience new transmedia worlds for ourselves over and over again. There's *Star Wars*, *Star Trek*, *Battlestar Galactica*, *Harry Potter*, *Twilight*, *The Matrix*, *Halo*, and *Avatar*, and others. Our fascination with them says as much about our desire for open encounters with the transcendent as it does about our fascination with other planets, witchcraft, technology, or other life forms.

We roll up our identities, dreams, moral values, rituals, stories, beliefs and relics into Katamari balls of our very own, transmuted by our encounter with media, shaped by our own creation as we interact with massive story worlds and the believers who invest themselves in them. We are, indeed, becoming experts at the manufacture of transmedia worlds, which is to say, we are becoming experts at the manufacture of new and ephemeral religions. Transmedia is never finished; whereas the traditional revealed religions are "stuck" to varying degrees with a fixed, written text, the "Halo Bible" is fluid, incomplete, evocative in its main characters and mythology but far from existing in any single, fixed form, and the form that it has is continually being updated, expanded, revised, transformed.

Yet desire for full comprehension alongside reveling in the immenseness of the "text" is clearly evident in immense traditions of interpretation in traditional religions and in transmedia. This desire is itself a hierophany generated through fascination with the other world and a deep desire to be *there* rather than *here*. Thus, transmedia forms of storytelling have usually involved what Sanes (n.d.) calls "ports of entry" that "allowed audiences to physically and psychologically immerse themselves in the situations and environments that have been portrayed" in theater, religious ritual, gameplay, and dramatic storytelling. Such entry points are also deliberately crafted by contemporary storytellers, designers of ARGs, who produce "rabbit holes," which are "designed to entice people to find out more" about the game. Rabbit holes might take the form of letters, e-mail, websites, videos, billboards, taglines in film credits, or information on t-shirts, advertisements, or other media (Sinead Rafferty 2008). This view is akin to the performed "belief" that enables players of the *Go Game* to see their world as enchanted, and that allows Christians to see Jesus appearing in a water stain, a bone, or a moth's wings.

Christian Connie Neal uses *Harry Potter* as an allegory to describe salvation, using Harry Potter as a metaphor to describe the Christian "portal" into heaven. Jesus, she postulates, might draw a parallel between the invitation to enter the otherworldly realm of Hogwarts with the Christian's invitation to enter the kingdom of God; and he might show children that just as Harry entered a magical door to platform nine and a half, the "magic door" to God's kingdom is the "magical transport" that is Jesus (2001, 90). Heaven and the transmedia world of Hogwarts are symbolically identified. McGonigal sees this desire as the "simulation of belief" that is "borne from virtual play and pointing, like virtual reality, to the unmet promise of [truly] experiencing its real counterpart" (2003, 4). Eliade would likely call this desire a form of the "nostalgia for paradise," that inscrutable wish on the part of the human for the Platonic Original, for the Sacred (1961, 92).

I suggest that such a desire is instead what *precipitates* belief. Desire *is* belief in its striving toward the real, in its hunger for the sacred, perfection, order, sense, cosmos. Desire *is* performance. In the case of transmedia, desire is generated in the audience for an ultimately unachievable comprehension of the whole story, driven by a participant's wish to fit the pieces of different streams of story content from different types of media into the core story world.

Gomez explains of fans that "when they're doing that work and it fits well, there's kind of like this ecstasy, this thrill of actually formulating it all together." This, I propose, is the thrill of the Sacred, the other, the transcendent. Gomez explains that "repeat customers" of a particular transmedia world may even become "evangelists" for the media world: "These people will light torches and claim ownership over [the producer's] universe, [or] story world – worlds like *Harry Potter*, *Twilight*, *Star Trek*" (2010 interview). He also helps us understand why some fans veer into deep devotion: "They want to know the whole story, to understand its structure, its order, and most importantly, they want to be *part* of it." This is why fans will show up in full costume and make-up, with props, fully immersed in a storyline of a transmedia world. They want to enter it, and pretending to do so is nearly good enough.

The *Wizarding World of Harry Potter*, a theme park at Universal Studios, is a perfect example of our increasing ritual engagement with transmedia worlds. Theme parks like this are built upon the premise that we *do* desire entry into these story worlds, that we want the deep immersion and the order that such stories offer, and that we'll choose to pay for the experience. As the theme park's website reports: "Join Harry Potter and his friends as you venture into a world where magic is real." You are invited to "[p]ass through the towering Hogwarts castle gates and explore the familiar passageways, classrooms and corridors" and "then get ready to soar above the castle grounds as you join Harry Potter and his friends on an unforgettably thrilling adventure" into which Universal Studios has injected "a little magic" (Universal Studios n.d.).

Conclusion

To engage with transmedia is to *choose* to engage. In some ways, too, it is to enter into a contract with the rules, expectations, and attitude that entry entails: to play by the rules of the game. Similarly, to play a religion is also to *choose* to play that religion. Salen and Zimmerman describe the "lusory attitude" as "the peculiar state of mind of game players" when they adopt unnecessary limitations and step into the world of the game's rules (2004, 77). This investment involves belief: "To play a game is in many ways an act of 'faith' that invests the game with its special meaning – without willing players, the game is a formal system waiting to be inhabited, like a piece of sheet music waiting to be played" (98). Religions work much the same way.

If we were able to generate stunningly vivid, immersive technology such that our experiences in the virtual "world" were utterly indistinguishable from this world (the kind of technology imagined in the *Matrix* trilogy, perhaps, but without the A.I. conspiracy), what would be the difference between that world and this one? If the immersion was complete enough, there would be no difference at all in sensory perception, and depending on how we choose to project our digital selves, we may look exactly the same and we can assume, would have the same sensory experiences. If such immersion were possible, the only difference between that world and this would be *the way* we participated in it – the assumed order or cosmos that the game would display. The algorithms would be assumed to be consistent, and we could assume the world had been crafted with some rules in place, put there by the game's Designer. After all, that is what a game is: the voluntary imposition of rules onto an arena of people or things that dictates how we are to interact with them and usually gives us a goal to achieve. So might we see our drive toward greater immersion into the structured worlds we've made as a form of hunger for the real, a hunger for order, cosmos, structure, and control? A world in which we know exactly who to trust and why? A world in which there is a fixed goal, in which the things we experience have rich contextual meaning, and in which we can experience the miraculous, the unexpected, the powerful?

This deep immersion seems to be precisely the direction we are taking. Researchers are developing new and more "haptic" (touch-based) modes of virtual interaction. Immersive spaces such as rooms, spheres, and full-blown sets are wired with virtual "walls" and sometimes enhanced with visual technology in the form of goggles and virtual tools or weapons. The popular new sci-fi show *Caprica* (a prequel to *Battlestar Galactica*) takes up this fascination with a storyline obsessed with a virtual world accessible via "holobands" that pull the participant into a virtual world that seems as real as our own – but which is fully designed by others and thus presumably with some defined order. *Avatar* takes them up a notch by offering us organic avatars and an intrinsic "programmer" in Eywah, the mother goddess of the Nav'i moon. Our fascination with virtual reality may signal our disillusionment with the postmodern, the fragmented, and the uncertain. We want rules and gods, adventures and heavenly worlds.

However, instead of buying completely into pre-packaged institutional forms of religious games and the rules they impose, increasingly, *we* write the rules for our own games and lives. *We* decide what to roll up into our own personal Katamari "sticky-ball-thing." And although we may find, if we land within a particular received religious tradition and worship with like-minded peers, that our "sticky-ball-things" resemble each other, we will not be easily convinced anymore that they are identical. If we meet this challenge head on, we will find ourselves constructing a shared world with respect for differences, with curiosity about potential similarities, and with the awareness that whatever we do in virtual environments, the world we build here together in our embodied form is the only one of its kind that we're going to get.

And thus, might we see our investment in virtual spaces as a reflection of what in other contexts we might easily consider the "religious" impulse? If viewed this way, then our desire for the virtual can in fact be viewed also as a hunger for the real – for a sense of meaning, order and definition in our own real lives. If religion is about finding meaning, order, and a sense of predictability – if it is about imagining the way the world might be – if it is about stories that animate our lives, rituals that shape our consciousness, and modes of interacting that define who we are, then it seems to me that virtual engagement is doing some of the very same things. Our desire for greater and greater immersion, coupled with the structure and order that come with that very immersion, may signal a "hunger for the real" that looks an awful lot like religion. And how can we really tell the difference?

Chapter 10

Expansion pack

Every good online game world offers expansion packs. Expansion packs are supplements for existing gameplay adding new areas to be explored, new tools to employ, and new adventures to embark upon. Because online worlds are streaming, they are never complete and thus our engagement with them is ongoing as well. A book like this requires the recognition that the story doesn't end here. In a couple of years, all of the examples I cite here will be woefully out of date. New technologies will be on the move that I have not imagined. New forms of haptic engagement, new levels of immersion, new ease of interface with virtual environments will be taken for granted. At best, these ideas will have some staying power as generators of an ongoing conversation that will last beyond the latest craze in video game play. At worst, my proposals here will seem stilted and naive to readers a decade from now. By acknowledging the vast speed with which everything is changing, I hope at least to indicate a trajectory into which scholars interested in this area might move – perhaps not a real expansion pack, but the gesture of one.

Throughout *Godwired*, I have struck a number of deliberate chords, calling your attention to what seem to be the shared conversations going on about virtual reality's place in our world across a variety of disparate fields. My goal here is to be a collector, a synthesizer, an observer, pulling together threads from as many different thinkers as I could get my hands on. Each chapter is focused on a key idea that seems important to hosts of scholars exploring our relationship to technology, ideas that recur repeatedly and intensely in the conversations of scholars of religion, communications, gamer theory, psychology, sociology, computer science, and philosophy. In *Godwired*, we have looked at: virtual storytelling and textuality; the relationship between rituals, games and stories; virtual identity; virtual community; virtual and sacred space; virtual evil; video games as apocalypses; and transmedia as religion. In a way, we have moved from some of the oldest forms of religious practice (ritual) to the newest (transmedia). However, one could as easily argue that transmedia is nothing new; it is just taking new and increasingly mass-mediated secular forms. When looking at these themes in a larger sense, one theme that emerges is the desire for order-making in an increasingly complicated, connected, and

diverse world. Could it be that our desire for entry into programmed environments is a contemporary form of a very old drive, one that used to take
much more traditional forms through the "programmed environments" of
institutionalized religion? This theme runs throughout all of the chapters,
raising new insights about each in light of the others.

Today's stories are increasingly interactive, and this shift is affecting how
people read sacred stories as well (Chapter 2). We want to be active agents in
the stories we imbibe, co-creators of meaning. Murray points out that "in a
postmodern world, everyday experience has come to seem increasingly gamelike,"
and "we are aware of the constructed nature of all our narratives" (2004, 3).
Accordingly, the similarity between games, rituals and stories makes us
increasingly aware of the game-like and story-like activities of ritual. The new
media available today help us to "retell age-old stories in new ways" as we
"imagine ourselves as creatures of a parameterized world of multiple possibilities" and come to comprehend our own role in rule-making all around us.
The hope is that we will increasingly recognize ourselves as "authors of rule
systems which drive behavior and shape possibilities" (8). We are world
builders: ritual crafters, storytellers, and game players, but what this means for
us we will have to decide for ourselves.

Perhaps our fascination with the ritual–game–story thing (Chapter 3) is that
it does, after all, provide us with some sense of order and structure in a world
increasingly shaped by fluidity and individual decision. Rituals, games and
stories all have "rules" that shape interaction. In rituals, these rules consist
largely of liturgical and processional requirements that urge particular behaviors over others. In games, the "rules" shape the experience itself, and can be
read in the procedural make-up of the programming, or in the rules accepted
by players before the game begins. In stories, rules are integrated into the
larger hermeneutical principles of the interpreting community and into the
ways that viewers and readers choose to engage with a received story, both
visual and textual. Such experiences are both intellectually engaging and
metaphysically comforting in their assumption of a degree of order combined
with the obligation to interact with them.

Our fascination with virtual sacred space also reveals our desire for structure.
Based on an application of Eliade, I have argued that one of the attractions of
the virtual construction of any space, including sacred space, is our own ability
to create something meaningful, predictable, and comprehensible in an otherwise
disordered space like *Second Life* or the *Minecraft* universe (Chapter 4). If our
encounter with sacred space online is in some ways a reflective process, and if
these encounters are constructed, circular, and performative, then another way
of putting this is that we are talking *to ourselves*, attempting to create meaningful order for ourselves apart from existing authoritative religious structures.
Grimes has remarked that ritual, "like television, is a medium of communication,
an enacted one ... ritual is a multimedium, a synthesis of drama, storytelling,
dance, and art" (2006, 11). Ritual is transmediated. Hillis agrees: "Rituals

performed through networked digital settings are indices pointing to the assumptions undergirding sociocultural institutions and political economies within which a ritual's performers find themselves ideologically and as embodied human beings" (2009, 63). Virtual worlds – what we might call the "virtual sacred" – are reflections of our own assumptions and beliefs. This "virtual sacred" manifests visually what *we* want, what *we* dream, and what *we* imagine, however sublime or ugly that may be.

Wade Clark Roof, Stewart Hoover, Diana Eck, David Chidester and others have all pointed out the remarkable fluidity of identity that characterizes our sense of self today. I have called this kind of self-conscious identity-crafting the "iPod self," and identified the myriad ways that our media reflect back for us our own developing values (Chapter 5). Roof says that contemporary, syncretistic religion is typified by "a direct relation between the consuming practitioner and spiritual goods in a religiously deregulated and demonopolized world" (1999, 69). Through focusing on the individual's experience of religion, media products have the ability to:

> remake religion into a more dynamic, self-reflexive activity on the part of the individual and reinforce the view that, whatever else it might be, religious consciousness involves an active process of meaning-making, of interpreting one's own situation in relation to media discourses as well as those in traditional religious institutions. Bombarded by media input, the individual is left having to do a lot of cognitive negotiating and bargaining.
> (70)

Such contemporary negotiation of individual identity appears to include the choice of whether or not to see a given experience as a game, a ritual, or both. Roof defined in 1999 what he calls "reflexive spirituality," seeing in our multimediated world "a situation encouraging a more deliberate, engaging effort on people's part for their own spiritual formation, both inside and outside religious communities" (75). Roof points out that in today's world, "[r]esponsibility falls more upon the individual – like that of the *bricoleur* – to cobble together a religious world from available images, symbols, moral codes, and doctrines, thereby exercising considerable agency in defining and shaping what is considered to be religiously meaningful" (75). That is to say, the individual must "play" with received traditions and decide for herself what to believe. This kind of media-motivated experimentation with identity is remarkably enjoyable, generating role play, community experience, personal creativity, and a host of engaging activities with a quasi-ritual component. There is no predetermined goal or end to reflexive spiritual work; it is, by definition, ongoing and transformative. With many transmedia worlds today, it can also be simply *fun*.

Acknowledging the personal nature of religious identity in today's culture, Jolyon Mitchell and Sophia Marriage argue that religious identity "is not *absolutely* any of these, but tends to be more *private, subjective, implicit*, and *reflexive* than in the past." Today, they say, "[a]utonomous selves tend to pick and choose from among traditions, and this has the effect of making the symbols of those traditions … less embedded in their received histories" (2003, 12). This is transmediation, with the "self" choosing what to adopt from the story hub of tradition. Roof gestures toward the reflexive quality of much of contemporary religious practices, and says that "[b]ecause ours is an age when it is possible to appropriate religious symbols from many times and places, we are forced to become more self-conscious about all such choices" (1999, 110).

If we are drawn to virtual environments because they represent order, we are met at the same time with their resistance to solidify the self into any single entity. Instead, our sense of self is multiplied in the many virtual environments into which we enter. When we are online, we are not exactly the same "selves" as those who sit in computer chairs sipping tea and pecking at keyboards; what is networked online – the virtual-ship selves that sail the digital seas – are merely what Hillis calls "visual assemblages of graphic traces." We are the "search as map." The internet, in this case, is "monad as nomad," the hope for unity but the reality of constant seeking. Even though anything that happens behind a digital screen is ordered in some respects for being programmed, our own selves cannot ever fully participate in that consistency. Instead, the hope for ordered identity, the *desire* for meaning *itself* becomes the purpose of our digital wandering. An online community is "anywhere, everywhere, and nowhere but always on the move" (2009, 2). We are restless, searching, alone, and also searching together. The paradox of the human condition is highlighted for us in high definition when we encounter it online, and the ordered environment it offers us is painfully ephemeral, always just out of permanent reach. The questions raised about who or what we are when we go online may be seen as more developed forms of the problem of the alternate "selves" we project in our many flesh-and-bones relationships, with the added dimension of separate websites, avatars, game rules, or other frames to remind us that we really are splintered selves – that we have less and less of a sense of grounded community when we "distribute" ourselves online (Chapter 6).

The same kind of desire drives us to nonetheless *seek* community online, where we can choose who to interact with, where algorithms can protect us from unsavory individuals, and where the hope for the perfect love connection is always just a few clicks away. A number of religious studies scholars have pointed out that the thing that makes religion work is precisely the community of believers that defines it, and the sense of belonging such groups can produce. Our fascination with elusive online community suggests that we may also be driven by the *desire* to find a sense of belonging, even if it is never fully achieved. Morgan has argued that community "must be envisioned in the things believers do" so that they can "realize in a concrete, corporeal way that they belong to this world or clan or tradition and that doing so ensures them of the benefits of membership, such as an enduring identity and sense of purpose" (2005, 59). But our communities online are never concrete, are markedly non-corporeal, and offer us so many different options of identification with clan or tradition that we can hardly sit still long enough to receive many of the benefits of membership.

Today's "texting tribes," consisting largely of youth and young adults, are fully aware of the potential of this new technology for social purposes (Rheingold 2002, 2). Youth today report that if they don't hear from their peers in regular text messages, they feel a loss of affection and a decreased sense of connection (21). But no matter how it may reinforce a sense of connection with loved ones, texting cannot fully replace embodied relationship. As Rheingold observes, texting can be used to briefly touch base with relatives and friends, no matter the distance between them, and this is clearly a positive thing (21–23). But although social groupings do not appear to be necessarily weakening according to Rheingold's research, they are surely transforming. We are at once more connected to those in different places than we have ever been, and as disconnected from those directly around us as we have ever been.

For Turkle, our deep dependence upon technology is troubling: "Tethered to technology, we are shaken when that world 'unplugged' does not signify, does not satisfy." Technology, she suggests, "offers us substitutes for connecting with each other face-to-face" and "redraws the boundaries between intimacy and solitude," encouraging us to "choose keyboards over the human voice" (2011, 11). The implications of such changes for religion might mean that our religious relationships – with other people or even with God – are seen as "real" only when issued through the virtual realm, and thus implicitly endangering preexisting real-life commitments and lessening the likelihood that we'll build relationships with those physically right next door. For Turkle, this is precisely why confessional sites and prayer walls won't create meaningful encounters: "Communities are places where one feels safe enough to take the good and the bad. In communities, others come through for us in hard times, so we are willing to hear what they have to say, even if we don't like it" (2011, 238). In virtual communities, the obligation to work through problems with online friends may be tempered by the ease with which we can simply tune out, blocking future interaction.

Indeed, instead of addressing the world's moral and cultural complexity, we may instead be most attracted to online environments that allow us to ignore the lived diversity around us by offering us an intoxicating, if temporary, sense of cosmic order (Chapter 7). Although I believe direct cause-and-effect arguments about violent video games as training modules for violence to be overly naive, I do think that repeated engagement with simplistic and dualistic algorithms may encourage a failure to imagine alternative possibilities in real-life conflict, instilling in us preferred cognitive structures of engagement with difference that deposit all people into one of two categories: friend or enemy. In so doing, such modes of thinking may excuse us from meaningful and deep encounter about conflicting issues of religion, belief, culture, education, politics and personhood. If games have any procedural rhetoric at all, and it seems that they must, it seems likely that the lasting lessons learned by most players are probably not about how to use a real weapon. More likely for the average user, especially those playing games that mimic actual, recent conflict, is the lesson that the world is simple and can be solved by demonizing those with whom we disagree. Is it any wonder that we are drawn to such scripted environments, when they can offer us temporary respite from difficult political and social problems that seem insolvable? And can we find a way to allow such temporary virtual escapes to coexist alongside more meaningful and ongoing conflict management about real life social problems? Or are we doomed to view the real world too in dualistic, eschatological terms, such that our video games become apocalyptic prototypes, blueprints for how to think in limited, scripted and violent ways (Chapter 8)?

Sanes argues that as humans we have a "built-in impulse to create world replicas" and that we do so "using the insubstantial images of the world's first virtual reality computer, the mind." These world replicas, he argues, say something important about us because they reveal our dreams: "In imitation worlds such as stories or dramas, we have merely externalized these creations of the imagination, and given them an objective and more elaborate form." This "externalization" of the human imagination is reflected in many different modes of contemporary world-building, especially in the virtual worlds and spaces that we create and maintain in online worlds like *Second Life* and in the video games we design and play. Such synthetic world spaces, says Sanes, work as "symbolic arenas" that afford us the ability to "explore alternative modes of existence." We "create world replicas to transcend the limits imposed by life" and overcome the "tyranny of actuality," in order to "achieve a kind of freedom afforded by the imagination" (Sanes n.d.). The virtual, in this case, is identified with the imagination, and virtual modes of experience are viewed as visible representations of our desires and dreams. Perhaps, then, we should think deliberately and carefully about what we choose to put up on our digital screens, and what we choose to consume there. We've made our dreams visible in waking life.

Eliade has argued that "modern" non-religious people are subject to the "terror of history" in their deprivation of the "Sacred," stuck in a meaningless linear flow of time and deprived of spiritual dreams (1954/2005, 141–62). Whereas Eliade sees this poverty as an obvious feature of contemporary life, it seems that with our fascination with virtual reality, re-enchantment is taking place, albeit of a self-designed form. As Landy and Saler remark, "there are, in the modern world, fully secular and deliberate strategies for re-enchantment of which … no one, however hardbitten he or she may be, need be ashamed" (2009, 2). Virtual reality is the most powerful of these forms of re-enchantment, providing us with rich "symbolic toolboxes" for the development of meaning in our own ways and on our own terms. Indeed, the emerging popularity of transmedia story worlds reveals our fascination with religion-building, with human-driven meaning-making (Chapter 9). Murray claims that "to be alive in the twentieth century is to be aware of the alternative possible selves, of alternative possible worlds, and of the limitless intersecting stories of the actual world" (1997, 38). We have the capability to corporately construct a world that is ever-evolving, taking into account the glorious differences among its co-creators and co-participants. We can see who we are, who we want to be, and what we most fear just by looking at what we create in our digital spaces. Our media are an apt reflection of what we *wish* were true, but they are also a reflection of our deepest fears. The challenge, of course, is to cultivate the former and resist letting the latter limit our ability to show compassion for one another.

Our dreams are beginning to move off the screens into our real lives, as well. Increasingly, game players' experiences are enhanced by new levels of ease of interface between the real body and the virtual environment. Martti Lahti has noted that rapid developments in game technology "intensify [the] bodily dimension of our experience, heightening the impression of sensory immersion and a physical link to an imaginary environment with data gloves, joysticks with feedback mechanisms such as rumble packs, pedals and wheels, motion-sensing technology (for example, moving seats), and surround sound." Such innovations serve to "fuse" the player with the computer or game, enveloping the space around the player's physical body (2003, 162). New developments also include headsets that can allow players to communicate with one another and, in some cases, to "see" the virtual world with a minimal amount of physical space between vision and screen, increasing the drive to identification of the player's point of view with the avatar's point of view as displayed on the monitor. The distinction between player and avatar, real world and game world, becomes increasingly harder to draw, as "this delirium of virtual mobility, sensory feedback, and the incorporation of the player into a larger system thus tie the body into a cybernetic loop with the computer" (163). Technology is in the works for an immersive sphere in which players can act and move with headsets, surround sound, and the ability to run and jump within a virtual environment. The virtual is surpassing physical hardware in another way through research like the experiment completed in 2006 at St Louis University, which allowed a teenager to play *Space Invaders* via thoughts alone, as he sat wired to the computer (Fitzpatrick 2006). New developments with the Wii and the Kinect system already involve us bodily in our virtual spaces.

As more technological advances increase the ability of the physical body to easily interface with the computer, the "differentiation between artificial and real or between outside and inside [increasingly] will be blurred" (Filiciak 2003, 98). Throughout their history, one of the characteristics of video game design has been "an attempt, with the help of various technologies, to erase the boundary separating the player from the game world and to play up tactile involvement." As Lahti notes, "much of the development of video games has been driven by a desire for a corporal immersion with technology, a will to envelop the player in technology and the environment of the game space" (Lahti 2003, 159). In this sense, the role of the war video game as ritual of cosmos-crafting becomes a conundrum of serious proportions: without a clear distinction between the world of the game and the real world, discussions about sacred and profane fall apart. And without a conscious sense of what we want to build, we will easily fall into the trap of creating limiting, small options that prevent human flourishing.

Roof has remarked that "[r]eligion – like jazz – involves an ongoing reconfiguring of possibilities" (1999, 133). Such fluidity may make some people nervous, but there is also good news. As Filiciak observes, the fluid or "postmodern identity" is "a self-aware identity" (2003, 96). Eck says something similar when she calls upon her readers to pay attention to what they believe, whatever that may be. She says: "just being awake, alert, attentive is no easy matter. I think it is the greatest spiritual challenge we face" (2003, 145). If our virtual spaces indeed mirror our current dreams and desires, then it is here that we should look to see just how alert and attentive we are.

Notes

1 Walkthrough

1 Summary material comparing rituals and video games in this chapter echoes material that will appear in the entry "ritual" in Mark J. P. Wolf (ed.), *Encyclopedia of Video Games: The Culture, Technology, and Art of Gaming*, two volumes, ABC-CLIO/Greenwood Press, 2012.

2 The stories we play

1 Portions of this section of the chapter originally appeared in a different form in *Religion Dispatches* under the title "Sacred Texting: When Religious Writ Gets Wired," October 23, 2008. Used by permission.
2 For some, we should even distinguish between "story" and "narrative," a complex distinction that I address more fully in Chapter 3. Here I use the terms interchangeably.
3 Portions of this chapter are adapted from "The Play is the Thing" in Craig Detweiler (ed.) *Halos and Avatars: Playing Video Games with God*, Louisville, KY: Westminster John Knox Press, 2010. www.wjkbooks.com. Used by permission.

5 Me, myself and iPod

1 Select portions of this chapter also appear in modified form in Heidi Campbell's forthcoming book *Digital Religion* (2012, Routledge).
2 This paragraph echoes material that first appeared in "Our Lady of Persistent Liminality" in Eric Michael Mazur and Kate McCarthy (eds.) *God in the Details*, second edition, London and New York: Routledge, 2011.
3 Portions of this unit first appeared in *Religion Dispatches* in "Dreaming Cyborg Dreams," February 13, 2009. Used by permission.

8 Xbox apocalypse

1 Portions of this chapter appear in a briefer, modified form in "Xbox Apocalypse," in the *SBL Forum* online (2009), and also in "Halo as Apocalypse," in Luke Cuddy (ed.) *Halo and Philosophy* (Open Court, 2011). The latter version includes additional insights about *Halo* by co-authors and previous Ithaca College students Tyler DeHaven and Chris Hendrickson, some of which appear here also. I am deeply grateful for their assistance.

2 Recent game developers have recognized the kinship between Enoch's vivid other-worldly journeys and videogame play. A game called *El Shaddai: Ascension of the Metatron*, a third person fantasy game modeled directly on Enoch's story, is currently in development by Ignition Entertainment and expected to be released in 2011.

9 Making belief

1 Christy Dena catalogs a number of related terms for this phenomenon, citing "transmedia storytelling" (Henry Jenkins 2006a), "distributed narratives" (Walker 2004), "pervasive games" (Montola *et al*. 2009), "ubiquitous games" (McGonigal 2006), "networked narrative environments" (Zapp 2004), "superfictions" (Hill 2001), "very distributed storytelling" (Davenport 1998). With Dena, here I see all as "subsumed under the term transmedia practice" even though "the area is in flux and crosses a wide range of creative sectors" (Dena 2009, 16).

2 Portions of this section draw on material that first appeared in "The Scholar's Code: Biblical Interpretation, Postmodernism, and *The Da Vinci Code*," in Bradley Bowers, (ed.) *The Da Vinci Code in the Academy* (Newcastle, UK: Cambridge Scholars Publishing, 2007), pp. 31–47. Used by permission.

3 For a more complete discussion of some of the most pressing issues relating to Christianity and postmodernism by a variety of modern theologians, see Myron B. Penner (ed.) *Christianity and the Postmodern Turn* (2005) and Kevin J. Vanhoozer (ed.) *The Cambridge Companion to Postmodern Theology* (2003).

Bibliography

Aarseth, Espen (2004) "Genre Trouble," in Wardrip-Fruin and Harrigan (2004), pp. 45–55.

ACIP (Asian Classics Input Project) (n.d.) Asian Classics Input Project website. <http://www.asianclassics.org/> Accessed October 25, 2010.

Aish.com (n.d.-a) "Window on the Wall," *Aish.com*. <http://www.aish.com/w/> Accessed July 2, 2011.

——(n.d.-b) "Place a Note," in "Window on the Wall," *Aish.com*. <http://www.aish.com/w/note/> Accessed July 2, 2011.

Ansell-Pearson, Keith (2005) "The Reality of the Virtual: Bergson and Deleuze," Comparative Literature Issue, *MLN* 120, no. 5: 1112–27.

Anti-Defamation League (2006) "*Left Behind: Eternal Forces* – The Video Game," review at the Anti-Defamation League website, December 19. <http://www.adl.org/Interfaith/leftbehind.asp> Accessed March 22, 2008.

Arab News (2009) "Shariah court approves SMS divorce," *Arab News*, Thursday, April 9. <http://archive.arabnews.com/?page=24&section=0&article=121367> Accessed September 21, 2011.

Artaud, Antonin (2007) Excerpt from "Sorcery and Cinema," in Mitchell and Plate (2007), pp. 54–56.

Ashcraft, B. (2009) "Love Plus Has Your Virtual Girlfriend Experience Covered," *Kotaku*, May 7. <http://kotaku.com/5243198/love-plus-has-your-virtual-girlfriend-experience-covered> Accessed February 5, 2011.

Au, James Wagner (2004) "Where Two or More Are Gathered," *New World Notes*, April 19. <http://nwn.blogs.com/nwn/2004/04/where_two_or_mo.html> Accessed May 14, 2008.

Augustine (1887) *On Christian Doctrine*, trans. James Shaw. From Nicene and Post-Nicene Fathers, First Series, Vol. 2, ed. Philip Schaff, Buffalo, NY: Christian Literature Publishing Co. Available (Kevin Knight rev. and ed.) from the New Advent website. <http://www.newadvent.org/fathers/12021.htm>

Aune, David (2005) "Understanding Jewish and Christian Apocalyptic," *Word & World* 25, no. 3: 233–45.

Bartle, Richard (2003) *Designing Virtual Worlds*, Indianapolis: New Riders.

Bateman, Chris (ed.) (2007) *Game Writing: Narrative Skills for Videogames*, Boston: Charles River Media.

Bateson, Gregory (2006) "A Theory of Play and Fantasy," in Salen and Zimmerman (2006), pp. 314–29.

BBC News (2007) "Violent Video Game Maker Forgiven," *BBC News*, October 24. <http://news.bbc.co.uk/1/hi/england/manchester/7059429.stm> Accessed June 21, 2008.

Beaudoin, Tom (2000) *Virtual Faith*, San Francisco: Jossey-Bass.

Bell, Catherine (1992) *Ritual Theory, Ritual Practice*, New York: Oxford University Press.

Benedict XVI (2010a) "The Priest and Pastoral Ministry in a Digital World: New Media at the Service of the Word," Message of His Holiness Pope Benedict XVI for the 44th World Communications Day, Sunday, May 16. <http://www.vatican.va/holy_father/benedict_xvi/messages/communications/documents/hf_ben-xvi_mes_20100124_44th-world-communications-day_en.html>

——(2010b) "New Technologies … Can Make the True and the False Interchangeable," Papal Address to the Catholic Press, *Zenit: The World Seen from Rome*, October 7. <http://www.zenit.org/article-30576?l=english> Accessed November 5, 2010.

Berger, Arthur Asa (2005) *Media Analysis Techniques*, 3rd edn, Thousand Oaks, CA: Sage.

Berger, Peter (1990) *The Sacred Canopy: Elements of a Sociological Theory of Religion*, New York: Random House.

Bernstein, Mark and Diane Greco (2004) "*Card Shark* and *Thespis*: Exotic Tools for Hypertext Narrative," in Wardrip-Fruin and Harrigan (2004), pp. 167–82.

Blake, William (1979) "On R. Watson, Bishop of Llandaff, An Apology for the Bible … addressed to Thomas Paine," in Mary Lynn Johnson and John E. Grant (eds) *Blake's Poetry and Designs*, New York: W. W. Norton & Co.

Blanchard, Anita L. and Lynne Markus (2002) "Sense of Virtual Community: Maintaining the Experience of Belonging," *Proceedings of the 35th Annual Hawaii International Conference on System Sciences (HICSS'02) – Volume 9*, Washington, DC: IEEE Computer Society. Available from the ACM Digital Library. <http://portal.acm.org/citation.cfm?id=820747&picked=prox&preflayout=tabs>

Blumenthal, Max (2007) "Kill or Convert: Brought to You by the Pentagon," *Nation*, August 7. <http://www.thenation.com/blogs/notion?pid=220960> Accessed June 21, 2008.

Bock, Darrell (2004) *Breaking "The Da Vinci Code,"* Nashville, TN: Nelson Books.

Bogost, Ian (2007a) "Art Does Not Take Exit Surveys," *Ian Bogost – Videogame Theory, Criticism, Design*, April 16. <http://www.bogost.com/watercoolergames/archives/art_does_not_ta.shtml> Accessed 26 July 2011.

——(2007b) *Persuasive Games: The Expressive Power of Videogames*, Cambridge, MA: MIT Press.

Boissevain, J. (1968) "The Place of Non-Groups in the Social Sciences," *Man* 3: 542–56.

Boon, Richard (2007) "Writing for Games," in Bateman (2007), pp. 43–69.

Boorstein, Michelle (2006) "In a Tech-Savvy World, the Word of God Goes Mobile," *Washington Post*, November 5. http://www.washingtonpost.com/wp-<dyn/content/article/2006/11/04/AR2006110400738.html> Accessed July 14, 2011.

Borg, Marcus (2001) *Reading the Bible Again for the First Time*, New York: HarperCollins.

Boyes, Emma (2007) "Sony under Fire from Church of England," *GameSpot*, June 11.

Brasher, Brenda (2001) *Give Me That Online Religion*, San Francisco: Jossey-Bass.

Briggs, J. R. (2009) *J. R. Briggs*, blog, May 9. <http://www.jrbriggs.com/facebook-jesus-or-twitter-jesus/05/> Accessed July 16, 2010.

bruder4321 (2010) "Judson Memorial Church Flash Mob in Washington Square Park 27 June 2010," *YouTube*, June 28. <http://www.youtube.com/watch?v=Fa9jo30oFkU>

Burell, Clay (2011) "Organize Smart Mobs to Defeat Creationism in Schools," online petition, *Change.org.* <http://education.change.org/petitions/view/organize_smart_mobs_to_defeat_creationism_in_schools> Accessed March 12, 2011.

Caillois, Roger (2006) "'The Definition of Play' and 'The Classification of Games'," in Salen and Zimmerman (2006), pp. 122–55.

Campbell, Heidi (2005) *Exploring Religious Community Online: We Are One in the Network.* New York: Peter Lang.

——(2010) *When Religion Meets New Media*, London: Routledge.

Campbell, Heidi and Patricia Calderon (2007) "The Question of Christian Community Online: The Case of the 'Artist World Network'," *Studies in World Christianity* 13, no. 3: 261–77.

CAN (Catholic News Agency) (2010) "Mexican Claims Responsibility for Cyber Attack against Vatican Google," *CAN*, July 21. <http://www.catholicnewsagency.com/news/mexican-claims-responsibility-for-cyber-attack-against-the-vatican-on-google/> Accessed June 10, 2011.

Careaga, Andrew (2001) "Fishing on the Net," *Online Evangelism.* <http://www.fishthe.net/e-vangelism/e-vangelism2.htm> Accessed February 4, 2011.

Castronova, Edward (2005) *Synthetic Worlds: The Business and Culture of Online Worlds*, Chicago: University of Chicago Press.

Charles, R. H. (ed.) (2004) *The Apocrypha and the Pseudepigrapha of the Old Testament*, vol. 2: *Pseudepigrapha*, Berkeley: Apocryphile Press; first published in 1913 by the Clarendon Press.

ChathNews (2010) "'Google Bomb' on Vatican Website," *CathNews*, July 20. <http://www.cathnews.com/article.aspx?aeid=22458> Accessed July 24, 2010.

Catholic Online (n.d.-a) "A Guide for Confession," *Catholic Online.* <http://www.catholic.org/prayers/confession.php>

——(n.d.-b) "Stations of the Cross: Act of Contrition," *Catholic Online.* <http://www.catholic.org/prayers/station.php>

CBS News (n.d.) "Boston Flash Mob for United Way," *CBS News.* <http://wbztv.com/local/flash.mob.charity.2.1039794.html> Accessed December 20, 2009.

Charny, Ben (2004) "Pope to Ping the Faithful," *CNET News*, April 6. <http://news.cnet.com/2100–1039_3–5185965.html> Accessed May 15, 2011.

Cheong, Pauline Hope (2009) "Christianity-Lite, in 140 Characters or Fewer?" *Religion Dispatches*, April 12. <http://www.religiondispatches.org/archive/culture/1346/christianity-lite,_in_140_characters_or_fewer> Accessed October 9, 2010.

Chidester, David (2005) *Authentic Fakes: Religion and American Popular Culture,* Berkeley: University of California Press.

Cobb, Jennifer (1998) *Cybergrace: The Search for God in the Digital World*, New York: Crown Publishers.

Collins, John J. (1979) "Introduction: Towards the Morphology of a Genre," *Semeia* 14: 1–20.

——(1998) *The Apocalyptic Imagination: An Introduction to Jewish Apocalyptic Literature,* Grand Rapids, MI: Eerdmans.

——(2005) *Encounters with Biblical Theology*, Minneapolis: Fortress Press.

Connerton, Paul (1989) *How Societies Remember*, Cambridge: Cambridge University Press.

Coppens, Philip (2003) "Cave Paintings: Entrancing the Otherworld," *Frontier Magazine* 9, no. 6 (November/December). Available on Philip Coppens' website. <http://www.philipcoppens.com/cavepaintings.html> Accessed February 15, 2011.

Costikyan, Greg (2006) "I have No Words & I Must Design," in Salen and Zimmerman (2006), pp. 192–211.

Crabtree, Shona (2007) "Finding Religion in *Second Life*'s Virtual Universe," *Washington Post*, June 16. <http://www.washingtonpost.com/wp-dyn/content/article/2007/06/15/AR2007061501902.html> Accessed January 17, 2008.

Craven, Kathy (2009) "What Is Machinima?" *MediaRights*, March 16. <http://www.mediarights.org/news/what_is_machinima> Accessed March 13, 2011.

Crawford, Chris (1982) *The Art of Computer Game Design*, Berkeley: McGraw-Hill Osborne Media,. Currently maintained online by Washington State University, Vancouver, WA. <http://www.vancouver.wsu.edu/fac/peabody/game-book/Coverpage.html#TOC> Accessed June 23, 2008.

——(2003) "Interactive Storytelling," in Wolf and Perron (2003), pp. 259–74.

Daily Radar (n.d.) "First Apple Store Wedding Flash Mob," pt 1, video, *Daily Radar*. <http://macblips.dailyradar.com/video/first-apple-store-wedding-flash-mob-part-1/> Accessed July 5, 2010.

Daily Times (2009) "Indian Clerics Issue Fatwa on Ringtones," *Daily Times*, Saturday, April 18. <http://www.dailytimes.com.pk/default.asp?page=2009\04\18\story_18-4-2009_pg7_15>

Dal Fiore, Filippio (2007) "Communities versus Networks: The Implications on Innovation and Social Change," *American Behavioral Scientist* 50, no. 7: 857–66.

Dansky, Richard (2007) "Introduction to Game Narrative," in Bateman (2007), pp. 1–23.

Davenport, Glorianna (1998) "Very Distributed Media Stories: Presence, Time, Imagination," in David Pritchard and Jeff Reeve (eds) *Proceedings 4th International Euro-Par Conference on Parallel Processing*, New York: Springer-Verlag, pp. 47–54.

Dawson, Lorne (2005) "The Mediation of Religious Experience in Cyberspace," in Højsgaard and Warburg (2005), pp. 15–37.

Dawson, Lorne and Douglas Cowan (2004a) Introduction to Dawson and Cowan (2004b), pp. 1–15.

Dawson, Lorne and Douglas Cowan (eds) (2004b) *Religion Online: Finding Faith on the Internet*, London: Routledge.

DeLuca, Michele (2009) "A Gift for Savilla: Niagara Falls Native Receives Gift from a Near Stranger," *Niagara Gazette*, August 23. <http://niagara-gazette.com/features/x1896317391/A-GIFT-FOR-SAVILLA-Niagara-Falls-Native-receives-kidney-from-a-near-stranger> Accessed February 5, 2011.

DeMarle, Mary (2007) "Nonlinear Game Narrative," in Bateman (2007), pp. 71–84.

Dena, Christy (2009) "Transmedia Practice: Theorising the Practice of Expressing a Fictional World across Distinct Media and Environments," PhD thesis, School of Letters, Art and Media. Department of Media and Communications, Digital Cultures Program, University of Sydney, Australia.

Derrickson, Krystina (2008) "*Second Life* and The Sacred: Islamic Space in a Virtual World," in Vit Sisler (ed.) *Digital Islam*, online research project,supported by Charles University in Prague. <http://www.digitalislam.eu/article.do?articleId=1877> Accessed October 16, 2008.

Detweiler, Craig (2010) (ed.) *Halos and Avatars*, Louisville, KY: Westminster John Knox Press.

Dokoupil, Tony (2007) "Downloading Heaven," *Newsweek,* August 5, p. 58.

Dorsky, Nathaniel (2007) Excerpt from "Devotional Cinema," in Mitchell and Plate (2007), pp. 407–15.

Doty, William (1986) *Mythography: The Study of Myths and Rituals*, Tuscaloosa: University of Alabama Press.

Douglas, Christopher (2010) "Multiculturalism in *World of Warcraft*," *Electronic Book Review*, June 4. <http://www.electronicbookreview.com/thread/firstperson/intrinsically> Accessed October 14, 2010.

Douglas, Jeff (2004) "Game Resurrects Waco Tragedy and Challenges Video Game Conventions," *Wichita Eagle*, July 3. <http://wacoresurrection.com/media/ap/9071356.htm> Accessed February 22, 2008.

Douglas, J. Yellowlees and Andrew Hargadon (2004) "The Pleasures of Immersion and Interaction: Schemas, Scripts and the Fifth Business," in Wardrip-Fruin and Harrigan (2004), pp. 192–206.

douglaseye (2010) "Flash Mob Response to Westboro Baptist Church in West Virginia," *YouTube*, April 27. <http://www.youtube.com/watch?v=DogjbopNBVg> Accessed January 1, 2011.

Dozier, John and Sue Scheff (2009) *Google Bomb: The Untold Story of the $11.3M Verdict That Changed the Way We Use the Internet*, Deerfield, FL: Health Communications.

dreamuknet (2009) "Liverpool Flash Mob – Guerilla Worship," *YouTube*, April 6. <http://www.youtube.com/watch?v=7-ghnXBWP4E> Accessed November 13, 2010.

Driscoll, Mark (2010) "Jesus and Demons," Mars Hill Church sermon, February 14. <http://www.marshillchurch.org/media/2010/02/14/20100214_jesus-and-demons_english_transcript.pdf>

Durkheim, Emile (2001) *The Elementary Forms of Religious Life*, trans. Carol Cosman, New York: Oxford University Press.

Eagleton, Terry (1983) *Literary Theory: An Introduction,* Minneapolis: University of Minnesota Press.

Eck, Diana (2003) *Encountering God: A Spiritual Journey from Bozeman to Benares*, 2nd edn, Boston: Beacon Press.

Egenfeldt-Nielsen, Simon, Jonas Heide Smith and Susana Pajares Tosca (2008) *Understanding Video Games: The Essential Introduction*, New York: Routledge.

Eickelman, Dale and Jon Anderson (eds) (2003) *New Media in the Muslim World*, 2nd edn, Bloomington: Indiana University Press.

Einstein, Mara (2007) *Brands of Faith*, London: Routledge.

Eliade, Mircea (1954/2005) *The Myth of the Eternal Return: Cosmos and History*, Willard R. Trask, trans., Bollingen Series, Princeton, NJ: Princeton University Press.

——(1961) *The Sacred and the Profane: The Nature of Religion*, trans. Willard Trask, New York: Harper & Row.

Epstein, Jean (2007) Excerpt from "On Certain Characteristics of Photogénie," in Mitchell and Plate (2007), pp. 49–53.

Eskelinen, Markku (2004) "Towards Computer Game Studies," in Wardrip-Fruin and Harrigan (2004), pp. 36–44.

Evans, Ruth (2010) "Surviving in an Alien Environment: Human + Christ as Medieval Natural-Born Cyborg," *Quiet Babylon*, blog of Tim Maly. <http://quietbabylon.com/2010/surviving-in-an-alien-environment-human-christ-as-medieval-natural-born-cyborg/> Accessed March 13, 2011.

Eve, Eric (2007) "All Hope Abandon: Biblical Text and Interactive Fiction," *Digital Humanities Quarterly* 1, no. 2. <http://www.digitalhumanities.org/dhq/vol/001/2/000010.html>

Fantz, Ashley (2008) "Forgive Us, Father; We'd Rather Go Online," *CNN Living*, March 13. <http://articles.cnn.com/2008-03-3/living/online.confessions_1_web-site-confessions-priests?_s=PM:LIVING> Accessed July 1, 2011.

Filiciak, Miroslaw (2003) "Hyperidentities: Postmodern Identity Patterns in Massively Multiplayer Online Role-Playing Games," in Wolf and Perron (2003), pp. 87–102.

Fine, Gary Alan (2006) "Frames and Games," in Salen and Zimmerman (2006), pp. 578–601.

Fitzpatrick, Tony (2006) "Teenager Moves Video Icons Just by Imagination," Washington University in St Louis, University Communications press release, October 9. <http://news-info.wustl.edu/news/page/normal/7800.html> Accessed June 23, 2008.

Flanagan, Mary (2009) *Critical Play: Radical Game Design*, Cambridge, MA: MIT Press.

Flannery-Dailey, Frances (1999) "Non-linear Time in Apocalyptic Texts: The Spiral Model," *Society of Biblical Literature Seminar Papers* 38: 231–45.

Fonda, Marc (1994) "Postmodernity and the Imagination of the Apocalypse: A Study of Genre," *Religious Worlds: An Internet Portal for Information about Religions and Religious Studies.* <http://www.religiousworlds.com/fondarosa/dragon.html> Accessed September 10, 2010.

Foster, Derek (1996) "Community and Identity in the Electronic Village," in David Porter (ed.) *Internet Culture*, London: Routledge, pp. 23–37.

Foucault, Michel (1998) "What Is an Author?" in *Aesthetics, Method, and Epistemology*, ed. James D. Faubion, trans. Robert Hurley *et al.*, vol. 2 of *Essential Works of Foucault 1954–1984*, New York: New Press, pp. 205–22.

Fox News (2009) "Man Marries Virtual Girlfriend … With Public Reception," *Fox News*, November, 22. <http://www.foxnews.com/us/2009/11/22/man-marries-virtual-girlfriend-public-reception#ixzz1D8FPBJPE> Accessed February 5, 2011.

Frasca, Gonzalo (2003) "Simulation versus Narrative: Introduction to Ludology," in Wolf and Perron (2003), pp. 221–36.

Frei, Hans (1974) *The Eclipse of Biblical Narrative: A Study in Eighteenth Century and Nineteenth Century Hermeneutics*, New Haven, CT: Yale University Press.

Garlow, James L. and Peter Jones (2004) *Cracking Da Vinci's Code*, Colorado Springs, CO: Cook Communications Ministries.

Geertz, Clifford (1983) *Local Knowledge: Further Essays in Interpretive Anthropology*, New York: Basic Books.

Genesis Works (2010) *Heaven*. <http://www.heaventhegame.com/>

Girard, René (1977) *Violence and the Sacred*, trans. Patrick Gregory, Baltimore, MD: Johns Hopkins University Press.

<http://www.timesonline.co.uk/tol/comment/faith/article2036423.ece> Accessed March 20, 2008.

Gledhill, Ruth (2007a) "Sony Apologises over Cathedral Computer Game," *Times Online*, June 15.

——(2007b) "Manchester Cathedral Says Sony Apology Not Enough and Issues New Digital Rules," *Times Online*, July 6. <http://www.timesonline.co.uk/tol/comment/faith/article1940286.ece> Accessed March 23, 2008.

Gomez, Jeff (2009) "Jeff Gomez on Creating Transmedia Experiences," interview by Digital Media Wire, Nordic Game and Film Lounge, *YouTube*, July 11. <http://www.youtube.com/watch?v=YfH8WwClSx0&feature=related>

——(2010) "Jeff Gomez, 'Storyworlds: The New Transmedia Business Paradigm'," paper presented at the O'Reilly Tools for Change in Publishing Conference February

22–24, 2010, *YouTube*, February 25.<http://www.youtube.com/watch?v=81Ol6Tbjt5k& feature=related>

Gonzales, Vincent (2011) "Crowdsourced Catholicism: New iPhone App Lets Users Forgive Sins," *Religion Dispatches*, January 10.

Good News Blog (2005) "Text Mary Service Brings Prayer into Digital Age," *Good News Blog*, November 5. <http://www.goodnewsblog.com/2005/11/05/text-mary-service-brings-prayer-into-digital-age> Accessed May 1, 2011.

Google Bomb Project (2005) "Googlebomb Jerry Falwell," *The Google Bomb Project: Exposing the Hard Right through Google Bombing*. <http://googlebombproject. blogspot.com/2005/05/googlebomb-jerry-falwell.html> Accessed February 9, 2011.

Govender, Rogers (2007) "Full Text of Letter From Church to Sony Over 'Sick' Video," *Times Online*, June 11. <http://www.timesonline.co.uk/tol/comment/faith/article 1917035.ece> Accessed March 19, 2008.

GozoGozo (n.d.) *Running Jesus*, Internet-based game. <http://www.onlinegames.net/ games/689/running-jesus.html> Accessed October 15, 2008.

Grady, Rachel and Heidi Ewing (dir.) (2006) *Jesus Camp*, New York: Magnolia Pictures.

Grimes, Ronald (1996a) "Ritual Criticism and Infelicitous Performances," in Grimes (1996b), pp. 279–93.

——(ed.) (1996b) *Readings in Ritual Studies*, Upper Saddle River, NJ: Prentice Hall,

——(2006) *Rite Out of Place*, Oxford: Oxford University Press.

Grodal, Torben (2003) "Stories for Eye, Ear and Muscles: Video Games, Media, and Embodied Experiences," in Wolf and Perron (2003), pp. 129–55.

Gromala, Diane (2004) Response to "From Work to Play," by Stuart Molthroup, in Wardrip-Fruin and Harrigan (2004), pp. 56–60.

Handelman, Susan (1982) *The Slayers of Moses: The Emergence of Rabbinic Interpretation in Modern Literary Theory*, Albany, NY: SUNY Press.

Hanegraaff, Wouter J. (2003) "How Magic Survived the Disenchantment of the World," *Religion* 33: 357–80.

Hardin, Richard (1996) "'Ritual' in Recent Literary Criticism: The Elusive Sense of Community," in Grimes (1996b), pp. 308–23.

Helland, Christopher (2000) "Religion Online/Online Religion and Virtual Communitas," in Douglas E. Cowan and Jeffery K. Hadden (eds) *Religion on the Internet: Research Prospects and Promises*, Religion and Social Order 8, London: JAI Press; Elsevier Science, pp. 205–24.

Hellholm, David (1986) "The Problem of Apocalyptic Genre," *Semeia* 36: 13–64.

Hill, Peter (2001) "Superfictions: The Creation of Fictional Situations in International Contemporary Art Practice," PhD thesis, RMIT University.

Hillis, Ken (2009) *Online a Lot of the Time: Ritual, Fetish, Sign*, Durham, NC: Duke University Press.

Hiltz, Starr Roxanne (1985) *Online Communities: A Case Study of the Office of the Future*, Norwood, NJ: Ablex Publishing Corp.

Hobson, Theo (2006) "Towards a Flash Mob Eucharist," *Guardian*, May 8. <http://www.guardian.co.uk/commentisfree/2006/may/08/theliberationofritual> Accessed July 23, 2010.

Hodgson, David and David Knight (2007) *Assassin's Creed: Prima Official Game Guide*, Roseville, CA: Prima Games.

Højsgaard, Morton and Margit Warburg (eds) (2005) *Religion and Cyberspace*, London: Routledge.

Hoover, Stewart (2001) "Religion, Media, and the Cultural Center of Gravity," in Daniel A. Stout and Judith M. Buddenbaum (eds) *Religion and Popular Culture: Studies in the Interaction of Worldviews*, Ames: Iowa State University Press, pp. 49–60.

——(2006) *Religion in the Media Age*, London: Routledge.

Hu, Alena (2010) "First Slash: Jesus/Judas," *LiveJournal*, January 31. <http://alena-hu. livejournal.com/162109.html#cutid1> Accessed October 14, 2010.

Huizinga, Johan (1955) *Homo Ludens: A Study of the Play Element in Culture*, Boston: Beacon Press.

Irenaeus (1885) *Against Heresies*, trans. Alexander Roberts and William Rambaut, *Ante-Nicene Fathers*, vol. 1, ed. Alexander Roberts, James Donaldson, and A. Cleveland Coxe, Buffalo, NY: Christian Literature Publishing Co. Available (Kevin Knight rev. and ed.) from the New Advent website. <http://www.newadvent.org/fathers/0103. htm>.

Jacobs, Stephen (2007) "Virtually Sacred: The Performance of Asynchronous Cyber-rituals in Online Spaces," *Journal of Computer-Mediated Communication* 12, no. 3: article 17. <http://jcmc.indiana.edu/vol12/issue3/jacobs.html> Accessed January 15, 2008.

Jenkins, Henry (2004a) Response to "The Pleasures of Immersion and Interaction: Schemas, Scripts and the Fifth Business," by J. Yellowlee Douglas and Andrew Hargadon, in Wardrip-Fruin and Harrigan (2004), pp. 197–98.

——(2004b) "Game Design as Narrative Architecture," in Wardrip-Fruin and Harrigan (2004), pp. 118–30.

——(2006a) *Convergence Culture: Where Old and New Media Collide*, New York University Press.

——(2006b) *"Star Trek*: Reread, Rerun, Rewritten: Fan Writing as Textual Poaching," in his *Fans, Bloggers, and Gamers: Exploring Participatory Culture*, New York: New York University Press, pp. 37–60.

——(2009) "Transmedia Missionaries," *YouTube*, July 23. <http://www.youtube.com/ watch?v=bhGBfuyN5gg&NR=1> Accessed October 4, 2010.

Jennings, Theodore (1996) "On Ritual Knowledge," in Grimes (1996b), pp. 324–34.

Juul, Jesper (2004) "Introduction to Game Time," in Wardrip-Fruin and Harrigan (2004), pp. 131–42.

——(2005) *Half Real: Video Games Between Real Rules and Fictional Worlds*, Cambridge, MA: MIT Press.

——(2006) "As Questions Go, This Is Not a Bad One: Do Games Tell Stories?" in Salen and Zimmerman (2006), pp. 33–36.

Kadushin, Max (1952/1972) *The Rabbinic Mind*, New York: Bloch.

Kearney, Richard (2002) *On Stories*, London: Routledge.

Kent, Jonathan (2003) "Malaysia Reviews Texting Divorce," *BBC News*, Asia Pacific News, July 31. <http://news.bbc.co.uk/2/hi/asia-pacific/3112151.stm> Accessed March 1, 2010.

Kiesler, S., J. Siegel and T. McGuire (1984) "Social Psychological Aspects of Computer-Mediated Communication," *American Psychologist* 39, no. 10: 1123–34.

Koo, Gene and Scott Seider (2010) "Video Games for Prosocial Learning," in Schrier and Gibson (2010b), pp. 16–34.

Kotaku (2009) "Eyes on with Invizimals: When Pokemon Meets Ghostbusters," *Kotaku*, 4 June. <http://kotaku.com/5279078/eyes-on-with-invizimals-when-pokemon-meets-ghostbusters> Accessed October 3, 2010.

Kuma Games (n.d.-a) *Attack on Iran Forum*, Kuma Games. <http://www.kumawar.com/ubbthreads/printthread.php?Cat=&Board=Iran_nuclear&main=14803&type=thread>

——(n.d.-b) *Kuma\War: Real War News, Real War Games*, Kuma Games. <kumawar.com> Accessed July 6, 2011.

Lahti, Martti (2003) "As We Become Machines: Corporealized Pleasures in Video Games," in Wolf and Perron (2003), pp. 157–70.

Lall, Ramshee Roshan (2009) "Video War Games Satiate My Feelings of Aggression," interview with the Karmapa Lama, Trinley Dorje, *Times of India*, September 20. <http://timesofindia.indiatimes.com/home/sunday-toi/all-that-matters/Video-war-games-satiate-my-feelings-of-aggression/articleshow/5032672.cms#ixzz12KrZTKA5>

Landy, Joshua and Michael Saler (eds) (2009) *The Re-enchantment of the World: Secular Magic in a Rational Age*, Palo Alto, CA: Stanford University Press.

Laurel, Brenda (1993) *Computers as Theater*, Reading, MA: Addison-Wesley.

——(2004) Response to "Interactive Fiction as 'Story,' 'Game,' 'Storygame,' 'Novel,' 'World,' 'Literature,' 'Puzzle,' 'Problem,' 'Riddle,' and 'Machine'," by Nick Montfore, in Wardrip-Fruin and Harrigan (2004), pp. 310–15.

Leavitt, Alex (2010) "Fan Edits: Improving the Original (Without Changing the Original?)," *Futures of Entertainment*, Comparative Media Studies, MIT, May 14. <http://www.convergenceculture.org/weblog/2010/05/fan_edits_improving_the_origin.php>

LeBlanc, Marc (2006) "Tools for Creating Dramatic Game Dynamics," in Salen and Zimmerman (2006), pp. 438–59.

LeDonne, Danny (dir.) (2008) *Playing Columbine*, self-produced documentary.

Lévi-Strauss, Claude (1966) *The Savage Mind*, trans. John Weightman and Doreen Weightman, Nature of Human Society, Chicago: University of Chicago Press.

Lévy, Pierre (1997) *Collective Intelligence: Mankind's Emerging World in Cyberspace*. Cambridge, MA: Perseus Books.

——(2001) "Collective Intelligence: A Civilisation," *eJournal of Art and Technology* 1, no. 1. <http://crossings.tcd.ie/issues/1.1/Levy/> Accessed March 14, 2011.

Liebhold, Mike (2010) "Digital Immersion: Augmenting Places with Stories and Information," *Nieman Reports*, Summer. <http://www.nieman.harvard.edu/reportsitem.aspx?id=102426> Accessed October 3, 2010.

Lövheim, Mia and Alf G. Linderman (2005) "Constructing Religious Identity on the Internet," in Højsgaard and Warburg (2005), pp. 121–37.

Lyden, John (2003) *Film as Religion: Myths, Morals and Rituals,* New York: New York University Press.

Lynch, Gordon (2007) "What Is This 'Religion' in the Study of Religion and Popular Culture?" in Gordon Lynch (ed.) *Between Sacred and Profane: Researching Religion and Popular Culture*, New York: I. B. Tauris, pp. 125–42.

Malkin, Bonnie (2007) "Church approves spire phone masts" *The Telegraph*, August 25. <http://www.telegraph.co.uk/news/1561285/Church-approves-spire-phone-masts.html> Accessed September 21, 2011.

Mark, L. (2008) "'Dangerous Cult,' Google Bombing and Scientology," *AssociatedContent*, Yahoo! Contributor Network, January 29. <http://www.associatedcontent.com/article/571371/dangerous_cult_google_bombing_and_scientology.html> Accessed May 4, 2011.

Martin, Adam, Brooke Thompson, Tom Chatfield *et al.* (2006) *2006 Alternate Reality Games White Paper*, Mt Royal, NJ: International Game Developers Association.

<http://archives.igda.org/arg/resources/IGDA-AlternateRealityGames-Whitepaper-2006.pdf> Accessed March 13, 2011.

Marwick, Alice and Danah Boyd (2010) "I Tweet Honestly, I Tweet Passionately: Twitter Users, Context Collapse, and the Imagined Audience," *New Media & Society*, July 7.

Mateas, Michael (2004) "A Preliminary Poetics for Interactive Drama and Games," in Wardrip-Fruin and Harrigan (2004), pp. 19–33.

Mateas, Michael and Andrew Stern (2006) "Interaction and Narrative," in Salen and Zimmerman (2006), pp. 642–69.

McDowell, Josh (1999) *The New Evidence That Demands a Verdict*, Nashville, TN: Thomas Nelson Publishers.

McGonigal, Jane (2003) "A Real Little Game: The Pinocchio Effect in Pervasive Play," Level Up Conference Proceedings, University of Utrecht, November 2003. Available at Digital Games Research Association (DiGRA) website. <http://www.digra.org/dl/order_by_author?publication=Level%20Up%20Conference%20Proceedings>

——(2006) "This Might Be a Game: Ubiquitous Play and Performance at the Turn of the Twenty-First Century," PhD thesis, Performance Studies and the Designated Emphasis in Film Studies in the Graduate Division, University of California, Berkeley.

——(2011) *Reality Is Broken*, London: Penguin Press.

MacKinnon, Ian (2005) "Kosher Phone Taps into New Market for Mobiles," *Times* (London), March 3. <http://www.timesonline.co.uk/tol/news/world/middle_east/article417509.ece> Accessed July 14, 2011.

McMahan, Alison (2003) "Immersion, Engagement and Presence: A Method for Analyzing 3D Video Games," in Wolf and Perron (2003), pp. 67–86.

Metz, Christian (1974) *Film Language: A Semiotics of the Cinema*, New York: Oxford University Press.

Miles, Margaret (1996) *Seeing and Believing: Religion and Values in the Movies*. Boston: Beacon Press.

Mims, Christopher (2010) "Chatbot Wears Down Proponents of Anti-science Nonsense," in "Mims's Bits," *Technology Review* (MIT), November 2. <http://www.technologyreview.com/blog/mimssbits/25964/> November 22, 2010.

Mirror (2005) "Vatican Pulls Plug on Sony Ad 'Blasphemy'," *Mirror*, October 1. <http://www.mirror.co.uk/news/top-stories/2005/10/01/vatican-pulls-plug-on-sony-ad-blasphemy-115875-16196475/> Accessed September 29, 2008.

Mitchell, Jolyon (2007) "In Search of Online Religion," *Studies in World Christianity* 13, no. 3: 205–7.

Mitchell, Jolyon and Sophia Marriage (2003) *Mediating Religion: Conversations in Media, Religion, and Culture*, London: T&T Clark.

Mitchell, Jolyon and S. Brent Plate (eds) (2007) *The Religion and Film Reader*, London: Routledge.

Montfort, Nick (2004) "Interactive Fiction as 'Story,' 'Game,' 'Storygame,' 'Novel;' 'World,' 'Literature,' 'Puzzle,' 'Problem,' 'Riddle,' and 'Machine'," in Wardrip-Fruin and Harrigan (2004), pp. 310–17.

Montola, Markus, Jaako Stenros and Annika Waern (eds) (2009) *Pervasive Games: Theory and Design*, San Francisco: Elsevier Science & Technology.

Morgan, David (2005) *The Sacred Gaze: Religious Visual Culture in Theory and Practice*, Berkeley: University of California Press.

——(2007) "Studying Religion and Popular Culture: Prospects, Presuppositions, Procedures," in Gordon Lynch (ed.) *Between Sacred and Profane: Researching Religion and Popular Culture*, New York: I. B. Tauris, pp. 21–33.

Morgan, Justin and Celestianpower (2006) "The Bible Retold: The Bread and the Fishes," interactive game, *Interactive Fiction Database*. <http://ifdb.tads.org/viewgame?id=u2faar89zkgv7961>

Mortensen, Torill (2003) "The Geography of a Non-place," *dichtung-digital* 4. <http://www.brown.edu/Research/dichtung-digital/2003/issue/4/mortensen/index.htm>

Mother Theresa (2007) *Come Be My Light: The Private Writings of the Saint of Calcutta*, ed. Brian Kolodiejchuck, New York: Doubleday.

Moulthrop, Stuart (2004) "From Work to Play: Molecular Culture in the Time of Deadly Games," in Wardrip-Fruin and Harrigan (2004), pp. 56–69.

Moulton, Ryan and Kendra Carattini (2007) "A Quick Word about Googlebombs," Google Webmaster Central Blog, January 25. <http://googlewebmastercentral.blogspot.com/2007/01/quick-word-about-googlebombs.html> Accessed July 24, 2011.

Murray, Janet (1997) *Hamlet on the Holodeck: The Future of Narrative in Cyberspace*, New York: Free Press.

——(2004) "From Game Story to Cyberdrama," in Wardrip-Fruin and Harrigan (2004), pp. 2–11.

Neal, Connie (2001) *What's a Christian to Do with Harry Potter?*, Colorado Springs, CO: Waterbrook Press.

Nefesh B'Nefesh (2009) "Hanukkah Flash Mob in Israel," video, *My Jewish Learning*, November 24. <http://www.myjewishlearning.com/blog/holidays/hanukkah-flash-mob-in-israel/> Accessed July 5, 2010.

Netland, Harold and Keith Johnson (2000) "Why Is Religious Pluralism Fun – And Dangerous?" in D. A. Carson (ed.) *Telling the Truth: Evangelizing Postmoderns*, Grand Rapids, MI: Zondervan Publishing House, pp. 47–67.

Newman, James (2002) "The Myth of the Ergodic Video Game," *Game Studies* 2, no. 1. <http://www.gamestudies.org/0102/newman/>

——(2004) *Videogames*, London: Routledge.

News Tribune (2003) "Hezbollah Computer Game Takes Propaganda War on Israel to Virtual Battlefield," *News Tribune*, May 25. <http://www.newstribune.com/articles/2003/05/25/export16774.txt> Accessed June 23, 2008.

Ng, Keane (2009) "Russian Priest Pitches Idea for a Religious MMOG," *Escapist*, September 1. <http://www.escapistmagazine.com/news/view/94368-Russian-Priest-Pitches-Idea-for-a-Religious-MMOG> Accessed July 20, 2010.

Nhât Hanh, Thich (2004) *Freedom Wherever We Go: A Buddhist Monastic Code for the 21st Century*, Berkeley: Parallax Press.

Nicholson, Judith (2005) "Flash Mobs in the Age of Mobile Connectivity," *Fibreculture Journal* 6. <http://journal.fibreculture.org/issue6/issue6_nicholson.html>

Nieuwdorp, Eva (2005) "The Pervasive Interface: Tracing the Magic Circle," online proceedings of Changing Views: Worlds in Play, Vancouver, WA, University of Vancouver, June. Available at Digital Games Research Association (DiGRA) website. <http://www.digra.org/dl/db/06278.53356.pdf>

Noble, David (1999) *The Religion of Technology*, London: Penguin Press.

Nogueira, Paulo Augusto de Souza (2002) "Celestial Worship and Ecstatic-Visionary Experience," *Journal for the Study of the New Testament* 25, no. 2.

Ocampo, Jason (2006) "*Left Behind: Eternal Forces* First Impressions: Putting Religion into Real-Time Strategy," *Gamespot,* April 7. <http://www.gamespot.com/pc/strategy/leftbehindeternalforces/news.html?sid=6147323> Access March 22, 2008.

Oldenberg, Ray (1999) *The Great Good Place,* New York: De Capo Press.

O'Leary, Stephen (2005) "Utopian and Dystopian Possibilities," in Højsgaard and Warburg (2005), pp. 38–49.

Olson, Carl E. and Sandra Miesel (2004) *The Da Vinci Hoax,* San Francisco: Ignatius Press.

Osu, Chris (2007) "Sony Says 'Sorry'," *Manchester Evening News,* July 6. <http://www.manchestereveningnews.co.uk/news/s/1010/1010666_sony_says_sorry_.html> Accessed March 23, 2008.

Palfrey, John and Urs Gasser (2008) *Born Digital: Understanding the First Generation of Digital Natives,* New York: Basic Books.

Pals, Daniel (2006) *Eight Theories of Religion,* New York: Oxford University Press.

Paradiso, Joseph and James Landay (2009) "Cross-Reality Environments," *Pervasive Computing* 8, no. 3: 14–15.

Pearce, Celia (2004) "Towards a Game Theory of Game," in Wardrip-Fruin and Harrigan (2004), pp. 143–64.

——(2007) "Communities of Play: The Social Construction of Identity in Persistent Online Game Worlds," in Pat Harrigan and Noah Wardrip-Fruin (eds) *Second Person: Role Playing and Story in Games and Playable Media,* Cambridge, MA: MIT Press, pp. 311–18.

——(2009) *Communities of Play: Emergent Cultures in Multiplayer Games and Virtual Worlds,* Cambridge: MIT Press.

Penner, Myron B. (ed.) (2005) *Christianity and the Postmodern Turn,* Grand Rapids, MI: Brazos Press.

Penny, Simon (2004) "Representation, Enaction, and the Ethics of Simulation," in Wardrip-Fruin and Harrigan (2004), pp. 73–84.

Perlin, Ken (2004) "Can There Be a Form between a Game and a Story?" in Wardrip-Fruin and Harrigan (2004), pp. 12–18.

Perron, Bernard (2003) "From Gamers to Players and Gameplayers: The Example of Interactive Movies," in Wolf and Perron (2003), pp. 237–58.

Petre, Jonathan (2007) "Threat to Church Phone Masts 'That Relay Porn'," *Telegraph,* March 12. <http://www.telegraph.co.uk/news/uknews/1545215/Threat-to-church-phone-masts-that-relay-porn.html> Accessed July 14, 2011.

Phillips, Max (2009) "Missionaries of the Digital Age," *Escapist,* June 9. <http://www.escapistmagazine.com/articles/view/issues/issue_205/6149-Missionaries-of-the-Digital-Age.2> Accessed July 20, 2010.

Pierre-Louis, Errol (2010) "Microsoft Shows Off 'Milo' Virtual Human," *PC Mag,* July 14. <http://www.pcmag.com/article2/0,2817,2366470,00.asp> Accessed February 5, 2011.

Pinchbeck, Dan (n.d.) "Ludic Reality: A Construct for Analysing Meaning-Mapping and Epistemology in Play," *thechineseroom,* game studio. <http://www.thechineseroom.co.uk/PinchbeckPCG07.pdf> Accessed July 1, 2011.

Piselli, Fortunata (2007) "Communities, Places, and Social Networks," *American Behavioral Scientist* 50: 867–78.

Plate, S. Brent (2007) "The Footprints of Film: After Images of Religion in American Space and Time," in Mitchell and Plate (2007), pp. 427–37.

——(2008) *Cinema and the Re-creation of the World,* London: Wallflower Press.

Poremba, Cindy (2007) "Critical Potential on the Brink of the Magic Circle," online proceedings of Situated Play, University of Tokyo, September, pp. 772–78. Available at Digital Games Research Association (DiGRA) website. <http://www.digra.org/dl/db/07311.42117.pdf> Accessed October 30, 2009.

Preece, J., and Maloney-Krichmar, D. (2005) "Online communities: Design, Theory, and Practice," *Journal of Computer-Mediated Communication* 10, no. 4: article 1. <http://jcmc.indiana.edu/vol10/issue4/preece.html>

Rachman, Tom (2003) "Vatican Official Praises 'Passion' Clips," *Worldwide Religious News*, September 13. <http://wwrn.org/articles/15181/?&place=vatican&section=general> Accessed 29 June 2011.

Radhakrishnan, S. (1939) *Eastern Religions and Western Thought*, London: Oxford University Press.

Rafael, Vincente (2003) "The Cell Phone and the Crowd: Messianic Politics in the Contemporary Philippines," *Public Culture* 15, no. 3: 399–425.

Rafferty, Sinead (2008) "What Is an ARG?" *YouTube*, October 8. <http://www.youtube.com/watch?v=V2b3Yx3B0OI&feature=related>

Rappaport, Roy (1996) "The Obvious Aspects of Ritual," in Grimes (1996b), pp. 427–40.

Raschke, Carl (2004) *The Next Reformation: Why Evangelicals Must Embrace Postmodernity*, Cedar Rapids, MI: Baker Academic.

Rehak, Bob (2003) "Playing at Being: Psychoanalysis and the Avatar," in Wolf and Perron (2003), pp. 103–28.

Reid, Elizabeth (1995) "Virtual Worlds: Culture and Imagination," in Steven G. Jones (ed.) *CyberSociety: Computer-Mediated Communication and Community*, Thousand Oaks, CA: Sage, pp. 164–83.

——(1996) "Text-based Virtual Realities: Identity and the Cyborg Body," in Peter Ludlow (ed.) *High Noon on the Electronic Frontier: Conceptual Issues in Cyberspace*, Cambridge, MA: MIT Press, pp. 327–46.

Ren, Yuqing, Robert Kraut and Sara Kiesler (2008) "Applying Common Identity and Bond Theory to Design of Online Communities," *Organization Studies* 28, no. 3: 377–408.

Reuters (2008) "Bezeq Launches Porn-Free 'Kosher Phone', Service," Reuters website, February 3. <http://www.reuters.com/article/2008/02/03/us-bezeq-idUSL0373275320080203> Accessed July 14, 2011.

Rheingold, Howard (1993) *The Virtual Community*, New York: Harper Perennial.

——(1996) "A Slice of My Life in My Virtual Community," in Peter Ludlow (ed.) *High Noon on the Electronic Frontier: Conceptual Issues in Cyberspace*, Cambridge, MA: MIT Press, pp. 413–36.

——(2002) *Smart Mobs: The Next Social Revolution*, New York: Basic Books.

——(2008) "A Smart Mob Is Not Necessarily a Wise Mob," text of the OhmyNews 2008 Forum Keynote by Howard Rheingold, *OhmyNews,* June 30. <http://english.ohmynews.com/articleview/article_view.asp?at_code=434721&no=382983&rel_no=1> Accessed March 13, 2011.

Roma Victor (n.d.) *Roma Victor* website. <http://www.roma-victor.com> Accessed October 10, 2008.

Roof, Wade Clark (1999) *Spiritual Marketplace: Baby Boomers and the Remaking of American Religion*, Princeton, NJ: Princeton University Press.

Rushkoff, Douglas (2010) "Why Johnny Can't Program: A New Medium Requires A New Literacy," *Huffington Post*, October 3. <http://www.huffingtonpost.com/douglas-rushkoff/programming-literacy_b_745126.html> Accessed October 3, 2010.

Russell, D. S. (1964) *The Method and Message of Jewish Apocalyptic*, Philadelphia, PA: Westminster John Knox Press.

Ryan, Marie-Laure (2006) *Avatars of Story*, Electronic Mediations 17, Minneapolis: University of Minnesota Press.

Rymaszewski, Michael, Wagner James Au, Mark Wallace, Catherine Winters, Cory Ondreika and Benjamin Batstone-Cunningham (2006) *Second Life: The Official Guide*, Indianapolis: Sybex. <http://www.sybex.com/WileyCDA/SybexTitle/Second-Life-The-Official-Guide.productCd-047009608X,navId-290543.html>

Sack, Warren (2004) "What Does a Very Large-Scale Conversation Look Like?" in Wardrip-Fruin and Harrigan (2004), pp. 238–48.

Salen, Katie and Eric Zimmerman (2004) *Rules of Play: Game Design Fundamentals*, Cambridge, MA: MIT Press.

Salen, Katie and Eric Zimmerman (eds) (2006) *The Game Design Reader: A Rules of Play Anthology*, Cambridge, MA: MIT Press.

Sanes, Ken (n.d.) "Virtual Realities: Then and Now," in *The Age of Simulation: Phony Transcendence in an Age of Media, Computers and Fabricated Environments*, Transparency website. <http://www.transparencynow.com/lascaux.htm> Accessed October 23, 2010.

Schechner, Richard (2002) *Performance Studies: An Introduction*, New York: Routledge.

——(2004) Response to "The Pleasures of Immersion and Interaction: Schemas, Scripts and the Fifth Business," by J. Yellowlees Douglas and Andrew Hargadon, in Wardrip-Fruin and Harrigan (2004), pp. 192–96.

Schechter, Anna (2007) "DoD Stops Plan to Send Christian Video Game to Troops in Iraq," *ABC News: The Blotter*, August 15. <http://blogs.abcnews.com/theblotter/2007/08/dod-stops-plan-.html> Accessed March 22, 2008.

Schrader, Paul (2007) Excerpt from "Transcendental Style on Film," in Mitchell and Plate (2007), pp. 176–82.

Schrier, Karen and David Gibson (2010a) Introduction to Schrier and Gibson (2010b).

Schrier, Karen and David Gibson (eds) (2010b) *Ethics and Game Design: Teaching Values through Play*, Hershey, PA: Information Science Reference.

Schultze, Quentin J. (2002) *Habits of the High-Tech Heart: Living Virtuously in the Information Age*, Grand Rapids, MI: Baker Books.

Seaman, Bill (2004) "Interactive Text and Recombinant Poetics: Media-Element Field Explorations," in Wardrip-Fruin and Harrigan (2004), pp. 227–35.

Ship of Fools (2003) *The Ark*, Ship of Fools website. <http://ark.saintsimeon.co.uk/> Accessed October 12, 2006.

Simkins, David (2010) "Playing With Ethics: Experiencing New Ways of Being in RPGs," in Schrier and Gibson (2010b), pp. 69–84.

Smith, Jonathan Z. (1987) *To Take Place: Toward Theory in Ritual*, Chicago: University of Chicago Press.

——(1996) "The Bare Facts of Ritual," in Grimes (1996b), pp. 473–94.

——(2005) Introduction to *The Myth of the Eternal Return: Cosmos and History*, by Mircea Eliade, trans. Willard R. Trask, Bollingen Series, Princeton, NJ: Princeton University Press.

Smith, Wilfred Cantwell (1991) *The Meaning and End of Religion*, Minneapolis: Fortress Press.

Sniderman, Stephen (2006) "Unwritten Rules," in Salen and Zimmerman (2006), pp. 476–503.

Spiegel Online (2006) "The Wailing Wall 2.0 – E-mailing the Almighty," *Spiegel Online International*, October 5. <http://www.spiegel.de/international/spiegel/0,1518,441010,00.html> Accessed July 14, 2011.

Squire, Kurt and Henry Jenkins (n.d.) *The Art of Contested Spaces*, MIT website. <http://web.mit.edu/cms/People/henry3/contestedspaces.html>

Staal, Frits (1996) "The Meaninglessness of Ritual," in Grimes (1996b), pp. 483–94.

Starlight Runner Entertainment (2009) "What Is Transmedia?" *YouTube*, May 3. <http://www.youtube.com/watch?v=zyjg6-7LJPg>

Steinkuehler, Constance and Dmitri Williams (2006) "Where Everybody Knows Your (Screen) Name: Online Games as 'Third Places'," *Journal of Computer-Mediated Communication* 11, no. 4: article 1. <http://jcmc.indiana.edu/vol11/issue4/steinkuehler.html> Accessed March 1, 2011.

Stern, Eddo, Peter Brinson, Brody Condon, Michael Wilson, Mark Allen and Jessica Hutchins (n.d.) *Waco Resurrection* website. <http://wacoresurrection.com> Accessed May 23, 2009.

Stone, Michael (1984) *Jewish Writings of the Second Temple Period*, Assen, Netherlands: Van Gorcum; Philadelphia, PA: Fortress Press.

——(2006) "Pseudepigraphy Reconsidered," *Review of Rabbinic Judaism* 9: 1–15.

Suits, Bernard (1990) *The Grasshopper: Games, Life and Utopia,* Toronto: University of Toronto Press.

Sulic, Ivan (2004) "Katamari Damacy: Happiness in a Box," review, *IGN Entertainment Games*, September 16. <http://ps2.ign.com/articles/548/548201p1.html> Accessed October 23, 2010.

Szulborski, Dave (2005) *This Is Not A Game: A Guide to Alternate Reality Gaming*, New York: New Fiction Publishing.

Tait, Robert (2009) "Find God, Win a Trip to Mecca (or Jerusalem, or Tibet)," *Guardian*, July 2. <http://www.guardian.co.uk/world/2009/jul/02/turkey-penitents-compete-gameshow> Accessed October 26, 2010.

Tambiah, Stanley J. (1981) *A Performative Approach to Ritual*, Radcliffe-Brown Lecture in Social Anthropology 1979, London: British Academy.

——(1990) *Magic, Science, Religion, and the Scope of Rationality*, Cambridge: Cambridge University Press.

——(1996) "A Performative Approach to Ritual," in Grimes (1996b), pp. 495–510.

Taylor, T. L. (2006) *Play between Worlds: Exploring Online Game Culture*, Cambridge, MA: MIT Press.

Tedeschi, Bob (2010) "Seeing the World around You through Your Phone," *New York Times*, July 28. <http://www.nytimes.com/2010/07/29/technology/personaltech/29smart.html>

Telegraph (2011) "Catholics 'Cannot Confess via iPhone'," *Telegraph,* February 9. <http://www.telegraph.co.uk/news/newstopics/religion/8313894/Catholics-cannot-confess-via-iPhone.html> Accessed February 10, 2011.

Totilo, Stephen (2005) "Wanna Part the Red Sea on a PlayStation? Behold 'The Bible Game'," *MTV.com*, May 11. <http://www.mtv.com/news/articles/1501675/gamers-behold-bible-game.jhtml> Accessed March 6, 2011.

Turkle, Sherry (1997) *Life on the Screen: Identity in the Age of the Internet*, New York: Simon & Schuster.

——(2011) *Alone Together*, New York: Basic Books.

Turner, Victor (1969) *The Ritual Process: Structure and Anti-Structure*, Chicago: Aldine Publishing Co.

TurnToIslam (n.d.) "Tajahud," discussion board, *TurnToIslam* website. <http://www.turntoislam.com/forum/archive/index.php/t-12093.html> Accessed January 9, 2010.

Universal Studios (n.d.) *The Wizarding World of Harry Potter*, theme park, Universal Studios website. <http://www.universalorlando.com/harrypotter>

US DOD (United States Department of Defense) (2008) "Virtual Dialogue Application for Families of Deployed Service Members," solicitation, *Opportunities*, November 12. <http://www.dodtechmatch.com/DOD/Opportunities/SBIRView.aspx?id=OSD09-H03> Accessed February 5, 2011.

USC (University of South Carolina) (n.d.) *Sunna and Hadith*, Hadith online database, Center for Muslim–Jewish Engagement, USC. <http://www.usc.edu/schools/college/crcc/engagement/resources/texts/muslim/hadith/> Accessed May 29, 2011.

Utterback, Camille (2004) "Unusual Positions: Embodied Interaction with Symbolic Spaces," in Wardrip-Fruin and Harrigan (2004), pp. 218–26.

van Gennep, Arnold (1996) "Territorial Passage and the Classification of Rites," in Grimes (1996b), pp. 529–35.

Vanhoozer, Kevin J. (ed.) (2003) *The Cambridge Companion to Postmodern Theology*, Cambridge: Cambridge University Press.

Vargas, Jose Antonio (2006) "Shock, Anger Over Columbine Video Game: Designer Says Web Creation an 'Indictment' of Society," *Washington Post*, Saturday, May 20. <http://www.washingtonpost.com/wp-dyn/content/article/2006/05/19/AR2006051901979.html>

Various Commentators (n.d.) "Comments by Those Who Have Seen 'The Passion of Christ'," *The Premier International Fan Website: Mel Gibson's* The Passion of the Christ. <http://www.passion-movie.com/promote/comments.html> Accessed July 14, 2011.

Vaughan, Kevin and Brian Crecente (2006) "Video Game Reopens Columbine Wounds," *Rocky Mountain News*, May 16; repr. at "The Noise Boston," *thenoiseboard.com*, May 16, 2006. <http://www.thenoiseboard.com/lofiversion/index.php?t130297.html> Accessed March 10, 2011.

Veith, Gene Edward (1994) *Postmodern Times: A Christian Guide to Contemporary Thought and Culture*, Wheaton, IL: Crossway Books.

Vesna, Victoria (2004) "Community of People with No Time: Collaboration Shifts," in Wardrip-Fruin and Harrigan (2004), pp. 249–61.

Wagner, Rachel (2009) "Xbox Apocalypse: Video Games and Revelatory Literature," *SBL Forum* 7, no. 9. <http://www.sbl-site.org/publications/article.aspx?articleId=848>

——(2011) "Our Lady of Persistent Liminality," in Eric Michael Mazur and Kate McCarthy (eds) *God in the Details: American Religion in Popular Culture*, 2nd edn, London: Routledge, pp. 271–90.

Wagner, Rachel, Tyler DeHaven and Chris Hendrickson (2011) "Apocalypse Halo," in Luke Cuddy (ed.) *Halo and Philosophy*, Chicago, IL: Open Court, pp. 101–24.

Walker, Jill (2004) "Distributed Narrative: Telling Stories Across Networks," in Mia Consalvo and Kate O'Riordan (eds) *Internet Research Annual*, vol. 3, New York: Peter Lang, pp. 91–103.

Wardrip-Fruin, Noah and Pat Harrigan (eds) (2004) *First Person: New Media as Story, Performance, and Game*, Cambridge, MA: MIT Press.

Wardrip-Fruin, Noah and Nick Montfort (eds) (2003) *The New Media Reader*, Cambridge, MA: MIT Press.

Webdale, Jonathan. (2010) "Defining the Future: C21 Media on Jeff Gomez's MipTV Appearance," *Starlight Runner Entertainment* website, April 10. <http://www.starlightrunner.com/news/c21-media-on-jeff-gomezs-miptv-appearance> Accessed March 17, 2011.

Weber, Aimee (2007) "Belgian Police Patrols *Second Life* to Prevent Rape," *Second Life Insider*, April 21. <http://www.secondlifeinsider.com/2007/04/21/belgian-police-patrols-second-life-to-prevent-rape/> Accessed June 23, 2008.

Wellman, Barry and Milena Gulia (1997) "Net Surfers Don't Ride Alone: Virtual Communities as Communities," in Peter Kollock and Marc Smith (eds) *Communities and Cyberspace*, London: Routledge.

Wertheim, Margaret (1999) *The Pearly Gates of Cyberspace: A History of Space from Dante to the Internet*, New York: W. W. Norton & Co.

Whittaker, Tony (2010a) "Internet Evangelism Idea # 4: Facebook as an Opportunity to Share Faith," *Christian Web Trends*, April 7. <http://blog.ourchurch.com/2010/04/07/internet-evangelism-idea-4-facebook-as-an-opportunity-to-share-faith/> Accessed August 8, 2010.

——(2010b) "What Is Augmented Reality?" *Digital Evangelism Issues*, June 28. <http://www.internetevangelismday.com/blog/archives/2054> Accessed February 17, 2011.

whytraveltofrance.com (n.d.) "Cluny, France, and the Abbey's Augmented Reality," *Why Travel to France*. <http://www.whytraveltofrance.com/2009/10/26/cluny-france-the-abbeys-augmented-reality/> Accessed March 13, 2011.

Wink Back, Inc. (n.d.) Introduction to *The Go Game*, Wink Back, Inc. <http://thegogame.com/brownie/game/description/intro.asp>

Wolf, Mark J. P. (2001a) "Narrative in the Video Game," in Mark J. P. Wolf (ed.) *The Medium of the Video Game*, Austin: University of Texas Press, pp. 93–111.

——(2001b) "The Video Game as a Medium," in Mark J. P. Wolf (ed.) *The Medium of the Video Game*, Austin: University of Texas Press, pp. 13–33.

Wolf, Mark and Bernard Perron (eds) (2003) *The Video Game Theory Reader*, New York: Routledge.

Wolter, Michael (2000) "Revelation and Story: Narrative Theology and the Centrality of Story," *"Revelation" and "Story" in Jewish and Christian Apocalyptic*, Aldershot: Ashgate, pp. 127–44.

Wooden, Cindy (2008) "In txts, BXVII Urges WYD Pilgrims to Proclaim Christ & His Luv," *Catholic News Service*, July 18. <http://www.catholicnews.com/data/stories/cns/0803734.htm> Accessed July 14, 2011.

Xanadu (2008) "Remembering Our Friends, Memorial in *Second Life*," *The Grid Live*, April 27. <http://thegridlive.com/2008/03/04/remembering-our-friends-memorial-in-second-life/> Accessed October 23, 2010.

Young, Glenn (2004) "Reading and Praying Online: The Continuity of Religion Online and Online Religion in Internet Christianity," in Dawson and Cowan (2004b), pp. 86–97.

Zaleski, Jeffrey (1997) *The Soul of Cyberspace: How New Technology Is Changing Our Spiritual Lives*, San Francisco: Harper Edge.

Zapp, Andrea (2004) "'A Fracture in Reality': Networked Narratives as Imaginary Fields of Action," in Andrea Zapp (ed.) *Networked Narrative Environments: As Imaginary Spaces of Being*, Manchester: MIRIAD, Manchester Metropolitan University, pp. 62–81.

Zimmerman, Eric (2004) "Narrative, Interactivity, Play, and Games," in Wardrip-Fruin and Harrigan (2004), pp. 154–64.

Index

agency 12–13, 37–38, 41, 70, 176, 184–85
apocalypticism 7, 12–13, 43, 84, 170, 187–204, 206, 222, 224, 235, 240
apps 24–25, 90, 100, 102–8, 136, 138, 147–50
ARG (alternate reality game) 91–92, 97, 215–16
Aristotle 31, 42, 47, 69, 70
Assassin's Creed 187, 190–95, 197–200, 202, 204
Augustine, St. 36, 39

the Bible: apps 103–4, 119, 138, 148; as digital prop 91, 119, 41; biblical characters 122; and belief 220; and games 40, 95, 137, 178; and interactive fiction 42–46; and interactive storytelling 23, 27, 30–32, 43, 61, 66, 225; and linear time 34–36, 48, 51, 65; and textuality 18, 22, 147; and transmedia 210, 221, 224; as a world 7, 50, 206, 209, 219, 222, 230; *see also The Bible Game and* Midrash *and* Bible Champions
Bible Champions 40–41
The Bible Game 32–33, 71–72
Bartle, R. 116–17, 122, 152–53, 193, 198
Bell, C. 55–57, 60–61, 72–73, 76–77, 180, 221
Blake, W. 209–10, 216
board games 54–55, 61–62
Bogost, I. 58, 60, 162, 167–68, 177–80, 183–84, 189–90; *see also* procedural rhetoric
Border Patrol 59, 168
Borg, M. 30–31, 65
bricolage 99, 101, 105, 107, 125, 237
Buddhism: apps 105; Dalai Lama 121; and games 54–55, 75, 182; and social networking 138, 140; and the internet 18, 106, 113; and ritual 50; and technology 118
Buffy the Vampire Slayer 213

Caillois, R. 86
Campbell, H. 9–10, 20, 104, 106, 119, 131, 133–35

catharsis: and games 72, 162, 183; and narrative 11, 27, 46–47, 48, 52, 69–70, 210; and ritual 49, 71, 73, 182; and *Second Life* 166
Catholicism: and apps 103, 149; and community 136, 138; Google bomb 139; pope 23–24, 218, 222; Mother Teresa 216–18; and ritual violence 183; Stations of the Cross 28, 37–38; and the transcendent 95; and virtual reality 19, 113, 133, 222
Chidester, D. 5, 229–30, 237
Christianity: Amish 20, 119; and apocalypses 84, 188, 190, 195–96, 201, 203–4; and augmented reality 4–5; and belief 34, 213, 218, 231; and *Facebook* 121, 138; and films 28, 35, 47; and flash mobs 142–43; and games 33, 40, 55, 75, 164, 169–70, 179, 193, 222; and the internet 25, 37, 103, 114, 131, 133; and MMORPGs 123, 137; and online community 106–7, 129, 133, 136, 220; and online repentance 146–47; and religious dialogue 106, 159, 178, 221; and sacred stories 16, 18, 30, 35–36, 38–39, 48, 65, 187, 206, 220; and sacred texts 22, 71–73; and *Second Life* 114, 137, 166; and transmedia 95–96, 223–25; and violence 124, 183; *see also* e-vangelism *and* Catholicism
Christ Killa: 117
communitas 12, 153–54, 156, 163–64 *see also* Turner, V.
community: and commitment 132, 238; and *Facebook* 135; and fan culture 46; and interreligious dialogue 100; and networks 106–7, 130–31, 140; online community 11–12, 20, 101, 104, 126–27, 133–34, 137, 150–52; and ritual 2, 6, 12, 18, 63, 71, 76, 135, 153–56, 236; and *Second Life* 154, 166; and sense of belonging 3, 107, 127–34, 143, 238, 158–59, 161; and virtual worlds 151–61; *see also* Durkheim, E.
Crawford, C. 65, 171, 175

Dalai Lama *see* Buddhism
Durkheim, E. 11–12, 127, 135, 157, 158, 205, 212, 229

Eck, D. 99–101, 105–6, 112, 114–15, 118, 223, 225–27, 237, 242
Einstein, M. 229
Eliade, M. 11, 78–80, 97, 172–74, 205, 231, 236, 240
Enoch, Book of 191–92, 194, 197,
Eskelinen, M. 27, 39, 60, 73
Ethnic Cleansing: 59, 168
e-vangelism 129, 136–40

Facebook 24, 104, 120, 121, 129, 135, 138–39, 143
film: and stories 5, 10, 28, 34, 38–39, 45, 48, 61, 65, 67, 69; and ritual 32, 47, 61, 81, 93, 164, 181; and montage 66; and religion 8, 18, 34–35, 38; and the transcendent 80, 84; and ARGs 91; and other worlds 80, 83, 92; and transmedia 85, 181, 212, 227–28; as iconic 174; *see also The Last Temptation of Christ* and *The Message* and *The Passion of the Christ*
Flanagan, M. 54–55, 59
flash mobs 135, 140–43
Food Force 59, 180
Frasca, G. 38, 66, 69, 170

game mechanics: 77, 87; "force" 72; "illusion" 72, 189; "ticking clock" 72, 195; *see also* immersion *and* agency
games: and control 37, 40, 172, 189, 198, 202; and community 12, 151; and ethics 184; and identity 100, 108, 119, 122, 199–200; and immersion 87, 200, 216, 241; and online worlds 2, 110, 152, 158, 206; and ordering of space and time 155, 168, 195–96, 233; and movies 39; and otherworldly spaces 17, 49, 82–84, 163, 175, 191–94, 197, 208, 231–32; and relics 85; and religion 8, 41, 43, 115, 137, 149, 161, 187, 203, 219, 222; and storytelling 27–32, 38, 47–48, 50–52, 66–67; and texts 36, 51, 224; as configurative 28; as environments 49, 118, 156; compared with rituals and stories 5–7, 10–11, 54–77, 167, 180, 201, 207, 209, 235, 237, 242; definition of 43, 221; and racism 59, 111; and reality 4, 88–89, 154, 160, 171, 214, 217–18, 236; and violence 13, 162–65, 169–70, 176–85, 188, 190, 240; see also rules *and* ARG *and* board games *and* procedural rhetoric *and* game mechanics *and* magic circle
Geertz, C. 83, 205–7, 210
Girard, R. 12, 71, 182–83 *see also* violence
The Go Game 92, 215, 231

God: and control of history 30, 33, 38, 48, 146, 188–90, 192, 195, 198, 201–2, 215, 220–22; and belief 75, 217–18, 225; and the internet 23, 26; and film 80; and texts 16–18, 27, 31, 34–36, 61, 65, 224; and Twitter 148; and video games 189; and virtual prayers 19, 25, 103, 116, 149–50; and the virtual sacred 97; God-mobs 140–43; in virtual reality 106, 115, 121, 143, 147, 231
Gods and goddesses 1, 16, 197, 233; and avatars 117; as totems 158
Grodal, T. 31, 34, 38, 47, 82, 168, 189, 208

hajj 1, 94
Halo: 68, 84, 187–88, 190, 192–93, 195, 197–98, 200–202, 204, 212, 228–31
Hardin, R. 68, 74, 76
Harry Potter: 13, 84–85, 95, 206, 212, 219, 228–32
Heaven: The Game: 193–94
Helland, C. 133
hierophany 30, 78–81, 85, 87, 91–92, 95, 172–73, 221–22, 229, 231
Hillis, K. 4, 10, 57, 81, 94, 105, 107, 109, 117, 128–29, 134–35, 236, 238
Huizinga, J. 2, 76, 86
Hush 59
Hinduism 1, 16, 49, 118
Hoover, S. 99, 101–2, 160, 237
hypertext: 37–38, 50, 108

identity: 11, 24, 99–125; 219, 237; and apocalypses 199–201; embodiment as 113; fluidity of 12, 65, 167, 227; hybrid 87, 124, 200–201; in community 132, 134, 142, 145, 152, 156–58
imagination 1–261
interactive fiction 41–45
Irenaeus, St. 36, 50–51
Islam: and apps 138; and authority 21; and *Facebook* 139; and games 75, 179; and images 35; and religious dialogue 179, 221; and ritual 17; and rules 50; and *Second Life* 79, 94, 110; and technology 1, 19, 21–22, 103; 113–14; imam 21, 138

Jesus Camp: 219
Judaism: and apocalypses 7, 13, 84, 187–90, 194–97, 199, 201–4; and cell phones 20; and flash mobs 142; and games 43, 59, 75, 168, 170; and the internet 26, 138, 140; and religious dialogue 114; and sacred stories 16, 18, 50–51, 206; and *Second Life* 110; and technology 1, 113, 159; *see also* Midrash
Juul, J. 8, 27, 29, 31 48–49, 51–52, 64, 163, 197, 208

Katamari 205–8, 212, 228, 230, 233
Kuma\War: 12, 162, 174, 177–79, 186

The Last Temptation of Christ 35
Laurel, B. 41, 75
LeBlanc, M. 70–73, 195
Left Behind 40, 139, 162, 164–66, 169–70, 186, 202, 221–22
Lévi-Strauss, C. 62–63
The Legend of Zelda 187, 192
liminality 11–12, 89, 127, 152–55, 159, 164–66, 175–76, 185; see also Turner, V. and persistent liminality
Live action role play (LARP) 68
Lyden, J. 8, 47, 80, 83, 164

machinima 124, 139
magic circle: application to virtual reality 86, 159; and apocalypses 187, 192–94, 204; and ARGs 92, 214, 216; and community 160–61; and games 2, 4, 10, 75, 86–89, 92, 156, 159–66, 171–72, 175–79, 184–87, 192–94, 204, 208, 214, 216; and ritual 10–11, 87; and violence 162–66, 172, 176–79, 184–86; and world-building 208, 214
The Matrix 85–86, 93, 95, 206, 212, 230, 232
McDowell, J. 30–31, 34
McGonigal, J. 9, 131, 214–17, 218, 231
The Message 35
Midrash 40–41, 43, 45, 46, 50–51, 61, 85, 216
Mitchell, J. 8, 133, 237
MMOG (massively multiplayer online game) 89, 91, 159
MMORPG (massively multiplayer online role-playing game) 108–9, 151, 207; see also MMOG
Molotov Alva and His Search for the Creator 124–25
Morgan, D. 17–18, 33, 167, 211, 215, 238
Moulthrop, S. 27–28, 48, 57, 151
Murray, J. 28, 36–37, 47–48, 50, 52, 57, 67–69, 76, 190, 204, 208, 236, 241

Noah's Ark 122

Oldenberg, R. 160

The Passion of the Christ 34–35, 47, 94
Penitents Repent 75–76
Pearce, C. 8–9, 70, 118, 151–52, 154, 156, 157, 159–61, 207
performance: and belief 13, 80, 106–7, 207, 213–14, 218–19, 231; and flash mobs 140, 142; and games 5, 69, 89, 150, 159, 168, 170–71, 180, 198, 217; and narrative 44, 55, 66; and ritual 3, 6, 9, 25, 28, 54–59, 60–63, 68, 74, 76, 84, 86–87, 103, 117, 121, 148,

163, 179, 208; and violence 154, 184–85, 203; theory of 8, 57, 213
persistent liminality 89, 159 see also liminality
Plate, S. B. 8, 35, 80–81, 83, 93, 97
play: concept of 6, 10, 35, 55–56, 61–64, 74–76, 215, 232; and apocalypses 196; and community 63, 151–52, 154–57; 163, 237; and conflict or violence 63, 73–74, 117, 162, 166, 171–72, 175–77, 181, 189, 201; and film 39, 66–67; and identity 11–12, 59, 105, 109–10, 116–17, 121–22, 200–201, 237; and the magic circle 2, 4, 75, 86–89, 92, 156, 159–66, 171–72, 175, 177–79, 184–86, 204, 208, 216; and narrative 16–17, 28–32, 36–37, 40–51, 66–73, 121–22, 189–90, 224; and ritual 2–4, 6–7, 10–12, 28, 32, 38, 48, 54, 56–57, 59–60, 62–64, 67–68, 70, 73–77, 86–89, 117, 153–54, 159, 160–66, 175–76, 179, 180–82, 185–86, 207–8, 214, 221; definition of 32
Pope see Catholicism
Poremba, C. 176, 177
prayer: and belief 213; and iPods or cell phones 17, 19; and online identity 1, 113, 133; and virtual space 169, 176; digital prayer wheels 1; prayer apps 102–3, 106, 138, 147–49; prayer flash mob 142; prayers to the Wailing Wall 26, 106, 115; prayer trees 104; prayer walls 24–25, 150, 239
procedural evil see procedural rhetoric
procedural rhetoric: and apocalypses 187, 189–90, 203; and rituals 58–60, 65; and sacred space 174; and storytelling 61; and violence 117, 163, 167–69, 172, 175–79, 240; and virtual "evil" 162, 170, 180–81, 184–85

the Quran 16, 18, 28, 51, 103, 138, 178, 206, 221 see also Islam

the Ramayana 54, 221, 49, 50
Rappaport, R. 6, 57–58, 64, 74, 107, 179
Raschke, C. 223, 224, 225
reflexivity 12, 96–97, 118, 176, 185, 192, 229
Resistance: Fall of Man 12, 168–69, 172, 174–75, 186
Revised Pratimoksha 18
Rheingold, H. 8, 14, 126, 131, 134, 136, 140–42, 239
ritual: and apps 103–4, 106; and community 154, 158; and games 5, 7, 11, 28, 54, 57–58, 63, 74–76, 164–66, 179; and identity 142, 87, 167–68, 186, 200–201, 214, 237; and film 47, 69; and iPods 107; and media 16, 23, 84–85, 93, 97, 110, 142, 228, 232; and myth 4, 50, 68, 157, 206, 236; and virtual worlds 87, 117, 153, 160, 175, 207–9; as conflict 73, 221; as ritualization 58, 60, 77; definition of 2, 6, 55–56, 59, 62, 96, 180, 205; online

rituals 26, 37–38, 101, 115–16, 133–35, 185; *see also* play, concept of *and* violence *and* liminality *and* rules *and* magic circle
Roma Victor 122–24
Roof, W. C. 99, 101, 105, 125, 166, 213, 228, 237–38, 242
rules: and ARGs 91–92; and belief 12, 35, 75, 91, 112–13, 115, 190, 215–19, 221–23, 232–33; and community 11, 151, 154, 161; and the magic circle 86–88, 163, 204; and religious games 40; and the taboo 171, 177, 184; and world-building 27, 32, 87, 94, 207–10, 227; in games 2–3, 49, 64–65, 168, 171, 233; in rituals 2, 6–7, 18, 28, 55–56, 60, 64–67, 73, 179–80; in stories and texts 31, 39, 42, 44–45, 49–52, 65–69; rabbinic interpretation 51–52, 61; ritual-game-story thing 56, 60–64, 71–77, 154–56, 236; *see also* procedural rhetoric

sacred and profane: and Durkheim 157–58; and media 160; and texts 17; and the virtual 78–80, 93, 96, 163, 211, 242; in relation to space 11, 79, 97, 153, 172–74; in ritual 89, 159, 165, 221; *see also* Eliade, M.
Salen, K.: 3, 9, 27, 32, 41, 43, 49, 52, 56–57, 62, 73–74, 88, 112, 118, 151, 154, 156, 163, 166, 170–71, 177–78, 197, 208, 232
Second Life 6, 166; chat-bot 144; and community 12, 128, 143–44, 151–53, 156; and evangelism 137; and identity 112; and machinima 124; and pilgrimage 1, 79, 94; and places of worship 26, 174; and ritual 89, 110, 113–14, 154; and the sacred 90, 236; as world 226
Sikhism 79
Smith, J. Z. 63, 73, 97, 173
Staal, F. 57, 64, 179
Star Trek 45–46, 212, 229–30, 232
Star Wars 94, 206, 212, 214, 229–30
Super Columbine Massacre RPG! 12, 162, 180–86

Tambiah, S. 84, 207
Taylor, T. L. 89, 153, 159
technomediators 112–16, 133, 136, 138
technomonists 112, 116–18
technophobes 112–14
theater: 8, 34, 39, 47, 60, 91, 152, 209, 217, 231
Third World Farmer: 59

TINAG (This is not a game): 91–92, 215–17
the Torah 52, 65, 138 *see also* the Bible *and* Midrash
totem 110, 158, 161, 212, 229 *see also* Durkheim, E.
transmedia 6, 13, 84–86, 92–95, 97, 207, 209–12, 219–32, 235–38, 240
Turkle, S. 8–9, 87, 103, 106, 108–9, 119, 144–45, 148, 150, 160, 239
Turner, V. 11–12, 110, 127, 152–54, 156, 163–64, 218
Twilight 84–85, 95, 206, 214, 228, 230, 232
Twitter 1, 17, 25, 95, 104, 120–22, 126, 135, 144, 146, 148

van Gennep, A. 84, 153
virtual reality 8, 13–14, 24–26, 52, 57, 82, 87, 90, 103, 112, 114, 160, 166, 186, 207, 231, 233–35; and the "sacred" 78–80, 94–98, 172; and the magic circle 86–88; and religion 4–7, 9–10, 15, 81, 113, 118, 174, 222; and the streaming 88–89; and worlds 2, 83–86, 91–93, 116, 160, 194, 206–8, 240; as hierophany 80–83; definition of 1, 109
virtual worlds: and community 152, 155–56; and identity 116, 202; as otherworldly 80, 91, 93, 194, 233; boundaries of 125, 154, 157, 159, 222; effect on us 160; entry into 81–82, 90, 117, 153, 191, 193, 208, 230; *YouTube* 25, 67, 142, 169
violence 12–13, 162–86, 239; and apocalypse 187, 201, 203, 221–22, 240; and ARGs 92, 216; and "brink games" 176–77, and community 151; and "forbidden play" 171; and identity 119, 121; *see also* procedural rhetoric *and* Girard, R.

Waco Resurrection: 117, 119
The Wandering Jew 59
Wellman, B. 130
World of Warcraft 12, 85, 110–11, 129, 137, 151, 156, 159, 206
world-building 2, 13, 17, 207–9, 211–12, 240

Zimmerman, E.: 3, 9, 27, 29, 32, 35, 41, 43, 49, 52, 55–57, 62, 64, 67, 73–74, 88, 112, 118, 151, 154, 156, 163, 166, 170–71, 177–78, 197, 208, 221, 232